ALSO BY PAUL MARIANI

Gerard Manley Hopkins: A Life

The Broken Tower: The Life of Hart Crane

Lost Puritan: The Life of Robert Lowell

Dream Song: The Life of John Berryman

William Carlos Williams: A New World Naked

THE WHOLE HARMONIUM

The Life of Wallace Stevens

PAUL MARIANI

Simon & Schuster

New York London Toronto Sydney New Delhi

Simon & Schuster
1230 Avenue of the Americas
New York, NY 10020

First Simon & Schuster hardcover edition April 2016

Interior design by Joy O'Meara

Manufactured in the United States of America

3 5 7 9 10 8 6 4

Library of Congress Cataloging-in-Publication Data
Mariani, Paul L.
The whole harmonium : the life of Wallace Stevens / Paul Mariani.
pages cm
Includes bibliographical references and index.
1. Stevens, Wallace, 1879–1955. 2. Poets, American—20th century—Biography.
I. Title. II. Title: Life of Wallace Stevens.
PS3537.T4753Z6783 2016
811'.52—dc23
[B] 2015020110

ISBN 978-1-4516-2437-3
ISBN 978-1-4516-2439-7 (ebook)

See page 461, which constitutes an extension of this copyright page.

For Eileen

e là m'apparve, sì com' elli appare
subitamente cosa che disvia
per maraviglia tutto altro pensare,

una donna soletta che si gia
e cantando e scegliendo fior da fiore
ond' era pinta tutta la sua via.

PURGATORIO XXVIII

CONTENTS

THE WHOLE HARMONIUM

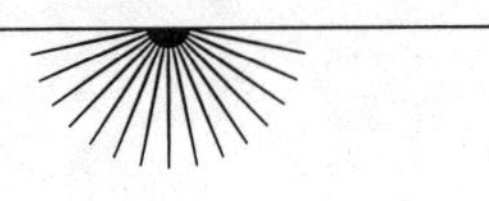

1

The Heaven of an Old Home: 1879–1897

I lost a world when I left Reading.

WALLACE STEVENS, 1907

Farewell to an idea . . . The mother's face,
The purpose of the poem, fills the room.
They are together, here, and it is warm.

WALLACE STEVENS, *THE AURORAS OF AUTUMN*, 1947

What strange places one wakes up in!" Wallace Stevens wrote his wife, Elsie, on September 4, 1913. He was thirty-three, had been married almost four years, and had just visited the city where he and Elsie had grown up: Reading, seat of Berks County, in Pennsylvania Dutch country. How different, how "unsympathetic," really, Reading had become for him since he and Elsie had settled in New York City, especially now, with both his parents gone. The problem was that he kept seeing the place not as it actually was but as he remembered it, which was largely through his mother's eyes: not an actual home but rather "the heaven of an old home." The Sunday before, he'd attended services in the old Grace Lutheran Church where he and Elsie had been married, and he'd been moved, far more than he ever expected, finding himself among old neighbors who still sat in the same pews they had twenty-five years earlier and he peering into what felt like "a mirror full of Hapsburgs."

Four years earlier, alone in a rented room in Greenwich Village, he'd written what he really felt about his first home in lines he'd translated from du Bellay. "Happy the man who, like Ulysses, goodly ways / Hath been," only to finally go back home decades later, where seeing once more smoke rising from the chimneys of the old houses would be more precious to him than the marble of palaces along the Tiber and sweeter than the "the sweetness of Anjou." A young man goes out from his native place to seek his fortune so that he might return in old age to the Eden of his first world. For an old dog like him, Reading felt then more like home than he thought New York City ever would.

He would spend the first twenty years of his life in the same mid-nineteenth-century three-story redbrick row house at 323 North Fifth Street, one of those buildings one sees in many of Edward Hopper's city scenes. It's still there, the place where Stevens was born and raised, and from the outside still looks much as he knew it, its façade facing west so that it catches the late afternoon sun between the shade trees lining the avenue and the drug deals on the street. West: the natural orientation for the autumnal Stevens, whether it was Reading or New York City or Hartford. That he also lived north of Penn Street, the main thoroughfare that divided Reading into its more affluent north and shabbier south districts, made sense, given the aspirations of both his parents, though he would have a hard time recognizing his native city today. With a population of forty-three thousand when he was born there, it proudly ranked as the nation's forty-first largest city.

He was the second child (and second son) born to Margaretha Catharine (Kate) Zeller and Garrett Barcalow Stevens. Both parents hailed from early Dutch German stock, folks who had settled in Pennsylvania well over a century earlier. Kate, who was thirty-one when she gave birth to Wallace, had herself been born in Reading to Sarah Frances Kitting and John Zeller, a shoemaker who died when Kate was thirteen, forcing her to quit school and work to help support her mother, brothers, and sisters with her schoolteacher's salary.

Like Kate, Garrett was born in 1848, but on a farm eighty miles east of Reading in Feasterville, Pennsylvania, one of six children of Elizabeth Barcalow and Benjamin Stevens. At seventeen he left home to begin teaching and then, five years later, moved to Reading to apprentice himself in the law offices of John S. Richards, passing the bar exams and becoming a lawyer in the Berks County courts in August 1872. His salary as a clerk, working six days a week, came to $100 a year, about what he'd made as a teacher, but now a world of promise had opened before him. To pass those exams he'd had to work nights and Sundays, including learning enough Latin and Greek to be able to translate passages at sight. For that he had had to hire a tutor. It was then in late 1871, when he was still clerking and she was teaching in the local schools that he met Kate Zeller. That Christmas he presented her with a copy of the *Poems of Alexander Pope.* For the next five years he courted her, comforting her after she lost her mother in 1872, and working hard, intent as he was on succeeding in life. Finally, on November 9, 1876, he had amassed enough income to marry Kate in the First Presbyterian Church, which she and her parents had regularly attended.

Thirteen months later, in December 1877, their first child, Garrett Jr., was born, either at 307 North Fifth, where Garrett and Kate first lived, or a few row houses to the north at 323 North Fifth, where the couple would live out their lives together. It was here, over the next dozen years, that all the other Stevens children were born and where the family would live together for the next several decades. Twenty-two months later, on October 2, 1879, their second son, Wallace, was born here, and fourteen months later their third son, John.

Both Garrett and John were family names. But, as often happens with second sons, Wallace was named for someone outside the family circle, christened, apparently, in honor of one of two (or perhaps both) Wallaces prominent in Reading at the time. The first was the Reverend Wallace Rackcliff, pastor of the First Presbyterian Church, where the Stevenses had been married, and whom Kate admired. The other was George Wallace Delamater, former mayor of Meadville, Pennsylvania, and a successful banker and insurance executive. Years later, when Stevens was in his late twenties and living in New York, Delamater—suffering from depression over the recent deaths of both his father and his son—would walk into his office at the Diamond Banking Building in Reading, shut the door, take out a pistol, and shoot himself.

From the birth of John in late 1880 until the summer of 1885, there were no more children, though it is possible that there was a stillborn infant. There may even have been twins who died shortly after childbirth in 1881 or 1882, both of whom may have been interred with other members of the Stevens family in the local cemetery a mile north of the Stevens home. Such deaths and burials were common in those days. The babies interred, life resumed its customary ways. Then two more children, the final two. On July 19, 1885, when Wallace was five and a half, his mother gave birth to Elizabeth, named for her father's mother. Four years later, on April 25, 1889, at the age of forty, Kate gave birth to Mary Katherine, the last to arrive and the first to depart.

• • •

LONG AFTER HIS MOTHER was gone, Stevens would remember how she would read to him and his siblings a chapter from the Bible each night before bed, or sit in the parlor on Sunday evenings, her little ones around her, playing the piano and singing old Christian hymns. He would remember waiting at the train station with his father and brothers for his mother to return from a day of shopping in New York City, her bags filled with boxes of candy for the children, or trailing his mother on market days, as she spoke with the farmers' wives in that strange Pennsylvania Dutch patois of theirs.

In the fall of 1884, just short of his fifth birthday, Wallace began his formal education. At first his mother walked him and Garrett to the school attached to the Presbyterian Church on South Fifth. A year later they went to the school attached to St. John's Evangelical Lutheran, more high church and more in the Stevenses' German Lutheran tradition, and a shorter walking distance to home. Often relatives showed up in Reading: his mother's sister, Aunt Mary, or his father's older bachelor brother, Uncle Jim Van Sant Stevens, who'd moved to St. Paul, Minnesota, some years before to pursue a business career selling artworks. Uncle Jim spoke French, Stevens remembered, "and had big dollars in his pockets, some of which went into mine." *There* was a man to emulate.

Back then Wallace was called Pat by family and friends and spent his summer vacations at the Stevens farmstead in Feasterville, where his father's brothers and sisters had grown up. When Pat was fourteen, his grandfather Benjamin Stevens died and the Feasterville farm was sold, so that the following summer Pat and his brothers were sent to Ephrata, to a large (180 beds) summer resort run by the von Niedas. The place was certainly no pleasure resort, young Stevens wrote his mother from there, and he found himself hanging out with either older or younger boys. Of the two boys his own age, he complained, one was a "damned ass and the other a G_ D_ one," preoccupied with girls all deluded by their own vanity. Oh to be home again baking on the locks of the Schuylkill. In the last day alone, all the "flotsam and jetsom [*sic*] of the scum-bedewed cities" had arrived, so that only the full moon in all its sad isolation and splendor offered him any solace. Still, within a week he was playing cards and shooting pool and singing in his fine alto in a barbershop quartet he'd formed with some of the Reading boys. He was even enjoying the company of the girls as well.

Following the death of his paternal grandfather, his grandmother had moved in with her daughter and her husband at their farmstead at Ivyland, and in the summer of 1896 the three Stevens brothers began spending summer vacations there. Aunt Mariah, his father's sister, sixteen-year-old Wallace reported in late July, was a "self-sacrificing whole-souled woman" (like his mother in this regard), both quiet and wise. Mariah's husband, Uncle Isaac, on the other hand, was "a Puritan who revels in catechisms and creeds, a hand-to-mouth man, earnest, determined, discreet." And Ivyland? It was a haven filled with red geraniums and quince trees. Each evening Garrett Jr. played piano tunes on the organ, while Wallace and John read whatever they could find.

In the fall of 1892 Wallace began attending Reading Boys' High School, where Garrett was two years ahead of him and where John would join him the following year. He took Latin and Greek, the highlights of the English literary tradition, grammar and composition, as well as geography, Greek history, algebra, and arithmetic. He played left end for the school's football team and poker with his classmates for Lucifer matches and cigarettes. He went about with the town rowdies, one of the young roughs himself.

While his older brother was more laid back and ethereal, his younger brother was as tough as Wallace and once, in a rage, nearly killed him. Just a year apart, they were constantly at it, all through their high school years. And because Wallace had to repeat his freshman year due to illness, he and John wound up in the same class for all four years, each trying to outdo the other. For Wallace this turned out to be a blessing because, up until then, he'd been content just to coast along.

Once, when he and John were behind the house chopping firewood, Wallace goaded John until he exploded and hurled an axe at Wallace. When John went to fetch it, he accidentally slashed his hand, the scar from which he kept for the rest of his life. They both had tempers, John's daughter-in-law would recall nine decades later. "That slow boil, but when it goes—watch out! I could see John get red up the back of his neck, and his face would get stern, and his eyes were absolute steel. I'm sure Wallace did exactly the same thing." But it was John who would keep the family together when their father had a nervous breakdown, by which time Garrett was married and practicing law in Baltimore and Wallace was walking the sidewalks of New York as a cub reporter. John, on the other hand, would remain in Reading all his life, practicing law and eventually becoming boss of the Democratic Party for Berks County. And it was John who made sure his mother and sisters were cared for after his father died, holding off getting married until he was thirty.

There were multiple reasons why Wallace did not fare well at the beginning of his time at Reading Boys', among them the various illnesses he suffered, including a bout of malaria, which permanently impaired the hearing in his left ear, no doubt contributing to his desire to be alone to think more clearly. Because of illnesses, his worried mother hovered over her Wal, as she liked to call him. It was she, in fact, who made sure he left Reading to spend several months with her sister, Mary Louise Zeller, and her husband, the Bavarian-born Reverend Henry Baptiste Strodach, along with their son, Paul—Wallace's own age—in the Williamsburg section of Brooklyn. That was where the Reverend Strodach was pastor of St. Paul's Evangelical Lutheran Church, located on the corner of South Fifth and Rodney Streets, as well as master of the school attached to the church, which Wal attended.

Later the Stevenses would welcome the Strodachs to Reading, after Strodach was forced to leave his Brooklyn congregation over a split that occurred in the church when a majority of members insisted on jettisoning the German language for services in English, this, after all, being America. When the dark, stern, handlebar-mustachioed Strodach refused to follow suit, the younger members left St. Paul's to found their own English-speaking Lutheran congregation a few blocks away. For Wallace, St. Paul's was as much a part of his history as the Presbyterian and Lutheran churches he'd grown up with in Reading, and Uncle Henry's church still held hints of its rose-colored aura when he revisited the church years later, after Uncle Henry himself was gone.

Eight years later, in 1900, living now in a tenement in lower Manhattan, Stevens searched the rear of the church for the small harmonium-like organ he used to marvel at. But even that was gone now, replaced by a ghostly piano in a dusty linen-covered shroud. As he was leaving, a woman who had shown him about the churchyard told him the sad story of his uncle's suicide. Strodach had frozen to death in a public park in Reading, near the hospital where he was being treated for severe depression. When she asked Stevens where he was from, he told her Massachusetts.

As he turned to go, he caught a glimpse of the iron steps in the schoolyard from which he'd once thrown kisses to the girls who had presented him with a pocketknife for his fifteenth birthday. Where were they now, he wondered. Even their names were gone, along with their faces and the letters they'd sent him. Two decades on, in a poem he called "Piano Practice at the Academy of the Holy Angels," he portrayed four of them in long, sad lines and christened them with new names: "Blanche, the blond, whose eyes are not wholly straight, in a room of lustres," her heart murmuring "with the music that will be a voice for her." Rosa, "disdaining the empty keys," and Jocunda, letting the rose leaves "lie on the water-like lacquer" as in a painting by Poussin. Then Maris, "wearer of cheap stones, who will have grown still and restless." And finally Wallace himself, in the guise of the young girl Crispine, whose knife blade, reddened now, would keep demanding of poems far more than they could give for one "needing so much, seeking so much in their music."

• • •

IF IT WAS HUMBLING to have to repeat his ninth year of school, at least he'd learned what the consequences of wasted time could be. So when he returned to Reading Boys' High in the fall of 1893, he was a changed young man. He even donned a white surplice and black cassock on Sundays and sang—first as a soprano, then as an alto—in the choir of Christ Episcopal on the corner of Court and Fifth. He was definitely more serious about his studies and—because of his intelligence and drive—soon found himself near the top of his class. In his front-facing bedroom on the third floor at 323 North Fifth, he stayed up past midnight each evening, reading as he smoked his small-bowled, long-stemmed pipe. He pored over Poe and Hawthorne and the classics, "all the things one ought to read."

It was then that he discovered his natural penchant for writing, and soon he was editor of *Dots and Dashes*, the school's newspaper. He took to heart his father's dictum that he was going to be able to prove himself only by dint of hard work. In March 1896, at sixteen, he won an essay contest sponsored by the *Reading Eagle*, proudly keeping for the rest of his life the two books he won. That Christmas he delivered the school's prize-winning oration, which he titled "The Greatest Need of the Age," earning a gold medal for his efforts, as well as a sketch of himself printed on the front page of the *Eagle* on Christmas Eve, much to his parents' delight.

When he graduated from Reading Boys' High the following June, the school chose him to deliver the valedictory oration. He called it "The Thessalians" and composed it in his best Gilded Age fustian. Calling to mind the Golden Age of Greece, he importuned himself and his classmates to hold true to their deepest Christian values if they were ever to realize their manifest destiny. He called upon his classmates to confound those conspirators who would destroy the country by their greedy self-interest. And, if even the classical virtues that had made Greece and America great should fail, there were the noble Christian virtues to keep young men on their true and steady course. Follow the cross, he ended, and "let every arm, let every breast, let every man defend the cross forever."

His Reading years over, that September he began a special program at Harvard which would allow him to complete his course work in three rather than the usual four years, because his father now had two young daughters at home, as well as three sons he was going to have to see through college, all at the same time. Garrett had started at Yale, then transferred to Dickinson College in Carlisle, eighty miles west of Reading. It was there that he would meet his future wife, the daughter of the college president. And John began classes at the University of Pennsylvania, even as Wallace entered Harvard.

Once, long after both his parents were dead, he went back to Reading to see the place where he'd grown up. He stayed at the six-story brownstone Mansion House on Penn Street in the center of town, in a room with a single window that opened onto an air shaft. Instead of a bathroom there was only a washbasin. Here he was, home again, imagining a land full of milk and honey, only to be "dumped into a hole in the wall with a couple of cigarette butts for company." No wonder it filled him with delight to learn later that the hotel had been razed.

One rainy May Tuesday in 1920, he'd stopped in Reading on his way back to New York on business and had walked up and down the train platform. But a few minutes of that had been enough. Seeing Reading in that light had been like finding oneself in "a hardware store on a misty day." From the platform the houses all seemed dirty and shabby and neglected, and Reading itself reduced to a miserable town. By then it was clear that the Reading he'd grown up in, "if it ever existed anywhere except in the affections," had long since disappeared.

"When you are young," Stevens would recall when he was seventy and his family long gone, "you look back to returning home. But when you become my age and go home you don't know anybody any longer. You have nothing but trouble at the hotel and the only person that takes any interest in you is the superintendant of the cemetery." By that point it had been years since he'd last been there. "I am out of touch with the members of the family at Reading," he wrote a cousin when he was just two years shy of his own death. Not *my* family, he said, but *the* family. A whole new generation of Stevenses lived there now, folks who had their own friends and—if they thought at all about his generation—thought about them as no more than nameless ghosts inhabiting sepia-tinted photographs on a wall. By then, of course, he himself had become a Large Red Man ensconced in a house in Hartford, alone in his sumptuous study, reading about a place he'd once inhabited somewhere called Reading.

2

Harvard: 1897–1900

I sang an idle song of happy youth.

WALLACE STEVENS, *SONNETS*, 1899

In September 1897, a month shy of his eighteenth birthday, "Pete" Stevens, having morphed his first name from his high school moniker, "Pat," moved into a room in a Victorian boardinghouse at 54 Garden Street in Cambridge, Massachusetts. Three elderly sisters, daughters of Theophilus Parsons, Dana Professor of Law at Harvard from 1848 until 1870, had for several decades been renting rooms to undergraduates and graduates, with several of whom Stevens shared a bathroom down the hall. The house is still there, although brick apartment buildings have long since sprouted up around it. The address was an easy fifteen-minute walk from classes at Harvard Yard, and from the beginning the sisters made him feel comfortable enough that he lived there during his three years in Cambridge.

By the time Stevens arrived, Harvard had become the liberal institution President Charles W. Eliot had spent the past quarter century shaping, a vision he would continue to promote until his retirement twelve years later, making of it a seat "of Unitarian optimism and untroubled positivism," a balance of both enlightened Evangelical Protestantism and modern science. Or, to see it from a more conservative perspective, as Eliot's cousin Charles Eliot Norton, Harvard's preeminent art historian and

Dante scholar, Harvard had given itself over to a progressive utilitarianism where scholarly contemplation had long become "an unfamiliar practice."

Nor was Norton alone in believing that President Eliot had changed Harvard for the worse. Norton's colleague, the Spanish-born philosopher George Santayana—the last Puritan, as he would call himself—also believed that Eliot had managed to undermine the core elements of a liberal education, especially in replacing the essential *Ratio Studiorum*, studied by all students in common, with a student's freedom to choose from a multitude of electives. Eliot believed that America was changing and that young men like Stevens were going to have to make their living in a world where technology and change were in the ascendency. That meant the classics and the study of languages would have to give way to other, more practical concerns, such as preparing for a future as citizens in a country that would, forcefully if necessary, make its mark on the world and offer its graduates an advanced living standard.

Stevens's father, with five children to support, of course agreed with Eliot, and constantly reminded Wallace that he was at Harvard to prepare himself to become a successful lawyer and businessman with important connections. Yet his son found himself drawn more and more to the humanistic concerns exemplified by Norton and Santayana. In time Stevens would see the wisdom of his father's thinking and go on to become a successful lawyer and insurance executive, but he would always harbor a deep attachment to the life of the mind: art, music, philosophy, language, and poetry. That life of the imagination, welded to his understanding of what after all constituted reality, would provide Stevens with a world in which he could breathe in its fresh oxygen.

Reading the Oxford scholar Benjamin Jowett on the classics, Stevens would take to heart Jowett's dictum that, as he inscribed it on the opening page of his freshman journal, *If I live I ought to speak my mind.* He would write essays and stories and plays and in time become editor of the *Harvard Advocate.* And he would develop an appreciation for Chinese and Japanese art with the help of a fellow student, Arthur Pope, who years later would become the director of the university's Fogg Museum. He would also befriend two young Harvard poets of promise: Witter Bynner and Arthur

Davison Ficke. And it was here that he would begin writing poems in earnest.

One of the first he wrote he called "Autumn," using a modified rhyming haiku form, which he published in the *Red and Black*, his high school's literary magazine, during his first year at Harvard. Here the strikingly handsome, six-foot-two eighteen-year-old freshman with hair parted fashionably down the middle, first caught the voice of the solitary singer contemplating the inevitable passage of time as day turned to night. He began in the best late romantic style, as reflected in the work of the Chinese masters. And why not? As he would remark half a century later, "a man's sense of the world is born with him and persists," so much so that it "penetrates the ameliorations of education and the experiences of life."

Soon he was sending his poems home for his mother's perusal and getting back chatty letters from his father, who, after all, was paying his son's yearly tuition of $150. The father's letters were witty in a heavy sort of way, often laced with outrageous puns and wreathed about with heavy irony. "Who knows," he wrote his son, someday Wallace's word painting might even be noticed by "some Yankee old maid," who would say that here, just here, Wallace had once "stood and saw the road to distinction." The real point was that, while "a little romance" was essential to one's being, the cold world rewarded only those bent on climbing the ladder to success. In the long run, success in America came down to "work and study, study and work," two things worth a whole "decade of dreams." That was, after all, why Wallace was at Harvard: to gain entry into the world beyond, and why Garrett Sr. was willing to allow his son to dwell for a moment among Harvard's hoity-toity privileged environs. As for Wallace, he had once again transformed himself, this time with a decided Harvard manner and a way of speaking that did not go over well at home.

Soon enough, however, the father was urging his son not to waste any more time on poetry. Instead he should keep himself busy widening his vision and learning to think for himself, and that meant privileging scientific and philosophical reasoning. Make every effort to search out the facts of the matter, Garrett urged all his sons, for that was how one reached the right conclusion. No son of his was ever going to play the dilettante, trying out first this idea and then that. Better to focus on what led to practical results, and that meant money in the bank. In this Garrett Sr. was no different from most American fathers raised in the Protestant ethic of hard work with its consequent rewards. Hadn't he himself arrived at where he was by sheer determination and hard work? Hadn't he himself made the necessary sacrifices to send all three of his sons to the best schools in the country? Keep up the good work, he urged Wallace, so that he could keep bragging about him to his law partner, Bill Kerper Stevens (no relation), back home in Reading.

Garrett was proud that Wallace was taking such a wide range of classes: Rhetoric and Composition, History of English Literature, French *and* German, Medieval and Modern History, and Constitutional Government and Law. And he was proud that his boy had earned A's in both English and French and B's in History and Government, his only B– earned for German. At the same time, though, Wallace should keep preparing "for the campaign of life" and learn "to paddle his own canoe without help from home of any substantial character."

Still, when Wallace told his father that he hoped someday to be a journalist rather than a lawyer like his father and brothers, Garrett tried to understand. If Wallace had set his heart on becoming a newspaperman, it would be best to try his hand at it in Boston or New York and see what such a life demanded of one, rather than return to Reading and work for the local paper. Surely a summer scurrying about as a cub reporter on the streets of New York would cure his boy of his fantasy. But Wallace lacked the self-confidence to try either Boston or New York, and soon he was begging his father to find something for him back in Reading. Garrett found him a position on the *Reading Times* for the summer. It didn't hurt that Tom Zimmerman, the paper's editor and a poet in his spare time, liked the poems Wallace had written, which Garrett had shown him.

Back at Harvard for his second year, Wallace read Jowett's translation of Plato's *Dialogues*, where Jowett noted that true poetry meant "the remembrance of youth, of love, of the noblest thoughts of man" and "of the greatest deeds of the past." Jowett also held out hope that it might be possible to reconcile poetry with religion, though such a reconciliation must give pleasure of the sort found in the poem, one capable of possessing the whole man. Real poetry, Stevens was coming to see, was—as with real painting—far more than mere technique, something that revealed the imagination in command of some deeper reality.

That November two of his poems appeared in the *Harvard Advocate*, the first of many to be printed there over the next eighteen months. One was an eight-line ballad-like piece titled "Who Lies Dead," while the other was a Petrarchan sonnet called "Vita Mea." Both pieces reveal a solitary young man, fearful of the isolation of death, though the latter poem does offer a glimmer of hope. In the end, though the poet weeps, he sees through the prison of his own tears a distant if cold light beckoning, "where Faith and Hope like long-sought stars / First gleamed upon that prison of unrest."

That Christmas he was back in Reading, amid the noise and smoke and grime of the city. To escape, he got up early the day after Christmas and hiked out to the Stone Tower, an observation post erected eight years earlier atop Mount Penn, though even there he could hear the Reading Railroad engines and boxcars. Coming down from the mountain, he watched the sun sliding under a smoke-filled sky, the darkness leaving him terrified "from an allegorical point of view," before adding, in his dry, comic fashion, "which was how allegories worked anyway." Forty-seven years later the image of that dark tower atop Mount Penn would still haunt him, though by then it had become for him nothing less than "the natural tower of all the world / The point of survey, green's green apogee." It would be on that final mountain, that final refuge created out of necessity against the encroachments of death, a place beyond place, that would have to transform itself into the "happiest folk-land" from which choired "mostly marriage hymns," and where one might stand, reading no book now, in a world beyond words themselves, because there would no longer be any need for them.

• • •

RETURNING TO HARVARD IN January 1899 for his fourth semester, he took English Composition with Barrett Wendell and a course in poetry writing with Charles Townsend Copeland, called Copey, and received A's in both. For Copey's class he composed a sequence of fifteen Petrarchan sonnets. Shelley's and Keats's and the *Rubaiyat*'s fingerprints are all over these thoroughly romantic and thoroughly derivative poems, but this was university Palgrave-inspired poetry in 1900, and William Carlos Williams, Ezra Pound, and T. S. Eliot would write in much the same manner in their time at college. These were dark, introspective *woe is me* verses, employing the sea and the moon and the darkness for their landscape, with a few Greek and Roman gods and heroes thrown in to show that the parents of these students had invested their money wisely.

About half the poems languished in Stevens's journals, while the others saw publication over the next year in the *Harvard Advocate* (whose staff he joined in March), the *Harvard Monthly*, and Columbia University's new undergraduate journal, *East & West*. Several in the *Advocate* had to be published under pseudonyms, such as R. Jerries, so that it would not appear that Stevens was packing the journal's pages with poems by himself. The truth was that there had not been enough submissions to fill each number.

Murray Seasongood, a friend of his at Harvard, would remember long afterward that the young Stevens struck him as someone who was "modest, simple, and delightful . . . large, handsome, healthy, robust [and] amiable, with light curly hair and the most friendly of smiles and dispositions." The two of them would take long walks together, though it was hard to keep up with Stevens, with either his rolling gait or his wit and frankness. At the same time, he found Stevens almost "diffident, and very tolerant and kindly" toward his colleagues and those who contributed pieces to the *Advocate*. Even then Stevens was a "magnificent craftsman" who wrote "noble sonnets, odes and mighty lines." But Stevens would look back at the poems he wrote then quite differently. Reading them decades later, he admitted, gave him the creeps.

• • •

ONE EVENING IN JULY 1899, his second year at Harvard behind him and back at the Ivyland farm with his brothers, Stevens, his long-stemmed pipe in hand, strolled up the hill overlooking the turnpike. He was nineteen now and had assumed the role of the Harvard *philosophe*. That very afternoon, in fact, he'd read Robert Louis Stevenson's *Providence and the Guitar* and found it somewhat artificial and Stevenson's protagonist merely "a paper doll."

Out here in the countryside, on the other hand, where he could breathe in the fresh air and watch the clouds and listen to the robins singing, it came home to him just how different "literary emotions were from natural feelings." Only the real world mattered. All the rest was mere literature.

Sitting in the modest piano room at John Wily's farm in Berkley, north of Reading, one afternoon later that same month, he read Keats's *Endymion* and listened to the rain falling on the trees outside. His eyes slowly followed a drop of rain as it slipped from leaf to leaf on a clematis as if he had all the time in the world, and he realized that it was "just such unexpected, commonplace, specific things that poets . . . jot down in their note-books," as he was doing now. What "a monstrous pleasure" it was to be so fully conscious of reality and then to write of that particular thing. Out in the fields the next evening he watched the blue sky turn pink, then a yellowish red, then gradually die "into thin whiteness," even as the moon began rising in the East, like the moon in *Endymion*. Ah, to wed what one saw or heard with the exact words that captured that wondrous reality!

That summer he was filled with ideas for new sonnets: how birds seemed to fly up from the "dark ground at evening . . . with golden spray on their wings," though it would take another seventeen years before he could translate that vision into lines like these:

Deer walk upon our mountains, and the quail
Whistle about us their spontaneous cries;
Sweet berries ripen in the wilderness;
And, in the isolation of the sky,
At evening, casual flocks of pigeons make
Ambiguous undulations as they sink,
Downward to darkness, on extended wings.

The landscapes of his beloved Pennsylvania filled his journals that summer. One morning that July he rose early and walked through the apple orchards at Wily's to take in "the apple pungency in the air." He studied the shadows of the trees reflected in the surface of the water along the creek and noted how the "trunks of the trees shook with light reflected from the rippling water," noted too the sound of a turtle dove suddenly interrupted by the scolds of a blue jay. Then it was a blue heron flying along a creek. Then a catbird singing in the rain. How tired he was now of the smutty jokes of his friends, desiring only to be alone with his thoughts.

He went fishing on Ontelaunee Lake with his old friend Ed Livingood and some others, including a young Miss Benz, whose "fine reserve and quietness" fascinated him, even if her head seemed to be filled only with the latest novels. He would be her Pygmalion, someone he could teach the differences between pulp fiction and the enduring works of literature, though he quickly despaired of that. "There must surely exist brains," he confided to his journal afterward, "that need the excitement of the 'latest' to keep them from sluggishness," and he wondered if Miss Benz had listened to him simply because his ideas seemed so novel. He promised to lend her his copy of George Edward Woodberry's *Heart of Man* with its essay "A New Defense of Poetry," which would show her that great literature did not mean famous old books but books of any age that revealed what truly mattered.

Still, he was infatuated enough with Miss Benz's beauty that ten days later he composed another Petrarchan sonnet, this one in imitation of Sir Philip Sidney, which he titled "To Stella," in parentheses wondering if indeed it was Miss B who had inspired his song, filled as it was with knights "on splendid pastures by the sea" who enacted feats of chivalry for "ladies [*sic*] soft applause," and of chaste young maidens in dim towers, like the one atop Mount Penn. He sang too of shady nooks where lovers carried on sweet trysts invisible to all but small birds. But, his poem ended, it was Miss Benz, his Stella, who surpassed all of these images. For the moment, he realized, he had indeed been smitten. But then one had to control such impulses if one was to get ahead in life. He could not afford to be a sentimentalist like Livingood, who'd confessed to him one night as they'd walked home from the Tower that he was feeling vulnerable to love's darts. To give oneself to someone, Stevens understood, inevitably meant being hurt by that person. Better to give oneself to nature's maternal largesse and to poetry, which asked for so little in return.

But if one's first day in the country, he observed that summer, began with a wild enthusiasm, how quickly the novelty faded. The real source of pleasure in nature came in meditating on some small part of its grand-ness. Not the horizon or some green field, but rather "the lyrics of song-sparrows, catbirds [and] wrens." Not a valley filled with corn, but the way the wind played on a single leaf. Or the way flocks of birds—an image he would revive years later in "Sunday Morning"—seemed to dash "toward the splendid clouds with a carol of joy" before suddenly "circling back to the clover and timothy."

And then there was John Wily, who rented the Stevens boys rooms who held Stevens captive with his talk of the country one afternoon while the rain poured down over a tent of lilacs. Weeks later, back in Reading, Stevens learned that Wily had just died as a result of injuries. Wily had three daughters—Kate, Rose, and Sally—two of whom Stevens had taken a liking to. Quite matter-of-factly he noted that the death of their father meant the end of a line going back to William Penn, who had entrusted the family with this very parcel of land. When Stevens returned to the farm later that summer, he sensed the loss and desolation which had settled on the daughters and which seemed to penetrate the landscape itself. Kate still had that mischievous streak about her, but the older sister, Rose, struck "the real note of despair" when she handed him the poems of an earlier John Wily, written back in 1719. It was as if she were reminding him of who the Wilys had once been. Forty years later Stevens would spend a small fortune attempting to prove his family had descended from the Dutch who had first settled New York. But for one or two spoilers in the mix—Germans who had come over just a bit too late—he came close to making good his claim to Dutch-American nobility.

When at last he said good-bye to the Wily sisters, Kate had bedecked his felt hat with fresh roses, which he thought of as a coronal bestowed on him at the end of some golden age. In fact, the green memories of that summer far surpassed anything he had ever experienced at Harvard. That was the poet effusing at nineteen. But five years later, on a hot, airless, summer's night in his cramped New York City tenement apartment, struggling to find a future which kept eluding him, he would read over the happy passage he had entrusted to his journal and dismiss it as nothing more than "silly, affected school-girl drivel."

• • •

THAT SEPTEMBER HE RETURNED to Harvard for his third and final year. He took a year-long course in Romantic and Victorian Poetry, a semester of Medieval and Modern German Literature, and another semester course in the Art of the Middle Ages and the Renaissance, as well as English Composition and American History. To his surprise, he received a mere C in French Literature, but then he knew he'd loafed and drunk his way through most of his senior year. Still, he managed to get elected to the Signet, an undergraduate society dedicated to the arts. And he continued to publish poems, including a sequence of four he titled *Street Songs*—one a sonnet about a woman he'd seen begging on the church steps of St. Paul's near Harvard Yard—as well as several short stories in the *Advocate.* In his final semester he was elected president of the *Harvard Advocate.*

Others would remember a wilder side to Stevens. On the evening of May 1, 1900, he read an ode he'd composed for the Class of 1901—his class, officially—at the Junior Dinner. Floyd DuBois, one of his younger classmates, who would become a world-renowned expert in metabolism and psychological stress factors involved in submarine and aviation warfare, recalled Stevens that evening reading "the most humorous poem I ever heard in my life." To prepare himself for the occasion, Stevens had downed a bottle of King William scotch just before addressing his audience, and then passed out, so that DuBois had to help him back to his room, thus missing the rest of the dinner.

Witter Bynner, a year behind Stevens at Harvard, would also remember this other Stevens sixty years later. Like many students and some of the younger faculty, Stevens was in the habit of frequenting a restaurant on Harvard Square called Ramsden's, or, more familiarly, Rammy's, where one could order buckwheat cakes to settle one's stomach after a night of heavy drinking. There was a seasoned waitress there named Kitty, well-liked by everyone for her Irish wit and ability to give as good as she got. One night that spring Stevens, drunk and with a silly grin on his face, staggered into Rammy's and announced to everyone that he was going to rape Kitty. And with that the six-foot-two virgin Stevens, hot to be de-virginated, vaulted the counter, where he and Kitty fell to the floor. When Kitty, old enough to be Stevens's mother, "screamed with enjoyably dramatic terror, a member of the English Department who was present left his buckwheats and severely interfered."

Stevens was no doubt reprimanded, but since he was so close to graduating, the matter ended there. In any event he was ready to forget all that and move on. Contrite, he spent a hot June day studying in the library for his finals.

A week earlier, in the company of his English instructor, Pierre de Chaignon la Rose, Stevens had dined with George Santayana at a restaurant in Cambridge. The twenty-nine-year-old La Rose, a devout Catholic and confirmed bachelor, with exquisite manners and a genius for creating heraldic emblems, had wanted to introduce his young poet from Reading, editor of the *Advocate*, and author of a number of fine sonnets, to Santayana. One of those sonnets so intrigued Santayana that he composed a sonnet of his own in response.

Born Jorge Agustín Nicolás Ruiz de Santayana y Borrás in Madrid, Santayana was thirty-six and the author of a recently published five-act verse play titled *Lucifer: A Theological Tragedy*, as well as *Interpretations of Poetry and Religion*, a treatise which celebrated religion and poetry as meaningful ways of understanding the human condition. Santayana had been raised a Catholic in the Spanish tradition and, while he no longer considered himself a believer, nevertheless maintained a deep respect for the old traditions, no easy feat in the liberal Protestant atmosphere that was Harvard. He preferred to describe himself as a Catholic atheist or, better, aesthetic Catholic. He also viewed American liberal thought with both suspicion and disdain. The university, he insisted, did not exist merely to prepare students for getting ahead in a dog-eat-dog capitalistic society. If anything, it should educate America's young leaders in the values of reason and beauty and thus step by step raise the cultural standards of this brash, vital young country.

Over dinner that evening, the conversation covered many topics, among them the figure of the fallen hero in Santayana's *Lucifer*, banished to an outcrop forever, but—as with Milton's Satan and Byron's and Shelley's dark heroes—at least master of his own dark destiny, so free forever from a Creator whom he did not trust and so would not serve. His rebellion also freed him from the ignorant masses who had rebelled against their Creator merely out of lust and greed. It had taken him ten years to compose his tragedy, Santayana explained, stroking his Van Dyke beard, and still he regretted that he'd not been able to make his songs lyrical enough to support the play's philosophical arguments. He'd even thought of calling his tragedy "The Temptation of Lucifer," of one who could see, as Stevens remembered it, "the beauty of love and ideals" without being able to participate fully in them, just as Santayana himself could see the beauty of Catholic thought as something superior to American Evangelical Protestantism without assenting to the Church's spiritual claims. Afterward the three went to Santayana's apartment to continue their discussion.

There Stevens shared his sonnet beginning "Cathedrals are not built along the sea," his poetic argument rejecting the faith in which he had been raised. To truly see and understand nature, he had decided, was something far superior to the pious feelings roused by the Sunday organ music which had mesmerized him as a boy. Cathedrals were not built along the sea for the simple reason that the sublimity of the sea in all its Kantian force would shake the church to its foundations and drown out its scrannel music:

And through the precious organ pipes would be
A low and constant murmur of the shore
That down those golden shafts would rudely pour
A mighty and a lasting melody.

But surely Stevens was being too severe, Santayana remonstrated mildly. Surely the cathedral had served its function in the evolution of the human species. So he answered with a sonnet of his own, entitled "Reply to a Sonnet Beginning 'Cathedrals Are Not Built along the Sea.' " The beauty of Christianity, fiction or not, Santayana explained, was that it had forged nature's clay into something of a higher order: a cathedral, that "cross-shaped temple to the Crucified," so that the wild winds which "through organ-pipes descended" had evolved "to utter what they meant eternally." Did not the cold moon itself gesture toward some greater reality, even as it shone through the stained-glass windows of Stevens's sonnet? And hadn't that same moon "devoutly mended / Her wasted taper, lighting Calvary," when the God-man sacrificed himself, thus lifting mankind beyond anything it had previously imagined for itself, so that "the sullen diapason of the sea" blended now with "a psalmody of angels"?

But, Stevens retorted, didn't even the sound that blows through the organ pipes issue from the sound of the wind blowing through space? But, Santayana replied in turn, didn't the wind act as a stimulus only, to which the scrannel pipe and in time the heavenly organ-pipe provide an answer? "We both held our grounds," Stevens noted, and then it was time to enjoy a couple of cigarettes and some decent whiskey. Therein lay the real pleasure of the evening. That and Santayana's thimble-size compressed CO_2 sparklets fastened to the top of a water bottle. "Sparklets were then something new," Stevens recalled, "and Santayana liked to toy with them as he charged the water which he used to make a highball or two." As for the debate: that would continue long after for Stevens in poems like "The Comedian as the Letter C" and "The Idea of Order at Key West."

A week later, when Stevens went to say good-bye to Copey, Copey asked him what he saw himself doing now that he was moving on from Harvard. First, Stevens told him, he meant to try his hand as a newspaper reporter in New York City as a way of paying his bills. But what he really hoped to be someday was a poet. Copey stared at him in disbelief. "Jesus Christ!" was all he could think to say.

No doubt Stevens's father felt the same way. Three years of college, and *this* was what his son had decided on? Hadn't Garrett Sr. made it clear that poetry was no way to make a living? But then, Wallace would learn soon enough that journalism was a dead end, which would then make law school the one viable alternative. But Stevens saw things differently. If being a reporter didn't work out, he meant to knock about and see the larger world. If he knew he could be happy dreaming his way through life, he also knew he would be just as happy to work for what he wanted. The question was how to accommodate both impulses.

What troubled him most, however, was not knowing how one went about becoming a success. Besides his youth and the endless possibilities open to him, he knew himself well enough to see that he had a strong work ethic, though he hated the thought of work for the sake of work. Likewise he was not going to write merely for the sake of writing. But for now, he would have to pack his trunk and ready himself for the cold, indifferent, vital world of lower Manhattan.

3

Starting Out: 1900–1903

> *Here am I, a descendant of the Dutch, at the age of twenty-five, without a cent to my name, in a huge town, knowing a half-dozen men and no women.*
>
> WALLACE STEVENS, FEBRUARY 7, 1904

Thursday afternoon, June 14, 1900, the freshly minted Harvard graduate, in New York with his trunk in tow, made his way downtown to the Astor House, that fortress-like building dominating lower Broadway between Vesey and Barclay. He would stay there his first night, using the hotel as an upscale address for his mail. This was the same hotel where, forty years earlier, Lincoln had stayed when he'd delivered his Cooper Union speech as a candidate for president, and it was from the Astor the following winter that he had left for Washington and his inauguration.

Stevens's arrival, of course, was on a far more modest scale. Armed with a letter of introduction from Copey, the twenty-year-old unpacked, then walked down Broadway to Pine Street and the offices of New York's oldest newspaper, the *Commercial-Advertiser*, where—looking for freelance work—he presented himself to Carl Hovey, who introduced him to the editor in chief, Lincoln Steffens, who had already earned a reputation as one of New York's fiercest muckrakers.

Stevens then made his way back up Broadway to the offices of the

Evening Sun and made an appointment to meet the editor the following Monday. Then it was dinner with a friend, Rodman Gilder, who'd graduated the year before from Harvard and, like Stevens, had also worked on the *Harvard Advocate.* Gilder was now a junior editor for one of the city's papers and had brought his portly Aunt Julia to liven up dinner with her droll wit. Afterward, Stevens listened to a band concert in East River Park, before returning to the Astor to write up his impressions of the music for the *Advertiser.* It was his first assignment.

The following day he found a room in a nearby boardinghouse in the slums, run by two single French women. The elder, he noted, was about thirty, with "a bosom a foot and a half thick," so that it was no longer a mystery to him why the French had acquired a reputation for amorousness, seeing as they came "with such accommodation for lovers." On a more mundane level, he squished what he thought were two bedbugs crawling on the wall of his room, only to discover they were lice. He treated himself to poached eggs, coffee, and three slices of bread at a nearby diner, then bought some newspapers from a street vendor and returned to his room. By then the city stoops and railings were crowded with boarders, many of them picking their teeth. All about him loomed darkened office buildings which looked "hard and cruel and lifeless." Back in his room he opened his windows to cool off, only to hear children playing on the streets below. The sound comforted him.

A week later, perusing the papers for something to write about, he picked up Robert Louis Stevenson's "Christmas Sermon," which ended with a quote from W. E. Henley's elegy for his daughter, Margaret, who had died at the age of five. "A late lark twitters from the quiet skies," Henley's poem began. It was one of Stevens's favorite motifs, and Henley's poem inspired him to begin a ballad-like piece he called "A Window in the Slums." Evening, and late birds singing in the streets about him, and "children in their fancied towers," swinging sticks like swords against the iron railings fronting the tenement steps, their song-like voices rising still, even as night fell over New York and no bird sang.

That Saturday he found a letter at the Astor from his father. What a "brave fellow" his boy was to try to find work in New York rather than return to Reading. For his part, Wallace had already had his fill of the city's brave fellows, many of them Italian immigrants with young families reduced to selling gelato on the streets, or Irish street sweeps working six-day weeks just to make ends meet, or young men just out of college like himself, hoping to make a start. On Sunday morning he headed west to the Hudson River and talked to an old man there who was walking six terriers and a Newfoundland and spent fifteen minutes playing with them. He found foreigners in a park shooting craps for ten-cent stakes and, over on Canal Street, draymen and street vendors, and bought a dozen shucked clams for a dime.

By midafternoon he was back in his room, already worrying whether he'd made the right decision to become a reporter. Was literature really a profession, he asked himself. Did one pursue literature after all? Or did literature pursue one? Was he ready to spend his life writing for some editor who would dictate to him what and how he should write? Except for the *Post* and the *Tribune*, most of the New York dailies were trash, and even they employed a chest of journalistic gimmicks. What journalists did, when one thought about it, was simply walk into a room filled with reference books and foreign phrase books and fill an article with high-sounding words ripped from their pages. Didn't that explain why one could find a sentence in an editorial in the *Evening Post* which sounded like someone trying to sound educated. "We may add," the sentence began, that the author "had not learned the biographer's art of *tout dire*—that *secret de ennuyer.*" Oh yes, Stevens could already see: New York was surely the best place to learn how to become Americanized.

Each day he walked the streets of lower Manhattan, familiarizing himself with a hundred different landmarks. Once he sat on a bench in Washington Square observing a man in an overcoat and rags hurrying by as if hiding something. He visited Trinity Church and was moved by the people praying there. On the other hand, he found Cooper Union "a dirty hole" compared to the Astor Library. He got a hair cut and had "four different kinds of oil" patted on his face, along with a dab of Vaseline in his hair "and a spray of water" up his nostrils, and came away feeling like some "embalmèd sweet." He ordered a packet of letters of introduction sent to various editors around the city to see if any of them might bite: *Munsey's*, the *New York Journal*, the *World*, and the *Herald*, then walked the six miles up to Columbia College on Morningside Heights, struck especially by the Beaux-Arts grandeur of the Seth Low library.

One afternoon he found his way to the top of the twenty-story *New York World* building on Newspaper Row, where the dailies vied with each other to build the world's tallest skyscraper, and enjoyed a bird's-eye view of lower Manhattan. The weather had been sultry for several days, and as he looked across at the twenty-three-story Tract Society Building opposite him he was suddenly knocked off his feet when lightning struck the Tract's flagpole. He wasted no time getting back down to the street.

His first regular assignment freelancing for the *New York Tribune* was to cover the funeral of Stephen Crane. The twenty-eight-year-old author of *Maggie* and *The Red Badge of Courage* had succumbed to tuberculosis in Bavaria, and his body had been shipped home for services at the Methodist Central Metropolitan Temple on Seventh Avenue and Fourteenth Street. Stevens found the whole affair frightful. The church had been only one-third full, and those present made up "a wretched, rag, tag, and bobtail" lot. He found the minister's address humdrum and absurd, certainly unworthy of the poet and novelist who had lived such "a brave, aspiring, hard-working life." When, afterward, the hearse rattled up the cobblestone streets, no one even doffed a hat. But then, this was New York.

A month after his arrival he rented an apartment at 37 West Ninth Street, which came with a bureau and an oval gilt mirror, along with numerous photographs of actresses as well as a library that included *The Divine Comedy* in Italian, the poems of Ralph Waldo Emerson, and something on the pleasures of solitude. From the window facing the street, he could see ivy clinging to the walls and a brush stroke of blue sky beyond. And from a window at the rear he discovered mountain asters and—to his delight—"several birds who make a little music for me in the morning."

He passed the evening hours in the *Tribune*'s outer offices, hoping for something to happen so he could write it up and get paid for it. But when nothing happened, he composed lines for sonnets in his head. One, he mused, might end with the mellifluous line "And hear the bells of Trinity at night." He hated the city's obsession with "infernal money-getting." But working the night shift now until four each morning, and reading Stedman's treasury of sonnets in *A Victorian Anthology* when he could, he wondered if things like sonnets really had a place in a city like New York, where life was "quick, unaccountable," electric, and which seemed interested only in the crisis of the moment.

The truth was that the sheer impersonality of the city overwhelmed him, whether it was the posh Harvard Club on West Forty-fourth, where, as an alumnus, he might dine, or the local saloon on the corner of Sixth and Eleventh, where he could order a beer and smoke a cigar and stroke a cat that had curled up on his lap while he talked to a stranger who had simply walked over and sat down opposite him, rolling "thin, sweet-smelling wisps" of marijuana and spinning yarns about life as a sailor and going around the Horn. At midnight Stevens said goodnight, then walked back to his apartment alone.

One night that September, walking home after his shift at the *Tribune* ended at 4:00 AM, he looked up to catch several shooting stars, then breathed in the fresh air and welcome stillness of the city. At other times he tasted the solace and cold beauty of St. Patrick's Cathedral, where he liked to come in out of the city's hustle and rest a while. Soon after, he began working daytime hours at the *Tribune*, making $15 a week, a little more than half of what he'd made freelancing. But a raise had been vaguely promised, and at least he could starve on his own terms now at a regular job. One of his first tasks was to cover the anti-imperialist, anti–gold standard Democratic candidate for president, William Jennings Bryan, who for the second time was trying to defeat the incumbent, William McKinley. In three hours' time he had heard Bryan address two crowds at Madison Square Garden, then another at Tammany Hall, and yet another at Cooper Union. Stevens found Bryan convincing enough to earn his vote, which meant returning to Reading. But once again, Bryan would fail to win the presidency.

Autumn in New York, with its clear cool days and leaves falling thickly and the wind kicking up again. He took long walks among the statues in Central Park and listened to the music he imagined whispering from the harp beneath the bust of Beethoven. His favorite spot was West Street, which ran parallel to the Hudson, because he too, like Whitman, was fascinated by New York's "clattering trucks and drays, tinkling and bouncing horsecars," and endless diners and restaurants and street vendors feeding the masses. He noted the hundreds of different flags hanging from the mastheads of steamships and sailing vessels, as well as "stevedores and longshoremen lounging about in the sun . . . dressed in overalls and a blouse, with a cap on their heads, a pipe in their mouths & their hands in their pockets," some of them "big-boned, husky fellows," others tubercular wrecks. He saw Jewish merchants selling "combs or cuff-buttons or cat's eyes [moonstones] from Mexico," as well as "hucksters, & fishmen, and grizzly oyster-openers, & ferry-keepers."

That fall he took in a number of plays, including Richard Mansfield in *Henry V*, delighting especially in Pistol's comic buffoonery. He saw Edmond Rostand's *L'Aiglon* at the Knickerbocker, an Englishing of the French production, and marveled at the Duke's anguished monologue as he faced the accusing wind, whose strange voice, Stevens suddenly realized, was coming from a wind machine. Though it was a serious moment in the tragedy, he couldn't help laughing out loud as the machine tried its damndest to double as the voice of the Furies.

The Duke's role had actually been created for Sarah Bernhardt, who'd performed it magnificently in the original French. He fell in love with Bernhardt in her role as Hamlet, which she likewise performed in French. He was in the audience that Friday night, December 28, 1900, and though the reviewer for the *Tribune* panned her performance, Stevens understood what Bernhardt had really achieved. She'd begun, he noted with the precision of Henry James, "in a level, unemotional, non-committal manner," then suddenly charged her monologue with emotion while her appearance remained the same. It was that exterior vacancy while the mind roiled beneath that he himself would come to master both as a business executive and as a poet. "Long ago," he recalled forty years later,

> Sarah Bernhardt was playing Hamlet. When she came to the soliloquy, "To be or not to be," she half turned her back on the audience and slowly weaving one hand in a small circle above her head and regarding it, she said, with deliberation and as from the depths of hallucination: "*D'être ou ne pas d'être, c'est là la question* . . ." and one followed her, lost in the intricate metamorphosis of thoughts that passed through the mind with a gallantry, an accuracy of abundance, a crowding and pressing of direction,

> which, for thoughts that were both borrowed and confused, cancelled the borrowing and obliterated the confusion.

"The intricate metamorphosis of thoughts." That too would become his own manner of composing over the years.

That New Year's Eve he sat in his room, pondering whether to go to midnight Mass at St. Patrick's to welcome in the twentieth century or simply stay where he was. In the end he stayed put. He considered making a series of New Year's resolutions, then let that idea go as well. Where, after six months in the city, was he headed? He thought of sailing for Europe or seeing Mexico or at least Arizona. But the farthest west he got that winter was Reading, where he'd spent Christmas having another of those man-to-man talks with his father, who advised him against doing anything as rash as traveling until he had a better idea of where his future lay. Suddenly he heard the ringing of church bells and the shouts of crowds on the street ushering in the twentieth century. Well, they might usher it in, he thought, but none of them, himself included, was going to be around to usher it out. He tried to say a prayer as he entered the infant century, then gave up that idea as well.

That February he moved once more, this time over to 124 East Twenty-fourth Street, to an apartment formed by partitioning off one end of the hall and shoving a bed and a few modest accoutrements into it. Still, he rather liked it, just as he had to admit that he was actually coming to like New York. One thing he knew: he was not going back to Reading as his brothers had. Soon he was taking long walks again, once that same month up to Central Park, arriving there in the yellow afterglow of the setting sun amid the jingling of horse-drawn sleighs, and kept on walking into the dark. Hours later, alone among the trees etched against the night sky, he heard the eerie hoot of an owl and suddenly felt "the mysterious spirit of nature." Then a moment later, he was once more looking at the hotels and apartment houses lined up like factories along the West Side.

A week later he saw Ethel Barrymore at the Garrick Theatre in the role of Mme. Trentoni in the comedy *Captain Jinks of the Horse Marines.* So charmed was he by her performance that he returned to watch her in two more performances. He even began composing a romantic comedy of his own, a light piece he called *Olivia*, about an American innocent somewhere in France (he would decide just where after he'd had a chance to consult his Baedeker and maps of the country). Then he added a dreamy poet, who remained nameless and who from the start had no chance with the charming Miss Olivia against her more worldly suitors and so simply disappeared from the stage. It was in fact a portrait of his own unhappy life.

There's a story—perhaps apocryphal, but indicative of Stevens's darker moods at the time—which William Carlos Williams no doubt heard from Stevens himself, of the young down-and-out Stevens "sitting on a park bench at the Battery watching the out tide and thinking to join it, as a corpse, on its way to the sea." Then, "as he sat there watching the debris floating past him he began to write—noting the various articles as they passed." Before long he'd become excited with what he was writing, so that he ended up taking back to the *Tribune* office an editorial that became famous in a small way.

He had an interview with John Phillips at McClure, Phillips & Co., which sold hundreds of articles by muckrakers like Ida Tarbell, who was exposing the illegal practices behind Standard Oil's huge profits, and Lincoln Steffens, who had revealed the corruption endemic to Tammany Hall. How, Stevens asked Phillips, did one actually make a living in the publishing world? Phillips, who was having a hard time keeping his publishing venture alive, told Stevens that publishing was mostly a clerical affair and paid very little. And with that, Stevens's dream of becoming a journalist went up in smoke. But when he wrote his father that he was ready to quit the *Tribune* and begin writing seriously, his father wrote back, tearing apart his son's suggestion as impracticable. "If I only had enough money to support myself," Stevens sighed, "some of his tearing would be in vain." But wasn't that the trouble? That the old man seemed "always to have reason on his side"?

• • •

THAT OCTOBER STEVENS ENTERED New York Law School at 35 Nassau Street. A decade earlier the founders of the school, which had followed Harvard's lead in basing classes on actual law cases, had split from Columbia's law school, which insisted on keeping the model of studying historical law tracts. The result was that, while Columbia's law school numbers dwindled, the New York Law School was on its way to becoming the largest of its kind in the country. No letters have survived from this period, and Stevens—busy with classes and finding the money to eat—stopped writing in his journal until the following summer. Nor do we have any letters from Garrett Sr., who had recently suffered a financial reversal with the failure of his real estate investments and his bicycle company, which in turn led to a nervous breakdown and a six-month rest cure in Saranac, New York. By the time Garrett Sr. returned home he was still far from cured. He was only fifty-four, but his shoulders stooped, haggard lines etched his face, and his earlier buoyancy was gone.

When his first year of law classes ended in mid-June 1902, Stevens began clerking in the law offices of William Gibbs Peckham. Thirty years Stevens's senior, Peckham had graduated from Harvard in 1867. The year before, he had cofounded the *Collegian* with his fellow student Charles Gage, and when the *Collegian* was banned after three issues for demanding cessation to compulsory attendance at chapel, Peckham and Gage had started the *Harvard Advocate* to replace it. After graduation Peckham had spent two years at the University of Heidelberg and had gone on to become a successful lawyer, defending several banks and winning several lawsuits against New York City's elevated rail lines. A dapper dresser with a prominent forehead and thick beard and mustache, he was also a member of several art societies, read Goethe and Heine in German, and had made himself an excellent horseman and outdoorsman. Now he took Stevens under his wing as he himself had been taken care of when he'd started out, thanks to Harvard's old-boy network.

Soon after, Stevens was invited to the Peckhams' estate in Westfield, New Jersey, where he rode horses with Peckham. In July he was invited to the Peckhams' summer lodge in the Adirondacks, where he reconnected with Miss Sybil Gage, a stunningly beautiful woman his age whom he had seen (at least from a distance) any number of times on his walks to and from Harvard Yard. She was the daughter of Charles Gage, who had become, among other things, a short story writer and a New York publisher. Gage had died some years before, but the families had remained close.

And so, by chance, here in the Adirondack Mountains, Stevens discovered his real-life sibyl.

Half a century later Sybil's image was as fresh in Stevens's imagination as when he first saw her in front of her home on Hilliard Street, across from Radcliffe Common, back when he had first arrived at Harvard. His principal interest in Charles Gage, he would explain to his fellow poet Richard Eberhart after a visit to Harvard in 1950, was not that Gage had founded the *Advocate* but that he'd founded Sybil. All those years later Sybil remained for him an angel, a beautiful woman who loved poetry.

He and Sybil spent a good deal of time together in the Adirondacks, walking through the woods and along the lake, and each was clearly drawn to the other. Trained as a teacher, Sybil had been studying Friedrich Froebel and Johann Heinrich Pestalozzi, two pioneers of early childhood education, and she discussed their ideas with a skeptical Stevens—skeptical because for Stevens life was harder and meaner than those two pedagogues seemed to understand. Still smitten, he composed a lyric for Sybil which began comically enough before it shifted to its real purpose, which was to remark on her compassionate nature:

Froebel be hanged! And Pestalozzi—pooh!
No weazened Pedagogy can aspire
To thrill these thousands—through and through—
Or touch their thin souls with immortal fire.

Only in such as you the spirit gleams
With the rich beauty that compassions give:
Children no science—but a world of dreams
Where fearful futures of the Real live.

It seems to have been an idyllic time, as such summer interludes can be, but when their time together was over, Stevens returned to his sweltering New York confines, a law student with very limited resources and years to go before he would earn anything like a living, while Sybil prepared to leave for the American West to teach. Whatever might have been remained only one more possibility in a world of infinite possibilities and infinite disappointments.

"Oh, Mon Dieu," he confessed to his journal. "How my spirits sink when I am alone here in my room!" He was tired of everything, even of reading and smoking and walking around the city. How he longed for the company of others. That evening he sought out a dark transept in St. Patrick's and spent an hour meditating there. But was the true religious force to be found in the church or in the mysterious callings of Nature and the "incessant murmurs" of the human voices which filled the church? In a pew in St. Patrick's or on the upper Palisades overlooking the Hudson? Or were these merely opportunities in which two entirely "different deities presented themselves"? If he had only a cloudy vision of either reality, it was the priest in him that worshipped God in one way, while the poet in him worshipped God in another way: the priest worshipped Mercy and Love; the poet worshipped Beauty and Might.

It was time to clear his head once again by taking long hikes. One Sunday he managed seventeen miles under a hot August sun, traveling by ferry across the Hudson to New Jersey, then by trolley from Hackensack to Spring Valley, Ridgewood, and Ho-Ho-Kus, before doubling back to Paterson. The following weekend he managed forty miles, hiking through the Oranges to Boonton, then climbing Torne Mountain to discover "one of the most beautiful scenes within a Christian distance of New York." Crossing the Meadowlands by train, he watched the evening sky turn gloriously pink above the smoke-sodden buildings of Manhattan.

The following Sunday he crossed over to Long Island and took the train out to Mineola, then another to Point Lookout facing the Atlantic. He'd never felt at home by the sea, and as he sat on the sands looking seaward and listening to the waves, all he heard was the empty sound of the wind blowing through the treetops. Better to imagine the sea, he thought, from the vantage of one's room, where one's imagination could feed on the idea of it, rather than the "dirty and dangerous thing it was in reality." And yet the sea too had its mysteries, and as night descended and he walked westward along the beach, he saw lights in heaven and on earth he'd never noticed before. Though there were hordes of noisome beach fleas swarming about him, there was the white strand of beach as well, with the setting sun throwing his shadow ominously behind him. Only the presence of two young women relieved the apocalyptic vision.

At the end of summer he finally discovered his Elysium, a place along the Palisades where he could spy on the Upper West Side of the city across the river. No one, he surmised, had ever found this spot, where "two thrushes fidgeted . . . in the boughs" and "stalks of golden rod burned in the shadows like flambeaux." He would come here often to lie under the trees and listen "to the showers of wind" and the water dripping among the rocks. But a month later, returning to discover eggshells scattered on the ground and realizing that the place was not his alone to enjoy, he abandoned it.

Just before his second year of law school began, he returned home, only to be stuck indoors by days of dreary rain. At least in New York he could fool himself into believing that he was living in a fine, false way. But in Reading even dreaming about a better future was useless, for work here reduced itself to going round and round without any deeper meaning. On his way back to New York, he stopped to see the Wilys in Feasterville and found the family more pathetic than ever. While there he called on a Miss Lewis and found her with even fewer manners than himself. Even an unattractive woman, he reasoned, could draw a man to her "by discreet flattery." But let a man flatter a woman and she would merely take it as her due. And if a man wasn't careful, he could be flattered "against his better sense." What fools men were, knowing just how rotten they were and yet so easily persuaded that they were all sweetness. With that, whatever comfort he hoped to find in Miss Lewis vanished.

• • •

FOR NEW YEAR'S 1903 he made four resolutions. First, to drink more water and less liquor. Not that he boozed much, he told himself. He loved temperance, or at least the idea of it, and even the smallest sip of liquor was by force of logic intemperate. Second, he would smoke more wisely so as to avoid the queasiness which often followed. Third, he would write something every night, for surely there was "gold there for the digging." Fourth, he would cut back on sleep by refusing to retire "before twelve candles of day gutter in their sockets & the breeze of morning blows, for sleep only means red-cheeks and red-cheeks are not the fit adornment of Caesar." One had to work, and work hard, if one were to succeed in this world.

Of course he kept none of these resolutions, and we hear no more from him until Sunday, March 1, when he attended services at Trinity Church on Broadway and Wall Street and listened to the seventy-five-year-old Episcopal rector Dr. Morgan Dix preach on "the powers and principalities of heaven." Ten days later he went up to Columbia to hear Alton B. Parker speak about the New York Court of Appeals, for which he served as chief judge. Stevens was struck especially by Parker's "great morality," determination, and kindness. Here was a man to emulate. But even those virtues would not prove enough when in 1904 Parker ran for president on the Democratic ticket against Theodore Roosevelt and was soundly defeated.

Now it was time for Stevens to think about life after law school. He would work in a law office, he imagined, work as hard as he could until he got "enough business . . . to hang out a shingle." But would even that be enough? Only a handful of people, it seemed, ever lived comfortable lives, while thousands lived on the verge of starvation. The Bible's first injunction was "to make the earth fertile and to earn one's bread in the sweat of one's brow." But how was he ever going to make enough to live comfortably, especially when he had nothing and had to admit that he spent endless hours loafing about? Would he now have to forgo his penchant for books and wine and fine food in order to make his way, beginning again at the bottom?

When he graduated that June, he resumed clerking for Peckham in his New York law office, which felt to him pretty much like undergoing an operation in a New York hospital. But, like his father and brothers, he knew now that law was how he was going to have to make his living. On Sundays he lay on the hot sands of Manhattan Beach, listening to those who passed cloud-like around him. And what did his fellow men reveal about the human condition as they discoursed? Nothing so grand as either lamentations or avowals but rather the dull, the comic, the eternal quotidian, the mundane: "Why there's Eddie—Hello, Ed.—Women's colleges—No, I'm from Louisville—There they go—Isn't the water extraordinarily cold?"

On the other hand, lying on the beach, he could philosophize in a more positive manner, looking up now and then to gaze upon a pretty pair of legs, and feeling a slight erotic tremor, which left him feeling "domesticated & friendly to people." Back in his apartment he sipped tea and smoked a Bock Panatela, then went to bed. But one evening in late July his fantasy was afire. As he dreamed of those pretty legs he saw himself rescuing a drowning beauty, which made him even more restless, so that by ten he was up again, telling himself he would read until he fell asleep. A month earlier he had promised himself to live the life of an ascetic, "a cigarless, punchless weary life," then remembered that he'd "smoked Villar y Villars & Cazadores, dined at Mouquin's on French artichokes & new corn etc. with a flood of drinks from crème de cassis mêlée, through Burgundy, Chablis etc. to sloe gin with Mexican cigars & French cigaroots." Once he'd even lunched on "a delicious calf's heart cooked whole & served with peas—pig that I am."

Perhaps, after all, things were beginning to look up. In two days he would head for the Canadian Rockies with Peckham to enjoy the great outdoors until September. But for now he sat musing alone, smoke from his cigar encircling him with visions that would have made even St. Anthony in the Desert blush. The faces he saw were "not the faces of St. Paul or St. Francis or of Mary or Ruth" but rather the face of some bloated fop at one table, while at another sat a good-looking girl chattering away, while at yet another sat "a coarse animal and its mate." Was that what life came down to, then? A world of meaningless chatter while the indifferent winds of life battered away at one? Mercifully, by midnight he had fallen asleep.

4

Two Versions of the American Sublime: 1903–1906

The pensive man . . . He sees that eagle float
For which the intricate Alps are a single nest.

"CONOISSEUR OF CHAOS"

At the beginning of August 1903 Stevens arrived in the Kootenay Rockies in the remote outback of Palliser, British Columbia, population eight. "What fat farms and astonishing prairies and capital mountains" there were to discover in Canada, he thought, as he gazed upon the sublimity of the mountains and the windswept barrenness of blank rock above the timber line, an image of earthly paradise he would remember half a century on as he lay dying.

On the morning of the 3rd he and Peckham and three of Peckham's hands set out by horseback along the Kootenay River, camping twenty miles south of Leanchoil on the far side of the snow-covered mountains. Stevens had brought along a copy of Ovid's *The Art of Love* to read while the others played a card game called Pedro. The men caught trout and shot fool hens and roasted them over a fire. In time Stevens managed to shoot a deer through the heart, but only after one of the hands had brought it down. He watched clouds move like ghostly camels across the mountains as the setting sun flared the pine tops and snowfields, and gazed on the blue-white skies above the Vermilion Pass.

That was one side of it—intimations of the Sublime, like something in a Bierstadt canvas. The other was fighting off the hordes of mosquitoes and black flies that buzzed incessantly through his tent. At night he sat by the fire wrapped in his white Hudson Bay blanket, reading the eighteenth-century French Jesuit Jacques Bossuet's *Lettres Spirituelles* while Peckham declaimed Heine in German to the hands, who passed the time spitting into the fire. There were two different worlds here: Peckham's and that of the mountain men, and before long tensions between the boss and his men began to mount.

Toward the end of August, after nearly four weeks in the wilderness, one of the hands named Hosey rode into camp, announcing that he'd bagged another deer, news which only infuriated Peckham, who had so far caught nothing. At first he refused to let Hosey bring his trophy into camp, then changed his mind. But the boss, Stevens noted, did not forgive easily, and Hosey was going around muttering under his breath that the goddamn boss was crazy. By then Stevens was all too ready to agree. The following day Peckham rode into camp to say he'd shot himself a lynx. True, it had been caught in a trap, but *he* was the one who'd shot it.

August 31, 1903: ice on the river and glistening frost on the logs. So far the hunting had proven difficult, the men inching their way "through burnt timber patches, willow swamps, slash etc. & not in watching or following game." Then came the rains. By early September everyone was ready to head home. The last night in the Kootenays they stayed at a rundown ranch house, where rats kept Stevens awake all night. Then it was two days of slogging through ankle-deep mud to Leanchoil, and from there back to the supply depot at Palliser. Finally they were back on the *Imperial Limited* heading east "through icy mountains [and] prairies of snow" to the lakes of Ontario. By the time he had made it back to New York, Stevens had stored in his memory enough visions of the American Sublime to last him the rest of his life.

• • •

THEN IT WAS BACK to clerking in Peckham's law offices at 54 William Street in the heart of the Wall Street district. After work Stevens would walk up Broadway to East Twenty-fourth Street, then climb the stairs to his hall apartment, where he might look out on "the distant company of strange yet friendly windows burning over the roofs" to the east as they caught the light of the setting sun. He dined with a friend and "guzzled *vin ordinaire* & puffed a Villar y Villar," balancing those epicurean pleasures by promising himself to "reassume the scrutiny of things as they are" the following morning. Henry Fielding had it right, he thought. One's desires were indeed shaped by one's education and penchants and not by nature. For the most part, poverty kept him a hearty Puritan. When you summed it up, all you really needed were "sound shoes, a pair of breeches, a clean shirt and a coat." And the occasional hearty meal. Hang all this talk of sweetness and light, of meekness and nonresistance. And hang philosophy. Only two things finally mattered: ambition and the gumption to realize one's ambition.

By February 1904 his perspective on life had soured even more. He had no money, no prospects, no friends, and did not know a single person in the apartments around him. He needed to "see somebody, hear somebody speak to me, look at somebody, speak to somebody in turn." He needed more than his work, his apartment, the occasional nod of an acquaintance. What he needed more than anything was companionship, female companionship. But given his shy, introspective nature, that seemed almost impossible to find.

That same month he took in three Shakespearean plays, hoping to lift his spirits. It didn't help that one of the plays he saw was *Hamlet*, in which he felt Johnston Forbes-Robertson had portrayed the main character as too sane and too cold. On the other hand, Ben Greet's Company's performance of *Twelfth Night* turned out to be "one of the finest comedies" he'd ever seen, and *As You Like It* "delightful up to the appearance of Phèbe and Silvius in the Fourth Act," when the play turned tedious. At the end of March he stood in the rear of the Cooper Union basement, with its reeking pillars and low ceiling, and listened to the Russian Symphony Society perform Tchaikovsky's Sixth Symphony, with its beautifully evoked sense of despair. But, American xenophobe and typical anti-Semite that he was, he was not happy with the largely Jewish audience from the Lower East Side, with their "suspiciously long hair," one of whom he was sure had passed a bedbug his way.

But his misanthropy went even deeper than that and helps explain why—in a city of four million, many of them immigrants—he felt so lonely. And if, by April, spring had finally arrived, robed in its brilliant violets and vermilions, yellows and whites, he also noted how pallid and sickly everyone looked, including the clientele at the Astor House Bar when he'd stopped there for a drink after work. *Everyone* looked blotchy, like bloodless bloated toads, "and many a good honest woman had a snout like a swine." A city of beggars, walking the filthy cobblestone streets. Worse, he had no idea what he was going to do when (if) he passed the bar exams. One Friday evening he and his old Harvard friend Witter Bynner, living now in Brooklyn, dined at the Café Francis on West Thirty-fifth Street and "sat & smoked & talked & drank St. Estéphe until after midnight." How was he supposed to read his friend, he asked, this fellow with "the manners of a girl, the divination, flattery & sympathy of a woman, the morbidness & reverie of a poet, the fire and enthusiasm & ingenuousness of a young man." The trouble was that, unlike himself, Bynner had yet to pass through the "sentimental, sketchy stage" of life.

With the arrival of spring Stevens returned to the Palisades again, lying on his stomach on the cliffs there and watching the seagulls circling below him over the Hudson as the sun went down. He could almost hear Blake's angels singing their hosannas in the night air. Another weekend, hiking along the cliffs toward West Point, he almost wept with awe at the blueness of the skies. "God!" he wrote, "What a thing blue is! . . . It pulls at the heart with an irresistible sadness . . . as if it were the dusk of the lost Pleiades, as if it were a twilight where any moment the fairies might light their lamps." Blue: the color of the vivid imagination.

Too often, one overlooked the beauty of the world, grinding out one's miserable living as he did among the trivia of law books. Yet if his time in the Kootenays and his long hikes along the majestic Hudson had taught him anything, it was this: that there was about the earth a terrifying and awesome sublimity, for the earth was a giant "full of solitudes & barrens

& wilds," capable of crushing us in an instant. We, on the other hand, were merely "an affair of cities," whose "gardens & orchards & fields" were the merest scrapings. If we had managed "to shut out the face of the giant from our windows," still the giant was out there. Romantic that he was, it was a question he would ask again and again of things as they are.

By the time he passed his New York Bar exams in late June 1904, he was already back in Reading. Both his brothers were practicing law there now, though Stevens had long ago decided to practice in New York. That same summer he met a young woman from Reading who had just turned eighteen. Her name was Elsie Viola Kachel, for him the embodiment of another, kindlier sublime, and—feeling he was now in a better position to allow himself to do so—fell head over heels for her. He met her at the home of her friend Claire Tragel, having been invited there by some old friends. He had, they confided to Claire, a reputation for being cultured and a very fine poet to boot.

Elsie lived with her mother, stepfather, and half-sister at 231 South Thirteenth Street, which meant she was (literally) from the wrong side of the tracks that divided Reading several blocks to the east of the Stevens home. Born on June 5, 1886, she was almost seven years younger than Stevens. Her parents, Ida Smith and Howard Kachel, had married only a few months before Elsie was born; a year later Elsie's father had died, and Ida raised Elsie by herself for the next seven years, before marrying Lehman Wilkes Moll. And while Moll never formally adopted Elsie, she eventually accepted that to most folks, including Stevens, she was Elsie Moll.

She'd attended school until she was thirteen and halfway through the ninth grade, when she had had to drop out to help support her family and also because her eyesight was so poor she could not make out what the teacher chalked on the blackboard. No doubt she needed glasses, but that was a luxury her parents could not afford. Because she'd taught herself to play the piano and play it with a sure light touch, she found work in a local department store selling sheet music, which she played for prospective customers from memory. To supplement her income, she gave piano lessons at home. At eighteen she was shy, awkward, and self-conscious, and walked stiffly, with her arms at her sides.

But she was also beautiful, and she caught Stevens's attention from the start. If she needed to be educated and shaped into the perfect woman, why, she was young enough, and Stevens, with his Harvard degree and book learning and fresh law degree, was more than eager to educate her. The attraction proved mutual, and by early August Stevens could confide to his journal how very happy he was to taste her warm mouth and touch her "ravishing hand; and that golden head trying to hide in my waistcoat somewhere; and those blue eyes looking at me sweetly though without intent."

Everything was altered now under the gaze of new love. That September he began practicing law with Lyman Ward, who had graduated from Harvard with him. Ward and Stevens, they called their partnership, but within months it was clear the practice was failing. Stevens liked Ward and found him "an extremely attractive fellow" who was also funding the venture, though, as Stevens noted in retrospect, Ward "knew nothing about making money." The trouble with Ward, Stevens soon realized, was that he was one of those men who actually believed what people told him. Before long Stevens was looking for another job.

What Stevens would remember most about Ward was his deep and powerful voice. Ward sang bass solo at Trinity Church on Sundays, Stevens recalled thirty years on. Because Ward had a tenacious mind, trial work suited him well, though it did not suit Stevens. Twenty years later Ward would become special assistant U.S. attorney for the Southern District of New York, whose job was enforcing Prohibition. Still later Ward would maintain law offices on lower Broadway, near where he and Stevens had worked together, and live in the swanky Hotel St. Moritz off Central Park. Then, in the spring of 1937, while vacationing in Jacksonville, Florida, he died in an auto accident.

That October 1904 Stevens invited his friend Arthur Clous, who had graduated with him from Reading Boys' High, to share his hall apartment. If moving in helped Clous to adjust to the big city, it also helped the cash-strapped Stevens. He hoped the two could get on together, though Clous had the annoying habit of being able to keep only one idea in his head at a time. If the man "were about to say 'Good Morning!'," Stevens wrote, "and you interrupted him and talked steadily about a thousand things for an hour, he would calmly go ahead with his stupid 'Good Morning' when you concluded." But knowing someone's liabilities allowed one to adjust one's demeanor, and for practical purposes Stevens was willing to adjust, though his deepest instincts were for solitude and reading and thinking about the Perfect Woman.

Though he kept working as hard as he could, he still found it difficult at times even to buy food. One Sunday he dined on Force Wheat Flakes and grapes, then pulled his sofa into the Hopper-like sunlight streaming through his window while he smoked and pored over Elsie's letters. That gave him comfort. If a letter failed to arrive, he wondered if the relationship was over. He had been delighted to see her at Thanksgiving back in Reading, but by now his own family seemed dull beyond belief and the country around Reading even duller. Yet he knew that Reading had shaped him and, however much he might mock it, it would always remain his first home.

On New Year's Day 1905 he and Clous took in an exhibition at the National Academy of Design and then walked through Central Park. A month later they dined over on Astor Place, getting drunk on Chianti and apricot brandy. That was his life now, he complained: "office and theatre and perpetual cold weather." A month later he was singing the same dirge: "Work, concerts, letters from Elsie, books, jaunts around town." A month later life had been reduced to "mere blots on the calendar." What a "monotonous Odyssey" his life had become. Sometimes he thought about just letting it all go, and then he would catch himself. At Easter he was back in Reading, mostly to see Elsie. Elsie: *une vrai princess* [sic] *lointaine*, he called her, "a truly distant princess," a lady to be worshipped, but only at a far remove. That Sunday they hiked over O'Reilly's Gap, gathering arbutus, cowslips, and violets, and Stevens found himself on the seventh rung of heaven.

Once there were letters in abundance from Elsie to Stevens and from Stevens to Elsie that documented these first years of their courtship. But after Stevens died, Elsie destroyed them because, she believed, they had been written only for the two of them. The effect is that, in the passage here and there which she, in her role as censor and severe editor, allowed to survive, Stevens often comes off sounding like some late Victorian

Polonius and Elsie an unwitting Galatea. To wit: "Are you really fond of books—paper valleys and far countries, paper gardens, paper men and paper women? They are all I have, except you; and I live with them constantly." And "I thought today that our letters were like some strange instrument full of delicate and enduring music—music just a little haunting, on which we played for each other." And "I want to be the only person who knows what you really like and think and are. Then you would be my Elsie in reality, and alone." And again "You are infinitely more a part of me than my family, or than any friend I ever have ever had. So that you must be constant."

He took communion at St. John's Lutheran in Reading that Easter morning, then fretted for a week about the efficacy of the sacrament he had received. How uncomfortable he'd felt—he a graduate of perhaps the finest college in America and now a young lawyer (even if a failing one), singing the "Gloria in Excelsis" among "the worn, the sentimental, the diseased, the priggish and the ignorant" he'd grown up among. As spring came around again, he felt the same vague disillusionment with the world. What, then, could he depend on to see him through? Health and physical well-being, for one thing, something his long Sunday hikes would help maintain. Love was another thing. And the consolations of Nature yet another. Add Friendship, Work and, yes, even Fantasy. Better perhaps, then, to stay at home of a Sunday morning rather than go to church. At least in his apartment he could let his imagination wander as Coleridge's Kubla Khan had, probing caverns "measureless to man, / Down to a sunless sea." If his church congregation fell short of what he needed, he would create his own philosopher's circle, a salon of men and women to which he would invite "Mary Stuart, Marie Antoinette, George Sand, Carlyle, Sappho, Lincoln, Hawthorne, Goethe and the like." He would continue to refine this fantasy, including in his interior Matisse-like space coffee and green cockatoos on a rug, as in his aptly named "Sunday Morning," which he would compose a decade later.

Still, he did attend Easter church services again that evening, only to rush home afterward, reciting over and over Shakespeare's "Tired with all these, for restful death I cry." Except for the fact that he would have to leave his beloved, the sonnet ends, the poet would just as soon leave a world where nothing was ever what it seemed. Oh, that the sonnet had been "a thousand times as long and a thousand times more bitter." He imagined himself walking down Broadway, head down and hands clasped behind his back, his black mood destroying everything before him. Yes, he was capable of delight. But man was certainly not a noble animal, nor was it often that his cup ranneth over.

Now, he decided, was the time to leave the city and his roommate and find something for himself over in New Jersey. By late May he'd located a room in a "cheerful" boardinghouse at 31 Halstead Street in East Orange, with decent food and a lawn and some trees. But he still felt terribly alone and, to fill that void, spent his evenings "drinking gin & courting the moon," until he realized that he needed more discipline. Then, for the first time since his expedition to the Rockies, he was on the road again, working for a New York firm which did surety claims, a job which, as it turned out, took him to the most god-awful places in the hottest months of the year.

By mid-July he was back in Reading with Elsie for a two-week stay. The highlight of his time there was a trip by horse and wagon twenty miles north to Strausstown, where he treated Elsie to an early dinner of ham and eggs before they headed southwest through the Blue Mountains to Womelsdorf. That was when the sun finally came out, he recalled, transforming every barn into a castle and every rooster into Chanticleer, and for a moment he was "as happy as a lark in a cloud of gold," as he pulled Elsie close to him. It had been, he told her, *their* day.

Another time he rode down to Ephrata and found old Von Nieda, still at the resort hotel, with the "same whiskers, same glasses," and the same scent of old soap on him. He searched for and found "names and initials crying loudly from the walls," among them his own initials, W.S., the S. carved backward in the bench, and almost wept. Now, ten years on, he had a mother and a father and a younger brother all sick in a house that seemed to have gone to hell, about which he could do nothing. Sometimes he cared and cared deeply about them. But not now. Now he didn't "care a damn." Which troubled him. Was he really all ice? Surely, he mused, someday someone might even discover "human bones . . . among my ashes."

In mid-August he moved from 31 Halstead Street to an attic room in another Victorian house a few houses over at 24 Halstead Place. Still depressed about where his life was headed, he wondered if he really did have a "vicious, dark mind." He called it his "New York gloom," the "creature of rainy Sundays and hideous miscellanea," alleviated now and then by the sounds of crickets and katydids coming from the other side of the window screens on late summer evenings.

Then he was on the road again, this time for a New York law firm whose business was bonding cattle herds and investigating why beef cattle were not reaching their destination. Like Whitman before him, he recorded the America he found: "women chopping wood, wash drying on fences, bare legs: black, white and yellow, Greek temples, rotten melons in a creek, women . . . with men's hats on, ox-carts, . . . [a] mule on [a] kitchen door-step . . . fried chicken, po' white trash leaning against things, rain," as well as razorback hogs which his landlord informed him was "pow'ful disagreeable prop'ty to have 'round." Add to this mélange rooming house beds too short for his six-foot-two frame, terrifying thunderclaps, bedbugs, and hordes of flies buzzing about his body at half past five in the morning, while outside roosters crowed, cows lowed, babies yowled, and a man hawked up phlegm. No wonder that finding Elsie waiting for him when he finally made it back to Reading, and how she'd taken his hand between hers, made him feel "wonderfully welcome."

Back in New York he lunched with his old friend and former classmate, Walter Arensberg, at the Harvard Club. He read Austen and Hardy and Henri Murger's *Scènes de la Vie de Bohème* and studied Japanese culture with its "minute knowledge . . . disclosing minute pleasures," and wrote and in turn received love letters from Elsie. He saw her at Thanksgiving and Christmas and thought every day of what he wanted his future wife to be like. In late December he sat in the top gallery of the Metropolitan Opera House and took in a performance of Humperdinck's *Haensel und Gretel*, and in the following months attended performances of Tchaikovsky, Mozart, and Rimsky-Korsakov by the Russian Symphony Orchestra. When he could, he visited various New York galleries, enjoying landscapes by Lockwood de Forest and Corot and Bierstadt, but especially one by Jean Charles Cazin titled *The Departure of Night.* He bought a decorative screen adorned with painted irises and attended a dance at a Miss Morehouse's and enjoyed himself, for he was a good dancer. But when he felt a subtle quiver rising in him as he moved across the dance floor, he thought of Elsie and abruptly left the party, waiting till the following morning to retrieve his hat. Had he not left when he did, he confessed, he "should soon have become blacker than Moses."

To settle himself, he walked long and furiously all that day, until he could feel the blood pounding through his veins and his black thoughts lifting. In the evening he went to Christ Church and sat in a pew near "a doddering girl of . . . twenty," with her "idiot eyes, spongy nose, and shining cheeks." The girl was accompanied by two women, one middle-aged, the other elderly, both "hungry-respectable looking" and all wearing homemade bonnets. Looking at such specimens, he saw, made it impossible "to be religious in a pew." Better some "great nave, quiet lights, a remote voice, a soft choir and solitude," or, if not that, a sacred grove somewhere.

He was tired of his lack of faith, tired of having always to question everything, of being bedeviled by so much self-consciousness. How much easier life would be if everything were simply spelled out for you. Oh, to have the black-and-white conscience of an executioner or a Russian policeman! How many passing moods made up his daily consciousness, each one of which someone somewhere had spent a life living out. Did one have to accept the baffling incertitude of the human condition and the despair that ensued, or should one struggle against that and lift one's spirits in any way one could? What was he, after all, if not some New Jersey Epicurean who took long walks and smoked and read the maxims, axioms, and adagia of Leopardi and Schopenhauer and Pascal and Rochefoucauld and called such things the knowledge of the world?

• • •

ON APRIL 22, 1906, the first Sunday after Easter, he thought of just lying down on his bed with a pistol nuzzled against his right temple and pulling the trigger. "It is such splendid melancholy," he mused, "and, mixed with a little beer and whiskey—divine. If only one could look in at the window when they found one's body—one's blood and brains all over the pillow. How terrible the simple books would look,—and the chairs and curtains so carefully drawn! How empty, for a moment, the lawns would seem,—the Sunday twittering of the birds! How impotent all the people!" Then he would tap on the window and say, "It is all a mistake. Let me come in again. I know how foolish it all is. But what is one to do?"

And yet what did life amount to after all, his black moods hissed. Where did it all lead? Wasn't it true that "the Christian fears life and loves death?" One became a clerk (or a lawyer) and died a clerk (or a lawyer). That was the given. The trouble was that the clerk too often imagined "marvels for his old age, a life in splendid retirement." Or one entertained one's sexual fantasies that, acted upon, would simply go to support some pimp. But what a bore not to give in to such fantasies. He imagined his own Victorian *Esthétique du Mal*, something taken from Beardsley, perhaps, the cunning serpent in the guise of some hypnotic vampire "coiled round the limbs and body of a woman, . . . its fangs in her pale flesh, sucking her blood." Or that same serpent coiled around someone like himself, the body "fainting in the distorting grip, the fangs in the neck—the victim's mouth fallen open with weakness, the eyes half closed." And the spent serpent "triumphing, horrible with power, gulping, glistening." If only he had Elsie here, and he some noble warrior, whispering sweet nothings to her. How content he should be then, instead of living in an attic and feeding himself on such sexual fantasies.

• • •

THAT JULY HE SAW Elsie again, then it was back to work in his New York office in the stifling heat. He watched some stray cats slinking along West Twenty-second Street, "starved, nonchalant, dingy things," one with its foot in a garbage can "blinking at a cloud of flies buzzing around its nose," like those four street urchins he'd seen whose ribs had so protruded he wondered if they really were intelligent creatures. Or that Saturday afternoon, when he'd walked through Hoboken and Jersey City and on to Newark. So many broken-down places and vile shops. Or that sign he'd read for a picnic gathering of the Hog-Slaughterers Association, or that huge pile of horse dung along the turnpike, or those Italian workers building a street-railway.

One night in mid-August, after dinner at the boardinghouse, he accompanied a harp, a violin, and a bad piano on his rusty guitar while two women sang hymns. But the company was so awful that once again he fled, this time to a nearby park, pebbles crunching beneath his feet as he watched young men and women caressing. Was it really worth all this trouble to make a decent life for oneself? Perhaps, he concluded, but only if you managed to succeed where so many had failed.

Note for September 5: "Read such things as may rather yield compunction to thy heart, than occupation to thy head." Dear old Thomas à Kempis, he smiled. And this: "The noble love of Jesus impels a man to do great things, and stirs him up to be always longing for what is more perfect." He would try to remember that as well.

By mid-September he was once again without a job. Then, at the beginning of October, he moved once more, this time to the Bronx, where he found a room on Sedgwick Avenue in the Fordham Heights section of the city. Having been let go by one law firm because of the economic crisis facing the country, he found a temporary position with the firm of Eaton & Lewis at 44 Broad Street. He began there Monday morning, October 8, taking the El from the northern to the southern tip of Manhattan each morning, then reversing himself each evening, a fifty-minute ride each way. "New office, new room, everything new," he journaled. But was it, really?

By late 1906, after five and a half years in New York and more years of the same to come, he was mired in his black abyss once again. "I am afraid to review the last two months," he confessed, because he knew they had changed him for the worse. He no longer read or even thought much these days, his brain having morphed like his daily subway vision into some worm-like creature tunneling "its way through everything" and leaving "everything crumbling behind." Once more life had been reduced "to a walk, . . . a little music, a few pages, a trip home at Thanksgiving." It was certainly "no Iliad" recounting such a humdrum failure of a life. And nothing, he now saw, was going to change that anytime soon.

5

Wingèd Victory: 1907–1913

My wings shall beat all night against your breast,
Heavy with music—feel them there aspire
Home to your heart, as to a hidden nest.

WALLACE TO ELSIE, FROM "A BOOK OF VERSE"
FOR HER 22ND BIRTHDAY, JUNE 1908

Sunday, March 10, 1907: It was snowing and it was going to snow. He'd been shoveling wet snow from in front of his apartment on Sedgwick Avenue, so that his arms still shook as he wrote Elsie. During a lull in the storm, he'd run along the Bronx River and escaped into the summer world of the greenhouses of the New York Botanical Garden. He found large palm trees there under the glass dome as well as sparrows, he told her, "just coming out of sparrow church," while, just beyond the glass, the blizzard raged on. Camellias, a Japanese bush in bloom, a pool with carp flashing their golden backs. It was a fitting image for the interior world Stevens tried always to carry with him. Though he still said his prayers each night, he wondered if that was merely the remnant of some half-unconscious habit, for he no longer felt he had to rely on those prayers. Still, there was something Santayana had said to him years before: how in Salamanca, Spain, there was "a pillar in a church . . . worn by the kisses of generations of the devout," and Stevens understood now that just "one of their kisses" was worth all his prayers, for something about the church remained alive for those flocks of pilgrims, as it did, at odd moments, in spite of everything, for himself as well.

By then his office, like so much else around him, had turned dingy, and his travel to and from work each day had become a passage through the same Dantesque underground. Occasionally there was a view of the Washington Bridge over the Harlem River, "all very Roman and wonderful," and walks up through Yonkers and New Rochelle, and the occasional glimpse of a purple mist-like twilight settling over Long Island Sound. But there was no real country for miles around. Worse, with the advent of spring, his black moods descended like succubae, and his revulsion against people and places deepened. How sad that the sun itself in all its majesty should have to shine on "nothing but mud and bare trees and the general world, rusty with winter." Part of his gloom no doubt stemmed from his still not knowing—because of the financial panic of 1907—if he had a job from one week to the next. Part was visiting his family that Easter and finding them as depressing as ever, and even Elsie for the moment "more or less unmanageable."

To keep his mind active and off his habitual blackness, he read Keats's *Letters* and Boswell's three-volume *Life of Johnson* and Matthew Arnold's *Notebooks*, with its learned quotations in six different languages, as well as a volume of lectures on ancient Greece effusing a "noble conception of a pagan world of passion and love and beauty and life." He read whatever of value he could find—in spite of how hard it was even to find a decent bookstore in New York—and dreamed of someday lining the walls of his living room with books and spending his days and nights lost in reading. It was the only ardor he still felt. He threw away things he no longer had any use for, including the Bible he'd been given for attending Sunday school as a boy. He had grown to hate the look of that Bible and was glad to see the silly thing gone. And though he held on to his college books as well as his father's copy of Robert Burns's poems, he knew that someday he'd rid himself of those as well.

That May he took the train to Darien, Connecticut, for a weekend to visit his old friend Charles Dana and his wife, and walked with them and their two dogs down to the beach facing the Sound and loafed on the rocks there, contemplating the crashing of blue waves. As a ward against his loneliness, he bought himself a large photograph of Rembrandt's *The Prodigal Son in the Brothel*, which shows a young rake with a young woman sitting on his lap as he holds up a glass of liquor. Rembrandt had used his wife, Saskia, as his model for the young woman, and Stevens had bought it, he told Elsie, rather than a Madonna because it was just the image he needed now to lift his spirits. He did not, however, tell her the title of the picture.

"I am in the mood for suddenly disappearing," he confessed in his journal in early June, and then wrote nothing for the next two months, by which time he was back in Reading and out of work again. Meanwhile he did some legal work in his father's office and took to hiking the roads around home. He became preoccupied with the concept of *l'art pour l'art*, art for the sake of art alone, and pondered a hundred different aspects of the Pennsylvania landscapes he had walked through over the years, the way a prisoner might stare at postcards of landscapes papering his cell. By late September he was back in New York again, still looking for work, "intent on getting something of consequence," though that prospect was beginning to look more and more improbable.

That October, as he turned twenty-eight, he found temporary work as a legal advisor for the Equitable Life Assurance Company, and within a month he was down in Washington, consulting with President Theodore Roosevelt and Charles Joseph Bonaparte, the U.S. attorney general, who were working to get the country back on its feet in the wake of the financial downturn. Then it was back to New York, where he found work with the law firm of Eustis and Foster at 80 Broadway, while, as he phrased it, other plans simmered.

Finally, in early December, with a real job on the horizon, he moved into the six-story redbrick Benedick at 80 Washington Square East in Greenwich Village, an exclusive apartment building for bachelors (cleverly named for the bachelor in Shakespeare's *Much Ado About Nothing*), which sported exotic bohemian apartments. In the evenings he read to Robert Collyer, an eighty-four-year-old Unitarian minister who had been rector at the Church of the Messiah on Thirty-fifth Street and whose eyesight was now failing. He also visited the National Academy of Design to view the new impressionist landscapes, which he dismissed as mere "transcripts of common-place Nature."

Twice he returned to Reading—once at Christmas and again for New Year's—to be with Elsie. He inscribed a copy of Bliss Carman and Richard Hovey's popular anthology, *Songs from Vagabondia*, for her, along with some verses he'd composed for her eyes alone. Nuances, innuendoes, and little secrets peeked through the lines. "Suppose some glimmering / Recalled for him," he winked,

An odorous room—
A fan's fleet shimmering

Of silvery spangle—
Two startled eyes—
A still trembling hand,
With its only bangle.

A bangle, a glass ornament worn by the bride on her wrist on her wedding day. Eastern tradition had it that the honeymoon would last as long as the bangle remained unbroken.

Finally, on Monday morning, January 13, 1908, he began regular employment in the insurance business, which—given his personality and the difficulties he had working with people—made more sense to him than a law career. This was in the New York offices of the American Bonding Company of Baltimore, in the sixteen-story Royal Insurance Building at 84 William Street, where he would work for the next five and a half years. He wrote legal briefs in the office and, in the evenings, poems in his Washington Square apartment. On June 5, Elsie's twenty-second birthday, he presented her with a "Book of Verses," made up of twenty poems, a few composed in a classically restrained free-verse form, though most were written in variously rhymed candy-box quatrains. Some were impressionistic in a Whistlerian sort of way; others were peculiarly dark and foreboding. A ferry ride in fog, for instance, reflecting perhaps the formlessness and incertitude of a journey (or marriage) undertaken, where only the will—embodied in the insistent beats and clanging of dissonant vowels and rhymes—propelled the speaker forward:

Fog now, and a bell,
A smooth, a rolling tide.
Drone, bell, drone and tell,
Bell, what vapors bide. . . .

Toll now, a world resolved
To unremembered form.
Toll the stale brain dissolved
In images of storm.

But such lines were the exception. His more quotidian patois remained the legal jargon of the world of contracts.

When, that fall, his father asked him pointedly if the only reason he kept coming back to Reading was so that his mother could do his laundry—since otherwise he seemed to spend all of his time with that girl across the tracks—Stevens stormed out of the house. Then, thinking it over, he brought his shy, blond, blue-eyed girl home to meet his family. She dressed spectacularly for the occasion in clothes she herself had sewn, and wore a new broad-brimmed hat with flowers adorning it. But Garrett Sr., whose depression had deepened in the wake of his disastrous financial losses, had hoped his son's dalliance with Elsie would have ceased by then. When it hadn't, he could no longer hide his real feelings and made the girl feel unwelcome in his home.

That was when the Stevens anger rose up and Wallace again stormed out of the house, telling his father that he did not intend to set foot there again as long as the old man was alive. It was a promise Wallace kept, one which would cause him unspeakable pain until his dying day. "Wall was in town," his mother wrote Wallace's sister Elizabeth that Thanksgiving, her pain almost palpable. But he had not come home to visit her or his father.

From now on Stevens would stick by Elsie. He needed her and felt desolate without her. Once, he'd gone to see a performance of *The Prima*

Donna which had cheered him as he sat alone in the upper gallery, that is, until he'd looked down on all the happy people and nearly wept. Couldn't she write him more, telling him everything she did from the time she got up until she went to bed? "Tell me what you wear," he begged her, "what time you get my letter—where you read it—every little thing. I want to have a peep into one of your ordinary days—as if I were watching you without your knowing it. No embellishing, mind you." He asked her for a photograph for Christmas, one with her facing him "but not looking right out of the picture," and wearing the simplest dress she had. She could even wear a hat, "the one with the black thing-a-ma-jig on it—not the one with the wide brim," for such hats were out of fashion now. He was bewitched by her, he admitted. Or at least by the idea of her. That Christmas Elsie presented him with the photograph he'd asked for, and he in turn gave her a diamond engagement ring purchased at Tiffany's. Business was booming, and he had his hands full these days. The insurance business consisted mostly of thinking without anything to show for it, but it paid the bills, and come September they could finally get married.

As 1909 roared in, he continued writing her long letters almost every evening. He read Henry James's *Washington Square*, which painted the very place he was living now as it had been thirty years before. Back then the Square was still a suburb of the city, which had now morphed into Manhattan's new "down-town—the very last place, in fact, in which people still lived, all below it being exclusively business, except for the tenement intermissions." He also read Poe, whose centennial it was; the revival in interest in him happened, he believed, because those who questioned the supernatural had found a substitute for it in a world of hallucinations and mysteries.

After all, the imagination had to be served, because most people—himself included—lived far too ordered lives and moved in the same monotonous groove day after day after day. Life was what humans cried out for, and that was not to be found in going to and from work on the subway. What mattered most was breathing in the pure oxygen of the imagination. Wasn't Poe's short, tragic life far more exciting than the life people like himself led, surrounded as they were by walls: office walls, apartment walls, yes, and the walls of the subway stations they found themselves imprisoned in each day?

Then there was the sensitive issue of one's pedigree, which had caused such deep damage with his family. All that really mattered, he reassured Elsie, was what one made of oneself. Every family had its poor relations. They had both come from respectable families; what they did with that fact was up to them. Nothing was "more absorbing than to trace back the good and evil in us to their sources"—to blame one's bloodlines—and yet nothing was more "unjust or more ungenerous." Then too there was the deep depression which ran in his family and had left his father crippled. He hated depression—*hated* it—and yet he had to admit that there were times when he suffered greatly from it himself.

What he hoped to be someday was a simpler and wiser human being, someone who could handle whatever life sent his way, though such wisdom and forbearance would come, if it came at all, only with time. Ten years before, while vacationing in Pennsylvania Dutch country, he'd jotted down a single line: "Oh, what soft wings shall rise above this place." Now, returning to that line, he composed a Petrarchan sonnet he called "In a Garden." The garden he meant was his own imagination, his own enclosed space, his *hortus inclusus*, filled with heavenly wings which lifted skyward, while at the same time sheltering within them the one necessary angel: the "odor and dew of the familiar earth."

• • •

HE RETURNED TO READING often that spring to be with Elsie, or wrote her letters about the philosophy of Paul Elmer More, or about music, or about Hispanic and classical Chinese art and American landscape painting and archetypal theory, much of which could not have deeply interested her. But he needed an audience of at least one, and that role he had bestowed on her. On the last Sunday in April he and Elsie hurried downtown to catch the early trolley from Reading to Blandon, where they got off to wander along the banks of Maiden Creek. He watched his girl with admiration as she ran ahead of him to gather cowslips and dandelions. Then it was on to Evansville to look down over the valley below. That was when the wind came up and they rested by a fence while she fixed her golden hair. Then she was riding on his giant shoulders, pretending all the while not to like it, though he knew better. Afterward they rested in a grove, their backs against a tree trunk, and ate tongue sandwiches, eggs and pickles, and tangerines and cake. Later he stole a kiss from her in the lane, then drank cold spring water from a magic goblet they found at a farmer's pump. This was their world, at least for the moment.

Back in the city he hired two English sailors off the street to move his belongings to 117 West Eleventh Street, about a half mile north of Washington Square. The new flat was part of a series of four-story row houses off Sixth Avenue and much larger than his old apartment, equipped with a closet, *two* windows, and a fireplace. It even came with a small table, so that he no longer had to balance a suitcase on his knees to compose his letters. The following Sunday he walked down to St. John's German Lutheran Church on Christopher Street an hour before services and sat in the last pew, thinking. He'd just read a life of Jesus in the Astor Library and wanted "to see what symbols of that life appeared in the chapel," though the only thing he could find that evoked anything of Christ's actual life was the plain gold cross on the altar. How impoverished the cross seemed when compared "with the wealth of symbols, of remembrances . . . created and revered" in the Church in former times.

If the Church was ever to be more than merely a moral institution, he realized, if it was actually to have an influence on the way one lived now, if it was ever to be more than some quiet gloomy space "to mystify and enhance the spirit," then it would have to return to those earlier sacred spaces "built by men who felt the wonder of the life and death of Jesus—temples full of sacred images, full of the air of love and holiness—tabernacles hallowed by worship that sprang from the noble depths of men familiar with Gethsemane, familiar with Jerusalem." No wonder the church he'd grown up in had become a mere relic, for didn't its very life, its vitality, "depend on its association with Palestine"?

As he sat there in the church that morning, it was as if he were remembering something long forgotten, as if "seeing something new and strange in what had always been" in his mind. Suddenly, he realized that Jesus and God were actually two separate realities, which was why someone might deny some of the incidents in Christ's life, like the Ascension into Heaven. But how could anyone deny God? Everyone, he was convinced, had to admit that God existed "in some form or other, "even if God be no more than the mystery of Life." Didn't the very idea of God, after all, make the world a sweeter place to dwell in?

For Elsie's twenty-third birthday that June, he presented her with *The Little June Book*, twenty poems he'd gathered for her over the past year. The poems were filled with flowers—blue convolvulus and roses and brilliant white birds—as well as small fishes that swam around in tiny couplets, bloodred and shadowy blue and "amber sheen / And water-green, / And yellow-flash / And diamond ash." In the lacquered tea boxes of those poems he carefully placed Japanese fans and newborn swallows and thrushes grieving in blossoming pear trees, along with exploding galaxies and even an Arab moon.

A few weeks later he began looking for a place for Elsie and himself. He'd hoped they might live just off Washington Square, but the rents there were prohibitive, so he looked uptown. By early August he'd found a worthy home for the two of them: a third-floor apartment at 441 West Twenty-first Street consisting of "two very large rooms with abundant light" occupying an entire floor, with the front room looking out over the General Theological Seminary just across the street.

He was in his office six full days each week, with only Sundays to enjoy the sun before it was back to the grind. There was so much to do at work, and so many people to see, that he'd taken to chain-smoking cigarettes to calm his nerves, which left him at day's end in a stupor without any energy at all, except to glance at the newspapers. If he didn't smoke, his nerves tingled and he needed "to walk violently, work violently, read, write, study—all at a bound." Cigars made him "intolerably irritable" and made life miserable for everybody in the office.

Because he'd become short and sharp with those he had business with, he tried not smoking for two whole days and part of a third, but that only made him snap at everyone. On the third day he smoked during his entire lunch hour and became as docile as a lamb. He regretted not being able to break himself of the habit and admitted that there was something "terribly insidious and seductive" about tobacco. "But," he added, "was there ever a smoker who was not bidding farewell to the weed with one hand and reaching for a perfecto [cigar] with the other?"

A week before he returned to Reading to fetch his beloved, he once again began throwing away things he'd accumulated over the years: books, papers, piles of legal documents, college notebooks filled with pen-and-ink sketches of queer noses, the backs of heads, all drawn while the professor droned on at the lectern. He kept only his diaries and poetical scribblings, all of which he could carry in one hand.

Finally, after five years of courtship, he and Elsie were married. The simple service took place in Reading on September 21, 1909, at Grace Lutheran, which Elsie had joined after she'd met him. None of Stevens's family was present. There was a small reception at Elsie's house, then the couple was off on a modest weeklong honeymoon which took them to Boston and Cambridge, where Stevens showed her around Harvard Yard. They went to Stockbridge and Pittsfield and Albany, where they boarded a steamboat and sailed down the Hudson, arriving at their new home, where they would live until it was time to leave New York behind.

One of the first things they did at West Twenty-first Street was send Elsie's mother a picture postcard of the Chapel of the Good Shepherd on the grounds of the General Theological Seminary, with their apartment just visible in the background, and above which Stevens drew an arrow. "Our house is under the mark," he wrote. "Our floor is the next to the top." The chapel was directly across the street and chimed every evening. *"We are not a part of the chapel,"* he joked, "but apart from it. Hence, the word apartment." Elsie, reading what he'd written, added, "Wallace is crazy. Don't mind him."

In the beginning the couple was happy in their life together. But Elsie was a Reading girl, and it wasn't long before she was missing her family. She still had every hope that she and Wallace would someday return to Reading and settle there, though nothing could be further from her husband's mind. There were arguments, of course, as Stevens and Elsie adjusted to each other, and from time to time their landlord, a German immigrant named Adolph Alexander Weinman, and his family could hear Elsie slamming the closet doors in their upstairs apartment, behind one of which they could also hear Stevens regularly reading poetry aloud to himself. Weinman, nine years older than Stevens, was a prizewinning sculptor who had studied with Philip Martiny and Augustus Saint-Gaudens and had worked with Daniel Chester French, the designer of Lincoln's statue in the Lincoln Memorial. A few years later Weinman would sculpt Elsie's profile, submitting it to the U.S. Mint in Washington, where this very private face, its hair alight with the wings of Mercury, would be chosen to adorn millions of American dimes and half dollars from 1916 to 1945.

For their first Valentine's Day together, Stevens wrote Elsie a poem in which he beseeched St. Valentine to speed them both through the winter months, first "her that I love—and then / Her Pierrot . . . Amen." That first April together they traveled to Annapolis and Baltimore, where Stevens was being considered for a position in the home office of the company he'd been working with for the past two years. His brother Garrett was also living in New York at the time, working for a law firm just down the street from Wallace at 100 William Street, but whether the two crossed paths at all seems unlikely. Garrett Jr. too was married by then, but the couples never socialized, though Garrett did make a few attempts. Hard feelings died hard among the Stevenses, especially with Wallace.

Often, but especially during the torrid, damp summers before air-conditioning, Elsie returned to stay with her mother, grandmother, and sister in Reading. In late May 1910, she was there again, and Stevens was once again living his monk's life in New York. To fill the time he took his customary solitary walks along the Palisades. He dined at a local boardinghouse, where nothing, he told Elsie, ever seemed to change, including the clothes the boarders wore. Once again dust seemed to settle over everything. He missed her, missed her presence, but was often as shy as she was about mentioning such things. How he wished he could tell her how sweet she was. What he could say was that he was happy, and that she would know the reason why.

Though he often joked about Reading and its people, he also knew that his very being was rooted in that ground. He loved to think of Elsie out there sitting at her window, "looking at an old scene, and thinking old-far-off-thoughts." When he thought of an image that might sum up his life, it was of the two of them on Tulpehocken Creek, or sitting on a fence along the Bernville road. One's native earth: *that* was what made one a giant. But a month into Elsie's return to Reading, he was begging her to come back to New York. He knew that country air and good friends were essential to her well-being, but he was desperate for her company and needed her to enliven the place and—yes—take care of *him* for a while.

That Christmas the couple returned to Reading, and when Stevens went back to work, Elsie stayed behind because her grandmother was mortally ill and would be dead before the New Year. There had been a bright moon over the new, seven hundred feet Metropolitan Life Tower on New Year's Eve, he wrote Elsie, but 1911 had entered with so much rain he'd been forced to stay indoors. The following morning he'd gone to the Metropolitan Museum of Art to see Henri Bouchard's bronze statue of a girl feeding a faun. He was also struck by a bronze bust of John La Farge by Edith Burroughs, the head resting on the left hand, the eyes half shut.

That July his father died, and he and Elsie went to Reading for the services. Elsie stayed on with her mother and was still there in August, when Stevens learned that he'd been bypassed for a position as surety manager of the recently formed insurance agency of Whilden and Hancock. The promotion had gone instead to a young southerner, J. Collins Lee, who would continue to be trouble for Stevens for years to come. Stevens had had good reason to expect the promotion, for by then he'd done well in the surety business, where complex monetary calculations had to be made to insure that the insurance company could assume fiscal responsibility for the insured and see a job through to completion.

No doubt if he'd returned home years earlier he would now be doing well by Reading standards, but disappointed as he was, he was *not* moving back to take over his father's law practice. If he ever did go back home, it would be to go into some business that would require capital (which he did not have) as well as "experience and a willingness to make money 1-3/4 cents at a time." Perhaps—he held out the carrot to Elsie, who was anxious to return to Reading—once he was on a firm footing financially, they might find an inexpensive summer place to come back to. In the meantime he would continue along the lines he'd drawn for himself, because it gave him a living and because it offered other possibilities. Things were bound to get better, he promised Elsie. After all, there were thousands all around them struggling just to survive. What kept him and Elsie going would have to be a dream of what was possible rather than the hard reality of things as they were.

But then seeing things as they were had many positive facets as well. Take those black-eyed Susans he'd seen along the Palisades. Or those three yellow birds he'd spotted, "swinging on the yellow flowers" and chattering. Or the moon soft and glowing over Washington Square as he'd exited the Earle Hotel one night after dinner. Such evenings, he sighed, were "like wells of sweet water in the salt sea" or "like open spaces in deep woods." Ah, to be the moonlight itself, and recite lines of poetry and be poetical. But then, did his trifling poesies amount to anything more than those designs one saw on ladies' fans? If Elsie had read between the lines of her husband's letter, she would have seen that what was really keeping him in New York was the long-deferred dream of one day becoming a poet.

• • •

JUNE 25, 1912: "ABOUT a year ago (July 14, 1911) my father died," he confided to his journal. His father had been only sixty-three. His mother was just sixty-four, and now she lay dying. He'd not seen her much over the past ten years, and when he visited in late May, she looked wasted, "sleeping under a red blanket in the old blue-room," the same room where she used to dress, "sitting on the floor to button her shoes, with everything she wore . . . so fresh and clean, and she herself so vigorous and alive."

Soon the house where the Stevenses had lived for the past thirty years would be emptied of furniture and sold. There were the chairs, the closets, the sideboard in the dining room, his mother's old piano on which she used to "play hymns on Sunday evenings" in her "absorbed, studious way." He returned to see her a week later and was relieved that she'd been happy to see him again. Both his sisters were there to take care of her, Catherine reading to her from the same Bible his mother had read to him. His mother had looked at him, he had to believe, with great affection as she whispered her last good-bye to him before he returned to New York.

On Tuesday evening, July 16, a telegram arrived telling him his mother had died, and he left for Reading the following day right after work. The funeral took place that Saturday, and he was back at his desk on Monday morning. All this time Elsie had stayed at a hotel in Vinemont, ten miles west of Reading, without ever once visiting her mother-in-law or attending the funeral. Nor did he see Elsie. It was probably just as well, for he was nearly inconsolable and would have made poor company. While in Reading it was the look of things he wanted to think about: the rugs, the chairs, the old piano, just as his mother had placed them, before it all disappeared. He wrote Elsie from New York to say he might come out to see her in mid-August, but in a subsequent letter he explained that he didn't have the money to make the trip. Did he, on an unconscious level at least, blame Elsie in part for the rift that had kept him from his father until it was too late and from his mother until the fear of losing her as well had finally called him home?

Life went on. In April 1913 he took Elsie on a business trip to Atlantic City, where she strolled along the boardwalk while he attended meetings. She spent the hot summer months at Pocono Manor, Pennsylvania, ninety miles west of New York, while Stevens continued sweating away in his office. Then, in early July, he received an invitation from his former boss Heber Stryker, who had left Whilden and Hancock to become vice president of the First Reinsurance Company of Hartford. He suggested to Stevens that he take the train to Connecticut for a visit and talk about Stevens's eventually joining him in Hartford. On the 3rd Stevens left for a five-day visit with the Strykers at their home at 22 Arnoldale Road in Hartford. It was almost like being in the country again, he told Elsie, and he'd reveled in the blue lobelias and Canterbury bells and hollyhocks. Even better, his bedroom had looked out onto a field of freshly mown hay, the sweet scent of which had filled his room, while a hundred blackbirds had held an impromptu convention outdoors.

Most weekends he visited Elsie in the Poconos and learned to play golf on the greens surrounding the estate. In August he visited the Strykers a second time, all of them guests of a Mr. Hublein at his beach residence on Eastern Point, New London, Connecticut, where they went sailing out to Fisher's Island. Back in New York and refreshed, he began writing poems again. It was just "a little collection of verses," he wrote Elsie, like the things he'd written for her birthdays, though he was as yet finding it difficult to get back into the rhythm of writing. Still, the exercise elated and satisfied him. The poems were to be their secret, he told her, since most people found it absurd that a man should write verse. His habits, in fact, were becoming, as he noted yet again, more and more ladylike.

Stryker had helped Stevens find a Steinway baby grand piano encased in ebony down on Grove Street in the Village, and Stevens had paid a Mr. Vitale half down. Now he was setting it up in the apartment to help Elsie get through the evenings more enjoyably. He had the Steinway polished in anticipation of her return, playing on it in the late summer evenings, sometimes into the early morning hours alone as he was once again.

6

An Explosion in a Shingle Factory: 1913–1916

Just as my fingers on these keys
Make music, so the self-same sounds
On my spirit make a music, too.

He was not at the point where he could write these lines—that moment lay two years in the future. But he was approaching it as he listened to Elsie playing on the new baby grand Steinway in their apartment on winter evenings, he sitting across from her, reading or composing poems. He kept in touch with his sisters, Elizabeth (twenty-seven), a schoolteacher now and living in Philadelphia, and Mary Katherine (twenty-three), living with their brother John in Reading. When Elizabeth was hospitalized in late 1912, Wallace wrote her, trying to comfort her with his wry sense of humor and promising to send money if she needed it (though he added that he was pretty much strapped for cash himself at the moment). Elsie had turned out to be a "stunning cook," the best he knew, and had roasted a big chicken for the two of them for Thanksgiving. They'd also been to a string of plays, all light musicals like *The Lady & the Slipper, Oh, Oh, Dauphine*, and *The Merry Countess*, all three "in less than a week," because in a town like New York theaters were "an easy mode of amusement."

At work things were looking up again. By February 1914, at the age of thirty-four, he'd been made resident vice president of the New York office of the Equitable Surety Company of St. Louis. His offices were in the stunning new Beaux-Arts skyscraper dubbed the Liberty Tower on Liberty Street, half a mile west of the Brooklyn Bridge. And, being the young capitalist he was, he was looking for even greater opportunities for getting ahead. On August 11, with war about to break out in Europe, he wrote Elsie, back in Reading with her mother once more, that he'd taken the train up to Hartford to see the Strykers yet again. It had been a pleasant enough trip, except that Stryker had been extremely nervous and unable to sleep, full of the rumors of a war they were both eager to ignore. They'd spent most of a Sunday afternoon walking about Hartford, including Cedar Hill, "an uninteresting cemetery in which lie the bones of J. P. Morgan" (and where eventually his and Elsie's bones would also come to rest).

He wondered if Elsie would mind staying somewhere around Reading for a few more weeks, promising to send her money as soon as he could, since his bank account at the moment looked like an airship that had been hit by anti-aircraft fire. On another note, he told Elsie that some things he'd been working on over the past year, together with five poems from *The Little June Book* he'd written for her years before, would soon appear in a New York magazine called *Trend*, though waiting to see his first poems in print in almost fifteen years felt like waiting to have one's will read. It was Pitts Sanborn, one of his Harvard pals, who had asked him for the poems. When they appeared the following month, they did so to little fanfare, except from the half dozen or so literati who made up New York's avant-garde. Three of those associated with *Trend* had been classmates of his at Harvard: Witter Bynner, Walter Arensberg, and Sanborn. The fourth to take notice was Carl Van Vechten—tall, blond, and bisexual—who had graduated from the University of Chicago in 1903, fallen in love with Chicago's black jazz culture, and then come to New York, where in 1909 he became the first American critic of modern dance for the *New York Times*. A decade later he would be one of the most visible white advocates for the Harlem Renaissance and a close friend of both Countee Cullen and Langston Hughes.

Stevens called his series of poems *Carnet de Voyage*. It was his imaginary travel journal, an exotic and mildly erotic colorist dream sequence.

The first of the pieces was in 3/3 time, a waltz-like trance, there and not there, a fiction of the mind, its evanescent sultana and seraph like something out of Matisse, coming around at the poem's end to lock onto death, decay, and the city streets with their ubiquitous horse dung:

An odor from a star
Comes to my fancy, slight,
Tenderly spiced and gay,
As if a seraph's hand
Unloosed the fragrant silks
Of some sultana, bright
In her soft sky. And pure
It is, and excellent,
As if a seraph's blue
Fell, as a shadow falls,
And his warm body shed
Sweet exhalations, void
Of our despised decay.

Of all the New York avant-garde, it was Donald Evans whose poems would have the greatest impact on the thirty-five-year-old Stevens. Unrecognized today, Evans offered poems with a Wildean breath of fresh air mixed with prickly sachet scents. A few years on he would see action as a U.S. Army sergeant, in turn becoming so adamantly antiwar that he took to praising the Kaiser's army as much better trained than either the Americans or Brits and certainly far superior to the French. It was Evans, in fact, as William Carlos Williams would later point out, who most influenced Stevens's breakthrough poems of 1913–14, especially such Evans lines as these, which Williams thought went:

In what room shall it be tonight,
darling? (looking up at the
illuminated nightbound hotel) In
every room, my sweet.

The poem Williams was trying to recall in his own characteristically short lines was Evans's "Dinner at the Hotel de la Tigresse Verte," which he was sure had "a lot of early Stevens in it":

As they sat sipping their glasses in the courtyard
Of the Hotel de la Tigresse Verte,
With their silk-swathed ankles softly kissing,
They were certain that they had forever
Imprisoned fickleness in the vodka—
They knew they had found the ultimate pulse of love.

Story upon story, the dark windows whispered down
To them from above, and over the roof's edge
Danced a grey moon.
The woman pressed her chicken-skin fan against her breast
And through her ran trepidant mutinies of desire
With treacheries of emotion. Her voice vapoured:
"In which room shall it be to-night, darling?"
His eyes swept the broad façade, the windows,
Tier upon tier, and his lips were regnant:
"In every room, my beloved!"

"What . . . has impelled me to write to you today," Stevens would report to his friend and fellow poet Ferdinand Reyher in June 1921, "is the appalling, devastating news of the death of Donald Evans." Evans had just died in New York's Bellevue Hospital, his body interred in his native Philadelphia a few days later. His last year had been unbelievably stormy, Stevens explained, after Evans's wife had run off with some "lounge lizard." Evans had gone to Bermuda to recuperate and had come back seemingly better. But the truth was that Evans had been "more deeply stricken than one's frivolous eye disclosed." He had been "one of the great ironists, one of the pure litterateurs." And now he had taken his own life.

One of the great ironists and *one of the pure litterateurs.* That was high praise coming from Stevens. It had been Gertrude Stein who had helped transform Evans's French decadent style, providing it with a new suppleness and dreamlike directness which evoked the strange new poetic space of Evans's imagined lotus-land-like *Sonnets from the Patagonian.* In the first of his sonnets, a fine Petrarchan piece titled "Love in Patagonia," Evans had written of his breakup with Fania Marinoff, a stunning Russian Jewish actress, who had left Evans for Carlo—Carl Van Vechten. In the poem Evans ironically wondered why Fania left him, abandoning her tentative, "mauve vows" to him. Had he not performed all the proper devotions, kissing and then biting her "sleek young body" until she bled? Ah, but Carlo! Carlo "shone like a new sin," and, after dressing his wounds in sweet pearl powder, the poet realized that his poor bleeding heart might—given a week of so—recover unscarred. To console himself, he slipped off to

a shop where shoes were sold within,
And for three hundred francs made brave my feet,
And then I danced along the boulevard!

It was a pose, of course, borrowed and updated from the Wildean 1890s, and it mocked the new consumerism of New York's upscale Francophile department stores, where one's broken heart might be mended by a decent shopping spree.

As Van Vechten remembered it, he'd read Stevens's poems in *Trend* that September 1914, then asked Sanborn about him. Van Vechten was especially keen to learn more because he would be editing the November issue of *Trend* and needed additional poems. Sanborn promised to talk to Stevens to see what else he might have. Soon after, as Van Vechten was leaving his office on a Saturday afternoon, there was a knock at the door and he found himself staring at a tall fellow who seemed to be "blushing and holding forward a tiny piece of paper," muttering something about Sanborn asking him to drop off some poems. Then he turned and disappeared down the hall. What Stevens had handed him on "an absurd half sheet of women's note paper in the tiniest scrawl" turned out to be two poems, "From a Junk" and "Home Again," both of which Van Vechten published a few weeks later.

Now he queried Walter Arensberg about Stevens, and Arensberg arranged for the three of them to have lunch together at the Brevoort, with its fine French cuisine, on West Ninth Street, a block north of Washington Square, on Saturday, November 21. As it turned out, Van Vechten had to meet with the board of directors of the financially troubled *Trend* that same afternoon, and, in short order, following Van Vechten's abrupt resignation, the board was dissolved and Van Vechten returned to the Brevoort to find Stevens and Arensberg deep in lighthearted banter over a bottle of good cognac.

An astute Jamesian observer of social behavior, Van Vechten saw in Stevens "a dainty rogue in porcelain," who struck him as "big, blond, and burly," but with a "refinement of mentality" and "a tiny reserved spirituality," not unlike Stevens's handwriting on that "absurd" sheet of paper. At once Arensberg altered Van Vechten's description of Stevens to "that rogue elephant in porcelain," an apt-enough phrase. What Van Vechten saw in Stevens's graceful hands seemed to explain who the man was beneath the linebacker's body: someone who was both expressive and poetic.

When Arensberg asked Stevens to show Van Vechten some more new poems, Stevens handed him "Peter Quince at the Clavier." It was, Van Vechten thought, "a really lovely little thing, showing how music awakens our natures, and bringing in a striking figure of Susannah and the elders, their blood pulsing pizzicatos of hosanna." The other poem was "Tea," in which every line seemed to convey an impression of tea. But what struck him most was Stevens's utter "lack of poise," his inability to accept praise of any kind. For his part, Stevens so enjoyed himself that afternoon that he decided to stay for dinner, sending a telegram to Elsie rather than telephone her. She would, of course, be expecting him home—they always dined together on Saturday evenings when she was in New York—and the telegram would let her know what his plans were without having to confront her directly. And dine out they did, at Bustanoby's on West Sixtieth and Broadway, where, with the help of bottle after bottle of wine, Arensberg recounted the story of Stevens at Harvard kneeling at the feet of some "pie woman" named Lucy. This was no doubt Kitty, the waitress at Rammy's whom the twenty-year-old Stevens had declared he was about to rape.

Afterward the three went to Arensberg's apartment on West Sixty-seventh, where Stevens played the piano and Arensberg gave his wife's maid tickets to a popular comic farce playing at a local theater so she wouldn't be around to hear the men's ribald banter. As Stevens looked about the salon-like room with its imposing seventeen-foot ceilings, he mentioned that, even with ceilings that high, the paintings on the wall were too large for the room, and the room too big for his comfort. Domestic intimacy was what made Stevens comfortable: a couch before a fireplace, with seasoned wood and flames flickering from the grate. With that, Arensberg pushed the couch closer to the fireplace, dimmed the lights, and—presto!—a cozy fire in the fireplace.

Soon, having downed several drinks on top of the wine at dinner, Stevens was telling the men just how much his wife objected to his drinking and smoking. Even when she was already in bed, though he shut all the doors and went into a corner of their apartment to smoke a cigar, Elsie would invariably detect what he'd been doing as soon as he crept into bed. Around midnight Stevens and Van Vechten left together, Stevens taking the El downtown and Van Vechten the subway. As he said good-bye, Stevens confessed that he dreaded what awaited him when he got back home.

Arensberg decided he wanted more of Stevens's company, an idea which was going to prove difficult if Elsie did not like being around people who drank or smoked. That was when Van Vechten came up with the idea of a post-decadent gathering of New York poets. All it would take, really, was getting "five or six men who live in the same town and hate each other" in the same room.

With the demise of *Trend*, Arensberg was eager to start another little magazine, this one to be called *Rogue*. He figured it would cost fifty bucks a month, so long as the magazine wasn't circulated. An avant-garde magazine "not for sale at fifty cents." It would include poems by Arensberg, his literary friends, and of course Stevens, and Van Vechten would serve as biographer of the movement.

A week later Van Vechten spotted Stevens at the Opera House, where *Boris Godunov* was being performed. He could see that Stevens was trying to quietly avoid him, but when the final curtain came down, he went over to say hello. Stevens had avoided eye contact, he confessed, because he didn't know Van Vechten very well and wasn't sure what to say to him. Van Vechten invited him back to his apartment on West Fifty-fifth, where

Stevens refused a drink for the first half hour. Finally he asked his host if Vichy left a smell on one's breath. The truth was, he told Van Vechten, he'd had a terrible time of it since he'd last seen him. He'd snuck into the apartment as quietly as he could that night, only to find Elsie waiting up for him. She'd said nothing, then glanced up icily at the clock, turned, and stalked off to bed. Next morning, a Sunday, she was up at seven, waiting for her derelict husband to get up as well, that is, unless he just wasn't up to it. All he'd done, he lied, was to go over to the Harvard Club to celebrate the news of his alma mater's victory over Yale (15–5, and that at the grand opening of the brand new Yale Bowl) and had then gone to Arensberg's apartment to spend a few quiet hours. When her eyes reproached him, he tried to make amends by taking her to the Metropolitan Museum of Art that afternoon. In spite of which, Elsie refused to smile at him for another four days.

Did he enjoy living with his wife? Van Vechten asked. No, but then what choice did he have? He loved Elsie, but was "too timid to assert his authority." Oh, to be like a friend of Stevens's, who had "tramped bootfully," Van Vechten quipped, a very Petruchio, into his wife's bedchamber at dawn and assailed her ears with frightful oaths, and how she had begged him to come to bed and love her once more. While Stevens always told himself he would never talk about his fear of Elsie, somehow he found himself doing just that. What he did not share with Van Vechten was that, though Elsie wanted a baby, he had told her that the time was not yet propitious for assuming such a responsibility, and would not be until he had the wherewithal to support a family. A baby grand was one thing. A grand baby was another.

Would Stevens be interested in a gathering of the post-decadents, Van Vechten asked, changing the topic. Stevens grew enthusiastic. How delightful to spend an evening with other poets reading and discussing their work. He looked at his watch. It was time he got back home to Elsie. As he was going down the stairs, Van Vechten called out to him. His friend Louise Norton was giving a dinner at Pogliani's the following week. Was he interested? "We are quiet, mouse-like people, so timid," Stevens replied. "We would die in the company of eight people."

Van Vechten took that as a yes. But to accommodate Stevens, it was decided that Arensberg and his wife, Louise, should ask him and Elsie to his apartment some night *after* dinner, after they and Van Vechten and his fiancée, Fania Marinoff, would have had time to drink and smoke to their hearts' content. When the Stevenses finally arrived, Elsie anchored herself to the couch. She was even prettier than he'd expected, Van Vechten thought, with wavy blond hair and violet eyes. She seemed timid and naive as well. Then too there were those crooked teeth.

When Stevens was asked to recite a few of his poems, Elsie began talking nervously, interrupting herself with "a painful nervous gulping laugh." Stevens explained that his wife did not like his poems, but Elsie contradicted him. She *did* like them, but only "when they weren't affected." The trouble was that so much of what her husband wrote these days, she laughed, was just that: affected. Nevertheless Stevens began reciting his poems in what Van Vechten recalled as a "strange word-dropping monotone." The first poem he read was "Dolls," a piece about "the thought of Eve, within me," a fantasy creature who will do whatever the poet desires. She is his angel, this woman, an angel among "the cherubim and seraphim, / And of Another, whom I must not name." That unnamed other might point to God, but the poem is really an homage to someone he "must not name." In fact, among the tortured sibilants and wordplay, there does seem to be a "solid game" here, one which evoked for Stevens the long memory of that young woman whose house he'd passed each day on his way to Harvard Yard and with whom he'd enjoyed a dreamlike interlude in the Adirondacks: the Impossible Perfect Woman, Sybil Gage.

Like the others, Elsie listened, not fully understanding but disliking the poem because she found it so "affected." Afterward Stevens passed around a copy of the poem, careful to deflect what it was really about, and then moved on to another piece, titled "Infernale." Van Vechten and the others liked this one even more, though they understood it even less, including the part that mocks "the bondage of the Stygian concubine," the one chained forever to a wife from hell.

But Stevens had saved the best for last: "Cy Est Pourtraicte, Madame Ste Ursule, et Les Unze Mille Vierges" (This Is a Portrait of Madame Saint Ursula and the 11,000 Virgins), at which the group oohed and ahhed.

Elsie disliked this one even more for its mocking spirit. It was a mixture of Voragine's *Golden Legend*—where the number of virgin martyrs increases from eleven to eleven hundred to eleven thousand—and of Apollinaire. In Stevens's rendering, the maiden Ursula makes an offering of radishes and flowers to the Lord as she kneels alone among the tall grasses. And the Lord, summoned by the music of her words, feels "a subtle quiver, / That was not heavenly love, / Or pity." What the Lord feels that evening as he gazes at the woman alone there in the garden is not unlike what the red-eyed elders felt when they lusted after Susannah, alone in her garden, bathing. But of course that feeling of the Lord's had not been "writ / In any book."

Later that evening Allen and Louise Norton arrived, the poems were read again, first by Van Vechten and then by Stevens, and the discussion as to the meaning of the poems continued. How often Stevens came out of the bathroom, Elsie blurted out at one point, "with a poem in his teeth." When someone told her that Van Vechten liked writing about just such eccentricities, she froze, refusing to say another thing if that man was going to write down what she was saying. A short time later, as the Stevenses were taking their leave, Elsie asked Louise Arensberg if Van Vechten was really going to record what she'd said that evening. She didn't know, Louise answered, but he might. After all, he was clever. "Well then," Elsie replied, "I hope he's clever enough to be nice!"

• • •

IN MANY WAYS THE seismic shifts in New York's radical chic were being mapped and registered, thanks in large part to the explosion of new techniques and ideas among the painters who were exhibiting their work in the art and photography galleries along Fifth and Madison. In the past decade Alfred Stieglitz's two hundred ninety-one gallery on Fifth and Thirty-first Street had been instrumental in raising the new art of photography to the stature of Modern art by displaying photographs alongside the work of Matisse, Rodin, Cézanne, Picasso, Brancusi, and Duchamp.

But the event that singlehandedly changed the way America saw and appreciated art was the Armory Show, the international exhibit at the

69th Regiment Armory on Lexington Avenue held from February 17 to March 15, 1913. Many Americans were of course familiar with realistic art, which portrayed stylized historical and classical narratives in a somewhat heightened manner. And many were aware of the work of the French impressionists. But what they saw in the galleries of the Armory Show were the works of the European vanguard—fauvists, cubists, futurists—along with work by contemporary American artists. The Show also provided American painters—and by extension musicians and a new generation of poets—the opportunity to create a new aesthetic and a new language with which to express a new reality.

A year before the Armory Show was launched, the artists Walt Kuhn, Arthur B. Davies, and Walter Pach—the last a lifelong friend of Stevens—formed the Association of American Painters and Sculptors, bringing along with them two dozen other artists, including George Luks and William Glackens. The stated purpose of the AAPS was "to lead the public taste in art, rather than follow it," and that meant working outside of accepted academic standards. After months of planning, they chose the 69th Regiment Armory for their mammoth exhibition, with exhibitions to follow in Chicago and Boston. In September 1912 Kuhn sailed for Europe, collecting paintings and sculptures in England, Germany, the Netherlands, and France, visiting not only galleries but private collections and studios, contracting for loans at each.

In Paris, Kuhn caught up with Pach, who knew the art scene there intimately, and who also knew Matisse, as well as a young Parisian by the name of Marcel Duchamp. Two months later Davies joined Kuhn and Pach in Paris, and together they secured three paintings that would be among the Armory Show's most famous and polarizing: two by Matisse, *Blue Nude* (*Souvenir de Biskra*) and *Red Madras Headdress (Madras Rouge),* as well as Duchamp's *Nude Descending a Staircase, No. 2.* Only that December, when they had returned to New York, did they decide to allow their American compatriots, who had been sidelined, to participate in the exhibit as well.

When the Show opened in February, it displayed some 1,300 paintings, sculptures, and decorative works by over three hundred avant-garde European and American artists. The New York papers accused the show's organizers of immorality, insanity, even of fomenting anarchy. There were parodies, caricatures, doggerel, and mock exhibitions, Teddy Roosevelt snapping that what was on display at the Armory was not even art. But it was Duchamp's cubist/futurist *Nude*, painted the year before and portraying a kind of frozen cinematic abstract with successively superimposed images, that caught the attention of the press and spurred the *New York Times* art critic, Julian Street, to describe it as "an explosion in a shingle factory." Gutzon Borglum, who would become famous for his presidential sculptures at Mount Rushmore and who had helped organize the show only to withdraw both his paintings and his support, called Duchamp's painting "Staircase Descending a Nude." Even better was the *New York Evening Sun*'s title: "Rude Descending a Staircase or Rush Hour in the Subway."

• • •

THERE WERE, THEN, A multitude of aesthetic filaments threading through Stevens's consciousness in his last three years in New York before moving to Hartford in the spring of 1916. Besides the gatherings with the Arensbergs, Sanborn, the Nortons, and Van Vechten, there was the avant-garde's intense interest in the little magazines. There were also copious, none too subtle, erotic images and themes which the magazines they published borrowed, stole, or co-opted from the British Yellow Nineties, flavored now with a certain unmistakable bourgeois naughtiness. Finally, there was the Arensbergs' fascination with Duchamp, who, back in France in 1911, along with his two artist brothers, had begun hosting a regular gathering at their home in Puteaux, to which had flocked Francis Picabia, Fernand Léger, Jean Metzinger, Albert Gleizes, Robert and Sonia Delaunay, Juan Gris, Roger de la Fresnaye, and Alexander Archipenko, artists who sought to produce pure color harmonies analogous to the concept of pure music: rhythms pulsating through the universe, not unlike the oscillations of radio waves or the shimmering radioactive dance of those newly discovered atomic particles.

Out of these experiments Duchamp had produced his *Nude* in what he called his analytic cubist style, the painting that more than any other set off the modernist art movement in the United States. True, the Armory

Show was originally to have been a demonstration of what American artists were producing, but Pach, Van Vechten, and Sanborn, after meeting with the French postimpressionists and sizing up what they had achieved, saw that the New was to be discovered not in the United States but in Paris, and so what was originally conceived of as the American Association of Painters and Sculptors morphed into the International Exhibition of Modern Art, in which modern French art was privileged from the start, basically stealing the show from the Americans. Once again the Americans were seen as derivative, the new cultural colonials, dependent this time not on London but on Paris.

If George Bellows, Mary Cassatt, and Arthur Davies, along with Marsden Hartley, George Luks, Edward Hopper, John Marin, William Glackens, Charles Sheeler, Joseph Stella, and His Eminence James Abbott McNeill Whistler, were on display in the American wings that greeted viewers as they entered the Armory Show, they quickly became mere passageways leading to the work of Brancusi and Bonnard, Braque and Cézanne, Corot and Degas, Delacroix, Dufy, Gauguin, and Van Gogh, along with Toulouse-Lautrec, Léger, Manet, Monet, Renoir, Pissarro, Rodin, Rouault, and Vuillard, as well as Kandinsky and Picasso.

But even among these bright lights, it was Matisse's vaguely sketched nudes in Gallery H (whose *Blue Nude* William Carlos Williams would pay homage to a few years later) and, in the adjoining Gallery I, Picabia's *Dances at the Spring* and Duchamp's three radical paintings, including his cinematic *Nude*, which entranced or disturbed the crowds of gasping spectators. Within days of the Show's opening, Gallery I became the scandal of New York, dubbed both the Cubist Room and the Chamber of Horrors.

What the twenty-six-year-old Duchamp had been after in *Nude Descending a Staircase* was, it seems, to have the classic anonymous odalisque get up from her bed and walk downstairs as any woman might, much as Stevens, three decades later, would have his Mrs. Papadopoulos get up at the conclusion of "So-and-so Reclining On Her Couch" as the Muse assumed a modern Greek moniker and identity. The painting was also an attempt to freeze cinematic motion on a static canvas, and thus offer a radical attempt to replace traditional perspective in painting by revealing simultaneous multiple perspectives of a subject caught in a series of frames: a photograph, as it were, which captured something of the startling new notions of space and time, matter and motion, at the core of Einstein's theories of relativity.

Seeing that no painting could outdo the airplane propeller in terms of dynamic stasis, however, the ever-restive Duchamp had already given up his short career in painting—much as his countryman Arthur Rimbaud had left modern poetry behind, but not before tossing a grenade or two. But whereas Rimbaud had taken up a lucrative career in gun-running in Africa, Duchamp turned instead to philosophy, chess, mathematics, and ready-mades. It was the very concept of art which now came under the intense scrutiny of Duchamp, Picabia, and Apollinaire, their withering gaze quickly deconstructing the art object—the score, the painting, the poem—until it seemed no more than a haphazard structure unmoored altogether from the Real.

Unmoored himself by the reality of the Great War, and having been exempted from military service because of heart irregularities in January 1915, Duchamp soon became uncomfortable remaining in Paris and sailed for New York on the *Rochambeau*, arriving in the sweltering noon heat of June 15, where he was met by Walter Pach. "I do not go to New York," he had informed Pach after he'd decided to leave France. He had merely left Paris for a time. Pach invited Duchamp to stay with him and his wife at their Beekman Place apartment until Duchamp could settle in at the Arensbergs' far more spacious apartment while they were on holiday.

Arensberg, who had been well-provided for by his father's fortune, had already bought a second version of *Nude Descending a Staircase* (the original having been purchased, sight unseen, by a California collector) and would soon purchase the original. So fascinated had he become with Duchamp that in late 1913 he and his wife moved from Cambridge, Massachusetts, to Manhattan in the wake of the Armory Show, intent on creating a New World version of European Dada. Dadaism had risen from the ashes of European civilization, a world where language and art had been compromised and then deranged by the disjunction between political rhetoric and the primal screams of hundreds of thousands of young men dying in the trenches of France until their words and cries had been drained of human meaning. For them, as for others, the war had rendered all established values, including the moral and aesthetic, nothing more than the empty grating of toothless gums.

Early that August 1915, Pach telephoned Stevens, inviting him to dine with Duchamp and himself at the Brevoort in Greenwich Village. There the two Americans and the Parisian exile spoke French together, the conversation sounding to Stevens's ear "like sparrows around a pool of water." French was Stevens's special language, unlikely sister to his own American idiom—one-eighth Pennsylvania Dutch German and seven-eighths Harvardian—and he felt completely at home with it. His first poems in *Rogue* and *Poetry Magazine* would amply demonstrate this, set as they were in an imagined Paris and Belgium, but a world such as Claude Lorrain had painted rather than the war-ravaged landscape of the Somme.

For Stevens that dinner was the beginning of an arrangement of artists and poets which, over the next eight months, would gather at the Arensbergs, attracting mainly the avant-garde French exiles, including the fixed center of this new galaxy, Duchamp, as well as his brother-in-law, Jean Crotti, Francis Picabia, Albert Gleizes, and Edgar Varèse. Of course American painters like Charles Demuth, Sheeler, Man Ray, and Stella were also welcome. And then there were the "others": the Nortons, Mina Loy, Van Vechten, and the poet and editor of various little magazines, Alfred Kreymborg. It was here too that Stevens first met the thirty-two-year-old doctor-poet from Rutherford, New Jersey: William Carlos Williams.

Williams, the son of an English father and a Puerto Rican mother in a household where French and Spanish were spoken as much as English, had spent his entire life in the same town in the Meadowlands section of northern New Jersey (and would die there a half century later). While his poetry had begun very much in the same vein of formal verse as Stevens's, Williams had already undergone a transformation, and with the help of his friend Ezra Pound and others, was already heralding the new forms of free verse that were gaining traction, especially in New York and London. He and Stevens were already heading on different verse trajectories, but they took to each other from the start, watching each other's progress like hawks in the decades to come.

"Arensberg could afford to spread a really ample feed with drinks to match," Williams would recall thirty-five years later, and "you always saw Marcel Duchamp there." His *Large Glass*, or *The Bride Stripped Bare by Her Bachelors, Even*, still unfinished, "stood at one side and several of his earlier works hung from the walls," along with paintings by Cézanne and Gleizes. "It disturbed and fascinated me," Williams admitted. "I confess I was slow to come up with any answers." Nor did Duchamp do anything to make Williams feel welcome; the Frenchman had an unnerving way of cutting one short, of humiliating one with a quick, stinging quip. As for Williams, he—like the other Americans at the salon, including Stevens—were mere beginners, "no matter how we might struggle to conceal the fact: bunglers . . . unable to compete in knowledge with the sophisticates of Montmartre." And because French was the preferred language at the Arensbergs', there was the language barrier as well, though Williams, who had spent a year in Switzerland as a boy, did know French, though not the witty Harvardian kind which Stevens and Arensberg preferred.

On one occasion Williams was struck by Duchamp's *Yvonne and Madeleine Torn in Tatters* adorning the Arensbergs' walls. It showed five heads, simultaneously revealing and concealing themselves in pastel shades. Williams was eager to engage Duchamp about what the artist had achieved there. But Duchamp had been drinking, Williams remembered, while Williams was sober. "I finally came face to face with him as we walked about the room and told him I liked the painting. He looked at me and said, 'Do you?' That was all." Duchamp had humiliated him, Williams understood, so that "there wasn't a possibility of my ever saying anything to anyone in that gang from that moment to eternity—but that one of them, by God, would come to me and give me the same chance one day and that I should not fail then to lay him cold—if I could. Watch and wait. Meanwhile work."

Stevens must have felt something of this same wariness. Perhaps, after he'd relaxed with four or five martinis, he might say something revealing or outrageous. Otherwise the edifice stood erect, permanent, like the façade of a well-appointed New York apartment. Still, for all his familiarity with Arensberg and Duchamp, Stevens wasn't that far removed from Williams in being on his best behavior with the new wave of decadents to whom he was attracted yet of whom he was apprehensive. He was certainly never going to give Duchamp the opening Williams had. Forty years later, when he learned that several memoirs of Duchamp had been published in Paris, Stevens confided to a friend that here in America Duchamp had always been taken to be "a cheerful, healthy young Frenchman, serious enough and yet not too serious," though personally he'd always felt the man "was an intense neurotic and that his life was not explicable in any other terms."

As for Arensberg, despite his apparent bonhomie, he always remained on his guard and would as soon cut a man as offer him a handshake or a drink. In fact, shortly before the Arensbergs left New York permanently for California in 1921, something happened that ended Stevens's relationship with Arensberg. A friend of Arensberg had complained to Stevens that Arensberg was spending too much time with the French artists and neglecting his American friends, and he'd asked Stevens to say something to him. "I had not myself noticed this," Stevens confided to the poet Weldon Kees forty years later, but he was willing to tell Arensberg what he'd been told. When he mentioned it to Arensberg, however, "Walter froze up . . . and when he froze up, I froze up too."

When Van Vechten heard about this, he tried to patch things up between the two and took it upon himself to invite them and their wives to dinner at a restaurant on Bleecker Street. "When we went there," Stevens recalled, "there was no one there and after waiting ten minutes or so I told my wife that apparently this was a joke." Then, just as they got up to go, the Arensbergs walked in. Elsie spoke briefly to both of them, not knowing there was any tension between the two men, both of whom continued to remain on their "high horses." And then Stevens added, "I never saw him again."

A year after the Arensbergs had left for California, Stevens happened to see Duchamp walking the streets of New York. Duchamp had left the States in 1918 to live in Buenos Aires, abandoning his *Large Glass* and his artwork and spending his time there playing chess. Nine months later he returned to Paris, only to return to New York the following year. "He seemed like a cat that had been left behind," Stevens confessed. As for the rest of the old bon vivant New York crowd, all of them had long since disappeared.

• • •

AND THEN THERE WAS Chicago, that other New World artistic vortex. Carl Sandburg's Chicago, "Hog Butcher for the World," home of the new Beaux-Arts skyscrapers, "stormy, husky, brawling, / City of the Big Shoulders." And home of Harriet Monroe, where by sheer pluck and hard work and her "open door" policy of printing "the best poetry written today, in whatever style, genre, or approach," she'd managed in late 1912 to launch the only one of the little magazines still flourishing a hundred years later. Half radical, half conservative, as her sometimes heavy-handed edits of Stevens and Williams and Hart Crane would prove soon enough, she too had dismissed Duchamp's *Nude*. For her it had been merely "a pack of brown cards in a nightmare or a dynamited suit of Japanese armor." Still, she was open enough to embrace the radical vision behind it. It was high time, after all, that artists and poets threw "a bomb into the entrenched camps" of establishment art and gave "American art a much-needed shaking up." If the artists had brought into the new century a new vision of what art could be, she and others knew that American poetry still lagged behind, stuck in the moss-covered bedrock of an exhausted nineteenth-century romanticism. A poet herself, and much attracted to things "Oriental," she initiated—with the help of 107 patrons who pledged to donate $50 a year for five years so that poets might be paid for their work—*Poetry: A Magazine of Verse*, which, despite its redundant title, managed from the start to publish some of the most important early work not only of Sandburg, but of Pound, T. S. Eliot, H.D., Marianne Moore, Williams, and of course Stevens.

In the fall of 1914, with the flames of war raging in Europe, *Poetry* advertised that it was looking for the best new war poetry for its "War Issue," planned for that November. The response was so overwhelming that the editors found themselves sifting through some seven hundred entries. Stevens, completely unknown to Monroe, sent her a sequence of eleven poems called *Phases* under the pseudonym Peter Parasol, a name the canny Stevens had used in sending out his earliest poems to other magazines. All of the poems in his sequence dealt with the devastated landscape of Europe. Monroe, taken by the poems, chose four of them, including the first, which captured in imagistic form what wartime Paris now looked like, with its "cab-horse at the corner" waiting for a passenger in the grieving rain. Paris, which had been "silver once, / And green with leaves," was now doubly desolate, shivering in the cold autumn rains. Now, with the rat-infested mud trenches north of Paris a reality, Stevens provided his readers with a "salty taste of glory" far different from Homer's epic battles. This was a new kind of war, where British cavalry, horse and rider, could be cut down by German machine guns hidden among the trees, a war discovered by young men who had gone from the playing fields of England's public schools to the nightmare of a random bomb blast in the trenches, leaving behind "an eyeball in the mud, / And Hopkins, / Flat and pale and gory!"

That, and another image, this one of vines distended with autumn's "yellow fruit" falling "along the walls / That bordered Hell." What was there that the common Londoner amid the daily grind could compare to a bullet's "short, triumphant sting," bringing with it the indescribable, once-only "salty, sacrificial taste" of death? In a very real sense, the war had come to roost for good in Stevens's troubled imagination. As if to show the individual's insignificance, when Monroe asked Stevens to supply her with a short autobiographical note, he wrote back that to date he'd published nothing (though *Carnet de Voyage* had been published two months earlier in *Trend*). Intrigued by this unidentified entity from New York, Monroe simply noted that Mr. Wallace Stevens was "unknown as yet to the editor." Though that too was about to change, as he began to publish poems in other little magazines, all based in New York, such as *Rogue, Soil, Others*, and, a few years later, the *Little Review*.

In January 1915 Stevens offered Monroe several new poems, including "Cy Est Pourtraicte, Madame Ste Ursule, et Les Unze Mille Vierges" and "Disillusionment at Ten O'Clock," a poem about an old drunken sailor, "asleep in his boots," who caught "tigers / In red weather." But she returned them and several other poems, finding them "recondite, erudite, provocatively obscure," and "Aubrey Beardsleyish," all with "a kind of modern-gargoyle grin to them." Better, she advised Stevens, to chase your mystically "mirthful and mournful muse out of the nether darkness," at the same time encouraging him to send other poems. Those two poems would find a home instead in *Rogue.*

That May he sent her what would become one of his signature poems, "Sunday Morning," a piece in eight fifteen-line stanzas, which summed up what Sunday mornings had come to mean for him now that he found himself midway through life's journey. "Complacencies of the peignoir," the poem begins in Stevens's Harvardian Frenchified mode, as the poet assumed the part of a young, teachable woman, lounging in a chair facing the welcoming morning sun in her apartment on a Sunday morning. Perhaps that particular Sunday was Easter, which fell on April 4 that year, when New York City was blanketed in ten inches of snow, a fitting Easter now that so many soldiers lay piecemeal in the trenches.

Instead of attending church services, Stevens's muse enjoys the pungent, passing pleasures of "late / Coffee and oranges" and "the green freedom of a cockatoo / Upon a rug," her senses mingling synesthetically "to dissipate / The holy hush of ancient sacrifice." This is Keats, of course, the Keats of "To Autumn," transported now to an apartment on Manhattan's West Twenty-first Street, where an exotic cockatoo with its erectile crest struts across a green, sun-drenched living room rug. Over against that green freedom, as the woman hears the bells calling the faithful to Sunday services, her daydreams are suddenly interrupted by the "dark / Encroachment of that old catastrophe" which turns everything on its head: the thought of death—her death and ours—and of that final silence.

But what of the comfort of the Resurrection, of eternal life in Christ, which had consoled his mother in her final sickness two years before? To which the speaker answers that he has come to understand that life is a journey over "wide water, without sound," a meaningless "procession of the dead," in which Christ too lies dead, his Holy Sepulchre a mere memorial to his mortality. And if Christ is dead, why then should she "give her bounty to the dead," especially as there dwells in her a divinity of sorts: one that flourishes not in darkness and phantasmagoric shadow but in "the comforts of the sun, / In pungent fruit and bright green wings"? If there is a heaven, it must be here, in this world, to be enjoyed in the time we have, living as we must among the wide spectrum of feelings we are heir to in all weathers and all seasons:

Passions of rain, or moods in falling snow;
Grievings in loneliness, or unsubdued
Elations when the forest blooms; gusty
Emotions on wet roads on autumn nights;
All pleasures and all pains, remembering
The bough of summer and the winter branch,
These are the measures destined for her soul.

No God created us. Instead it was we who created God, humanizing him more and more until "he moved among us as a muttering king," an image not unlike Stevens's own dead father. With the passing of centuries, it was we who gave God a human face, "commingling, virginal, / With heaven" because we had to, creating as well a heaven no different, finally, from the earthly Eden we mortals created with our unappeasable longings. All we can ever hope for, the poem insists, is to inhabit the world, a world in which pain and suffering are inevitable. That, and the thing Stevens most hungers for and cannot seem to get in "this dividing and indifferent blue" of life: the dream of some "enduring love."

But what, really, endures for us? Not the pale, white thought of heaven. Nor some classical "golden underground, nor isle / Melodious," as the Greeks and Romans had it, "nor cloudy palm / Remote on heaven's hill," such as one might see on a Tiffany stained-glass window in the church one once attended. No, what endured was the eternal round of the seasons: "April's green" or, absent that, the memory of "awakened birds" and an evanescent June. Those and the consummation not of the dove as at the Annunciation but that other "consummation of the swallow's wings," disappearing from the darkening gray-black cobbled streets below.

The seasons come and go, and death reminds us that there is a season for new life, a time for erotic desire and reproduction, when the present generation brings forth the next before it goes its inevitable way. Which is why boys take the "disregarded plate" left by their parents and place "new plums and pears" upon it, offering these up, in this reversal of the

Genesis story, to the maidens, who will "taste / And stray impassioned in the littering leaves," to beget a new generation. "Death is the mother of beauty," Stevens tells us not once but twice, and in time even his girl, his Elsie, will become an image of his mortal earthly mother.

And he? What is he if not one among "a ring of men," reversing Matisse's version of *The Dance*, "supple and turbulent," singing his Whitmanian "boisterous devotion to the sun . . . / Naked among them, like a savage source." Who is he if not part of "the heavenly fellowship / Of men that perish" like so many young men perishing that very Sunday morning in anonymous trenches somewhere north of Paris, whose lives and deaths "the dew upon their feet shall manifest?" The final lesson the poet would impart to the young woman lounging in her peignoir this morning is this: that we live alone and we die alone,

> *in an old chaos of the sun,*
> *Or old dependency of day and night,*
> *Or island solitude, unsponsored, free,*
> *Of that wide water, inescapable.*

In the interstices between the then and the ever-fleeing now, Stevens concludes his poetic sermon with lines reminiscent of Wordsworth's *Prelude*:

> *Not in Utopia—subterranean fields,—*
> *Or some secreted island, Heaven knows where!*
> *But in the very world, which is the world*
> *Of all of us,—the place where in the end*
> *We find our happiness, or not at all!*

And so with this modern romantic as well, unwilling to surrender those mountains of his youth or those woods along the New Jersey Palisades, where deer still

> *walk upon our mountains, and the quail*
> *Whistle about us their spontaneous cries;*
> *Sweet berries ripen in the wilderness;*

And, in the isolation of the sky,
At evening, casual flocks of pigeons make
Ambiguous undulations as they sink,
Downward to darkness, on extended wings.

But even now, as the poem vanishes into its own silence, Stevens leaves us guessing as to what those ambiguous undulations might mean, if in fact they mean anything at all. Or what those extended wings, in a poem so heavily fraught with Christian symbols, might likewise mean, if they too are meant to be read as anything beyond a casual causality.

Monroe liked the poem well enough, though her midwestern sensibilities were once more disturbed by Stevens's too-modernist confrontations with Christianity. She agreed to take the poem, or at least half of it, and Stevens bowed to her decision because he felt he had to. The four sections she accepted were rearranged so that the first stanza would be followed by the last, which would in turn be followed by stanzas IV and V. And what did Mr. Stevens wish to tell the world about himself this time, she asked? The elusive Stevens: that he'd been born in Reading, that he was "thirty-five years old, a lawyer" who lived in New York City and had "published no books."

Two weeks later Monroe suggested that Stevens add a fifth stanza, provided he alter it. The phrase "disregarded plate" would have to go, she said. But, Stevens explained, the phrase means "the disuse into which things fall that have been possessed for a long time," so that "what the old have come to disregard, the young inherit and make use of." After all, wasn't that what death did: release us from the past even as it left us renewed? Still, if Monroe was unhappy with the phrase, he suggested—not without a bit of sarcasm—the alternative "ponderous piles." Of course, he added, her criticisms were always so "clearly well-founded," and he did appreciate her "very friendly interest." So the changes were made and the poem published in the November 1915 issue of *Poetry*, though when he included it in his first book of poems eight years later, he restored his "disregarded plate" and his disregarded stanzas, and rearranged the poem so that it assumed its original shape.

• • •

ONE SUNDAY IN LATE August, alone in his apartment while Elsie took in the salubrious airs of Woodstock, New York, he lazed about all morning while the rain continued outside. Finally he dressed and visited the New York Botanical Garden, only to find rain dripping everywhere between the cracked glass panes as couples beneath umbrellas walked about under the palms and banana trees. This time he paid especially close attention to the abundant erotic orchids. The night before, he admitted, he'd tried writing poetry, only to find himself getting bluer and bluer "about the flimsy little things" he'd done in the month Elsie had been away. Everything he wrote now, in fact, seemed "so slight and unimportant," and yet he was more interested than ever in composing verse. How he wished he might give all his time to poetry instead of a few hours in the evening, when he was exhausted after a day in his sweltering office. After all, it took "a great deal of thought" to compose a poem, and besides, he knew himself to be "an erratic and inconsequential thinker."

Still, that same month saw the publication of the second issue of Kreymborg's *Others: A Magazine of the New Verse*, which included Stevens's "Peter Quince at the Clavier" and "The Silver Ploughboy," along with four poems by Williams, including an unsettling piece called "The Ogre," about a doctor's sexual fascination with a little girl in the course of a routine physical examination.

Unlike Stevens's fellow Harvardians, Kreymborg was part of another world, which included the vital Lower East Side Jewish community, where Kreymborg's parents had run a cigar store. Back in September 1913 Kreymborg had partnered with the painter Man Ray to bring out the *Glebe*. That same summer Ray and another artist had started an artists' colony just across the Hudson in the rolling hills of Ridgefield, New Jersey. It turned out be the ideal place for an artist to live: quiet, pastoral, with cold, clear water drawn from a well, a welcome retreat from the streets of New York. Ray called the makeshift colony Grantwood; it consisted of several clapboard shacks on a bluff overlooking the Palisades directly across from Grant's Tomb on Manhattan's Upper West Side. Soon Kreymborg had fallen in love with "the view of the Jersey meadows, striped and streaked with the Passaic and Hackensack rivers, lazily rolling away to the horizon."

It was from there that Kreymborg had launched *Others* in July 1915—thanks to Arensberg's financial backing—and soon poets began arriving at Grantwood to picnic and read their poems, among them Mina Loy, Maxwell Bodenheim, Pitts Sanborn, Conrad Aiken, Mary Carolyn Davies, Skipwith Cannell, and Marianne Moore. Moore was Kreymborg's discovery, and he did everything he could to promote her unique and brilliant work. "I was a little different from the others," she confessed years later, and so might "pass as a novelty." Soon arguments over cubism and the new poetry filled the air, Williams remembered, when it seemed "daring to omit capitals at the head of each poetic line" and even "rhyme went by the board."

The inaugural number of *Others* had featured the work of Loy, Orrick Johns, and Kreymborg himself, while the second number included the work of Amy Lowell, Alanson Hartpence, Cannell, and Robert Carlton Brown, along with Williams and Stevens. In September it featured the work of a young American living in London named Thomas Stearns Eliot, whose work Pound had introduced to Kreymborg. The poem that appeared there was "Portrait of a Lady," and—in the interest of democracy—Eliot's modernist poem was immediately followed by John Gould Fletcher's "Songs of the Arkansas."

The March 1916 number highlighted the work of Stevens by publishing seven poems on as many pages: "The Florist Wears Knee-Breeches," "Song," "Inscription for a Monument," "Bowl," "Six Significant Landscapes," "Tattoo," and "Domination of Black," of which only the last three would make it into his first book of poems. "At night, by the fire," "Domination of Black" begins eerily enough, with the darkness outside encroaching on a solitary speaker sitting by the flickering peacock flames of a fireplace, painfully aware that there is no stay against the darkness that will eventually swallow the light and, with it, everything:

The colors of the bushes
And of the fallen leaves, repeating themselves,
Turned in the room,
Like the leaves themselves
Turning in the wind.

Yes, but the color of the heavy hemlocks
Came striding
And I remembered the cry of the peacocks.

ON A SUNDAY AFTERNOON the following month, the *Others* group, some with their wives, gathered at the Williamses' home at 9 Ridge Road, Rutherford. There they assembled in the front yard to have their picture taken. Missing from the photo is Stevens, who, just a month earlier, had accepted a position with the surety division of the Hartford Accident and Indemnity Insurance Company, which meant that he was already on the road dealing with claims adjustments. Writing to Stevens that June about "The Worms at Heaven's Gate," which, as acting editor of *Others*, Williams would publish, he assured Stevens that he would keep him informed "of anything of importance doing among the [*Others*] crowd when we get together again." From this point forward, Stevens would have to content himself with being a visitor to the city where he'd spent the past sixteen years.

When the Equitable, for which Stevens had worked for the past five years, dropped its surety division early in 1916, Stevens had found himself once more without a job. What saved him this time were his Hartford connections, Jim Kearney and Heber Stryker. By then both men were established in America's indisputable insurance capital, and that March Stevens was hired to oversee the Hartford's new fidelity and surety branch, an appointment highlighted in the company's magazine, the *Hartford Agent.*

Mr. Stevens, the article began, was taking charge of all claims and legal matters for the Hartford. A member of the New York Bar, he specialized in suretyship and eight years earlier had been hired by the American Bonding Company of Baltimore to work in its New York legal division. Later, when the American Bonding Company merged with the Fidelity and Deposit Company of Maryland, he'd worked for the latter in their New York office. It was of course of the utmost importance that surety claims "be handled in the usual broad and open-minded 'Hartford' way," and in Mr. Stevens the company had found a man peculiarly able to maintain those traditions.

For technical and legal reasons, Stevens had been brought on board as an officer of the company's subsidiary Livestock Insurance Company to handle its surely claims and oversee the legal aspects of the Hartford's rapidly expanding bond department. But in two years' time, as promised, a separate fidelity and surety claims department would be established, which Stevens would head for the rest of his life, after which it would be effectively disbanded, merging into another division.

For now, though, Stevens would take to the road once again. "You sign a lot of drafts," he would explain matter-of-factly years later. "You see surprisingly few people. You do the greater part of your work either in your own office or in lawyers' offices. You don't even see the country; you see law offices and hotel rooms. You try to do your traveling at night and often do it night after night. You wind up by knowing every county court house in the United States." Trips would often last two weeks or more, each sending him to yet another city. Once more he would be sleeping in overnight Pullmans and hotels, taking hot baths whenever he could to wash off the soot and sweat, then trying to grab a few hours' rest before he moved on to take care of the Hartford's business in places as far away as Texas and Nebraska.

7

The Eye of the Blackbird, 1916–1918

What syllable are you seeking,
Vocalissimus,
In the distance of sleep?
Speak it.

"TO THE ROARING WIND," 1917

On late Saturday afternoon, March 18, 1916, his leather briefcase stuffed with insurance papers from the Hartford, Wallace Stevens, thirty-six, impeccably dressed in a three-piece blue business suit, sits in a Pullman coach alone. He pores over a sheaf of documents and letters of introduction, sipping a martini. It is snowing and it is going to snow over the Pennsylvania hills beyond Reading. He is headed west, and when he wakes tomorrow after a night's twisting and turning in his too-small bunk, he will be in Indiana, where the sun will dazzle and the air will feel positively springlike. Then he will stop in Chicago and take a brisk walk, gulping in the fresh air along the edge of Lake Michigan before he boards, bound for St. Paul and Minneapolis, where the only two bright signs he will see as he travels through the Wisconsin countryside are billboards advertising Beechnut Bacon and Climax Plug, the Grand Old Chew. Ah, America!

When he arrives in St. Paul at ten that evening, he will hail a taxi to take him to the new million-dollar high-rise St. Paul Hotel, where he will take a long, hot bath, ridding himself of the grime from the smoke-belching engines, then get some rest before meeting with his clients at the Hartford's offices at Cushing, Dunn and Driscoll. Then he will be back on the Pullman, this time heading for Minneapolis, where he will stay at another high-rise hotel (with bath) and write Elsie to say he is going to have to be away for yet another week, though it will actually be closer to two before he gets back to New York, so that in the interim she may wish to return to Reading with her mother if her mother tires of New York and wants to go home. He may even call on his uncle Jack, his father's brother here in St. Paul, whom he has not seen in years. But to business first. Water the plants, he reminds her. It is such domestic missives that make up much of his married world now.

Returning home through Chicago at the end of March, he takes a room at a top-notch hotel on the Empire Block. It's another new skyscraper near the Chicago Loop, and he invites his aunt Anna, his mother's youngest sister, and her husband, Harry, for a drink in the lobby, and even considers taking them up on their offer to visit, but won't, as there is a portrait of Manet by Fantin-Latour and a superior collection of Renoirs and Monets on loan at the Art Institute in Chicago, plus the old World's Fair grounds and the Lakefront to enjoy.

There's also an unexpected telegram from Jim Kearney, his boss, informing Stevens that he will have to stay over in the Windy City for two more days, as there are clients to see and papers to sign. He had hoped to finally meet Harriet Monroe, but that too will have to wait for another time. Then it's back to New York for a few hours before he's on the road once more. And then home again, calling Kreymborg to see how things are going with *Others*, which—like many of the little magazines—seems to be in financial trouble. Then it's off on business again, this time heading south. But at least it will be springtime down in the Carolinas, where he will enjoy miles and miles of dogwood and cherry blossoms, while young girls parade about the streets in white for Easter.

Six days later it's the twelve-story Mason, its roof-line sign proclaiming that here indeed is the "Finest Roof Garden in the South." He dabs his pen into the inkwell in the hotel's library to tell Elsie it's summer here, with hibiscus, acacias, periwinkles, and pansies everywhere and that the trees are already heavy with leaves. Then it's on to Florida. Another week of this, and he and Elsie can finally leave New York behind and head to their apartment in Hartford. In the meantime he takes out a small scrap of cerise paper and writes in that terrible scrawl of his a few lines celebrating the world around him:

The lilacs wither in the Carolinas.
Already the butterflies flutter above the cabins.
Already the new-born children interpret love
In the voices of their mothers.

Timeless mother,
How is it that your aspic nipples
For once vent honey?

• • •

THAT EASTER HE WAS in Biscayne Bay and had to imagine the parade making its way along New York's Fifth Avenue, even as in the park a church choir was singing, much like the one he remembered in Reading. Was there anything "more inane than an Easter carol," which, when he thought about it, was nothing more than "a religious perversion of the activity of Spring in our blood"? Why a man who would prefer "to roll around in the grass should be asked to dress as magnificently as possible and listen to a choir" was a mystery to him, "except from the flagellant point of view," he told Elsie.

The truth was that the theater of his mind seemed to dwell in a place more like hell these days. And that theater, like the theater of the war raging across the Atlantic, constituted a world of darkness and oscillating shadows, upon which a raw red sun revealed things as they were. Earlier he'd written a one-act play called *Three Travelers Watch a Sunrise* and sent it to *Poetry*, and had just learned that it had been chosen from among some eighty plays to win a prize of $100 and publication in the July issue. What he had tried to do with his play, he told Monroe, was "create a poetic atmosphere with a minimum of narration." It was the first thing like it he'd ever done, and he was "delighted with the result."

"All you need, / To find poetry," one of the Chinese characters in the play says in the opening lines, "is to look for it with a lantern." But by the play's close, the scholar of one candle has been replaced by another, who sees that the very sunrise is not one thing, but as many things as there are observers. Stevens wasn't interested in a plot and character development, he told Monroe, for here—as in his poems—narrative and character development were at most secondary. The real point of the play came in the final sentence of the final speech, where reality was revealed as "many-faceted as the leaves of a forest reddened by first light."

In the June issue of *Poetry*, Monroe would go so far as to define Stevens's play as a "formative moment in our poetic drama," which Stevens felt was over the top. The play, he told Monroe's associate, Alice Corbin, was something "quite out of the question in the ordinary theatre." Still, he did think "that in the hands of people of imagination and feeling, it might do very well." He wanted to see it performed, but only if it were done "properly and sensitively," though, in a practical sense, that would have to be left to those footing the bill.

Four years later, on Friday evening, February 13, 1920, the play would have its sole performance at the Provincetown Playhouse on Macdougal Street in Greenwich Village. But by then its six characters would search in vain for their author, for, while Stevens was in New York that day, he did not go to see his play performed. "So much water has gone under the bridges since the thing was written," he told Monroe, "that I have not the curiosity even to read it at this late day," and that was the "truth, not pose." Thirty-five years after he'd written the play, he told a composer interested in turning it into a musical composition that he'd long since given up writing plays because he cared much more for the elegiac than he did the dramatic.

• • •

BY LATE MAY 1916 he and Elsie were settled in Hartford at the Highland Court Hotel at 38-40 Windsor Avenue, two and a half miles north of Stevens's office on Trumbull Street. The Highland was a five-story brick building with 250 apartments, sported a dining room, lobby, parlor, kitchen, barber shop, and servants' quarters, and advertized itself as "an Hotel for Homelovers with the Atmosphere of an English Inn and the Convenience and Comfort of an American Home of the Best Class." For years to come Elsie would have to live alone in Hartford much as she had in Manhattan while her husband traveled. Still, Hartford for her was infinitely better than New York. Just a week into their stay at the Highland, Stevens wrote Ferdinand Reyher that he already missed New York "abominably," though "Mrs. Stevens, with murderous indifference, pretends that Hartford is sweet to her spirit."

By then Williams was editing *Others* in Rutherford and writing Stevens about a batch of poems Stevens had sent him earlier. Among them was a draft of Stevens's unfinished "For an Old Woman in a Wig," written in rhymed terza rima, no doubt as a nod to Walter Arensberg, who had been translating the *Divine Comedy*. Many of Stevens's three-line stanzas still had gaps in them, and the rhyming remained for the most part plodding, but he did manage to catch something of Dante's masculine clarity and authority. The fragment was mostly scrawled in pencil with many erasures, and Stevens would soon abandon the form while he worked and reworked the ideas contained therein for decades to come. For his part, Williams liked the final lines especially, he told Stevens, because there he'd allowed himself to "become fervent for a moment." Forget the epic poetry of sky and sea, Stevens had written there. Better to push into the "unknown new" all around one and see what might be discovered there. The poem of the present, then: *there* was a worthwhile project.

A week later Williams wrote Stevens again, congratulating him "on winning 'ARRIET'S prize!" for *Three Travelers*. He was keeping a copy of Stevens's "The Worms at Heaven's Gate" for the July issue of *Others* because it was "a splendid poem," though "a change or two" would "strengthen the poem materially." The first edit was to change the second line from "Within our bellies, as a chariot" to "Within our bellies, we her chariot." Williams wanted the change because "THE WORMS ARE HER CHARIOT AND NOT ONLY SEEM HER CHARIOT," he wrote in bold caps. "'We her chariot' has more of a collective sense and feels more solid." Then he added, "What do you say?" He also urged

Stevens to remove two lines from another poem which he thought too sentimental. "For Christ's sake," he wrote, "yield to me and become great and famous," which was what Stevens did.

"The Worms at Heaven's Gate" is a dark poem. Macabre, really, dealing as it does with the fleetingness of a woman's beauty, even the beauty of a Badroulbadour lifted from the pages of *Arabian Nights*, reputedly the most beautiful woman in the world. It was not the lark at heaven's gate this time round, as Shakespeare had it, but worms lifting the body piecemeal toward the empty heavens. Nine lines, with the last line, following a long silence, returning the reader to the opening, with a new ring of horror:

Out of the tomb, we bring Badroulbadour,
Within our bellies, we her chariot.
Here is an eye. And here are, one by one,
The lashes of that eye and its white lid.
Here is the cheek on which that lid declined,
And, finger after finger, here, the hand,
The genius of that cheek. Here are the lips,
The bundle of the body and the feet.
. . . .
Out of the tomb we bring Badroulbadour.

From St. Paul that June, Stevens wrote Elsie that nobody seemed to recognize him for the "Eminent Vers Libriste" he was. In a parody of a newspaper report, he wrote that "Wallace Stevens, the playwright and barrister," had "arrived at Union Station, at 10:30 o'clock this morning," where "some thirty representatives were not present to greet him." When "asked how he liked St. Paul, Mr. Stevens, borrowing a cigar, said, 'I like it.' "

Just now the news was all about General "Black Jack" Pershing leading a large expeditionary force into Mexico in an attempt—unsuccessful, as it turned out—to capture Pancho Villa. Stevens was impressed with the squads of recruits—husky, virile young men—drilling in the square opposite the Minnesota Club, where he was staying. But he was not impressed with President Wilson's handling of the situation, feeling he'd made a serious mistake in sending American troops into Mexico without first declaring war. But then, he added, staunch Republican that he was, Wilson, a Democrat, had "an unfortunate ease" in getting the country into messes. "Why all this horror of what must be done," he wondered. After all, a good fight might be just the thing to settle the matter.

One evening, returning to the Club after work, he happened to pass his uncle Jim on the street, but instead of stopping to say hello, he just kept walking. "It was very nice to see him and not to be recognized," he wrote Elsie. After all, what was there to say? Family relations were stupid, and he was sure that, after asking each other a few questions, "there'd be nothing in the world to talk about except Japan," and he felt no need to talk about Japan. Three years later the scene would be repeated when Stevens was in Cleveland, where his brother Garrett was now practicing law. One afternoon he spotted his brother on the street, but—having nothing to say—crossed the street and just kept walking.

• • •

BUSINESS RELATIONSHIPS ON THE other hand did matter, and Jim Kearney certainly looked upon Stevens as a valued asset. It was Kearney who saw to it that the Stevenses had comfortable housing when they moved that summer from their hotel to Farmington, a fifteen-minute trolley ride along tree-shaded Farmington Avenue. Then, in late August, they were able to move to 594 Prospect Avenue, an extensive three-story dark brick apartment building on the corner of Farmington Avenue, two miles from Stevens's office, so that he could get in his daily exercise, breathing in the Connecticut air as he walked briskly to and from work.

At first he and Elsie hobnobbed with the best of Hartford's society, though in time, given Elsie's awkward shyness, they would isolate themselves more and more. But on January 26, 1917, with Elsie in Reading caring for her sick mother, Stevens attended a dinner at the Heubleins', an extremely successful German American family who had made a fortune with their A-1 Steak Sauce and then with ready-made bottled cocktails and later would make millions with Smirnoff's vodka, the "new white whiskey." That evening turned out to be "a regular blowout," with everybody, Stevens wrote, "dressed like a warlord" except himself, who looked more like that image of Ben Franklin one found on boxes of Quaker Oats. Among those he'd met was the Viennese Wagnerian soprano Melanie Kurt, "one of the best singers at the Metropolitan Opera," whose career would be cut short just months later when the United States, after declaring war on Germany, forbade Wagner's operas from being performed.

In February Stevens traveled with Kearney to Omaha on business, and when that project had to be aborted, the two returned to Minneapolis, where Stevens headed south to Houston by himself. There were high winds and snow throughout Minnesota, so that Stevens's train was delayed twelve hours. Even then it had to inch along, following a snow plow clearing the tracks while the winds howled incessantly. Houston, on the other hand, was like July, with japonica and peach in full bloom and people watering their lawns. The local agent there drove him out to Rice University, with its handsome buildings and faculty culled from Oxford, Harvard, and Princeton, who, Stevens believed, would in time transform Houston's prairie goats into civilized sheep. From there it was on to San Antonio and Cuero, before he headed back to Chicago.

• • •

WHEN LAURA SHERRY, PRODUCER for the Wisconsin Players, read *Three Travelers* in the pages of *Poetry*, she wrote Stevens asking if he would write a one-act play for her troupe, and Stevens happily obliged by writing *Carlos among the Candles*. His intention was not to produce something dramatic, he explained to Bancel LaFarge, who would design the set, but rather to show how people were affected by what was around them. Consider, he explained, the effect of a single candle upon the senses. Vary the number of candles lit or extinguished in a dark room, and one's emotions and sense associations were likewise affected. Thus at one point, Carlos, the lone speaker on the stage, tells his audience that a dozen blazing candles on the table are "like twelve wild birds flying in autumn," and that—as he extinguishes them one by one and the darkness becomes more visible—one imagines the twelve birds disappearing one after the other into the dark of winter.

On Saturday evening, October 20, Stevens was in New York to see the sole performance of *Carlos*. This took place in conjunction with several other one-act plays at the new, experimental Neighborhood Playhouse at 466 Grand Street, within sight of the Brooklyn Bridge, and was performed by the Wisconsin Players. Along with Providence Playhouse and the Washington Square Players, the Neighborhood Players in the largely Jewish section of the city was among New York's first "little theaters" and sat some three hundred, presenting work by O'Neill, Shaw, and Joyce. But, though a few critics were enthusiastic about the performance of *Carlos*, from Stevens's perspective the play was a disaster.

He was not, of course, interested "in proving anything to the critics," he explained to Monroe that Halloween, just days after another of his one-act plays, *Bowl, Cat and Broomstick*, was performed at the same playhouse by the same players. Ralph Block, reviewing *Carlos* for the *New York Tribune*, wrote that the purpose of this kind of entertainment . . . appears to be to say something that has no meaning at all with all the bearing of significance." The critics were justified in whatever they said, and "would have been in saying anything," Stevens admitted. Still, a play, even without action or characters, "ought to be within the range of human interests." But wasn't that the problem? Ever since Aristotle, plays had to have a "form . . . like a sonnet," with "passion, development and so on," even though the Players were interested in experimenting with new forms altogether. But, then, what did he know? It was "all Swedish" to him.

Two decades later he admitted that he would have "been more interested in the theatre" if the actual performance of his plays had not given him "the horrors." Take the stage set for *Carlos*, for instance, which had been cobbled together by some schoolboy. Or the actor who managed "to forget three pages of a text made up of only ten or twelve pages." No wonder the management had refused to allow the play to run a second night.

From the Hillsboro Hotel in Tampa in mid-November, he wrote his friend Reyher to say that the Players had finally "returned to Milwaukee, thank God." *Poetry Magazine* would publish *Carlos* in its December 1917 number, and, if Reyher read it, he would "have no difficulty in imagining the feelings of a Russian damsel among the Bolsheviki." Besides, he had more pressing things on his mind, among them seeing that Elsie was settled as smoothly as possible back in the Highland Court Hotel while a more spacious fourth-floor apartment was readied for them at the St. Nicholas complex at 210 Farmington Avenue, just a mile from Stevens's office. In early December they moved into apartment D1, where they would remain for the next six years and where Stevens would finish his first book of poems.

• • •

IN HIS PROLOGUE TO *Kora in Hell* (1920), William Carlos Williams quotes from a letter Stevens wrote him, dated April 9, 1918. Stevens had written to thank Williams for a copy of *Al Que Quiere* and added at the top of his letter a postscript: "I think, after all, I should rather send this than not, although it is quarrelsomely full of my own ideas of discipline." Williams included the letter because what Stevens said there spoke to how the two poets differed in their approaches to the poem. Stevens was "a fine gentleman," Williams began, a man whom their mutual friend Skip Cannell had nailed by likening him to a "Pennsylvania Dutchman who has suddenly become aware of his habits and taken to 'society' in self-defense."

What most struck him about Williams's poems was "their casual character," Stevens began, so that the books Williams had thus far published had about them the sense of a miscellany. That was an approach Stevens himself disliked, and the reason he had not yet bothered to publish a book of his own. For Stevens it was necessary to stick with an idea if one had any hope of conveying that idea to a reader. "Given a fixed point of view," he explained, whether realistic or imagistic, everything eventually "adjusted itself to that point of view." But to keep playing with points of view, as Williams did, led "always to new beginnings and incessant new beginnings lead to sterility."

"A single manner or mood thoroughly matured and exploited is that fresh thing," he explained, and the essential Williams was to be found in lines like those about "children / Leaping around a dead dog." A book of that would surely "feed the hungry." In any event, a book of poems was "a damned serious affair," and a book by Williams should contain only what was distinctive about Williams's style and nothing else. Stevens had found that quality everywhere in *Al Que Quiere*, "but dissipated and obscured." There were "very few men who have anything native in them or for whose work I'd give a Bolshevik ruble," he added. Williams should follow with full force his search for an American idiom and his New Jersey landscapes, and not fiddle with anything else.

But what would Stevens have him do with his Circe, Williams asked in his sexually fraught sleight-of-hand manner, now that he'd "double-crossed her game" and slept with her? Marry her? That was not what Odysseus had done. For his part, Stevens would hold out for a unified volume, excluding as many fine poems from the book he would title *Harmonium* as he would include, so that it would take another five years to craft the book he wanted.

In the meantime he kept composing. The December 1917 issue of *Others* published "Thirteen Ways of Looking at a Blackbird" along with four other poems. It may well be the first of Stevens's poems to include something of the world of Connecticut, his new home, in its wintry landscape, and with the war very much in the background. It is not the nightingale or the robin, but the blackbird which dominates the thirteen haiku-like sections of Stevens's signature poem, the poem which, with its thirteen marble markers, now greets—if that is the word—those who look for Stevens in Hartford today, between the place where he worked and the place he lived.

"Among twenty snowy mountains," the poem begins, "the only moving thing / Was the eye of the blackbird." The poem ends with the blackbird once more, this time sitting "in the cedar-limbs" in the long evening of a winter's afternoon, where "it was snowing / And it was going to snow." In the middle section of the poem, Stevens addresses "the thin men of Haddam." Haddam: one of those small American towns (population seven thousand) that sounds as if it should be a town in the Bible but instead lies twenty-seven miles south of Hartford along the Connecticut River. Why, the poet asks, should one spend one's time imagining golden birds when actual blackbirds walk "around the feet / Of the women about you"? No matter where our thoughts are, death the blackbird is a part of what we know and what we feel. In "the long window / With barbaric glass" out of which we look onto the world about us, or within us, one thing is sure: that "the shadow of the blackbird" has crossed and will continue to cross that window, its shadow tracing the unnamed, "indecipherable cause," death.

A year later his poem on the failure of his marriage, "Le Monocle de Mon Oncle," appeared. In a dramatic monologue in the voice of a fictive uncle, Stevens's play on the words of the title make light of the tragedy of what had come of his marriage: *Dans ces lignes, mon cher, je t'envoie mes regrets sincères pour les dix dernières années.* "In these lines, my dear, I send you my sincere regrets for the last ten years." The title itself calls to mind Donald Evans's sonnet "En Monocle," the lines themselves Stevens's reprise ten years on. Elsie was no longer his golden girl of eighteen, but a woman who at thirty-two still dressed in the style of thirty years before, Pennsylvania Dutch drab, her hair down now, and sex a strained affair at the least. "Born with a monocle he stares at life," Evans's poem begins:

His calm moustache points to the ironies,
And a faun-colored laugh sucks in the night . . .
Features are fixtures when the face is fled,
And we are left the husks of tarnished hair;
But he is one who lusts uncomforted
To kiss the naked phrase quite unaware.

Pound and Eliot were covering similar ground at the time, and even Williams had flirted with it. It was an attitude lauded among the decadents of the Yellow Nineties, but carried now on the fetid winds of the Great War and Dada, and Stevens had breathed in its air, basking in that sachet-scented wasteland as well. Whatever Elsie had meant to him in his loneliness in New York in those early years lay buried now in the same dark earth of Reading, along with memories of his parents. "Mother of heaven," "Le Monocle" begins, invoking Mary in a parody of the Catholic litany. Or is this Stevens's version of the Perfect Woman, this "regina of the clouds," this "sceptre of the sun" and "crown of the moon"? In any case this much he knows: that he has perfected a language with which to mock his own failed attempt to turn his golden girl from Reading into the Perfect Woman.

But does he mock her, or merely himself in such magnificent measures? Once she was his Venus rising full-blown from the sea, born of an imagination gone amuck, and now the unforgiving "sea of spuming thought" mocks him with "the radiant bubble that she was." Bleak reality returns things to what they are: "A deep up-pouring from some saltier well / Within me, bursts its watery syllable." A young man of fortune at last meets a man of forty. Yes, it is spring again, a time when birds build their nests and sing, to remind him that his own springtime is gone now, irretrievably, "past meridian," and that these spring "choirs of welcome" choir for him only farewells.

Consider those Japanese beauties brought to life in the prints of Utamaro in the eighteenth century, which influenced so many of the French impressionists. Consider the sensuous nuances the Japanese artist caught in the "all-speaking braids" of those ladies. Consider too "the mountainous coiffures of Bath," those London ladies of the Enlightenment on holiday with their luscious locks. Have "all those barbers lived in vain / That not one curl in nature has survived?" And why is it, he asks the woman with him in their bedroom, that "without pity on these studious ghosts / . . . you come dripping in your hair from sleep?"

Once you were Eve, the "Untasted" one in that "heavenly, orchard air" of Eden, and you proffered your apple, which in time ripened and then fell to the ground to rot there, as flesh will do. In the beginning, in Eden, love was "a book too mad to read." But now we have all the time to read it at our leisure. Think first of the budding amorist and then of the balding amorist at forty, when

amours shrink
Into the compass and curriculum
Of introspective exiles, lecturing.

Now our fall harvest has come, and we are its fruits: "Two golden gourds distended on our vines," hanging

like warty squashes, streaked and rayed,
Into the autumn weather, splashed with frost,
Distorted by hale fatness, turned grotesque.
The laughing sky will see the two of us
Washed into rinds by rotting winter rains.

The poem keeps circling itself with each end-stopped stanza, like concentric circles flowing from an open wound. "If sex were all," the poet mocks himself, "then every trembling hand / Could make us squeak, like dolls, the wished for words." And what is married life at forty? "Last night," the poet laments, recalling that the "first, foremost law" of life demands that we regenerate our kind before death takes us if we are to live on at all, last night "we sat beside a pool of pink, / Keen to the point of starlight, while a frog / Boomed from his very belly odious chords."

Sing as you will, weep and grunt and play doleful heroics, all life ends in death. When he was younger, he could afford to observe "the nature of mankind, / In lordly study," for love then was a subject he could swallow, a mere "gobbet in my mincing world." Later, "like a rose rabbi," he could pursue "the origin and course / Of love." But now what he sees is that all things flutter in a constant flux, that all shades of nuanced understanding must resolve themselves into the final shade of death. When the mind tires finally of beating its wings against the void, he too will flutter to the ground, dropping like that apple, to assume the final shade of death, from which there will be no escaping.

• • •

"I'VE HAD THE BLOOMING horrors, following my gossip about death, at your house," Stevens wrote Monroe in early April 1918, three weeks after his first visit to her. The war was well into its fourth year and America was now shipping out thousands of young men who would never return. Over three hundred of his Harvard classmates had volunteered to serve in some capacity in the effort to bring the war to end all wars to a speedy close. But Stevens was not one of them, and the failure to be part of that effort seems to have troubled him deeply. A million and more young men and women, his sister Katherine among them, had volunteered to do their part. So, if he had dwelt too long on death that evening, he told Monroe, it was because what absorbed him these days were war and death.

So many people were directly involved in the war, whereas for him it was essentially a thing to think about. He was approaching forty when he wrote this, so he might have been excused because of his age. If anything, his time to have served would have been during the Spanish-American War, as a number of his Reading classmates had done. But he was in college then, and that had certainly seemed a good enough excuse. Now he was married and had a wife to take care of. Excuses, surely, and decent ones. Still, the fact was that he was safe, while so many others, younger than he, were dying every day.

That spring he made several unbearably boring trips to Tennessee, dreaming only of getting back to Hartford, where he could finally "sleep in a big chair over a big book." But he'd seen something in Chattanooga just two weeks after America had entered the war that had deeply stirred him: the sight of young men in uniform, even if for the moment there was nothing for them to do but walk about or crowd into his hotel for a decent meal. Soon enough they would be on their way to France and, he believed, would get the job done for which they were being sent.

A few days later, now in Johnson City, he noted with unexpected but real pride that a trainload of "Negro" draftees had passed through the night before, and the local blacks on the platform had gone up and down shaking hands with the men on the train, cheering them on, to the amusement of the few whites there who regarded the scene as an absurdity. He'd tried to understand things from the southern white point of view and so take part in laughing "at these absurd animals," because that was what one was expected to do. But what he'd felt instead was a thrill at these young soldiers, so that he had wanted "to cry and yell and jump ten feet in the air," because it made no difference, finally, whether a man was black or white, for every one of them was his fellow countryman, and all stood ready to fight a common enemy.

He'd tried to acknowledge the reality of war by imagining what death by bullet or bayonet or bombardment might feel like, but he knew that the reality of war was too much for any poet to capture. The summer before, he'd read Eugène Emmanuel Lemercier's *Lettres d'un Soldat (août*

1914–avril 1915) and been deeply moved by it. A young landscape artist, Lemercier had joined the French Army at the outbreak of the war in August 1914. In the nine months following, until he disappeared during a heavy bombardment of his trenches by the Germans, he had continued to write to his mother about the terrible faces of war and of the consolations he looked for in his Catholic faith, his art, and, finally, in the band of brothers he fought beside. André Chevrillon had provided a preface to the letters when they were first published in 1916, and this too had resonated powerfully with Stevens. "To fight with his brothers," one translation reads, "with his eyes wide open, without hope of glory or profit, and simply because this is the law, here is the commandment that the god gives to the warrior Arjuna when he doubts that he must turn away from the absolute toward the human nightmare of battle. . . . Let Arjuna stretch his bow with the others."

To turn away, then, even from the consolations of the imagination, and with one's eyes wide open to the reality of war: that was the challenge facing Stevens. So he took what he could from the letters and turned them into taut, stripped lyrics as he tried to place himself imaginatively in the face of an overwhelming reality, one with the power to turn Emerson's transcendent all-seeing eye into a soldier's eyeball blown from its socket and lying now in the mud. "If I should fall, as soldier," Stevens wrote,

I know well
The final pulse of blood from this good heart
Would taste, precisely, as they said it would.

17 *mars* 1915, with three weeks left before Lemercier would die: *J'ai oublié de te dire que, l'autre fois, pendant la tempête, j'ai vu dans le soir les grues revenir. Une accalmie permettait d'entendre leur cri.* "I forgot to tell you that the other evening, during the storm, I saw the cranes returning. A lull allowed me to hear their cry." Lemercier's was a sensibility much like Stevens's, ever on the outlook for the cry of birds, even in hell. "The cranes return," Stevens wrote. "The soldier hears their cry. He knows the fire / That touches them." In time he would discard these lines as unequal to

the tragic loss of a soldier. All that would survive his scrutiny is a single quatrain in which he attempts to revive the ancient trope of the "theater of war," something older than Virgil or Homer or Ashurbanipal, something as old as the human race itself.

Nine sections of the antiwar poem's original thirteen made it into the May 1918 number of *Poetry*, after Stevens and Monroe had gone back and forth on which to include and in what order. They plotted this together in the offices of *Poetry* late on the afternoon of March 14, as Stevens was preparing to return home from Indianapolis, having completed some old business there. That was the day he'd gone on and on about the inscrutable banality of death in the trenches. And yet none of these war poems made it into the first edition of *Harmonium*, though in the revised version of 1931, "The Death of a Soldier," along with two others, would return.

"Life contracts and death is expected," Stevens wrote there, and though Lemercier had been killed in the spring of 1915, Stevens thought it more appropriate to alter the season to autumn. Nor was there any hope for Christian rebirth here. In death the soldier did not "become a three-days personage, / Imposing his separation, / Calling for pomp." The war had taught Stevens this: "Death is absolute and without memorial," and "as in a season of autumn," the wind would stop, and "the clouds go, nevertheless, / In their direction."

A month later, in the pages of the *Little Review*, Margaret Anderson published—along with a sizable segment of Joyce's *Ulysses*—three poems by Stevens: "Anecdote of Men by the Thousand," "Depression before Spring," and "Metaphors of a Magnifico." How to describe a troop—or a trope—of, say, twenty men "crossing a bridge, / Into a village"? Were they "twenty men crossing twenty bridges, / Into twenty villages"? Or was it "one man" only, "crossing a single bridge into a village"? Or, as Gertrude Stein might have said, were "twenty men crossing a bridge, / Into a village," simply "twenty men crossing a bridge / Into a village"? But what did such a statement tell us, if it told us anything? Or did the real come down finally to a prelinguistic sense of things, as in a series of fragmented aural and visual images? The sound of twenty men's boots clumping on the wooden boards of a bridge. That, and the "first white wall of the village" rising through fruit trees as the scene changed, as in Duchamp's *Nude*: "The first white wall of the village . . . / The fruit trees," the the . . .

• • •

ON CHRISTMAS EVE 1918, William Carlos Williams watched as his dying father slipped into a coma. At one point he turned to his mother to tell her that her husband was gone now, only to see his father, eyes shut, shake his head slowly from side to side. "Dear Stevens," he wrote that evening, "Three Amens! It might be three blackbirds or three blue jays in the snow—but it is three Amens!" His wife was downstairs trimming the tree and the boys were in the room next to him, already fast asleep. "What in God's name" could "a man say to Christ these days"? Christmas morning he added a postscript, thanking Stevens for his poetic criticism in the latest *Little Review.* He was referring to "Nuances of a Theme by Williams," Stevens's take on Williams's four-line poem "El Hombre." "It's a strange courage / you give me ancient star," Williams had written, one more poet among many remaking poetry now. Nor did it matter if his poems survived. What did matter was that—like the star—he continue to "shine alone in the sunrise" toward which he lent no part.

Stevens saw a chance to point out some of the differences between what Williams was up to and what he himself would have added to that spareness. "Shine alone, shine nakedly," Stevens wrote:

Be not chimera of morning,
Half-man, half-star.
Be not an intelligence,
Like a widow's bird
Or an old horse.

The eye of that blackbird again. A hard truth to grasp, especially on a Christmas morning with one's "poor dear father" dead. Who, after all, could really say what the loss of one's father might mean for oneself or one's work?

8

Hartford on the Harmonium: 1919–1921

Let these be your delight, secretive hunter,
Wading the sea lines, moist and ever-mingling.
Mounting the earth lines, long and lax, lethargic.
These lines are swift and fall without diverging.

STARS AT TALLAPOOSA

It was 1919. One war was over, while another brewed in Ireland with England's unleashing of criminals—the Black and Tans—upon the Irish. Six days into the new year Teddy Roosevelt died in his sleep, and Woodrow Wilson, now entering the seventh year of his administration, was preparing to go to Paris to help shape a new peace. That January would also see the ratification of the Eighteenth Amendment, prohibiting the sale of liquor a year hence. And that same month Stevens would find himself once more in Florida covering surety claims. Palm Beach and Miami, then north to Jacksonville, where he fumed on a porch waiting for someone to show up who owed the Hartford "a substantial sum of money"; when the man did appear and saw the size of the insurance agent waiting for him, he quickly signed the documents Stevens presented him with. Then it was west again by rail through the Florida Panhandle to New Orleans, Houston, Dallas, and Tulsa, with a night in Muskogee because of a missed train connection.

What he pined for most on these trips south was the tip of Florida, with its palm trees and blue horizons. He'd strolled about in Miami, winding up one evening in a public park, where he listened to the *oom-pah-pah* of a brass band. A chance before the next train north to taste fresh strawberries and corn on the cob—and this in January!—and a breeze blowing warmly, fevering his blood with the lusciousness of it all. And yet if Miami was "a heavenly change" from Hartford, he confessed to Elsie, Hartford gave him something he needed: exquisite springs and long autumns which these "lotus-eaters of the South must pine for."

By early May he was on the road again: New York to Washington this time, then west to Chicago, where he walked about and dined sumptuously—one of his deepest pleasures—before moving on to Milwaukee. For two weeks he sat in court each day from ten until four dealing with company business. What a bore the place was, like most of the Midwest: "dingy, grimy, and sooty," with March-like weather even now.

Worse was waiting for his associates to wake up and get down to business. Two had arrived from New York and done nothing but ramble on, before heading back to New York, their job unfinished, leaving him to work out the details of the case for yet another week. In between he spent hours in a dentist's office having his teeth drilled and working evenings on some poems he'd brought with him which he planned to leave with Harriet Monroe when he passed through Chicago on his way home. That batch would appear five months later in the October number of *Poetry* under the collective heading of *Pecksniffiana* and go on to win the Harriet Levinson Prize for Poetry, worth $500.

Pecksniffiana. As in Dickens's unctuously hypocritical character in *Martin Chuzzlewit*. "Some people likened him to a direction-post," Dickens writes of Pecksniff, "which is always telling the way to a place, and never goes there." Stevens loved inventing or reimagining his characters and then peppering them throughout his poems, early and late, so that they seemed a mixture of Lewis Carroll, Edward Lear, and Dada, resisting interpretation—as he said good poetry must do—almost successfully. When his first volume of poems appeared, it would be home to a host of characters with names like Peter Quince, Hoon, Don Joost, Crispin,

Remus, Ursula, the Infanta Marina, Fernando, Hibiscus, the Doctor of Geneva, Vincentine, Badroulbadour, Berserk, Scaramouche, Victoria Clementina, Jasmine, Rosenbloom, Bonnie and Josie, the Polish Aunt, and Chieftain Iffucan of Azcan in caftan.

Pecksniffiana. Peter Quince again, Act I, Scene 2: Stevens's mocking gesture about assuming the high road in poetry: the winking lawyer letting you in on the joke as he spread his bouquet of sophisticated punning poems before his readers. "Barque of phosphor," the first poem begins (and Stevens will show no signs of letting up). It's the opening of "Fabliau of Florida," an early medieval French tale written in octosyllabics, the content comic, satiric, and bawdy by turns. The poem itself opens and closes with a pun on the poem's first word, *barque* (bark, as in a ship, or the bark of a dog, say, or the cry of the poet), and its final word, *surf*, a homonym for serf, a laborer, a servant, like Stevens the lawyer and Stevens the poet at the beck and call of his Muse with his own "barque of phosphor," his poetic cry and thoughts "on the palmy beach" of Biscayne Bay.

In "Homunculus et La Belle Étoile," it is Venus who conducts "the thoughts of drunkards" as well as "the feelings / Of widows and trembling ladies." Let the rationalists look upon that evening star, bathing their hearts in the late light of the moon, before they return to their rigid thoughts by day. If they wish to live the lonely life of the scholar of one candle, so be it. Still, even for them their muse is "no gaunt fugitive phantom" but "a wanton, / Abundantly beautiful," to be found in the simplest of speech. After all, the ultimate Plato is the visionary, the dreamer, the poet, for whom the evening star is enough to soothe the buzzing torments of our workaday lives.

And the poem about the strange state of mind Stevens called Tennessean, which he gives us in "Anecdote of the Jar," a reworking, most probably, of Duchamp's *Fountain*, submitted to (and rejected by) the avant-garde Society of Artists in 1917: a porcelain urinal discovered in a hardware store—a true American objet trouvé—laid on its side and signed by one R. Mutt. A jar (a Dominion Jar?) taking dominion everywhere, much as Duchamp's urinal did: a jar placed on a hill in Tennessee, making Tennessee's "slovenly wilderness / Surround that hill" and taming it with its focus, so that we might see how round upon the ground that jar is, which "took dominion everywhere" and "did not give of bird or bush, / Like nothing else in Tennessee."

• • •

ON A SUNDAY MORNING in May 1919 Stevens took a trolley south from Milwaukee to Evanston, Illinois, to visit his uncle Harry, who had recently lost his wife, Stevens's aunt Anna. Now Uncle Harry was alone, except for the care provided by Eleanor, Stevens's brother John's sister-in-law, who brought Stevens up to date about the family he hadn't seen in so long. His sister Elizabeth had married a man twenty years older than she, a man of "fifty with white hair." Stevens gasped when he heard the news. Elizabeth had recently given birth to a girl named Jane. Eleanor showed him photographs of John's children, and then one of John's wife, who had grown "much stouter," though in truth he'd met her only once, and that was at his mother's funeral seven years before. His brother Garrett was still lawyering in Cleveland and trying to support a family, though there was the same old news about Garrett's money problems. Katharine, his favorite sibling, was now serving with the Red Cross somewhere in France, caring for amputees and gas victims. Still, for him, family news was such a bore. If his family had turned out to be successful millionaires, that might have made a difference. But since none of them had. . . .

Two weeks later the news came that Katharine had died in a military hospital in Saint-Nazaire on the coast of France. She'd taken ill early that month and had been operated on for mastoiditis just four days after Stevens had visited Uncle Harry. Then, on May 19, she had succumbed to meningitis. She was laid out in her Red Cross uniform, upon which a friend had pinned a large red peony plucked from a bouquet someone had sent her, and her body was shipped back to the States to be buried next to her parents in Reading. Katharine had just turned thirty and her tour in Europe was about to end. A friend of hers who had worked with her had written that everyone had loved her because she was always so friendly and happy and sang for the men in the hospital, something which meant so much more "over here than it does at home."

"I am completely done up by the news of Katharine's death," a chastened Stevens wrote Elsie. How horrible "to think of the poor child fatally ill in a military hospital in an out-of-the-way place in a foreign country, probably perfectly aware of her helplessness and isolation!" And yet, if she had made it back home, what was there for her here? For one thing, the home where they'd all grown up together was no longer theirs, so that she would have had to make her own way, a young soul who never complained and who had always been "loyal to what was good."

Standing in the crowd on the streets of Milwaukee during the Memorial Day parade, he found it almost impossible to look at the grieving mothers, each carrying a gold-star flag for her dead son or daughter, as they passed by, reminding him of his own loss. He noted too the large number of German Catholic priests marching by, because "all the great churches" here in Milwaukee were Catholic. That evening he tried writing Elsie a letter in the lobby of the Athletic Club, but so many women, all of them Swedes, had crowded into the place after dinner that he found it "a job for a man, even when he has only one good ear," to concentrate, which was one reason he preferred solitude whenever and wherever he could find it.

That July, on his way home from Philadelphia on business, he made it a point to stop in Reading for a couple of hours to visit the family graves where Katharine now lay buried. She'd done her part for the war effort, "unselfishly and devotedly," he wrote Elsie, and look at what had happened to her. He and Katharine, the two siblings most like their mother, while the other three were more like their father, which helped explain why he saw so little of them. Her presence here, even in death, further complicated his feelings about his birthplace, giving it an added sense of the sacred, something only the heart could understand whenever he thought of Reading now.

That summer he remained mostly in Hartford, a place that had by then become for Elsie and himself "as dismal as two grave-diggers spending a rainy night in a vault," he confessed to Harriet Monroe. Even so, it was better than spending time near the ocean or in the mountains, which would have surely given him the blues. On October 8, as he turned forty, he wrote to thank her for printing his *Pecksniffiana.* When he'd last seen her in Chicago, she'd introduced him to Carl Sandburg, who in turn had sent Stevens a copy of *Cornhuskers*, along with a note: "Here is one of thirteen ways of looking from a skyscraper." How delightful, he told Monroe, to see his own poetic reputation beginning to appear on the western horizon, even as far as Chicago.

• • •

THAT WINTER JOHN RODKER, a private publisher in London, sent Stevens a shipment of books he'd recently produced, including, prominently, T. S. Eliot's *Ara Vos Prec.* Stevens thanked Rodker, but added that the book contained nothing he hadn't already seen: "The Hippopotamus," "Sweeney among the Nightingales," "Sweeney Erect," "Burbank with a Baedeker: Bleistein with a Cigar," "Gerontion," and "Mr. Eliot's Sunday Morning Service." Many of these poems, in fact, shared a similar aloofness and chilliness with Stevens's own work, including "Cy Est Pourtraicte," "Le Monocle de Mon Oncle," and "Sunday Morning."

His summation of *The Waste Land* would fare no better. "Eliot's poem is, of course, the rage," he would write Alice Corbin Henderson in November 1922, just after it appeared in the *Criterion.* As poetry it was "surely negligible." If it was supposed to be the "supreme cry of despair," it was Eliot's only. Personally, he found it "a bore." He would continue to hold Eliot at greater arm's length than even Williams would, the difference being that, where Williams lashed out at Eliot as a wounded beast and Pound's ill-begotten creation, Stevens, being the good lawyer he was, preferred to keep his own counsel, at least in print.

By the spring of 1920, what with the incessant pressures of work, Stevens's own poetic output had begun to fall off. On the train to Indianapolis on April 25, he'd written Monroe a wry letter including an improvised miscellany of poems he'd composed that very day to keep boredom at bay. These were a send-up to show how far he'd drifted since *Pecksniffiana.* "The cows are down in the meadows, now, for the first time," the first poem begins, while the sheep grazed under thin trees, all of which "makes me happy." His last improvisation carries the grand title "Certainties cutting the centuries" and is composed in Stevens's impeccable French: *Je vous assure, madame, q'une promenade à travers the soot-deposit qu'est Indianapolis est une chose véritablement étrange. Je viens de finir une belle promenade. Le jour après demain je serai à Pittsburg d'où je partiri pour Hartford.* "I assure you, madam, that a walk through the soot-deposit that is Indianapolis is truly a strange thing. I have just finished a nice walk. The day after tomorrow I will be in Pittsburgh whence I shall go to Hartford." *Tum-ti-tum.*

"I have not had a poem in my head for a month, poor Yorick," he confessed to Elsie three weeks later, while on yet another business trip, this time to Erie, Pennsylvania. Early Sunday morning, May 16, he found time to write her from the brick and granite Lawrence Hotel there, complaining of how hard-pressed he was by the twists and turns of the five cases he was juggling in three or four places, so that he felt like a "Cuban chess-player trying to beat fifty antagonists all at a time." He'd been up late writing a report for Kearney and in a little while he would meet with a Mr. McAleer arriving from Baltimore, and a Mr. Connolly, coming in from Pittsburgh, to finish some business for the Hartford. At noon he would be on his way to Cleveland to meet with some clients, and then leave for Youngstown that evening. Then it would be back to Erie to undertake "the most difficult and dangerous cases" litigation-wise he'd ever had to handle for the company.

He was soaking in a tub when the phone began ringing, and soon he was "floating on a Gulf Stream of talk with lawyers, contractors, dealers in cement, lumber and so on." He'd wanted to attend services at the local Episcopal church that morning but was afraid his two Irish colleagues might object to his "worshipping the principle of things instead of the stuff that makes the mares go round." What made the mares go round, of course, was money. He begged Elsie to join him in Chicago in early June to celebrate her thirty-seventh birthday. That it was only her thirty-fourth spoke volumes about the state of their marriage.

By then he'd been away for over a month and could feel the strain of his life as a celibate. Worse, he could not afford to return to Hartford, for a single mistake in the high-stakes game of the insurance business could prove fatal for him. Old man Moore—Frederick C. Moore, the Hartford's watchdog in matters of special risk cases—had been sent out to oversee the Erie case and was planning to take up residence with his wife there in the countryside, where, as Stevens noted, he would "have little to do except spend [the Hartford's] money" and have "a good time."

Of course Stevens himself was all for making the mares go round. Most important, he made sure that Elsie was provided for. But she was of such a shy and retiring nature—in fact, agoraphobic—that it would take a miracle to get her to join him on his business trips. To compensate for her absence, he had three pleasures he refused to deny himself. The first was visiting art galleries, though purchasing originals would have to wait until he had more capital. The second was having his friends and acquaintances find objects which evoked the sense of a particular place, whether that was honey, candied fruit, a bronze statue of a lion or one of the Buddha, and which he himself paid for. The third was ordering books, rare books, especially from London and Paris book dealers.

That March, for example, he'd taken in Rockwell Kent's Alaska paintings, on exhibit at Knoedler's Gallery at Fourty-sixth and Fifth, though he'd been disappointed in what he'd seen there. Part of the problem, he told Carl Zigrosser, who ran the Weyhe Gallery farther uptown, was the woman behind the counter who, judging from his size and what he'd been wearing, had mistaken him "for a strayed Klondiker." But would any Klondiker have recognized in Kent's palette of "old gold, old rose and boudoir blue . . . any sense of Alaska that he had ever had"? The trouble with Kent's work was that it tended to the *miêvre*: the corny and mawkish. And while Kent could sometimes throw "a dart so tragic as to be instantly fatal," in these paintings the dart had "no more heft or sting to it than the little feathered thing one bats around in battledore and shuttlecock."

That fall he wrote Ferdinand Reyher, who was on his way to London, asking him to procure a copy of John Rodker's book of poems, *Hymns*, which, as with Evans's poems, contained such erotica that it would be "necessary to keep the book hidden in the piano" and away from Elsie. Better, perhaps, to have the book mailed to his office. He also asked Reyher to get him some Sicilian honey, which Amy Lowell had told him could be purchased "in a large grocery store in Piccadilly." Also some illustrated catalogues of prints and pictures, as well as one of Augustus John's etchings—if they weren't too expensive. Perhaps too a woodcut by Lucien Pissarro. And, while he was at it, Vernon Lee's *Studies of the Eighteenth Century in Italy*, Philippe Monnier's 1910 *Venice in the Eighteenth Century*, and John Black's 1814 translation of Goldoni's *Memoirs*. Anything in fact that dealt with life in eighteenth-century Venice. If Reyher couldn't find any of these, then a selection of Italian prints would have to do.

When, in turn, Reyher asked Stevens to send him copies of the most significant magazines being published in the United States, Stevens told him he was asking for the impossible. Williams and a young man from out west by the name of Robert McAlmon had just started something called *Contact*, and Stevens promised to send him a copy because it would be worth reading. Yet, while the idea behind *Contact*—to come in contact with the reality of the everyday—was a good one, it was so good that Williams and McAlmon were already "trying to explain it away." Another little magazine called *Rainbow* was already headed for oblivion, and another, the *Arts*, was merely full of hot air. Then there was Arensberg, who was now thinking of publishing something like the *Atlantic Monthly*, a "*summum bonum* . . . still in process of gestation."

Yet another was the brainchild of Harold Loeb, part owner of the Sunwise Turn Bookshop on East Forty-fourth Street, a gathering place for many of New York's radicals. Loeb, Stevens thought, had the right idea about these self-conscious little magazines and was thinking of starting something that wouldn't take itself so seriously, something along the lines of "Oh! Sal, the butcher's wife ate clams / And died amid uproarious damns." Scofield Thayer's *Dial*, to which Stevens would soon contribute, while it was doing very well, seemed to him "mere literary foppery." And even that was derivative of what the French were doing, so that anyone in direct communication with France got it all long before it came out in the *Dial*.

His old friend Pitts Sanborn, whom Stevens liked to visit whenever he could get down to Greenwich Village, was writing sonnets these days, some of which Stevens found so stale that it was like reading "fly dirt," though there was still "a good deal of incandescence in the old horse." Stevens had even stored a case of brandy in Sanborn's cellar, hoping that that might "invigorate him and get him away from" writing those god-awful sonnets. He'd taken Kreymborg to lunch in New York just the week before, and noticed that he'd consumed seven dollars' worth of food at Stevens's expense. But at least now Kreymborg would make it through the winter.

That April he wrote Alice Corbin to thank her for sending him a copy of her book of poems, *Red Earth: Poems of New Mexico.* He was in Norfolk, Virginia, on business and, because she'd lived there once, he described what the place looked like now that spring had arrived, with leaves on the trees and bushes and "nigger hucksters . . . selling shad in the back parts of the town for $.30 a piece." How good it felt to drop back into eighteenth-century America with so little trouble. "Mow the grass in the cemetery, darkies," he would write, recalling his time there:

Study the symbols and the requiescats,
But leave a bed beneath the myrtles.
This skeleton had a daughter and that, a son.

He'd read Corbin's poems the evening before, and, since their subject was New Mexico and its history, it had raised the question once again of what the American poet was "to do about the damned Indians." Most likely they would have to do what the pioneers had, and assimilate their influence. In any event, their native aesthetic came out clearly in the poem she'd titled "Buffalo Dance." "Strike ye our land / With curved horns!" it began. "Breathe fire upon us, . . . Let your hoofs / Thunder over us!" The native aesthetic of the Indian, "like the aesthetic of England, France, or Peru, "was something one had to assimilate rather than try to imitate. And trying to assimilate everyone's worldview in one's own poetry, he had long ago decided, was not something he was going to even try.

Kreymborg, he'd learned, was leaving for Italy to publish another little magazine, this one with Loeb, to be called *Broom*, which no doubt would end up adding nothing new, really, and certainly not the international character they'd hoped for. Still, living as he did in Hartford kept him too far out of the vortex of avant-garde New York to know what was going on anymore, though the turn to a new Americanism was in "tremendous swing at the moment," and a book like *Red Earth* was an important "part of the palette not only for its Indian colors but also because it contains the colors of our Spanish side, which is so often overlooked, and which nevertheless is one of our most fascinating phases." Perhaps Williams had had more impact on him than he realized.

In mid-May Stevens wrote Reyher again, this time to say that McAlmon, who had married a woman named Bryher on Valentine's Day, was now settled in England, so that Reyher might want to look him up. Bryher, whose birth name was Annie Winifred Ellerman, was the daughter of the shipping magnate Sir John Ellerman, purportedly the richest man in Europe, and had been carrying on an affair with Hilda Doolittle (H.D.), though Stevens probably did not suspect this then. It had been to get out from under her father's control and be with H.D. that Bryher had married McAlmon, who was himself bisexual. The couple, along with H.D. and H.D.'s daughter, Perdita, had sailed for Europe four days after the wedding and were now settled in London, where McAlmon could savor his new family and the immense wealth that came with it. What a young Lochinvar that McAlmon was, Stevens clucked. Lochinvar: Sir Walter Scott's fictional knight who had come "out of the west," in this case, South Dakota, taken off with the fair damsel, and then disappeared.

Stevens had never met McAlmon, but he had corresponded with him when McAlmon was editing *Contact* and living in New York. Stevens had given the magazine (a venture so strapped for money it had to be printed on mimeograph paper supplied by Williams's father-in-law) two of his lighter poems, "Invective against Swans" and "Infanta Marina," which McAlmon had published in the January number. Something about the young man had fascinated Stevens (and, for that matter, Williams as well). Perhaps it was McAlmon's bravado and good looks. He was enthusiastic, energetic, and convinced of his own views on things, Stevens told Reyher. "The evolution of this youth" was "one of the most extraordinary things going on in the world today." A few months ago you could not have distinguished "this particular almond" "from a hazel nut," and now, here he was, traveling, "spending his time in Paris, studying French by day and practicing it by night," having in short order become James Joyce's boon companion, and all thanks to Bryher's money.

"Kreymborg described your build to me," McAlmon wrote Stevens from the five-star Hotel Eden Palace au Lac in Montreux, Switzerland, situated on the shores of Lake Geneva. He'd also told McAlmon of Stevens's treatment of Scofield Thayer, "naughty, naughty Scofield, venturing into incorrect realms with a pseudo correctness, more English and Oxford than any Englishman." If that was true, then Mamma should take Stevens and "spank, panky pank" him hard. But then Thayer was a nonentity, something so bland it was hard even to satirize him. Then a wink at Stevens: "Emotionally, you aren't any more sophisticated than I am, for all your ironic whimsy, and grand display of cerebration and intellect."

McAlmon would shortly be "bicycling with Wyndham Lewis in southern France," typing out the manuscript of *Ulysses* for Joyce, and starting up his own Contact Press, which would publish Hemingway's first book, *Three Stories & Ten Poems*, Williams's *In the American Grain*, as well as Bryher, H.D., Mina Loy, Ford Madox Ford, Marsden Hartley, and Gertrude Stein. But with McAlmon in Europe, Williams's *Contact* had had to cease publication, which was too bad, Stevens thought, since the idea behind the magazine made sense. True, there was a great deal of free verse being written in the States these days, though none of it had any "aesthetic theory back of it." Most of the stuff wasn't very good because those who wrote it didn't "understand the emotional purpose of rhythm any more than they understood the emotional purpose of measure." As for himself, while he was not exclusively for free verse, he was not averse to it either.

• • •

THAT OCTOBER *POETRY* PUBLISHED Stevens's new set of poems, *Sur Ma Guzzla Gracile*, which, translated from the Spanish and Serbian, meant something like "playing on my small gusle," a Balkan single-string instrument. The poems took up the opening nine pages of the issue and included "Palace of the Babies," "The Misery of Don Joost," "The Doctor of Geneva," "Gubbinal," "The Snow Man," "Tea at the Palaz of Hoon," and "Hibiscus on the Sleeping Shores." At least one poet, Genevieve Taggard, who generally admired Stevens's work, told him over dinner one evening in New York that they amounted to "hideous ghosts" of Stevens, to which he replied, "It may be."

They are certainly dark. "One must have a mind of winter," "The Snow Man" begins in its Zen-like spirit, "to regard the frost and the boughs / Of the pine-trees crusted with snow." That is, merely to regard or notice the colder aspects of reality. And one would have to be "cold a long time / To behold" the reality of the "junipers shagged with ice" and the "spruces rough in the distant glitter / Of the January sun." *Behold*, then, rather than merely think

Of any misery in the sound of the wind,
In the sound of a few leaves,

Which is the sound of the land
Full of the same wind
That is blowing in the same bare place

For the listener, who listens in the snow,
And, nothing himself, beholds
Nothing that is not there and the nothing that is.

To listen long and hard, as one stood in the frozen snow until one could empty oneself—insofar as such a thing might be possible—and thus more clearly see the nothing that you are, alone in a world without hope or even the consolations of the imagination. Only then might one behold the void at the heart of existence: that strange oxymoronic nothing that is, holding onto that until *the snow man* becomes *this no man.*

At the other end of the imaginative spectrum was "Tea at the Palaz of Hoon," though even it contains an ironic take on the Emersonian poet as clairvoyant eye. Here Stevens does seem to wrap himself in a self-creating royal purple to confront the terrifying nihilism of Nietzsche and Schopenhauer. "Not less because in purple I descended / The western day," the poem begins, late as this late romantic comes in the romantic tradition, "through what you called / The loneliest air, not less was I myself."

It is the imagination here—not as fuzzy blanket but as roaring lion, fierce bear—which confronts the nothing that is. It is here too that the poet descends from his Jovian cloud, his regal beard sprinkled with heavenly ointment for his self-anointing, while high hymns buzz about his ears and the tidal force of the imagination sweeps through him, until

Out of my mind the golden ointment rained,
And my ears made the blowing hymns they heard. . . .
I was the world in which I walked, and what I saw
Or heard or felt came not but from myself;
And there I found myself more truly and more strange.

It is the imagination, then, which allows us to behold the full powers of which we are capable, so that we might transform ourselves into a brave new creation. Not the erotic, but the visionary. Thoughts of sex—free or not—had become such a commodity by 1921 that we could "put it in our pipes and smoke it." But such was not the case with the atomic radiance of the Imagination, itself reimagined and now set free. Though he would put this purple vision of the self back in his wardrobe for another ten years and shrink into the cipher of a single consonant, Stevens would return to the Palaz of Hoon, where the sleeping giant would awaken and blaze with the radiance of the radiant sun god Ra once more.

9

The Comedian as the Letter C: 1921–1923

something in the rise and fall of wind
That seemed hallucinating horn, and here,
A sunken voice, both of remembering
And of forgetfulness, in alternate strain.
Just so an ancient Crispin was dissolved.

THE COMEDIAN AS THE LETTER C

In December 1921 Stevens published four poems in the inaugural issue of Kreymborg and Loeb's *Broom*, a magazine which Stevens knew, as he'd earlier confided to Harriet Monroe, was not "such a must." The first of these was "The Bird with the Coppery, Keen Claws," one of Stevens's darkest poems about God and the imagination. It is also one of his tropical poems, this one in tercets with an unrhymed first line followed by a couplet, the hard K sounds luxuriating like tucked strings plucked throughout, in which the parakeet of parakeets—or the god of gods—prevails. This is a terrifying bird, really, outwardly gorgeous like some Aztec deity, surrounded by "the rudiments of tropics," but whose "lids are white because his eyes are blind." This is Ananke, Necessity, Fate, the indifferent God. It is the human imagination trapped in the cave of the skull, which "broods there and is still." And like the imagination, it is a force capable of creating a splendidly green panache of a universe, undulating outward in "turbulent tinges," but which itself remains indifferent, like some terrifying still point at the center of creation. Call it the Panurge, whose "pure intellect applies its laws," even as it munches on the dry shell of the human skull, exerting at all times its immanent will. It is a force, in fact, which, under many guises, would preoccupy Stevens for the rest of his life.

That same month *Poetry* announced the Blindman Prize, named after a long antiwar poem of that title composed by a Hervey Allen of Charleston, South Carolina. The prize was $250 and would be awarded for a long poem to be subsequently published by the Poetry Society of South Carolina. Amy Lowell would be the sole judge. Stevens knew Lowell personally and knew her work, which no doubt helped him decide to try his hand at what would become both his ars poetica and his apologia, once more presented, as with Peter Quince earlier, through the figure of the clown. All poems would have to be submitted by the first of the year, which meant Stevens would have to start working on his poem at once.

Within days he was so preoccupied with the long serenade he called *From the Journal of Crispin* that he'd "made life a bore" not only for Elsie but for everyone else around him, as he went on "churning and churning," only to produce "a very rancid butter." Still, he kept at it, determined to submit whatever he could "for what it may be worth, which at the moment, isn't much." This he confessed to Monroe on December 21, with *Crispin* "still very incomplete and most imperfect," and with only ten days left to work on it. No matter. He was "determined to have a fling at least and possibly go through the damndest doldrums of regret later on."

As it turned out, Lowell chose Grace Hazard Conkling's mediocre offering, *Variations on a Theme*, for the prize, with Stevens as first runner-up. "I have just come back from a trip to the west," Stevens wrote Hervey Allen five months later, thanking Allen for his "personal shock absorber" of a letter when he learned that he was an also-ran. "I hate like the devil to take anybody's dust," he confessed, though he didn't know "of anybody's dust that I could take more equitably than Mrs. Conkling's," whose "vivid and sensitive southern pieces," he fibbed, had always been a great delight to him. The next time he was down Charleston way, he added, he meant to look Allen up, for he knew after living with Prohibition this long how desirable it was "to have friends in places not altogether dry."

Now, with time to think about what he had wrought and what still needed to be done with his poem, he started refitting and reshaping it. He began by renaming the poem *The Comedian as the Letter C*, deleting over 125 lines from the original and adding more than two hundred new lines, including an additional two sections that would take Crispin onward and outward—or rather inward—on his journey. We have relatively little in the way of drafts for Stevens's body of poems because he was careful to discard them once he was finished with them, and we would not have *Crispin* either except that the astute Mrs. Gay, the landlord at 735 Farmington Avenue, where the Stevenses would reside for eight years beginning in 1924, discovered a sheaf of poems he had just relegated to the trash can. Knowing that the man who lived upstairs was an important poet, Mrs. Gay took it upon herself to rescue the poems, secretly keeping them in the family's possession until long after Stevens and Elsie were both gone.

Finally, in 1974, with Mrs. Gay herself gone, her son, the Reverend John Gay, donated the manuscripts his mother had saved to Yale's Beinecke Rare Book and Manuscript Library, explaining that, while his mother believed that what she had done in salvaging the poems from the trash can might seem "a very unlady-like thing to do," she also believed that those same manuscripts "might someday be of value." Among those papers was a nineteen-page, double-spaced typescript which Stevens had dictated to his secretary at the Hartford, titled *From the Journal of Crispin*, along with an almost complete carbon copy. Typed above the title were the words "Submitted for Blindman Prize" and, in pencil in the upper right-hand corner, two words that must have stung Stevens and yet prompted him to return to unfinished business: "Honorable Mention."

The Comedian by any measure is a roller coaster of lexical complexities, a blank verse send-up, the form of which provides the necessary traction for the up-and-down ride that bends toward one axiomatic resolution after another before it flies off into yet another of its giddy oscillations. The poem is and is not autobiographical, for the main character here is that French eighteenth-century commedia dell' arte valet Crispin, citizen of the old world of Bordeaux, with an "eye most apt in gelatines and jupes, / Berries of villages, a barber's eye, / . . . of simple salad-beds" and "honest quilts," bourgeois Crispin, the Stevens of Reading and Cambridge, man as *philosophe*, "the intelligence of his soil" and "sovereign ghost."

That is until, in crossing the vast Atlantic, Crispin the valet is nearly obliterated by a storm at sea, a "century of wind in a single puff," and realizes just how insignificant a thing he or any man really is. It is an encounter with Kant's terrifying Sublime: the force of the sea, the majesty of the Alps, a tropical full-force hurricane crashing through a *cabildo* and reducing the bellowing breeches that is Crispin to "a skinny sailor peering in a sea-glass." This is also, quite likely, that Mr. C, the protagonist of that German romantic Heinrich von Kleist's *On the Marionette Theater,* the send-up Kleist wrote the year before he shot his terminally ill beloved and then himself at her request, there on the shores of the Kleiner Wannsee, having at thirty-four given up any hope of making sense of the world. Crispin, reduced to the single letter C: Stevens's marionette-like comic figure—for which see vintage 1920 Krazy Kat or Harold Lloyd—in this instance a fat, bourgeois Enlightenment figure who will shortly be "washed away by magnitude," that monstrous force which was, is, and always will be "ubiquitous concussion, slap and sigh," something beyond any conductor's ability to shape into order, much less a symphony. On Crispin's journey we too experience the terrifying tsunami, interminable crescendo and blare of cacophonic horns, all of which are capable of reducing Crispin to a cipher of the sea.

What makes the poem even more difficult to comprehend is the way Stevens hurls the *Oxford English Dictionary* even more forcefully than usual right at our heads, not unlike the brick that Ignatz loved to hurl at the head of Krazy Kat, who took that bizarre gesture as a veritable sign that Ignatz cared about her (or him). How read such lines, for example, as these, which seem to sum up the benefits of conjugal love: "For all [Fate, Life] takes it gives a humped return / Exchequering from piebald fiscs unkeyed"? Or what of lines like these, to describe why Stevens/Crispin left behind his early love of the sonnet for an uproarious blank verse unlike anything in Marlowe or Shakespeare or Pope or Wordsworth, substituting his Mayan sonneteers for those New York Patagonians, ten years of verse experimentation along those lines as dead now as that premier Patagonian, Donald Evans, himself:

Crispin arraigns the Mexican sonneteers,
Because his soul feels the Andean breath.
Can fourteen laboring mules, like theirs,
In spite of gorgeous leathers, gurgling bells,
Convey his being through the land? A more condign
Contraption must appear.

The letter C, he explained years later, stood as "a cypher for Crispin" and was meant "to suggest something that nobody seems to have grasped," that is, "THE COMEDIAN AS THE SOUNDS OF THE LETTER C." Like St. Francis, who wore bells "around his ankles so that, as he went about his business, the crickets and so on would get out of his way and not be tramped on," just so, Crispin and the reader are accompanied throughout the poem by the letter C, which itself echoes the ever-looming presence of the sea and one's ultimate cessation. "I don't mean to say that there is an incessant din," he explained, "but you ought not to be able to read very far in the poem without recognizing what I mean." That C sound is surely in full panoply throughout the poem, both in its soft C's and hard K's, along with such derivatives as X, TS, and Z. Thus in a phrase like "Bubbling felicity in Cantilene," where the soft C of "felicity" morphs to the hard C of "Cantilene."

It is essential to the effect of the poem that one "hear all this whistling and mocking and stressing and, in a minor way, orchestrating, going on in the background." He had hoped the effect on the reader would be a comic one, but what often comes across is the sense of a boom box blasting in a monk's cell as the monk studies a complex passage of some sacred text, or the effect that boom box would have on a scholar trying to follow the twists and turns of a complex philosophical script amid uproarious, frantic laughter. The major pun in all of this, of course, turns on the failed and furious attempt of the mind to orchestrate the ubiquitous slap and sigh of the wind upon the dominant sea, which here stands in for the *Ding an sich* of the full force of Reality and its sister shadow, Death.

The mind, after all, Stevens had learned, was "a pretty hard thing to catch," and as he sought desperately for the harmonious center of *Harmonium*, hoping to discover a more modern version of romanticism, even as he was coming to see that he was merely on the tenuous periphery of the matter, trying "to get to the center." His poems had shown him that it was he who remained isolated from the world, and not the other way around, and he was now more anxious than ever to share the common life. He would say this to one of his closest readers twenty years later, explaining why his poetry had taken such a turn from the language of the *Comedian.* "People say that I live in a world of my own," he told Hi Simons, one of his earliest followers, so that he had long given up what he called his search for a "relentless contact" with reality, opting instead to achieve "the normal, the central." He did not "agree with the people who say that I live in a world of my own." He was "perfectly normal" in that regard, but he did believe there was a center somewhere to be found. "A photograph of a lot of fat men and women in the woods," he added, moving away from a topic so serious, "drinking beer and singing Hi-li Hi-lo convinces me that there is a normal that I ought to try to achieve." Except, of course, that drinking beer and singing Hi-li Hi-lo with his Pennsylvania Dutch neighbors as his father used to do up on Mount Penn, say, or as part of a block party in Hartford on a summer's evening, would never—could never—have satisfied Stevens's restless mind.

In fact what Crispin learns as he confronts the Sublime is what Stevens had learned in confronting that same immensity as a philosophical concept in his classes at Harvard, later in the vast solitude of the Canadian Rockies, and in his travels across the vastness of the American landscape, which sojourn had led in time to the virtual disappearance of God, reduced by then to a "negligible Triton" lurking in his imagination, and—in freeing himself of that anthropomorphic immensity—coming to believe he had somehow freed himself "from the unavoidable shadow of himself / That lay elsewhere around him." In severing himself from his early dependence on the idea of God—as he'd demonstrated years earlier with "Sunday Morning"—he had hoped that "the last distortion of romance" had at last forsaken "the insatiable egotist," leaving, as he saw it, only the shaken realist behind:

Crispin beheld and Crispin was made new.
The imagination, here, could not evade,

In poems of plums, the strict austerity
Of one vast, subjugating, final tone.

But then freedom from the falseness of what Crispin/Stevens had taken for his world had in fact left him only with a new austerity and a blank slate, which was not exactly a cause for elation. Instead it meant relying on the inward violence of a newly realized imagination which would be all he had to counteract the violence of the world as it was, absent the myth of a benevolent God at the center holding things together.

But what was at the center of it all, if indeed there was a center? And if not a center, then what? A balance between the pressures of Reality and the counterpressures of the mind that seeks to shape an order? For what else was there? Certainly Crispin, that comedic, vaudevillian ragdoll of Stevens's imagination, was not a sufficient force, not even Crispin remade. Finding that center, even if it turned out to be a fiction, was like awaking from the dream of the past into the dreamlike reality—incorrigible romantic that Stevens was—of the present moment, to find that only in the writing of green poems, in which he might discover who he was, could he counter the "green barbarism" of the world with "an aesthetic tough, diverse," and just as untamed. Not Wordsworth's Lake Country, then, as an example of what nature held, but rather a tropical plenitude manifesting the fearsome abundance of Nature, one "thick with sides and jagged lops of green," a world "of seeds grown fat, too juicily opulent, / Expanding" in the sun, with its gold "maternal warmth."

Time, then, for Crispin to head north from the Andes to Havana and walk the harbor streets of a place still south enough to be strange and unnerving to any Reading native, where he might inspect "the cabildo, the façade / Of the cathedral, making notes," until yet another version of the Sublime—a storm headed Crispin's way from Mexico—should announce itself, "bluntly thundering, more terrible / Than the revenge of music on bassoons." No theater set piece complete with orchestra this time, but one more manifestation of an elemental force capable of crumpling poor Crispin, until the cool observer took flight and "knelt in the cathedral with the rest," this clown who would be a "connoisseur of elemental fate." Except that Crispin has learned at least this much: that if he is ever to flourish as a poet, he will have to find a way to embody this elemental reality, this "span / Of force" and make of it a poetry "envious in phrase."

It is with a renewed spirit, then, a sort of secular Pentecost, vouchsafed Crispin as he feels for the first time the immense freedom of a New World Andean breath stirring in and through him,

In which the thunder, lapsing in its clap,
Let down gigantic quavers of its voice,
For Crispin to vociferate again.

Which is why the language shifts so rapidly between the florid baroque and the Arctic chill of lines which evoke the monosyllabic lexicon one associates with—as Stevens would increasingly do in the years to come—a mind of winter, where "nothing of himself / Remained, except some starker, barer self / In a starker, barer world."

• • •

AND SO, FROM HAVANA north to Carolina, a middle ground between tropical Florida and cold Hartford, "a Carolina of old time"—a tinkatink-tunk—"a little juvenile, an ancient whim," like a Currier and Ives print evoking that too too happy antebellum South. That and the South as "the visible, circumspect presentment" that it is now, circa 1922, drawn from what Crispin observes "across his vessel's prow." For now at last Stevens seeks entrance into the world of virtual contact where Crispin might tilt his nose to "inhale the rancid rosin" and the "burly smells / Of dampened lumber," much as William Carlos Williams was celebrating in his poems, the poet quickening his desires now to take in the "rank odor of a passing springtime."

Here is Crispin, then, savoring Carolina's "rankness like a sensualist," like Williams, but with more linguistic splash, noting "the marshy ground around the dock," along with "the crawling railroad spurs, the rotten fence," and "puffing engines [and] cranes, / Provocative paraphernalia to his mind." These, and the lilac-lined alleyways (shades of Whitman!) and "the cobbled merchant streets, / The shops of chandlers, tailors, bakers, cooks, / The Coca Cola-bars, the barber-poles," two tea rooms, and, yes, even a church. And yet for all that, it is a world in which Stevens has yet to feel at home. For "if the lilacs give the alleys a young air / Of sentiment, the alleys in exchange / Make gifts of no less worthy ironies." That is the problem, for whereas Williams could write of such things without mocking them or evoking such mundane things without irony, that is not so for Stevens, who wonders, as he struggles to work out his own rude aesthetic, "Are bakers what the poets will"? Or do those elemental makers "have, on poets' minds, more influence / Than poets know?"

Such insights are important, Stevens knows, and if, finally, they are merely some "curriculum for the marvelous sophomore," he has also come to understand how such images might purify the imagination and "make him see how much / Of what he sees he never sees at all." So, in the miasmic moonlight world of the romantic imagination falsified, he "grips more closely the essential prose" of things as the "one integrity" still left him, the antipoetic, if you will, though that phrase will provoke a dispute with Williams ten years hence. Still, it is the one

Discovery still possible to make,
To which all poems are incident, unless
That prose should wear a poem's guise at last.

• • •

IN THIS EFFORT HE and Williams, different as their personalities are, have struggled side by side. And so, in section IV, "The Idea of a Colony," Stevens imagines what his own blank-verse aesthetic manifesto might look like: a thing made up of equal parts "souvenirs and prophecies," a half looking back and a half looking forward. Not the world of the Arapaho, Sioux, or Comanche—those truer New World Primitives—with their "sapling gum" and "honeyed gore" trying to reimagine some prelapsarian world forcibly taken from them, a world "distilled of innocence." Nor Turk nor Eskimo, nor any outlander, but rather a New World according to "the man in Georgia waking among pines" who "should be pine-spokesman." Let too the poet of Florida "prick thereof, not on the psaltery, / But on the banjo's categorical gut, / Tuck tuck, while the flamingos flapped their bays," the bay of Biscayne and the bay of the poet.

It's a gorgeous send-up, all of it, on Stevens's part, as he follows the comic logic of his personal plan for a nativist poetry, until he sees that even that plan is bound to become a veritable cult, the melon and the plum served up once more on salvers as they were in "Le Monocle," their aromas steeped now in midsummer, a sacrament and a celebration, where in time "shrewd novitiates / Should be the clerks of our experience." Except, that is, that Stevens refuses to rest content with such a "masquerade of thought" cloaked in "hapless words." How easy to fall back into the "monotonous babbling in our dreams / That makes them our dependent heirs." Better to humbly serve a "grotesque apprenticeship to chance event." Better, if one must be a clown, at least to be "an aspiring clown."

Is there a place where an ars poetica such as Crispin has envisioned might flourish? "His colony may not arrive," Stevens closed *From the Journal of Crispin* at the end of 1921. And yet he knew "the site / Exists. So much is sure." If *Crispin*, at its best, concerned himself alone, still Stevens might read the tableau cheerfully enough. Just as Pound had to leave behind the alternate version of himself in *Hugh Selwyn Mauberley* if he were to create a newer, greater self in his epic *Cantos*, or just as Joyce had to leave behind his youthful poems to go on to the epic scope of *Ulysses*, Stevens too understands that the poet who for eight years had dabbled in his "trinket pasticcio" will likewise have to be dissolved in the creative destruction of the sea to pursue "veracious page on page, exact." So the original *Crispin* ends with the poet in his attic, trying to shape the poem that should somehow contain him and which might "discourse of himself alone, / Of what he was, and why, and of his place, / And of its fitful pomp and parentage."

• • •

WHEN, IN THE SUMMER of 1922, he returned to Crispin, recrispining it *The Comedian as the Letter C*, he added two new sections, V and VI, to expand upon what he had already written. This time he would take into fuller consideration his other roles as breadwinner and surety expert on the rise, the forty-three-year-old husband growing older and alas ever more apart, the hermit in his attic, and—should the Fates conspire with his wife and wallet—a father in the not-too-distant future.

If he had remained deeply discontent, he might have continued to search out and colonize "his polar planterdom" by attracting disciples, as Williams and McAlmon and others seemed intent on doing with their manifestos. What intervened, however, was the idea of finally possessing a "nice, shady home" of his own. How difficult, after all, to maintain a posture "of rebellious thought" when the sky was blue, a blue that infected the will and whispered, "Perhaps this is enough." Perhaps somewhere beyond the quotidian skies there lay a transcendent purple. Perhaps. But he was first and foremost a realist, and even the romantic who hunts a matinal continent—a New World Naked, say—"may, after all, stop short before a plum / And be content and still be realist." He had surely played with words long enough to know that, if the "words of things entangle and confuse," if they "harlequined and mazily dewed and mauved" the plum, still, the plum, Reality, the thing itself, "survives its poems . . . in its own form, / Beyond these changes, good, fat, guzzly fruit."

He would not, of course, "bray" his mood "in profoundest brass / Arointing his dreams with fugal requiems," as McAlmon had told him Eliot had done in *The Waste Land*, which McAlmon had read in its unfinished form. Who was any one individual, even Tom Eliot, to speak for the world and "company vastest things defunct / With a blubber of tom-toms harrowing the sky"? Being at heart a jovial clown, Crispin/Stevens was not about to dress the world in "calamitous crape" or "lay by the personal and make / Of his own fate an instance of all fate." What, after all, was "one man among so many men"? No, what Stevens would do was what millions of his fellow men did: build himself a house and plant a garden, then clasp his prismy blonde and close the bedroom door and—master at least of this single room—latch up the night so that solitude might cover him in a haven where St. Francis's crickets with their incessant clicking C's might finally come to rest.

Then, in the morning, in the fullness of the bright sun, Crispin would feast on a fig, and if on a fig, on cream for the fig, and if cream, then a silver pitcher from which to pour the cream, and then—voilà!—"a blonde to tip the silver and to taste / The rapey gouts." *There* was a quotidian he might settle on, composed "of breakfast ribands, fruits laid in their leaves," an imaginative space where he might pour "out upon the lips of her / That lay beside him, the quotidian / Like this, . . . true fortuner." Because for all life takes, it "gives a humped return / Exchequering from piebald fiscs unkeyed," laying out in vast returns such treasures as only a woman wooed and won and bedded may give.

Of course there would always be the workaday world to contend with—those long business trips and weeks on the road, as well as long hours in his office, so that the "return to social nature, once begun / . . . Involved him in midwifery so dense / His cabin counted as phylactery." In time Stevens too would help create a new generation with its own wants and needs as complex as anything Crispin had ever known, making of him too for a time one more "indulgent fatalist." Crispin's four daughters, then, each as different as the four seasons, each growing daily, and each demanding to be heard: the first his "goldenest demoiselle, inhabitant / . . . of a country of the capuchins." Then a second and a third, and finally the fourth, who would be "mere blusteriness that gewgaws jollified / All din and gobble, blasphemously pink." What Crispin has come to see at last is that the world, which seemed like

a turnip once so readily plucked,
Sacked up and carried overseas, daubed out
Of its ancient purple, pruned to the fertile main,
And sown again by the stiffest realist,
Came reproduced in purple, family font,
The same insoluble lump.

In the end Reality remained itself, Crispin the fatalist has come to understand. That being the case, there is nothing for it but to chuck reality like that insoluble lump of a turnip "down his craw, / Without grace or grumble." And "if Crispin is a profitless / Philosopher, beginning," like most young poets, "with green brag" and "concluding fadedly," a poet still prone "from a fancy gorged / By apparition" to poeticize "plain and common things," so that "what he proves / Is nothing," what can all this matter since the story, like the poet's journey, has come, "benignly, to its end?" And with that Stevens will sign off for another ten years, for when all else fails, as life itself must fail, "so may the relation of each man be clipped."

• • •

ON JANUARY 6, 1922, Stevens was in Atlanta again, only to learn that he and half a dozen of the Good Ol' Boys whom Judge Arthur Powell of the Atlanta law firm of Powell, Goldstein, Frazer and Murphy had invited along, should all head down to Miami at once to conduct business there. Stevens had hired Powell to represent the Hartford Accident and Indemnity Company in surety matters for the southern United States. He was a powerful, likable man, who had been elected to the Georgia Court of Appeals in 1907 at the age of thirty-five and had served for the next six years, when he'd left to enter private practice. It was Powell who would introduce the Pennsylvania Dutchman to the delights of doing business southern style in Long Key and Key West, where Stevens could dine and drink to his heart's content at the Hotel Casa Marina for years to come.

From Miami Stevens sent Elsie a postcard of a coconut tree, explaining that he'd somehow wound up here in southern Florida and hoping she wouldn't mind too much his basking in the sun in such clear, perfect summer weather. Within twenty-four hours, the boys had seen to it that everything was signed, sealed, and delivered as far as business was concerned, after which Stevens boarded the *Flagler Express* to Key West to see what that looked like, then headed back east to Long Key to meet up with the boys for a fishing expedition.

Long Key was small, he wrote Elsie, only about the size of the Hartford's new building complex at 690 Asylum Avenue: a simple haven replete with cottages and meals and brilliant white shards of coral strewn about which dazzled in the sunshine everywhere. The sea, just fifty feet from his cottage, beckoned him to step outside that first morning while he was still in his pajamas and partake in a delicious surf-bath. So this was what heaven looked and felt like, with the breezes tousling the long fronds of the palm trees amid brilliant blue skies and a blue-green sea. What a fool he would have been not to have mixed in a little fun with so much business. "We must come together as soon as we can," he told Elsie, "and every winter afterwards." But Elsie would accompany him only once to the Keys, and even that would have to wait a long time.

The truth was that he was not eager to bring Elsie along because he'd finally found the paradise he'd dreamed of in "Sunday Morning": a "ring of men," "supple and turbulent," who might "chant in orgy on a summer morn / Their boisterous devotion to the sun." In truth, there was another dimension to his time there with such glorious company as the boys provided. "Now that trip to Florida would have unstrung a brass monkey," he told Reyher once he was back in snowbound Hartford. He'd been to Miami "with half a dozen other people from Atlanta, . . . the only damned Yankee in the bunch," and been "christened a charter member of the Long Key Fishing Club of Atlanta," an initiation which "occupied about three days, and required just two cases of Scotch," so that by the time he'd started for home he could not tell whether he "was traveling on a sound or a smell." As he remembered it, "it was very much like a cloud full of Cuban señoritas, cocoanut palms, and waiters carrying ice-water." Those southerners, bless them, those southerners were great people indeed.

As for literature, he didn't really much care about that these days. After all, what was there to say? Kreymborg was still in Rome editing *Broom*, Williams was working away in Rutherford, and Arensberg had moved to Los Angeles, leaving Pitts Sanborn behind in Greenwich Village. A book of souvenirs by that late phenomenon Donald Evans was about to come out, and Allen Norton, that one-time literary provocateur, was now a reporter for the *World*. Just where the painter Charles Demuth was at the moment he did not know, though he'd had an exhibit at the Daniel Gallery back in the fall, which had featured his portrait *Aucassin and Nicolette*, composed of a silo resting against a smokestack. The New York art crowd, which had once held center stage for Stevens, just kept growing dimmer and dimmer. As a sign that it was time to move on—as Crispin had—he'd just rounded up all of his art catalogues, "which were really a pretty complete survey of what had been shown in New York for the last ten years," and donated them to Hartford's Wadsworth Atheneum.

"My poems seem so simple and natural to me," he explained to Alice Corbin Henderson out in Santa Fe, after she'd asked him to enlighten her about several of them. Why in heaven did people think his poems were so "deep, dark or mysterious"? *Épater les savants* was as trifling to him as *épater les bourgeois*, though it was true that one could not "always say a thing clearly and retain the poetry of what one is saying." Part of the problem with understanding what he was up to was that whenever someone sensed a symbol lurking somewhere in a poem of his, that someone instinctively tried to match that symbol with something in his or her own experience rather than let the poem show what the symbol meant in that poem. Imagine, he urged, someone "accustomed to potatoes studying apples with the idea that unless the apples somehow contain potatoes they are unreasonable." Or consider Charlie Chaplin flinging a pie at someone's face. For most Americans flinging pies like that needed no explaining. It was simply something incongruous and therefore hilarious. And yet hadn't some Englishman recently "raised his eyebrows at what he called 'pelting with puddings' "? The only real difficulty, after all, was in trying to understand the poet's point of view. As far as he could see, his own poems were "all perfectly direct and mean just what they say even when that may seem a bit neither here nor there."

As for news on the literary front, he'd just read Williams's latest book of poems, *Sour Grapes*, and had found it "very slight—very. Charming but such a tame savage, such a personal impersonal." So too with Marianne Moore's *Poems*, just published by H.D. and Bryher. The trouble with Moore, he opined, was that she concerned herself too much with the form of her poems, a fastidiousness which she then went to great lengths to hide. In fact, the real problem with all poems these days was that they lacked substance, even when one conceded that substance itself was more "a matter of nuances, sounds, colors etc instead of eighteenth-century avoirdupois."

Which was why there was so little of artistic interest going on in New York these days. Take the current Independent Show. Such a poor thing, really, and yet it still managed to attract crowds who had no idea what they were looking at. What these exhibits lacked was originality. Nor was there any independence about the independents, for you either did as they did or you risked becoming a laughingstock. The only real independence, after all, lay in the ability "to pull people by the ears and not be pulled by them." There was only "one real literary Deadwood Dick" just now, and that was McAlmon. True, the man's short stories and poems were awful, but what vitality he had!

Then there was the poet Yvor Winters, who had sent him a copy of his "recent attenuations." He liked Winters well enough, but only because Winters liked him, having recently called Stevens the "greatest of living American poets" in the pages of *Poetry.* Still, there was something anemic about a man like Winters, devoid of the smell of whiskey, a smell which made you feel you could trust a man. And then there was Sandburg, who'd visited the Stevenses in Hartford, bringing along his guitar to strum. "I expected to swallow my Adam's apple when he began to sing," he confessed to Corbin, "but the truth is that I enjoyed it immensely." As for Mrs. Stevens, she continued to be "perfectly happy here" in Hartford, which she much preferred to New York.

"I pride myself on being a member of the Long Key Fishing Club of Atlanta," he told Reyher a month later, "and I take damned little stock in conversation on philosophy, aesthetics, poetry, art, or blondes. Of course, I hanker for all those things as a fly hankers for fly paper. But experience has taught me that fly paper is one devil of a thing to get mixed up in." As for Hartford, that had long since become a "frightfully uncongenial place." It was worse in winter, when the place reached an almost unbearable "degree of staleness," where who you were boiled down to the work you did. But now it was early April, and he was panting for spring's return, for what Reyher, a Pennsylvania Dutchman like himself, would remember they called "the Frühlingswetter." With the robins back "in the trees in the evenings," one began to find staring into "one's aquarium a bore."

That same month he sent a group of poems to Gilbert Seldes, managing editor of Scofield Thayer's *Dial*, with the tentative title "Mostly Moonlight," which Seldes accepted immediately, though with suggestions for reordering the sequence. Weeks later, back from yet another business trip west, Stevens told Seldes that he did not wish "to be persnickety about the arrangement," as long as it had "a good beginning and a good end," which meant that the poems should begin with "Bantams in Pine Woods" and end with "The Emperor of Ice-Cream," two of Stevens's most delicious and successful pieces. But all six of the poems were splendid, and all would make it into *Harmonium.* As for a biographical note, once again he begged off. "I am a lawyer," he wrote, "and live in Hartford. But such facts are neither gay nor instructive."

But the poems were. "Chieftain Iffucan of Azcan in caftan, / Of tan with henna hackles, halt!" the first poem begins with its uproarious samba-like jigging cadences, the speaker in this case being a pine tree that puts the strutting poet / rooster firmly in his place. Intentionally or not, "Bantams" seems to spin that clairvoyant central eye of Emerson's—founder of the *Dial*—away from the poet as spokesman to let Nature speak for itself. Let the poet crow all he wants; it matters not since he has failed to take the true measure of the world about which he struts. And now a representative of that world, a pine tree, rebukes him and his blazing tale:

Fat! Fat! Fat! I am the personal.
Your world is you. I am my world.

You ten-foot poet among inchlings.
Fat! Begone! An inchling bristles in these pines,

Bristles, and points their Appalachian tangs,
And fears not portly Azcan nor his hoos.

"The Emperor of Ice-Cream" begins with a series of commands: first to "the roller of big cigars / The muscular one," bidding him "whip / In kitchen cups concupiscent curds," for he will need those muscles to churn the curds in the ice-filled, salt-laced bucket into ice cream. But why summon the muscular one at all? For what occasion? And why "let the wenches dawdle in such dress / As they are used to wear"? Why command the boys to "bring flowers in last month's newspapers," with their old, stale news? Because all things are evanescent, all things pass, and the only truth that remains is the truth Diogenes found: to "let be be finale of seem." The only thing we ought to pay attention to is the moment itself, as Walter Pater had urged years before: the Heraclitean flux of things, where assuredly "the only emperor is the emperor of ice-cream."

The first of the two stanzas reads like a disorienting riddle, as it is meant to, the dark truth of which is revealed in the second. Come, see for yourself. There's a modest bedroom down the hall, with a dresser made of cheap deal wood, "lacking the three glass knobs." And look, on top of the dresser there's a sheet, on which a woman "embroidered fantails once," something to gussy up her room with what little art she could muster. Now she lies there dead, and someone—perhaps you, the reader—must take that sheet, make of it a shroud, "and spread it so as to cover her face."

If the sheet is too short when you pull it up to over her face, so that "her horny feet protrude," well then, those poor, calloused animal-like feet—like the ancient Gates of Horn which manifest the truth of the matter—"show how cold she is, and dumb." Nothing for it but for Diogenes's lamp of truth to "affix its beam" there to remind us that this is what all life comes to in the end. What else can we do, then, but enjoy life's pleasures while we can? The pleasures of the language, for example, which enwraps the nothing within. Like ice cream, those deliciously concupiscent curds, which tastes good to us but which must be enjoyed now before it melts away. The only thing worth worshipping is pleasure, the carpe diem, the seizing of the day, for in the long and the short of it, the only emperor, the only one we must obey, is "the emperor of ice-cream."

• • •

WHEN STEVENS RETURNED HOME from yet another business trip, this one to Charleston, South Carolina, in mid-July, he found a letter waiting for him from Carl Van Vechten inviting him to submit a manuscript of his poems to Van Vechten's publisher, the young Alfred A. Knopf. As Stevens had told Williams four years earlier, publishing a book of poems was a damn serious affair. Even now, with so many of his poems published in the best literary magazines here and in Europe, he felt "frightfully uncertain" about the idea. Better, he told Van Vechten, to talk the matter over face to face the next time he came to New York.

It had been years since he'd seen Stevens, Van Vechten would remember thirty-five years later, but when Sanborn told him that July that Stevens seemed at last ready to publish a book of poems, Van Vechten had written Stevens asking if he might talk to Knopf about it, and Stevens had given him a tentative go-ahead. It was Knopf who had published Van Vechten's first book, *Music and Bad Manners*, six years earlier, and who would continue to publish Van Vechten over the years. "Alfred did desire to examine [Stevens's] manuscript and almost immediately agreed to publish it," Van Vechten recalled. Not only that volume, as it turned out, but every volume of Stevens's poetry and prose for the rest of Stevens's life—and after.

Within a week or two Stevens met with Van Vechten and Knopf, who agreed to publish the book he had tentatively decided to call *Harmonium*. "A few weeks ago I came to the substance of an agreement with Mr. Knopf for the publication of a book in the fall of 1923," he wrote Harriet Monroe in late August 1922. Though he asked her to say nothing to anyone for the present, he could think of no one more entitled to hear about it than her. *Harmonium* would be "a collection of things that have already appeared; for since the manuscript is to be ready by November 1 this year it will not be possible for me to do anything new in the interim." These long summer spells at home in Hartford were very good for him, and he'd been able to get a lot of reading done. There had even been moments when he'd been "in a most excellent state of spontaneity," though nothing had "survived the subsequent katzenjammer" of having at last found a publisher for his poems. Now he had two months to rework *The Comedian* as a central ars poetica and apologia for the volume and then carefully, meticulously, arrange the poems of the past eight years into a harmony of sorts: an order, a music played on the harmonium, and not just a lyrical miscellany.

Earlier that month Williams, driving up to his in-laws' farm in southern Vermont with his son Paul and their dog, Bobby, had stopped by the Stevenses' apartment at 210 Farmington. It had been a pleasure to see Williams, Stevens confided to Monroe, "although we were both nervous as two belles in new dresses." In short order he'd found a hotel room nearby for Williams and told him he hoped to see him "on his way back to New Jersey." What the two spoke about is unrecorded, including whether Stevens told Williams that his poems were finally going to be published as a book. The only thing, in fact, that Williams recalled was Stevens telling him how much he enjoyed receiving candied violets each Christmas from a friend. That friend was Pitts Sanborn.

Realizing that time was running short if she was going to get something new from Stevens, Monroe wrote him in mid-September, inviting him to submit the revised *Comedian*. "About the Crispin poem," he wrote back, he had already promised Sanborn the poem for *Measure.* During the summer he'd rewritten it so that "in its present form it would run to, possibly, the greater part of twenty pages in print." True, compared to *Poetry, Measure* was little more than a "miserable sheet," but Sanborn, who was at the moment in Paris along with everyone else, would be returning to New York shortly with a medley of "autumnal bon-bons" for him, and, since Sanborn would need a long poem to make up his issue of *Measure,* Stevens meant to keep his promise. As it turned out, the poem did not see publication there or elsewhere until its appearance in *Harmonium.*

For Stevens poetry had always been "a form of retreat," an exercise of the imagination that demanded undivided time and attention. And because he had never been one to write a great deal, the public's opinion as to how much he published was "neither here nor there." Still, if he did write another long poem, he promised to send it to her, *Poetry* being the place he liked to send the pieces he liked best. As for writing long poems, he had found that "attention to a single subject has the same result that prolonged attention to a signora has" in that "all manner of favors drop from it." The problem, however, was that writing one required "a skill in the varying of the serenade that occasionally makes one feel like a Guatemalan when one wants to feel like an Italian." Even *The Comedian as the Letter C*—fresh as it now looked—would in time no doubt "become rudimentary and abhorrent."

"Gathering together the things for my book has been so depressing that I wonder at *Poetry*'s friendliness," he wrote Monroe in late October, having just learned that he'd been listed for Honorable Mention in the magazine's November issue for four of his poems. Already many of his earlier pieces reminded him of "horrid cocoons from which later abortive insects have sprung." No doubt, then, even the book, once published, would amount to nothing except to teach him something. Still, reading over his "outmoded and debilitated" things made him want to "keep on dabbling and . . . be as obscure as possible until I have perfected an authentic and fluent speech for myself." The problem was that, by the time he had perfected his style, he would be like that decrepit old lover "Casanova at Waldheim with nothing to do except to look out of the windows." Still, what else could a poet do but swallow the rotten pill and keep on writing.

That November he wrote Van Vechten to say that the manuscript of *Harmonium* was now ready and that he would bring it with him when he came to New York again. It had been "an awful job to typewrite" the poems, and he didn't trust the mail to get the manuscript to him. "Knopf has my book," he wrote Monroe on December 21, "the contract is signed and that's done. I have omitted many things, exercising the most fastidious choice, so far as that was possible among my witherlings." How difficult, he added, "to pick a crisp salad from the garbage of the past."

It was Van Vechten, then, along with Sanborn, who found a publisher for Stevens. Perhaps that is why there is a hurt tone in Van Vechten's recollection thirty years later, when Stevens had all but forgotten him. By then Sanborn was long dead and Van Vechten and Stevens old men. "I do not remember that Wallace wrote me before the publication," Van Vechten recalled, "but he did send me a copy" of his *Collected Poems*. "I did not see him again until his seventy-fifth birthday in 1954, just before his death, when Alfred Knopf gave a luncheon in honor of this anniversary." That somnolent event would be held at the Waldorf in Manhattan, and, though there were a number of "important literary and journalistic figures . . . seated at small tables," Van Vechten was not invited to sit with Stevens. By then Van Vechten was "extremely deaf," and because he had forgotten to wear his hearing aid, much of what Stevens said had to be repeated to him by Mark Van Doren's wife, who was sitting next to him. It was she who reassured him that Stevens had thanked him for helping get *Harmonium* published in the first place.

• • •

JANUARY 24, 1923: FROM the Georgian Terrace Hotel in Atlanta Stevens wrote Elsie that the letterhead of the paper on which he was now writing, claiming "Golf All The Year," was "pure nonsense," as everything—including the golf courses—was presently coated with ice. There'd been a blizzard and the wind had "whistled loudly half the night" and rain and sleet had fallen in sheets, but at least he would be meeting up with the

Long Key gang in short order. The following day he was in Jacksonville, Florida, where the roses and cannas were already in bloom, though even here it was chilly. He spent the day going over "a matter of $700 which Mr. Hamilton wired me last night to try to collect from a former agent. I spent hours listening to the agent's reasons why he did not owe that large sum and, getting nowhere, I then employed a firm of lawyers to bring suit." But that business was over, and he'd stopped long enough to watch some "children on a lawn making lemonade, tennis games, camellias in full flower and so on."

Three days later he wrote Elsie again, this time from Long Key. He'd been "out at sea fishing all day with Governor Hardwick, of Georgia, and a man named Pidcock from Moultrie, Georgia," both friends of Judge Powell, and had managed to catch "four or five fish, some of them less than three feet long," so that he now brandished "a coat of tan which . . . burns like midsummer on my cheeks." He and the Long Key boys had settled into a large cottage and feasted on endless quantities of freshly killed quail, dove, venison, and steak in a private rail car which Pidcock's father had sent down from Georgia. They were seven in all, and, when they weren't fishing, passed the time playing cards. All, that is, except Stevens, who preferred to smoke a cigar and then turn in early. Mornings he loafed on the veranda, reading the papers and listening to Powell go on about life in Georgia. For lunch they'd dined on baked kingfish that one of the group, a banker from Atlanta, had caught the day before. In the evening they'd feasted on freshly killed wild dove served on toast, then walked under the full moon while the palms murmured in the breeze. Powell had gotten it right when he remarked that life here was like being drowned in beauty, sir, drowned in beauty.

When Powell and the boys left for Miami that Thursday evening, Stevens stayed behind, wanting to visit Havana for the first time. "Nothing but the most gorgeous weather," he wrote Elsie, with a "flaming sun by day and flaming moon by night." That night he'd lain awake listening to the sound of the wind pouring down like rain under the moon. When he'd awakened that morning, the palm tree at his door shone red in the sunlight.

At noon he left for Key West by rail and reached Havana by Flagler steamer that same evening. Havana was far more Spanish than he'd imagined. He'd asked "a nigger policeman to get my bearings," he wrote Elsie, but the officer could not understand him. He stayed that first night at the Hotel La Union but, finding the bed impossible, had moved to the Hotel Sevilla. In the afternoon he'd attended the popular horse races, only to find himself bored to death. In the evening it was a game of jai alai. The following day, Sunday, he'd walked about Havana, unimpressed by the sameness of home after home, each built around an inner open air court decorated with plants, their front rooms full of cheap statuary and decrepit furniture. Still, those courts, filled with half-naked kids playing and shouting, were the coolest places around. Evenings, on the other hand, were fresh and cool, so that he'd slept like a king.

He dined at the British Club with a representative from Aetna, then breakfasted at the Sevilla, before visiting every big church he could find. They were all Catholic churches here, gorgeous and shabby, most of them older than the oldest buildings back in Hartford. Then luncheon at El Telegrafo: "orangeade, a Cuban lobster, banana bread, cocoanut milk ice cream and a pot of Cuban coffee." Everything about the city fascinated him, from the bootblacks to the dark-skinned women smoking cigars to the Fords that took you almost anywhere for twenty cents. Yes, he admitted, he did feel "rather sinful" about coming here, though it was "not a very great sin," and even Elsie might see it as something he'd earned. Everyone here spoke Spanish, of course, even the Chinese vendors selling hot peanuts on the streets, which made him feel like an outsider. But the view! From his window he could look out over the Prado and down to the seawall and Morro Castle across the bay. Havana cigars were cheap as dirt here, though he found the Cuban cigarettes even better to his liking.

And the orangeade here, a word he used only once in his poetry. "Bellisimo, pomposo," he brayed in "The Revolutionists Stop for Orangeade," remembering that black uniformed traffic cop who spoke Spanish but not enough English to understand this northerner from los Estados Unidos:

Sing a song of serpent-kin,
Necks among the thousand leaves,
Tongues around the fruit.

Sing in clownish boots
Strapped and buckled bright.

A send-up, then, another manifestation of Stevens's writing of a subject out of his range and sensibilities. If there was a lack of communication on the policeman's part that day, Stevens's failed poem shows how misunderstanding might cut both ways.

By Tuesday he was back in Miami, where he met up with some of the Hartford's agents. His job was to look into the feasibility of insuring construction work on the Tamiami Trail, which would cut across the state from Miami to Tampa. He spent the day being driven about in a Model T Ford over rough roads, so that by nine that evening he was exhausted. The following morning he took a brisk walk along the beach, then boarded a bus for Palm Beach in heavy rain. That same evening, he boarded a Pullman sleeper and headed north, reaching Charleston, South Carolina, the following evening, where he visited with the poet Hervey Allen as he'd promised he would the year before. But instead of the Prohibition whiskey he'd hoped to enjoy there, Allen's elderly aunt offered him a cup of hot chocolate.

North Carolina proved to be one miserable hotel after another, even as the weather grew colder. Finally in Greensboro he managed to find a decent hotel. It was named for the short-story writer O. Henry. Fancy having your name on the soup ladle, as well as on the linen, he wrote Elsie. Fancy too Shrimps O. Henry, Salad O. Henry, Parfait O. Henry. Such was literary fame. Otherwise the town was pure business, home to Blue Bell Overalls, intent like so many places in the South on worshipping two things only: "the dollar and the Almighty." And everywhere the same signs: "Jesus Saves," "The eternal God is thy refuge and underneath the everlasting arms," "Prepare to meet Thy God." At the hotel he'd followed a huge crowd of young men, hoping to find something to amuse him, only to learn that they were going to the men's meeting at the First Presbyterian Church. If churches back in Hartford were "more or less moribund," here in the South—alas—religion took the place of everything, including society, art, and literature.

But, then, he reasoned, if he had to live here, "faced constantly by the poverty around me . . . and the despair that the land and the people are bound to create," he too might come to "depend on some such potent illusion as 'The eternal God is thy refuge.' " One thing you learned when you spent as much time as he did traveling the country was just how many people were "brought up in dirt and ignorance without a thing in the world to look forward to."

Back in Hartford again, having thought hard about it, he wrote Knopf asking him to change the title of his book to "THE GRAND POEM: Preliminary Minutiae." *There* was a title, he thought, that had "a good deal more pep to it" than *Harmonium*. Then more fussing and fretting, until finally, on May 18, less than four months before the book's publication, he sent Knopf a telegram. It read in full, "USE HARMONIUM WALLACE STEVENS."

10

A Baby among Us: 1923–1934

I have read very little and written not at all. The baby has kept us both incredibly busy . . . she dominates the house and . . . her requirements have to a large extent become our own. I have been moved to the attic. . . .

WALLACE STEVENS TO WILLIAM CARLOS WILLIAMS,
14 OCTOBER 1925

By the time Knopf published *Harmonium* on September 7, 1923, in an edition of 1,500 copies (at $2 a copy), poetry had taken a back seat to Stevens's other concerns. *The Comedian* had predicted that this would be the case, and Stevens wrote few poems that year, or the next, or the next. In fact he wrote only a handful and published even fewer over the next ten years. In the meantime he sent copies of *Harmonium* to various friends, Van Vechten among them since, after all, he'd been the book's "accoucheur." Knopf had done "very well by it," and Stevens was grateful to both Knopf and Van Vechten. Over the next few months he would also send copies to Harriet Monroe, William Carlos Williams, Robert McAlmon, and Alice Corbin in Santa Fe, telling her that it was his "first (and, no doubt, only) book." Nevertheless, he hoped she liked it.

That October he turned forty-four; Elsie was now thirty-seven. One piece of unfinished business for Stevens was finally taking his wife on a real honeymoon vacation and, with luck, making at least one of those daughters with curls he'd conjured in *The Comedian* a reality. The couple spent four nights at New York's Commodore Hotel, adjacent to Grand Central Terminal, then, on the 18th, set sail on a fifteen-day cruise aboard the Panama Pacific line's *Kroonland.* The trip would take them to California via Havana and the Panama Canal, then north along the Pacific and back to the States. From California they would return to Hartford by rail, stopping in New Mexico to visit with Witter Bynner. "The sea as flat and still as a pancake, before breakfast," Elsie entered in her journal on the 28th. It was not a particularly striking simile, but it made its point, and the calm seas were no doubt welcome, as Elsie was prone to seasickness. On November 1 she noted, "Cool this morning—Still plowing through the Pacific—just now near lower California. . . . Sun setting directly opposite the port side."

Something about the clouds, sea, and weather came together for Stevens then, in all likelihood the news that Elsie was finally with child, the result being a five-part poem in tercets which he called "Sea Surface Full of Clouds." If this poem is an announcement that Elsie was pregnant, it resonates even more, with its alternating moods of expectancy and anxiety over a future which of necessity remains unknown. Yet through it all there is a sense that the advent of a baby would turn out well. "In that November off Tehuantepec," each of the five sections begins. It is like a still point to which the flux of sea, cloud, and sky return at last, or like Monet's sequence of thirty paintings of the cathedral at Rouen. Stevens paints the sea's surface as first a rosy chocolate, then a chophouse chocolate, a porcelain chocolate, a musky chocolate, and finally a Chinese chocolate. Gilt umbrellas morph into sham, pied, frail, and, finally, large umbrellas.

There is throughout the five-part series a sense of things blooming: sea blooms, blooms of water, ocean blooms, morning blooms, white blooms with silver petals, and green blooms. It's Crispin at sea again—in all senses of that phrase—but older and a bit more hopeful, at home with the fact of new life springing from the old. There's also the vertiginous sense of some "turquoise-turbaned Sambo, neat / At tossing saucers," the poet's bastard spirit, the tenuousness of it all. But then too there's the sound of the conch trumping "loyal conjuration," with its echo of conjugation, the sea finally turning from crisped to "motley hue / To clearing opalescence."

There's the comedy of it all, and yet a seriousness as well, and with it a sense of conjugal unity, when, like the lovers, "the sea / And heaven rolled as one and from the two / Came fresh transfigurings of freshest blue." A new and richer life propounded, then with the news that, through all the daily "sloppings of the sea" and all the tossings and turnings of their machine-like life together, a new dimension was about to be added as the two rolled together as one. "Who, then, evolved the sea blooms from the clouds," the poet asks, "diffusing balm in that Pacific calm"? That peaceful calm indeed, to which the poet replies, *C'était mon enfant, mon bijou, mon âme:* "My child, my jewel, my soul."

• • •

BUT THERE WAS HIS "bastard spirit" too to contend with. One of the most personal poems Stevens ever wrote appeared in the August 1924 number of *Measure*, the same month Holly Bright Stevens was born. It is called "Red Loves Kit," and its language echoes the fear and incertitude one senses in parts of its unlikely companion piece, "Sea Surface Full of Clouds." "Red Loves Kit": words one might find on a wall or fence or underpass painted over with graffiti and for which one might well read "Wallace loves Elsie." Red, for instance, may be a pun on Reading. "Red Loves Kit" was published once and once only, in a small literary magazine, and was never republished in Stevens's lifetime. "Your yes her no, your no her yes," the poem begins, the man and the woman at cross-purposes from the very start:

The words
Make little difference, for being wrong
And wronging her, if only as she thinks,
You never can be right.

If Stevens saw himself as the man who might bring calm and security to his wife in "Sea Surface," here he is again, the man who would have

brought the incredible calm in ecstasy,
Which, like a virgin visionary spent
In this spent world, she must possess. The gift

Came not from you. Shall the world be spent again,
Wasted in what would be an ultimate waste,
A deprivation muffled in eclipse,
The final theft? That you are innocent
And love her still, still leaves you in the wrong.
Where is that calm and where that ecstasy?
Her words accuse you of adulteries
That sack the sun, though metaphysical.

Spent: there's a pun here too, as Stevens repeats the word three times in as many lines. *Spent*, as in sexually spent, as well as spending himself in agreeing at last to have a child who, by its very existence, must offer a hostage to Fate. And *spent* in the sense of money, and Elsie's face on the Mercury dime and half dollar that seems to have evoked that "virgin visionary spent / In this spent world." Having been relegated to the attic now by Elsie with the arrival of the baby, has it all been a waste, then? Has it been a terrible miscalculation on his part of the little that remains after one has spent oneself and been rejected? There is no evidence that Stevens ever had a fling with a woman down in Florida, Cuban lady or otherwise, and in any event he denies that possibility in his poem. But to be accused of adulteries, even though they may be metaphysical only, as in giving oneself over to one's poems, or if not, spending all of one's time in the attic, where he reads book after book and listens to music on the radio, or perhaps escaping with the Atlanta crowd down to the Keys. What does it matter, now that the light has gone out of his marriage and the Large Red Man is consigned to the attic? "The gift" of himself, he realizes, she will never see as coming from him.

Once, he and Elsie were in love, so that everything was transformed by that love, as the moon's light alters the earth's evening, as the sea is reflected in the sounds the waves make on the shore. Just so,

when in her mystic aureole
She walks, triumphing humbly, [*she*] *should express*
Her beauty in your love. She should reflect
Her glory in your passion and be proud.

Her music should repeat itself in you,
Impelled by a compulsive harmony.

And yet, though the poet sings of his love, the woman refuses to walk proudly in that love. Though "you may love / And she have beauty of a kind," it is not what he had hoped for, so that now more than ever "such / Unhappy love reveals vast blemishes."

What, then, is left for him? Nothing. Nothing beyond the nightmarish image of black crows resting on "the edges of the moon," which he bids now

Cover the golden altar deepest black,
Fly upward thick in numbers, fly across
The blueness of the half-night, fill the air
And darken it. . . .
Then turn your heads and let your spiral eyes
Look backward. Let your swiftly-flying flocks
Look suddenly downward with their shining eyes
And move the night by their intelligent motes.

Even the stars seem to mock the poet now, their shining morphed into crows' eyes in a waking nightmare. Let this poem, then, this good galliard, stand as sign "to enchant black thoughts," beseeching those black crows of the imagination "for an overwhelming gloom." If there is anything to be gained by knowing how things stand, then let that knowledge be fruitful and multiply and let it be "fecund in rapt curios," for what could be more curious than an estranged couple with a baby in the house, feasting yearly on each other's misery?

• • •

NOR WERE THINGS TO get any better in the coming years, if the poem Stevens wrote in 1930 is any indication. He called it "The Woman Who Blamed Life on a Spaniard," and withheld it from publication for another two years, before it finally appeared in another little magazine, *Contempo.* "You do not understand her evil mood," the poem begins:

You think that like the moon she is obscured
But clears and clears until an open night
Reveals her, rounded in beneficence,
Pellucid love; and for that image, like
Some merciful divination, you forgive.

But there is something truly malevolent about this woman, he has come to understand, this presence who

spreads an evil lustre whose increase
Is evil, crisply bright, disclosing you
Stooped in a night of vast inquietude.
Observe her shining in the deadly trees.

People speak of pain, of fate, but they often turn a simple mot into a dictum, a way of bracketing the real. But this woman is like a picador jabbing and jabbing at him as if he were a circling bull she would torment and torment again before finally bringing it down. Well, two can play a fiction: "Be briny-blooded bull," then, and

Flatter her lance with your tempestuous dust,
Make melic groans and tooter at her strokes,
Rage in the ring and shake the corridors.
Perhaps at so much mastery, the bliss
She needs will come consolingly.

Poetry as melic groan, where the would-be lover's words are reduced, as here, to a pitiful groan of sexual exasperation. But wouldn't that too be merely role-playing, the creation of a male fantasy doomed to end badly? Who is the belovèd bird, the fowl of Venus, then? Is she a cooing dove, or some silly goose? Does Venus possess the voice of the nightingale? Is she wise as a seraglio parrot with access to the knowing world of the harem? Does she show disdain like the haughty eagle? Yes and no to all of these questions, then. For, whatever else love is, the poet suggests, it "must have tears / And memory and claws" and yet sing "arpeggi of celestial souvenirs." Love should hold heavenly memories, as of the woman he wooed twenty years before, the one for whom he closed the door on his father. Nothing for it, then, but to compose a fiction of the perfect woman, some "hallowed visitant" here or elsewhere, whom he knows to be "chimerical": a woman who will never reveal herself, as even the cloud-covered moon glimpsed from his attic window in time will finally do.

• • •

BY DECEMBER 10, 1923, he was in his new office at 690 Asylum Avenue, catching up on his correspondence, among which he found a letter from Monroe Wheeler, whose Manikin Press had just published ten of Williams's poems culled from *Spring & All* and titled *Go Go*. Wheeler wondered if Stevens might also have a pamphlet-size batch of poems he could publish, along with collections by Janet Lewis and Marianne Moore. "At the moment I have nothing that I can send you," Stevens replied. "However, I shall keep your letter, and, if I happen to do something during the winter that I think might be of interest to you, I shall write to you again." But there would be no new poems.

He told Harriet Monroe the same thing seven months later. He'd sent "one or two things to people who seemed to want them," but most evenings he loafed and smoked cigars and meant to do so for a long time to come. He hadn't even been to New York City in months. And, to top it all, his "royalties for the first half of 1924 amounted to $6.70." With that sort of return on his poetic investment, he was thinking of chartering a boat and taking his friends around the world.

Of the handful of reviews of *Harmonium* few were positive. That irascible Arkansan and friend of fellow imagist Amy Lowell, John Gould Fletcher, had reviewed the book for the December 10 issue of the *Freeman*. He'd found Stevens's earlier poems, especially those Monroe had published, among the best things then being written by an American. But he balked at others, especially *The Comedian*. He called his review "The Revival of Aestheticism," an overview of American poetry published in the previous decade, singling out Stevens for praise, though he thought *Harmonium* as a whole a failure because it showed that Stevens had created merely a "fictitious reality" which disintegrated whenever it came up "against the banal, the ordinary, the commonplace, which is every-day reality." That was because, Fletcher suspected, the poet's own personality seemed to be disintegrating. Stevens had two choices open to him now: either "expand his range to take in more of human experience, or give up writing altogether."

Fletcher's review stunned even Williams. Two days after Christmas he wrote Marianne Moore, asking her to read the review and tell him what she thought. Clearly Fletcher seemed "somewhat misanthropic toward . . . the younger American poets." But then Fletcher was a failed poet himself, who had now stepped down "among the populace for mud to fling" at others. If Fletcher had managed to diagnose the shortcomings of Stevens's poetry, the fact remained that Stevens had anticipated Fletcher's criticism by giving *The Comedian* double endings and a final silence not unlike that of Achilles in refusing to leave his tent and join the melee raging outside.

By then too the critics had turned their attention to Eliot. In November 1922, "out of the blue, *The Dial* had published *The Waste Land* and . . . wiped out our world" of poetic experimentation, Williams would lament three decades on in his *Autobiography*. It was "as if an atom bomb had been dropped upon" his and Stevens's poetic world

> and our brave sallies into the unknown were turned to dust. . . . I felt at once that it had set me back twenty years, and I'm sure it did. Critically Eliot returned us to the classroom just at the moment when . . . we were on the point of an escape to matters much closer to the essence of a new art form itself—rooted in the locality which should give it fruit. . . . Eliot had turned his back on the possibility of reviving my world. And being an accomplished craftsman, better skilled in some ways than I could ever hope to be, I had to watch him carry my world off with him, the fool, to the enemy.

As it turned out, it was Moore, in her essay review "Well-Moused, Lion" in the January 1924 number of the *Dial*, who offered the most sympathetic, if also one of the most peripatetic, reviews of *Harmonium*. "There is the love of magnificence . . . in these sharp, solemn, rhapsodic pieces of eloquence," she wrote. As if to show that she could dance Stevens's dance as well, she compared the coloration of his Yucatan imagination to "vials of picrocarmine, magenta, gamboge, and violet mingled each at the highest point of intensity." Yes, Stevens could do all of that, and do it superbly. Indeed there was about his poetry "the effect of poised uninterrupted harmony" and a symmetry of movement such as one found "in figure skating [and] tight-rope dancing."

Yet she too had her caveats. "One resents the temper of certain of these poems," she wrote. For while Stevens was "never inadvertently crude," there was in him a "deliberate bearishness—a shadow of acrimonious, unprovoked contumely." If there appeared to be a surface nonchalance to his demeanor, the truth was that an ogre also lurked just beneath the surface. Even in a poem of such "masterly equipoise" as "Sunday Morning," she'd found a "mind disturbed by the intangible," oppressed by the things of the world which the poet meant to reshape with his own imagination. Add to these observations the abiding strain of self-mockery which kept getting in the way of his poems.

Two years later, in the November 1925 *Dial*, Gorham Munson's "The Dandyism of Wallace Stevens" appeared. "The impeccability of the dandy resolves itself into two elements," Munson explained: one was correctness, the other elegance. The problem was that both went beyond good taste, for correctness implied "a knowledge of the rules governing the modes of expression, feeling, thinking, conduct," and elegance consisted of "good taste that has been polished." On the other hand, American literature had never had a real dandy before. Oh, there had been plenty of Yankee Doodle Dandies and "swaggering macaronis." But "the grace and ceremony, the appropriate nimbleness of the dandy," was something American poetry lacked. Now, however, Stevens had given us our first real dandy. But this view of Stevens, which Munson had meant as high praise, would come back to haunt Stevens in the coming years.

• • •

SOON AFTER HOLLY WAS born on August 10, 1924, the Stevenses moved into the upstairs apartment of an attractive two-family brick house located at 735 Farmington Avenue in Hartford, a mile and a half west of their former apartment and a two-mile walk to Stevens's office along the main thoroughfare running from Hartford to Farmington and beyond. It was a road Holly would remember as "continually heavy and noisy with automobiles, trucks, and trolleys." The couple who owned the house occupied the first floor and had several young children, so the house was seldom quiet. There Stevens loved listening to music on his combination radio-Victrola, collecting a sizable number of classical records, many ordered from Europe. He also enjoyed time in his "big fat giardino," as he called it, installing rose and iris beds, as well as a large asparagus patch behind the house. And in honor of his daughter he planted a holly tree in the front yard.

"Holly grows prettier and jollier every day," he wrote Harriet Monroe twelve days into 1925. "We have never had the least trouble with her—have never lost a wink of sleep. She babbles and plays with her hands and smiles like an angel." Of course such experiences were "a terrible blow to poor literature," more distracting even than the siren call of the radio. He had written no poetry in months. Now he was preparing to leave for his annual trip to Long Key, where it might grow noisy enough for him to write something. But all he managed to compose that year was a Valentine's greeting to Elsie and the baby:

Though Valentine brings love
And Spring brings beauty
They do not make me rise
To my poetic duty

But Elsie and Holly do
And do it daily—
Much more than Valentine or Spring
And very much more gaily.

He signed it "W.S.," assuming that at least one of the recipients would guess who had sent it.

• • •

WHEN WILLIAMS, BACK FROM a sabbatical in Europe, wrote Stevens that October announcing the publication of his improvisational essays on the history of American literature from the Vikings through Lincoln, called *In the American Grain*, he asked him for some new work for the revival of *Contact*. Stevens confessed that he'd "seen very few litérateurs [*sic*]" during the last year or two, "read very little and written not at all." The baby kept him and Elsie "incredibly busy." While Holly was not under his "jurisdiction" and was as well-behaved "as a south-wind," she still managed to dominate the house. He himself had long ago been "removed to the attic . . . to be out of the way." There he could "smoke and loaf and read and write," though all he did these days was turn in early. He read mainly because, "as the Chinese say, two or three days without study and life loses its savor." He took the occasion to confess that he'd always found in Williams that "live contact" with one's world he himself wanted, but which seemed to elude him. It was the same vitality he found in that "uncaged animal" McAlmon. In any case, his job now was "to keep the fire-place burning and the music-box churning and the wheels of the baby's chariot turning and that sort of thing."

When Marianne Moore as editor of the *Dial* invited him to review *In the American Grain*, he told her that what Columbus had discovered was nothing to what Williams was looking for. Still, however much he might like to "evolve a mainland from [Williams's] leaves, scents and floating bottles and boxes," there was a baby at home, which meant all lights were out at nine. Perhaps one was "better off in bed anyhow on cold nights."

It was the same a year later, when she invited Stevens to present that year's Dial Award to Williams for *In the American Grain* ("Carlos the Fortunate," he called him), he declined, explaining that he was "incessantly and atrociously busy." Belatedly he would write Williams to say how much he regretted not having been at the award ceremony. How good that the *Dial* could offer "its foster-children veritable fortunes," he joked. "Your townsmen must whisper about you and, as you pass the girls, they surely nudge each other and say 'The golden boy!' "

In February 1926 he wrote Monroe to thank her for the Christmas ornament she'd sent sixteen-month-old Holly, which he and Elsie had placed on their tree. The baby had been "most curious about it," he bragged, having "a strange eye for detail. If you show her a bush, she does not see it but will see a bird in it, if you show her a picture her finger goes straight to some particularity." Holly would remember her father calling her his little Princess Wamsutta Percale. "It took a while for me to find out that that was a brand of bed linen"; she thought he'd named her that for helping him once with the laundry.

She also remembered how her father liked to listen to classical music when he came home from work in the evenings, and, if she let him listen to his music on the radio-Victrola combination before dinner, he bargained with her, she could have one new book a week of her choosing. And there was always music in the house. On weekends her father listened to opera or the New York Philharmonic. He also liked to listen to comedy shows after dinner, "particularly Eddie Cantor and Parkyakarkus," when he "would roar with laughter." Other evenings her mother played the piano while her father listened. Later Holly tried her hand at the piano—"Chopsticks" variations—which drove her mother crazy. On the other hand, her father taught her to whistle "melodies and bird calls," while he accompanied her.

• • •

DURING HIS TIME IN the Keys that winter of 1926, Stevens joined a sailing expedition with the boys on John Little's yacht, the *Ilah*, visiting the Keys and the Everglades. It was "a glorious trip, which . . . could have gone on for several months without protest." But what with Florida's land boom madness, even Miami, which until then had seemed "isolated and a place for exotic hermits," had become "a jamboree of hoodlums." Perhaps after Miami cleaned up after itself, something of its colonial flavor would re-emerge and he might feel at ease again. But then, in a few years' time, "the only true temples . . . to be found" would be in isolated places like Tobago or the mountains of Venezuela.

That same year Stevens began experiencing blurred vision. Shortly after his forty-seventh birthday, doctors diagnosed his large hands and feet and morphing facial features as signs of acromegaly, a rare disease of the pituitary gland, which results in an enlargement of the face and extremities. He also learned that he was seriously overweight and was suffering from high blood pressure. Exercise, they told him. Lose weight and cut back on alcohol. Stevens took the advice seriously and for the next year put himself on such a strict regimen that by the end of 1927 he was found to be anemic and underweight. At that point he began moderating his diet and exercise. Finally, in October 1928, as he turned forty-nine, he was relieved to be given a favorable medical report, which he mistakenly took to mean he could return to his old habits.

In mid-1927 Williams wrote Stevens with a request that had come directly from "the Pound" himself, now living in the northern Italian resort village of Rapallo, asking for something for an issue of *Exile*, a new magazine he was editing. It took Stevens three weeks to get back to Williams, and when he did, his answer was no. "Believe me, signor," he wrote,

> I'm as busy as the proud Mussolini himself. I rise at day-break, shave etc.; at six I start to exercise; at seven I massage and bathe; at eight I dabble with a therapeutic breakfast; from eight-thirty to nine-thirty I walk down-town; work all day [and] go to bed at nine. How should I write poetry, think it, feel it? Mon Dieu, I am happy if I can find time to read a few lines, yours, Pound's anybody's. I am humble before Pound's request. But the above is the above.

"Undecipherable letter from Wallace Stevens," Williams told Pound. "He says he isn't writing any more. He has a daughter!"

In March 1928 Stevens answered a series of questions a Leonidas Payne sent him about *Harmonium*. Stevens was forthright in admitting to a distaste for commenting on his own work (a procedure which felt rather like "converting a piece of mysticism into a piece of logic."), but he obliged Payne by dictating a response to his secretary at the office. Since reading the proofs of *Harmonium*, he had not looked at the book. But he could say this: that his early poems were not about ideas, but rather about sensations. Moreover, after writing a poem, it felt good "to walk round the block," and "after too much midnight," how "pleasant to hear the milkman." It was shocking, though, to have to talk about such things. "I don't mind your saying what I have said here," he added. "But I don't want you to quote me. No more explanations."

• • •

DURING THAT YEAR HE composed only one poem, jotted down one day in mid-June during a two-day business trip to New York. He called the poem "Metropolitan Melancholy" and sent it as a gift to Harriet Monroe to thank her for her birthday gift to Holly. It was for her perusal only, he told her, and not something he wanted published. It was another send-up, the subject of this one being Hoon's consort. "A purple woman with a lavender tongue," it began,

Said hic, said hac,
Said ha.

To dab things even nicely pink
Adds very little,
So I think.
Oh ha, Oh ha.

The silks they wear in all the cities
Are really such a million pities.

That same summer the poetry editor of one of the Hartford newspapers sent Monroe a note bringing her up to date on the local poetry scene. "No doubt you know that Robert Hillyer, Wilbert Snow and Odell Shepard live here," the editor wrote enthusiastically. Moreover Muriel Stuart's last book of poems had been published by Mitchell's bookshop, where the Poetry Club of Hartford met, so that—if anywhere—Hartford's poetry vortex centered there. Monroe printed the notice in the August number of *Poetry* but added pointedly that as far as she was concerned, the real poetry center of Hartford was "in the residence of Wallace Stevens." For his part, the poet remained in hiding.

The crop of poems for 1929, unlike Stevens's fat garden, fared little better. "Thanks for the pleasant letter," he wrote Louis Untermeyer, the poet and prolific literary editor, that June, after Untermeyer had written asking Stevens if he might include six poems from *Harmonium* in an upcoming anthology, plus anything new he cared to send along. "You can use anything of mine that interests you," he added, "but Knopf is the legal owner." He included the only new thing he'd written all year, "Annual Gaiety," a shorthand paean to Hartford and Florida, composed of equal parts pinked blue snow and those ominous alligators he'd seen lying "along the edges of your eye / Basking in desert Florida" and who seemed to follow him wherever he went, ready at any time to pull the poet, Père Guzz thumbing his lyre, under the water for good. Little as it was, Untermeyer used it.

On February 19, 1930, he wrote from Key West to his friend and former associate at the Hartford, Jim Powers. The two had met in Miami four years earlier, when Powers represented J. C. Penney and Stevens the Hartford in a case. So impressed had Stevens been with Powers that he offered him a job as his assistant at the Hartford, where Powers worked for the next two years, before returning to private practice in New York City and later in Portland, Oregon. He'd been in Miami for a week now, Stevens wrote, and felt he could go on living there for a long time to come. Just last night the wind at Key West had "lashed the palms to such an extent that it kept me half-awake all night long." But now the sun was back, and he had written something: a twelve-line poem in five unrhymed couplets followed by a rhymed heroic couplet, an ending very like that of one of Shakespeare's sonnets. The following month it would appear in the *New Republic.* He called it "The Sun This March," and in it he spoke about how dark his spirit had become over the past half dozen years. "The exceeding brightness of this early sun," the poem begins,

Makes me conceive how dark I have become,

And re-illuminates things that used to turn
To gold in broadest blue, and be a part

Of a turning spirit in an earlier self.
That, too, returns from out the winter's air,

Like an hallucination come to daze
The corner of the eye.

There was something about Connecticut, his element, really, which brought with it "voices as of lions coming down." The lions of March, bearing with them the sense of an old power recovered. It was to the sun, now, teacher and master and creator, ever old and yet ever new, venerable and veritable rabbi, to whom he turned as if in prayer, pleading for its saving light to descend again and break the dark of his tormented spirit:

Oh! Rabbi, rabbi, fend my soul for me
And true savant of this dark nature be.

Then the silence, like a great depression, descended over him again.

• • •

IN THE SPRING OF 1930 Alfred Knopf wrote Stevens that he was prepared to bring out a second edition of *Harmonium* the following year. Stevens waited months before answering, then, in October, wrote back to say yes to the proposal. But he wanted to add fourteen new poems—some of them going back more than a dozen years—and asked that three poems from the first edition be omitted: "The Silver Plough Boy," "Exposition of the Contents of a Cab," and "Architecture."

The new poems were to be added at the back, but with the two poems which had closed the original edition closing the revised edition as well. The group of fourteen he was adding were "The Man Whose Pharynx Was Bad"; three from *Lettres d'un Soldat* ("The Death of a Soldier," "Negation," and "The Surprises of the Superhuman"); "Sea Surface Full of Clouds," published in the *Dial* in July 1924; "The Revolutionists Stop for Orangeade," written after his first trip to Havana in 1923; "New England Verses," which had appeared in *Measure* in April 1923; "Lunar Paraphrase," from *Poetry* in May 1918; "Anatomy of Monotony"; "The Public Square," also in the April 1923 issue of *Measure*; and "Sonatina to Hans Christian," "In the Clear Season of Grapes," "Two at Norfolk," and "Indian River," all dating back to 1917, when they'd appeared in the long-defunct *Soil*. "To the Roaring Wind," published years earlier in *Soil*, concluded the volume. "What syllable are you seeking / Vocalissimus / In the distances of sleep?" the poet at thirty-six and the poet at fifty-one cry out as from a fitful nightmare from which neither can awaken. "Speak it."

• • •

TWICE, ONCE IN JULY 1930 and again nine months later, Lincoln Kirstein, editor of the prestigious *Hound and Horn*, had written Stevens for new work. The first time Stevens explained that his muse was asleep somewhere. The second time, when Kirstein held out the carrot that R. P. Blackmur would be writing a thirty-page essay for the magazine highlighting Stevens's achievement, Stevens explained that, though he was pleased by their interest, "nothing short of a coup d'état would make it possible for me to write poetry now." And when Harriet Monroe wrote him in August 1932, asking for a new poem, he had to tell her, "Whatever else I do, I do not write poetry nowadays." Stevens, it seemed, had simply disappeared from the poetry scene.

• • •

"DEAR LOUIS UNTERMEYER," A thirty-two-year-old poet, brilliant in his own right, wrote from his father's house in Chagrin Falls, Ohio, in mid-August 1931. The year before he'd published his epic of the United States, which he called *The Bridge*, and was preparing now to sail to Mexico on a Guggenheim to compose an epic piece about the Spanish conquest of an America far more south than Key West. He would fail at that and in despair jump to his death from the SS *Orizaba* as it sailed back to New York the following April. Why was there no fresh work by Stevens anymore, he wondered. "I miss fresh harmonies from him almost more than I can say. There never was anyone quite like him, nor will there be!" Then he added, "I don't think any critic has ever done him full justice, either, and it's a temptation to attempt it sometime oneself. . . . I hope he's going into your anthology." He signed the letter, "Faithfully yours, Hart Crane."

• • •

IN SEPTEMBER 1932, WITH the Great Depression about to enter its fourth year, one of every four workers in the United States out of work, and breadlines longer than ever, the Stevenses were at last ready to move into the first and only home they would ever own. They had looked at two other houses before settling on this one, built just before the Wall Street Crash and now, like so many other houses, for sale in an economically stressed market. Ironically, only now did Stevens feel he had the resources to purchase a home and pay for it in cash. No more rented rooms, no more apartments. A real home this time, like the one he'd grown up in, with a playground with swings nearby where he and Elsie could take their daughter. They also hired a full-time housekeeper who could help look after eight-year-old Holly.

From the age of five until she was seventeen, Holly attended the Oxford School for Girls at 695 Prospect Avenue, a half mile northeast of their Farmington Street apartment. The Oxford School was (and is, though it long ago merged with the Kingswood School for Boys) a secular private day school which believed that "wise parents know they must share with teachers the shaping of the minds and character of young people." Its motto was *Vincit qui se vincit.* "One conquers by conquering oneself." When the Stevenses moved to their house at 118 Westerly Terrace, the distance to school increased to a mile and a third, but a car from the Prospect Park Livery (the same which took the Stevenses wherever they had to go since neither drove) would arrive promptly each morning to take Holly to school and return her home each afternoon. Both parents believed they'd given Holly free rein to do as she wished, within limits, of course, though Holly would remember her upbringing as far more restrictive. For a headstrong girl, not unlike her father, those restrictions, imagined or otherwise, led inevitably to conflicts, especially with her mother. As Anthony Sigmans, one of Stevens's closest business associates remembered it, all the time Holly "was growing up, she must have experienced a lot of want in her life because[,] her father being what he was" and her mother being such an odd sort of person, Holly didn't get to "see much of life."

• • •

"IS THERE NOT FUNDAMENTALLY a kinship between the sensory discriminations and comfortable tranquility of Wallace Stevens' poetry and the

America that owns baronial estates?" This was the question Gorham Munson had posed in his review of *Harmonium* in the *Dial*, catching something at the heart of Stevens's and secular America's search for fulfillment. And if there was a heaven, wouldn't it have to be here? "The American nation drives passionately toward comfort," Munson wrote. "Wide, accurately barbered lawns, . . . the silvered motor-car, the small regiment of obsequious servants": these were what people like Stevens wanted. But there was a sly caveat as well on Munson's part: "Naturally, in paradise one would not wish to be annoyed by a suspicion that all was a brilliant fake, a magnificent evanescent dream, but rather, to refine upon one's luxurious means of existence." This was where the American poet might "enter and play, . . . adding splendour to the circumstances of one's comfort." Both Baudelaire and Eliot, Munson pointed out, had manifested aspects of the dandy. But Baudelaire's dandyism had turned out to be a "metallic shell secreted by a restless man against a despised shifting social order," and Eliot's dandyism, especially in *The Waste Land*, had turned "his promenade through . . . modern life into bitter melancholy." Stevens, on the other hand, had learned "to sit comfortably in the age, to enjoy a sense of security, to be conscious of no need of fighting the times." It came down to this: for Stevens the world was "a gay and bright phenomenon" which he feasted on "without misgiving."

Munson was half right. He'd caught the gaiety, the parasols and chocolate, the complacencies of the peignoir, even the blaze of the tiger's eye. But he missed what others hadn't: the unhappy Stevens, the angry man, the raging bull piqued by the picador. "I do not discover in him the ferocity that some critics have remarked upon," Munson insisted, "but there is at least a flair for bright savagery, for 'that tuft of jungle feathers, that animal eye, that savage fire.' " In truth, both sides of Stevens had come to occupy the second-floor study and hideaway he claimed on Westerly Terrace.

It was a large, comfortable white-sided colonial house on a half-acre of green turf in an upscale section of Hartford, within easy walking distance of Elizabeth Park, with its pond and walks and trees and rose gardens, the same park he and Elsie and Holly had visited so often over the years. The house sat on a terraced street with a wide grassy knoll between the two levels, where cherry trees would later blossom. The holly tree which

Stevens had planted outside the apartment where Holly was raised had been transplanted just outside the front door of their new home, along with the rose and iris beds Stevens had also originally planted on Farmington Avenue.

"The only thing of any interest concerning myself," he wrote Jim Powers that Christmas, "is the fact that we bought a house . . . out on Westerly Terrace, which is a twig running off from Terry Road, which, you may remember, is a branch running off the main stem of Asylum Avenue." Though the house might look "very much like other houses," it was *their* house now, and they were delighted with it, even if it still lacked furniture. In fact the first thing they were going to buy as soon as they could afford it was a sofa for Holly. His salary had been frozen in 1930 and reduced the following year, yet the feeling at the Hartford these days was that things were "going to grow better rather than worse." It didn't look as though there would be any further salary reductions, for while business had "not been so good, nevertheless when compared with what other companies have been doing," it wasn't all that bad either.

Of course there were signs of domestic fracture to consider. From the beginning Stevens, who had not shared a bedroom with his wife for years now, moved into the master bedroom with its attached study on the second floor, with a communal room to the left and two small bedrooms to the left of that: one for Holly and the other for Elsie, one of which—Elsie's—was originally a housekeeper's quarters. An elegant set of stairs which could be approached from left or right ran through the center of the house, connecting the first and second floors, while another set of stairs, far more modest, off to the left and hidden, connected the smaller bedrooms to the kitchen and pantry on the first floor and a maid's room (though they did not keep one) and attic on the third floor. There was a large parlor and a sitting room downstairs where guests might be entertained, though, given the Stevenses' intense desire for privacy, such a thing rarely happened.

"Good Man, Bad Woman" appeared in *Poetry* a month after the Stevenses moved into their new home. Its bitter, exasperated tone could serve as a harbinger of things to come. "You say that spite avails her nothing," the poem begins, using the same fifteen-line form as "The Woman Who

Blamed Life on a Spaniard," as if the new poem were broken off from that longer one, like a sliver of ice. "You rest intact in conscience and intact / In self." It was as if in poetry Stevens had found a way to protect himself from what he perceived as Elsie's steely cold behavior. And yet, when spring came around again and the poet "walked / Among the orchards in the apple-blocks / And saw the blossoms, snow-bred pink and white," so that for a moment he forgot the mask of cold indifference and bared himself to her, wasn't it always received as an empty gesture? And so the poem ends, "She can corrode your world, if never you." A shield, then, to protect oneself, but at what cost?

In early January 1933 William Rose Benét wrote Stevens that he was planning an *American Auto-Anthology*, which would feature the favorite poems of fifty poets, inviting Stevens to include one. Stevens chose "The Emperor of Ice-Cream" because, he explained, it wore such "a deliberately commonplace costume" and yet contained "something of the essential gaudiness of poetry." He liked it, he said, because in it he had let himself go. "Poems of this sort are the pleasantest on which to look back" because they remained fresher than others "with the least possible manipulation."

In late February he sent Holly a group of postcards from the Big Easy. It was Mardi Gras season, and New Orleans was electric with "dances, feasts, parades en masque and similar galas," which would explode on Fat Tuesday, February 28. By then business would have taken him elsewhere, but already the shop windows on Royal Street were filled with "fantastic costumes, mostly of paper, false faces, streamers, and so on." While he waited to meet with Manning Heard, a New Orleans attorney he had co-opted for the Hartford, Stevens had strolled about the French Quarter, finding it "dilapidated, dank [and] dirty." He'd walked through the black section of the city and found "a very great negro population," one "very much alive, a thing of the present and not like the French Quarter a thing of the past." The place was full of pathos and "equally full of fun," especially a street band performing while children danced. One of the sites he would have come across was the St. Louis Cemetery, the City of the Dead, with its litter stuccoed to the headstones of the dead black population, a stark image which would shortly find its way into his poetry.

When Morton Dauwen Zabel, acting editor at *Poetry*, now that Monroe, approaching seventy, had given Zabel responsibility for the day-to-day operation of the magazine, wrote Stevens that March, asking for some new work, Stevens wrote back that he was unwilling to send *Poetry* some old "unpublished manuscript," and he did not much like his new things. "Writing again after a discontinuance seems to take one back to the beginning rather than to the point of discontinuance," he confessed. And because Harriet Monroe had always been friendly, he wanted to send fresh work good enough for the magazine. The probability of doing that, however, still lay some months off. But he wanted to send Zabel something, especially as Zabel had written a review of the second edition of *Harmonium* for *Poetry* a year earlier, a piece Stevens had found "uncommonly sensitive and intelligent."

"Since Stevens has passed now safely beyond the need of any comparison with his contemporaries," Zabel had written in his review, he wanted to note "that the 'modern' devices" which now appeared to be "the trickery of a topical vaudeville" had in fact "proceeded from an interior vision and necessity." But Stevens's style was not in fact "an expression for ideas of no given date, of which he remains in many cases our only exact recorder." His poetry had created a much needed balance between the poles of lexical plentitude and starkness, where, "between indulgence and austerity," the two had been harmonized: "bravado and terror disciplined in fortitude, and . . . chaos and rectitude reconciled in order." Munson, Zabel explained, had not helped readers understand what Stevens was about by calling him a self-contented dandy. Dandyism, after all, was a "style without significant motive or conviction," and contentment merely implied a "resigned will." For Stevens, however, order was something the imagination necessarily created out of chaos with patience and stoicism, without succumbing to a chic cynicism. If poetry was the supreme fiction, it still remained for Stevens that and that only: a fiction which, try as it might, could never quite evade "the strict austerity / Of one vast, subjugating, final tone."

On the surface of things, Blackmur explained the following year in his essay, there did seem to be a preciousness to Stevens's language in his use of words "uncommon in English poetry." He catalogued nineteen such examples from *Harmonium: fubbed, girandoles, curlicues, catarrhs, gobbet, diaphanes, clopping, minuscule, pipping, panicles, carked, ructive, rapey, cantilene, buffo, fiscs, phylactery, princox*, and—most deliberately—*funest*. Such words had given Stevens "a bad reputation among those who dislike the finicky, and a high one, unfortunately, among those who value the ornamental sounds of words but who see no purpose in developing sound from sense."

But both classes of readers were wrong. "Not a word listed above is used preciously," Blackmur insisted, "not one was chosen as an elegant substitute for a plain term; each, in its context, was a word definitely meant." Stevens gave abstract statements "a concrete, sensual force," turning an idea or a conviction "into a feeling which did not exist, even in his own mind, until he had put it down in words." Stevens's real circle of philosopher-poets included Pound and Eliot as well as Milton and the great romantics. By extension, E. E. Cummings was a mere shadow of a poet, while Blackmur did not even deign to mention Williams, Moore, or Hart Crane.

By the mid-1930s, then, Stevens had been offered a place at the high table of the Academy. But he would also come to find Blackmur and other critics like him unnecessarily prolix. In a letter to a young Cuban friend, José Rodríguez Feo, who would play a significant role in Stevens's literary life a decade later, he would confess that, while he found Blackmur intelligent and much superior to someone like Yvor Winters, Blackmur still had one serious defect, and that was that it took him "twenty-five pages to say what would be much better said if said in one," so that after one had read twenty-five pages of Blackmur's, one didn't have "the faintest idea what he has been talking about." And what ideas, if any, could one identify as actually Blackmur's? He would tell Feo this in confidence, in part, perhaps, because Blackmur had smiled favorably on him.

• • •

IN MAY 1933 STEVENS updated Jim Powers on the house he'd bought, enclosing a photo of the place. "It seems to be rather like your own," except of course, he wrote, tongue in cheek, that his own was "much handsomer." Westerly Terrace was "situated on one of the slopes of Prospect Hill," and the declivity behind his house ran "towards a public dump surrounded by Jews, and Jewesses," he noted with the characteristic casualness of the times. That fact would find its way into one of his finest poems of the Depression era, "The Man on the Dump." Buying the house had been one of the best things he'd ever done. Yes, it was expensive, but that prevented him from throwing his money away "on unimportant things" or, for that matter, throwing it away on anything.

Then too, because of the Depression, there were

> so many burglars and bums about that instead of living in a neighborhood that is poorly lighted, the neighborhood is in reality brilliantly lighted. People actually go to bed leaving lights burning all over the house in order to fool the bums. . . . Holly and Mrs. Stevens have been trained, in the event of a break, to offer to make breakfast and show any visitors round, whether I am absent or not. I am afraid that, if I hear burglars in the house, no one will be able to determine whether I am absent or not.

The trouble was nationwide, of course, so that, when he and Judge Powell had made their annual visit to Key West that winter, they'd found things "so low down there" that even the Depression made no difference.

That summer Stevens went to New York to take Jim and Margaret Powers out on the town. By then the Powerses were living on the West Coast, each summer coming east for a week or so, when Stevens made sure to see them. Jim, after all, was "his boy," the young lawyer he'd taken under his wing, and he enjoyed Margaret's company just as much. Half a century later Margaret would remember the first time she ever met Stevens. That was in 1929; she and Jim had been married two months when Stevens came over to their place to "see what kind of a person that boy of his had married." When Stevens arrived, Jim was in the shower, so she had to meet Stevens herself. "There I was, this little girl absolutely in awe" of the man who had written *Harmonium*.

> I thought, Oh, my lord—I'm as intellectual as the *Reader's Digest*. Well, he realized the situation, so what did that darling person do but just have me rolling on the floor telling me about somebody's funeral. It sounds

> blasphemous, but he made it so funny. When Jim came out, I was just madly in love with Wallace Stevens. He certainly put me at ease, and I enjoyed him ever since. . . . How considerate to understand that here was a young girl absolutely green.

Stevens and Jim took care of business in New York and afterward met Margaret for dinner. First they went to a couple of upscale speakeasies where Stevens was known, and then to dinner, where he got the woman singer to play "La Paloma," tipping her handsomely to sing of a girl down in Cuba:

When I left Havana nobody saw me go
But my little gaucho maid who loves me so.

Though it was nearly midnight, Stevens took the couple to the new, ultra-chic art deco Starlight Roof atop the Waldorf Astoria, New York's first skyscraper hotel with a retractable roof that opened onto the stars. Soon Stevens was asking Margaret to dance. He "was doggone good," she remembered. He had "a wonderful sense of rhythm" and seemed "to enjoy it thoroughly, and that was a new experience for him. . . . It was an impetuous evening." He loved "doing things that he'd never done before." "He kissed me—the only time in his life—he wasn't that type. I understood the evening and what it meant to all of us," though when he turned the evening into a poem, she had to admit she couldn't follow him as she had on the dance floor.

"Melodious skeletons, for all of last night's music," he would recall in a "A Fish-Scale Sunrise," the bittersweet aftertaste, knowing that too was now no more than a memory still clinging to him, and the new day, with its fish-scale clouds hiding the sun, portending rain and more rain, when "today is today and the dancing is done." Then he named them: "You Jim and you Margaret and you singer of La Paloma." He wrote the poem in couplets, the first line dancing outward as in a waltz under a starlit sky, followed by a short, heavy line bringing the dreamer back to things as they are:

my mind perceives the force behind the moment,
The mind is smaller than the eye.

The sun rises green and blue in the fields and in the heavens.
The clouds foretell a swampy rain.

• • •

WHEN THE YOUNG POET Louis Zukofsky decided that year to publish a volume of William Carlos Williams's *Collected Poems* from 1921 to 1931 for his Objectivist Press (five hundred copies at $2 each), he asked Williams who he wanted to write the preface. Stevens, Williams told him, for personal as well as for professional reasons, for they had known each other for twenty years. Stevens agreed, and that November wrote something he must have thought Williams would surely like.

First of all, he began, Bill Williams, now fifty, was still a romantic, though calling him that would no doubt horrify him. A romantic in the accepted sense, yes, but even more, someone who had "spent his life in rejecting the accepted idea of things as they were." Yes, Williams had his sentimental side, but it was his acute reaction to that which so vitalized his work. He had a passion for the antipoetic that kept him sane because it kept him grounded in reality, and real poetry was the result of a constant tension between the sentimental and seeing things as they were. The romantic in 1933 was the one who dwelt in an ivory tower but who insisted "that life there would be intolerable except for the fact that one has, from the top, such an exceptional view of the public dump and the advertising signs of Snider's Catsup, Ivory Soap and Chevrolet Cars"—in other words, the "hermit who dwells alone with the sun and moon, but insists on taking a rotten newspaper." Williams was like Lessing's Laocoön: "the realist struggling to escape from the serpents of the unreal." But if Williams was our Laocoön, he was also our Diogenes of contemporary poetry, seeking to discover the truth inherent in the poem.

Williams was initially happy to have Stevens's preface, but in time he became more and more unhappy with Stevens's depiction of him as the antipoet. Fifteen years later Williams would confess that he was "sick of the constant aping of the Stevens' dictum that I resort to the antipoetic as a heightening device," even though it was Williams who had described himself in just those terms as far back as *Spring & All*, ten years before Stevens had ever thought to use the term. Poetry and prose were not antithetical to one another, Williams had insisted there, but were part of the same matrix out of which language was generated, with poetry antedating prose by God knew how many centuries. The fact that the common vulgate might come from below Fourteenth Street was no more of a problem for the poet than that Dante's language and Eliot's footnotes came from the other end of town. But of course Stevens was speaking of the tension between the real and the imagined in his own poetry as much as he was describing what Williams was up to.

On February 8, 1934, Stevens attended the world premier of Gertrude Stein's comic opera *Four Saints in Three Acts*, with music by Virgil Thomson, at the Avery Memorial in Hartford. While the opera was an "elaborate bit of perversity in every respect: text, settings, choreography," Stevens told Harriet Monroe, "it is most agreeable musically, so that, if one excludes aesthetic self-consciousness from one's attitude, the opera immediately becomes a delicate and joyous work all round." Still, he'd had to put up with "numerous asses of the first water in the audience" that evening, New York having sent a train load of them up to Hartford. By asses he meant people "who walked round with cigarette holders a foot long, and so on." Bryher too had been in the audience that evening, though he hadn't known that at the time, tied up as he'd been "with some pretty awful people. But she sent me a note," he added, "which it was delightful to have."

Two weeks later he was back in Key West. One morning after breakfast he and Judge Powell left the grounds of the Casa Marina and strolled about downtown. Off in the distance to the south lay Cuba, Havana rife just now with strikes, a reminder of why the USS *Wyoming* lay at anchor off the beachfront, which meant that crowds of sailors filled the streets each evening. Because the bars were still off-limits—thanks to Florida's state laws still prohibiting liquor, even though Prohibition had just been repealed—the sailors had been reduced to occupying every ice-cream shop and drug store in Key West, all of them looking like sad "holiday-makers without any definite ideas of how to amuse themselves."

How "old-fashioned and . . . colonial in aspect the town really was," Stevens couldn't help noticing, with what seemed the entire U.S. Navy congregating just outside his hotel room, laughing and talking into the early morning hours.

Still, in spite of Key West's prohibitionary laws, he and the Judge managed an awful lot of drinking. In fact "if the Communists were to destroy the existing state of society," he told Jim Powers that March, "the result would not be any more remarkable than the result of repeal on the speakeasies." As for himself, he'd been on the wagon since returning home from Key West, "very largely because I did not have sense enough to go on before I went." Now that he'd finally been promoted to vice president at the Hartford Accident and Indemnity Company, he would have to act with more propriety. His salary had been raised to $20,000 a year, equivalent to about $350,000 today. And this at a time when many Americans were out of work, searching through trash cans for food.

That June Stevens was approached by a certain Martin Jay, requesting some poems for a classy, new poetry quarterly to be called *Alcestis*. Intrigued by the idea, Stevens wrote back to say that what Jay had in mind was "wildly needed," provided he "could keep it alive" and "vigorous." In time he sent Jay—who by then had morphed himself into J. Ronald Latimer—eight poems for the magazine's inaugural issue: "The Idea of Order at Key West," "Lions in Sweden," "Evening without Angels," "Nudity at the Capital," "Nudity in the Colonies," "A Fish-Scale Sunrise," "Delightful Evening," and "What They Call Red Cherry Pie." These would be followed by another five in the magazine's second number.

By then Stevens the poet was once more alive and thriving, having in the year and a half since his promotion to vice president written some of his best poems in a decade. At a time when poetry had become a luxury for many, he found himself in good company with the younger generation Latimer had gathered, which included Robert Fitzgerald, John Peale Bishop, Herbert Read, Foster Damon, and Willard Maas, who worked with Latimer on the quarterly. *Poetry* took notice as well, with Morton Zabel commenting in his column that Stevens had appeared in the pages of *Alcestis* "with his best work since his virtual lapse in creative activity ten years ago." Zabel also observed that Latimer himself remained strangely faceless, and even Stevens—who owed Latimer a special debt of gratitude in providing an upscale forum for him to begin publishing again—noted that *Alcestis* did in fact seem "impersonal to the point of constituting a special ambiguity."

None of this, however, concerned Stevens very much. So when Latimer at Alcestis Press approached Stevens with the idea of publishing a book of his new poems, Stevens was enthusiastic. But could he gather together fifty pages that satisfied him? Someone like Williams managed to write "every day or night or both," so that his house had to be filled with manuscripts. But such was not the case with him. Still, after a hiatus of ten years, Stevens was ready to publish another book. But who was this Latimer? Trying to find out who the shape-shifting figure was had proven difficult. "Dear James Albert Mark Jason Ronald Lane Latimer," his assistant, Willard Maas, had addressed him in a letter dated that December, then added, "I leave out the Leippert." James Leippert, it turns out, was the name Latimer had been given at birth. He had graduated from Columbia University in 1932 and lived for a time in Greenwich Village. But over the years he would assume at least half a dozen identities before disappearing somewhere in Asia to become a Buddhist monk.

We know that Latimer/Leippert published two volumes of Stevens's poetry in beautiful limited editions, *Ideas of Order* (1935) and *Owl's Clover* (1936), under the imprint of the Alcestis Press, along with limited editions of books by Williams, Marianne Moore, Allen Tate, Robert Penn Warren, John Peale Bishop, and others. "He was a bisexual avant-gardist living and publishing books in Greenwich Village," the scholar Alan Filreis writes, at the same time "being a semi-secret Communist, while enrolled in a school preparing him for the priesthood upstate, while engaged to a young woman in Albany . . . while corresponding crucially with Stevens and other poets, while running away from certain demons." By gathering up all of his various pseudonyms, Filreis learned that Leippert/Latimer was by turns a "Buddhist in flowing robes in New Mexico, then expatriate in Japan, finally Episcopal priest in Florida (while living with a young man whom he told neighbors was his son—and who might have been his son . . . but doubtful)."

Back in April, Stevens had written to Witter Bynner, who had moved from Santa Fe to Florida and been in contact with Latimer about publishing a volume of Bynner's poems. But Bynner was suspicious about the shape-shifting, elusive Latimer, and told Stevens so. "Dear Bynner," he wrote, "I don't know that Leippert is all that you say he is; I don't know anything at all about him, and don't care." Williams would publish two volumes with Alcestis Press: *An Early Martyr* in 1935 and *Adam & Eve & the City* the following year. He too wondered who this elusive figure really was, writing Stevens in May 1936 about his concerns. "Dear Sherlock Holmes," Stevens wrote back. No doubt there was something strange about the secrecy surrounding Latimer, but that was the way some people were. All Stevens really cared about was acting intelligently (i.e., cautiously) in dealing with the man. "What Latimer is is nothing to me so long as he does not involve me," Stevens told Williams. "It is very easy to say of a man of this sort that he is a slop-over. His letters are full of little nursery turns, but the books that he has published up to now certainly show discipline, whether it is his or his printer's." After all, if he and Williams went along, were they "any worse off than going along with almost anybody else"? In any event, Stevens's most extensive correspondence with anyone during the mid-1930s would be with this phantom editor who intrigued him, but whom he trusted, inasmuch as he trusted anyone.

11

The Idea of Order at Key West: 1934–1936

These voices crying without knowing for what,
Except to be happy, without knowing how.

The first among the poems which Latimer's inaugural issue of *Alcestis* published in October 1934 was "The Idea of Order at Key West." The placement was fitting because that poem was an announcement—and a powerful one—that Stevens had once again found both his voice and his subject; now only death would be strong enough to stop him. It is a threshold piece, with the poet on the shore, the tenuous sands of the known beneath his feet, facing the immense uncharted depths before him. Here is Crispin, come back to face once more the sublime immensity of a sea which had nearly drowned him even as it baptized him into the knowledge of just how little we really know. "She sang beyond the genius of the sea," the poem begins, thus announcing Stevens's reinvigorated muse, and surely not the paltry nude of his earlier verse.

Nature, in the guise of the *genius loci*, the genius or spirit of the place (in this instance the world in and about Key West), contains its own reality, the speaker realizes. But so does the woman, the singer, the poet, the one who would render reality in a language supple enough to contain reality's ever-changing fluctuations. And when she sings, she has the ability to sing *beyond* what the sea is capable of singing. For the sea is like some uncouth giant who makes recurring slapping sounds, slurping sounds, sea sounds, C sounds, much as Crispin the Comedian once heard, even as this speaker understands that humans need something more: a meaning, a music, subtle registers to satisfy the restless mind. And yet a music that somehow contains the real, for without a sense of the real undergirding one—shifting as that foundation may be—one sings mere nonsense, however modulated and beautifully arranged.

Though we speak of it as an entity with a self, the sea is never really that, can never be that. We give it a self, and if a self, a spirit, a ghost, whether we call it Nature or Neptune or Proteus. The truth is that "the water never formed to mind or voice / Like a body wholly body, fluttering / Its empty sleeves." And yet

its mimic motion
Made constant cry, caused constantly a cry
That was not ours although we understood,
Inhuman, of the veritable ocean.

In its mimicry the sea seems to cry out constantly, as if pleading to be understood or at least acknowledged. That cry, that sound of the sea in its various shapes, creates in us a cry as well, as if it called out to us and we answered with our own cry, our own words, the human addressing the inhuman. Nature, not in the sense of harmful or cruel, but simply a thing apart, though we depend on it for our very being.

If we, islands in ourselves, are to provide a meaning for things which can be communicated to other human islands all about us, we will have to use signs of some sort, and these will for the most part entail sounds, and, if sounds, words. Therein lies the difficulty, for the sounds of a song or a poem can never be one with the sounds of water, "even if what she sang was what she heard / Since what she sang was uttered word by word." That is, even if the poet could re-create the sensation of the sea, "the grinding water and the gasping wind," still it would be the poet, the maker, the *makar* we would be hearing, not the sea. Can the poet, no matter how skilled, ever actually embody the real? No more than the element of air can ever embody the element of water. Or human sounds, however modulated, contain the "dark voice of the sea," with its "meaningless plunging of water and wind." Or poems ever be more than "bronze shadows heaped/On high horizons," mere still lifes—*mortes natures*—of the ever-fluent Real.

All poetry is by its nature elegiac, so that it is the song that makes "the sky acutest at its vanishing," that captures an emotion, a feeling, a gesture, a living thought, even as these slip from us and vanish, or remain behind to taunt us with what we have lost. Only the poet, the woman singing, remains as

the single artificer of the world
In which she sang. And when she sang, the sea,
Whatever self it had, became the self
That was her song, for she was the maker. Then we,
As we beheld her striding there alone,
Knew that there never was a world for her
Except the one she sang and, singing, made.

We speak of the world, but there is no world for us except the one we create in our imagination and which is constantly being created—and re-created—only as we sing or write, composing our world even as we attempt to compose ourselves.

In the closing stanza the speaker turns to the one beside him, Ramon Fernandez, the philosopher, and dares him to tell us, if he knows (and he doesn't, any more than the poet finally knows)

Why, when the singing ended and we turned
Toward the town, tell why the glassy lights,
The lights in the fishing boats at anchor there,
As night descended, tilting in the air,
Mastered the night and portioned out the sea,
Fixing emblazoned zones and fiery poles,
Arranging, deepening, enchanting night.

We are witness to an order here, a song sung note by note and word by word by the poet, and now, as we watch the lights on the Lilliputian fishing boats tied up in the harbor, much as the old seamen sought out the stars, forming them into constellations and assigning them myths and stories to try to tame the terror of the dark and the vastness of the sea, we do so by "arranging, deepening, enchanting" what cannot be so ordered except as the capable imagination is able to ward off, for the moment at least, the depths of darkness and death. "Oh! Blessed rage for order, pale Ramon," the speaker ends his meditation, because it is the romantic's one weapon against the encroaching chaos not only without but, more frighteningly, within us, as we keen in ever-keener sounds, crying out for a fiction that will sustain us, at least for now, in

Words of the fragrant portals, dimly-starred,
And of ourselves and of our origins,
In ghostlier demarcations, keener sounds.

What, after all, can the poet offer by way of comfort in the midst of the calamitous 1930s? What song should he play? It is a question central to Stevens's second book of poems, *Ideas of Order*, and the very question he asks in "Mozart, 1935." The speaker here will instruct the poet on music suitable to the exigencies of the times. "Poet, be seated at the piano," the speaker begins, as at that baby grand in his living room at Westerly Terrace, ordering him to

Play the present, its hoo-hoo-hoo,
Its shoo-shoo-shoo, its ric-a-rac,
Its envious cachinnation.

If Stevens has employed a more elevated and ironic stance in his poems up to now, this is not the time for that. It is an issue which the poet will continue to face throughout the decade: how to music the moment when that moment is ugly, unnerving, unsettled, and people merely mock the music the poet has to offer. One hears that laughter in the subhuman nonsense sounds of "hoo-hoo-hoo" and "shoo-shoo-shoo" and "ric-a-rac" and even in the underlying suggestion of the belly laugh in the word *cachinnation*, with its phonic intimations of kaka: shit, *merde*. This is not a poet happy with the political and economic realities of the times, but one who has come to see that he must find a language that speaks to the times. This is an angrier time, a time of winter and snow, when the poet might be targeted as a parasite, and when, even as yet another corpse in rags is carried from some tenement, the poet fears his own house may soon be pelted with stones:

If they throw stones upon the roof
While you practice arpeggios,
It is because they carry down the stairs
A body in rags.
Be seated at the piano.

That lucid souvenir of the past,
The divertimento;
That airy dream of the future,
The unclouded concerto . . .
Strike the piercing chord.

As much as one might want to, this is *not* the time to be practicing Mozartian arpeggios on one's baby grand. Rather it is a time for striking the fatal chord which in turn will strike at the heart, and thou—not you, but thou, *thou*—must be a Shelley for our time, with a voice that embodies a deeper seriousness. Thou must be the voice "of angry fear" and of a "besieging pain," transforming the country's cry of pain into a music consonant with the times, like

the great wind howling,
By which sorrow is released,
Dismissed, absolved
In a starry placating.

Perhaps someday "we may return to Mozart" and the harmonies of youth in a more innocent time. But not now, for "we are old" and "the snow is falling" and—yes—the streets are really "full of cries."

In another poem published in the same number of *Alcestis*, a poem he called "The American Sublime," Stevens asks directly not how one should seat oneself at the piano, but rather how one should stand to "behold the sublime" and—with a jab at Walt Disney's vision of the world as cartoon—confront "the mockers, / the mickey mockers / And plated pairs" (plated pears), with its punning reference to his own "Sunday Morning" and its vision of the sublime twenty years before. Even General Andrew Jackson's and Stonewall Jackson's equestrian statues must succumb to the passage of time with the evidence of birds visible on their bronze figures. Even the idea of the Sublime is subject to the same stresses as everything else, which comes down in the end

To the spirit itself,
The spirit and space,
The empty space.

Given that reality, what heavenly vision, what logos, what sacrament, what center can hold? In a time of hunger and homelessness and world despair, what can the poet with a baby grand piano in a house situated on a terraced street offer us? "What wine does one drink?" the poem ends—not with an answer but a question, followed in turn by another question: "What bread does one eat?"

• • •

POETRY NOT AS LITERATURE, then, but as garbage, litter, without meaning for a desperate people in a desperate time. "If you do not like these," Stevens wrote Zabel at *Poetry* in December 1934 when he sent him a collection of fifty short pieces he titled *Like Decorations in a Nigger Cemetery*, which *Poetry* would publish two months later, "do not hesitate to say so. It is very difficult for me to find the time to write poetry, and most of these have been written on the way to and from the office." The title, he explained, "refers to the litter that one usually finds in a nigger cemetery and is a phrase used by Judge Powell last winter in Key West." It is difficult to gauge the full impact such a title would have had on an American readership in 1935, except to say that it leaves one unnerved and wondering where the poem is going to take us. For a young American Communist like Stanley Burnshaw writing for a magazine like *The New Masses*, the title was so appalling, so racist, that it soured his reading of the entire volume of *Ideas of Order*. For many black readers, it would have been both offensive and a sign of business as usual in white America. For a later writer like the feminist Adrienne Rich, the title represented everything that was wrong with the poetry of the white male patriarchy that dominated her growing up in post–World War II America.

But for Judge Powell of Atlanta, it simply described the litter and trinkets and graffiti he and Stevens saw as they passed a fenced-in enclosure in Key West in February 1934. "I explained," Judge Powell remembered, "that I thought the fence enclosed a graveyard, as some of the rubbish looked 'like decorations in a nigger cemetery.' [Stevens] was interested when I explained the custom of negroes to decorate graves with broken pieces of glass, old pots, broken pieces of furniture, dolls' heads, and what not." The poem itself was therefore "an olio, and the title . . . fitting."

In fact, cindery as it tastes, there is a sense in which, given the bleaker realities of American culture, the idea behind the title—if not the words—fits the subject, for by it Stevens tells us that even poems and philosophical aperçus and maxims crumble finally to the same level as those shards of decorations in an overlooked cemetery, for beneath whatever vitality those gauds might represent, the fact of death and annihilation awaits everyone. The cemetery, the final resting place of the poor and the rich, reminds us of the essential poverty death bestows on everyone, in much the same way "The Emperor of Ice-Cream," another Key West poem written ten years earlier, did.

Like so many of his poems, this one is about death, and what death reminds us of is the importance of living as fully as we can. It's a fall poem, really, one approaching the final winter, and Stevens will evoke that fall season again and again, even though it begins with a contretemps evoking the passing of Walt Whitman. "In the far South" an autumnal sun is "passing / Like Walt Whitman walking along a ruddy shore." But Whitman was the spokesman—at least in the years leading up to the Civil War—of a more optimistic phase of America, as he strolled the ruddy shore, singing of a world in which "nothing is final," where "no man shall see the end." Whitman as the poet-prophet full of the present, the phallic poet whose "beard is of fire and his staff is a leaping flame." But this initial vision of hope is undercut as quickly as it was evoked, replaced by a weary singer who sings among the oaks of Hartford and yet who, even with such dark harbingers as the Nazi rise to power, pines for a better time. "Sigh for me, night wind," he pleads,

In the noisy leaves of the oak.
I am tired. Sleep for me, heaven over the hill.
Shout for me, loudly and loudly, joyful sun, when you rise.

The setting of the poem is November, with—as Stevens had said of Williams's *Collected Poems, 1921–1931*—the unmistakable scent of aged tobacco in the air. With the foliage stripped and the bare skeletons of the trees again visible, their blackness has become apparent, and one sees for oneself the disorder at "the base of design." Three stanzas which lie half-hidden in the underbrush of the poem—XVII, XVIII, and XIX—evoke the current situation, with the Japanese incursions into China and the Far East and the rise of the Third Reich as destroyers with a new set of directives to "avoid the museums," that is, a more comprehensible way of dealing with those who would oppose the New Order. "The sun of Asia creeps above the horizon," Stevens writes, evoking the symbol of Japan's rising sun, "into this haggard and tenuous air," and the operatic precision drill of Nazis saluting the Führer on parade is evoked in the Wagnerian image of a new Götterdämmerung:

An opening of portals when night ends,
A running forward, arms stretched out as drilled.
Act I, Scene I, at a German Staats-Oper.

At the heart of the poem lies the image of a shattered mirror, a cubist portrait of the artist at fifty-five, a figure consisting merely of the fragments of a self: an idea of order that accumulates by one's dwelling in a place, a self assembled from the scraps of maxims, aperçus, newspaper clippings, newsreel images, radio reports, opera on the radio juxtaposed with the parade music of Hitler's marching armies, a self assembled from the memories of a failed marriage and the poet's incessant search for a language that might adequately reflect the times. Not summer, then, not even the images of a summer painted by Corot when that summer has gone, nor the comforts of human contact nor even the comfort of escaping human contact. If this poem is a sequence, it is a sequence of sausage links, reminding us repeatedly that the "union of the weakest," as with a mob or an army, "develops strength, not wisdom." Leaders like that business associate who talks the talk but fails to produce results: that hen-cock, as Judge Powell once put it, who "crows at midnight and lays no egg." Or those "iron dogs and iron deer" Stevens passes each day on the way to his office: the Hartford landscape of 1935, which will have to suffice now that the English landscapes of Constable are gone.

And yet, is not poetry, that "finikin thing of air / That lives uncertainly and not for long," far more radiant than those "much lustier blurs" of a thousand billboards and advertizing slogans? What is there to say, then? What to do? Is it not the case that "if ever the search for a tranquil belief should end," or the future stop "emerging out of the past," a past so full of ourselves, then there would be no direction or even illusion that we needed a direction. And yet is it not our fate that one's "search / And the future emerging out of us seem to be one"? Notes, then, scraps not unlike those fragments Eliot needed to shore against his own ruins in the midst of his journey through the wasteland. And yet might there not also be discovered a few purple scraps for a purple bird, the royal one, "notes for his comfort that he may repeat / Through the gross tedium of being rare"? Might it not even be possible at some point to compose notes which might reach toward some supreme fiction, notes to sustain one if one ever hoped to behold Hartford in a purple light?

• • •

"YESTERDAY I PUT ON ear muffs," he told Latimer in mid-December, as he searched for the fragments he might quilt together into his second book of poems, his first in a dozen years. Then he wrapped himself "in a blanket, and spent several hours in the attic," where he searched for whatever reliquiae he could find to fill out the book's pages. Then, "after returning downstairs and thawing out, I put together everything that I have, and I think that it will not make more than 35 pages, which could be expanded very easily by set-up to about 40." He'd made "a tentative arrangement of the material," only to discover that "the tone of the whole" was still "a bit low and colorless." And since the book's tone would be most important, he wanted to add another "10 or 15 pages, in order to give it a little gaiety and brightness." After all, his mind was "not ordinarily as lamentable as some of the poems suggested." But then, if one did not write poetry constantly, it tended to become "cheerless to anyone except the poet." With a little time, however, he could change all that.

A month later he followed up with a progress report. "I sit down every evening after dinner," he wrote Latimer on January 8, 1935, and, "after a little music, put my forefinger in the middle of my forehead and struggle with my imagination." The other night, for instance, he'd taken it into his head "to describe a deathbed farewell under the new regime. And I am bound to say that I liked the result immensely for the moment. So you see what happens when one tries to pump up floods of color." To write poetry one needed an impetus, and that meant "one had to be a poet constantly." It had been "a great loss to poetry when people began to think that the professional poet was an outlaw or an exile," for while poems sometimes happened, it was better that they were caused. "If all this is true," he added, "then it may be that in a few weeks time my imagination will be such a furnace that I can stroll home from the office and fill the house with the most iridescent notes while I am brushing my hair, say, or changing to the slippers that are so appropriate to the proper enjoyment of Beethoven and Brahms on the gramophone."

Shortly after, he sent Latimer three lines for his eyes only, lines which could never be included even in so bleak a book as the one he was composing. The little poem was called "The Widow":

The cold wife lay with her husband after his death,
His ashen reliquiae contained in gold
Under her pillow, on which he had never slept.

"Reliquiae": the remains of what was once a man contained in a golden text, not unlike Yeats's golden nightingale or Mallarmé's golden text, words that would come in time to replace the living man himself.

• • •

BY MID-FEBRUARY HE WAS back in that haven, Key West, enjoying the sun and the martinis at the Casa Marina with Judge Powell, the man to whom he'd dedicated "Decorations," one of only two poems he would ever dedicate to anyone, excepting of course his early verses to Elsie. It was from there that he wrote an old friend and lawyer colleague, Phil May, up in Jacksonville, on the 21st: "Many thanks for everything, except God, who seems a nuisance from the point of view of Key West." But even Key West was losing its old charm. After all, who wanted "to share green cocoanut ice cream with these strange monsters who snooze in the porches of this once forlorn hotel," now filled with noisy strangers? With a wink he added, "It is unnecessary to say that we are patterns of propriety."

A few days later he wrote Elsie to bring her up to date on his perambulations: the sun was hot; in spite of which he and the Judge had "walked up the boulevard, returning about eleven. From then until lunch time, one o'clock, I loafed on the dock and beach, sunning myself." That morning he'd spotted the two-time Pulitzer Prize winner Robert Frost walking along the beach. It was Frost's first visit to Key West, though he too would find a rustic cabin by the sea and become a regular at Key West in the years to come. Stevens presented him with a bag of sapodillas, a sweet tropical fruit he had come to love, and then invited the poet to sup with him and Powell on conch chowder.

But before the chowder Stevens and the Judge hosted a cocktail party, where—to Frost's horror and amusement—Stevens downed a few too many martinis. "The cocktail party," Stevens would recall, "along with the dinner with Frost, and several other things became all mixed up, and I imagine that Frost has been purifying himself by various exorcisms ever since." It was the first time he'd actually met Frost, and he'd taken the occasion to argue over the right way to write poetry, with Frost complaining that he didn't like Stevens's poetry very much because it purported to make him think, and later telling an audience at the University of Miami about Mr. Stevens's abysmal behavior.

Seated behind his desk at the Hartford amid stacks of claims reports early that March, Stevens wrote Frost, saying that a copy of the first edition of *Harmonium* was on its way to him, as well as a Latin dictionary so that Frost could "look up such things as *lotus eaters*, and so on," the knowledge of which he thought Frost might benefit by. After commenting on the weather, he added a farming metaphor he thought Frost might like: "But the grass is coming through, matted down like the hair on a horse that has been in the stable too long." The early end of March: "that special season" in Connecticut Stevens had come to look for, that brief moment "after winter and before spring."

Eventually word got back to Stevens of Frost's gossip about that evening, and Frost in turn wrote Stevens to apologize. He'd meant only to be playful in his remarks, he explained, and treasured the memory of their meeting, at the same time ribbing Stevens that he had been in a better condition than Stevens to appreciate that night. Nor did he see any real conflict about their contrary views about what a poem should be. It had all amounted, simply, to "the prettiest kind of stand-off." Besides, wasn't it true that he and the Judge and Stevens all liked one another and that he and Stevens really did like each other's work? "At least," he explained, "down underneath I suspect we do. We should. We must. If I'm somewhat academic (I'm more agricultural) and you are somewhat executive, so much the better: it is so we are saved from being literary and deployers of words derived from words."

• • •

THAT MARCH STEVENS SENT Latimer a new poem for the collection Alcestis Press would bring out in four months' time, telling Latimer that the title for the collection he'd decided on was *Ideas of Order.* He had also decided that the book should open with the new poem he was sending, which he called "Sailing after Lunch." Perhaps, he explained, the poem meant more to him than it should, being "an abridgment of at least a temporary theory of poetry." Most people took the word *romantic* pejoratively. But poetry by its very nature was "essentially romantic," and the romantic was an idea that was constantly renewing itself and so "just the opposite of what is spoken of as the romantic." Without this new and vitalized "sense of the romantic," one got nowhere. With it, even "the most casual things" took on transcendence, "and the poet rushes brightly, and so on."

But how did one keep company with the great romantics in an unpropitious time like the present, he wondered. And so the poem tries—and seems to fail—even to get under way. "It is the word pejorative that hurts," the poet laments, being, after all, "a most inappropriate man / In a most unpropitious place." The false romantic was like an old sailing boat in a time of oil-powered ships, its "heavy historical sail" trying to make headway "through the mustiest blue of the lake / In a really vertiginous boat," the whole endeavor "the vapidest fake." But the true romantic had always to be pressing ahead, sailing into uncharted waters, for there was no going back, no copying of the great masters like Shelley or Wordsworth or Keats or Whitman or, more specifically, that American transcendentalist Emerson. It was a matter of feeling, then, to be able to say, and say convincingly, that poetry was a matter of expunging all people and becoming instead a pupil

Of the gorgeous wheel and so to give
That slight transcendence to the dirty sail,
By light, the way one feels, sharp white,
And then rush brightly through the summer air.

The poem was a send-up, really, a mimicking and mocking of the Emersonian transcendent eye, expunging all connection with the human race and becoming instead a pupil (a student, yes, but also the pupil of the eye), which might provide not a transcendent vision but merely a "slight transcendence": what Williams would call a grasshopper transcendence—up, up, and then back to earth again—that momentary feeling of "sharp white," as in Shelley's vision of unrefracted light, all colors merging into one, gaining sail and rushing "brightly through the summer air." The trouble here is that the Sleight-of-Hand Man has fumbled his pack of words, and—as the stage light shines on him—one sees that the too happy ending was just that: a grand romantic finale willed, but convincing no one, including Stevens himself. Which helps explain why, when Stevens published *Ideas of Order* with Knopf in a trade edition in the fall of 1936, he added a new overture to the volume, one that was plangent, determined, and inconsolable.

That spring T. C. Wilson, associate editor of *Life and Letters Today,* wrote Stevens, asking if he would be interested in reviewing the *Selected Poems* of Marianne Moore. Stevens replied enthusiastically, saying that for him Moore was a real poet, "not only a complete disintegrator," but "an equally complete reintegrator," a poet, if the truth be told, whose poems were "a good deal more important than what Williams does," because Williams represented an "exhausted phase of the romantic," whose major attraction was its form. Moore, on the other hand, represented a new phase of the romantic, whose break with the more traditional forms was in fact "an attempt to free herself for the pursuit of the thing in which she is interested: a vision of what a fresh romanticism might look and sound like." Three months later he sent Wilson his essay review, "A Poet That Matters," inviting him to send it on to Moore herself. He'd written the review simply because he'd wanted to, and he didn't care whether it was "published in Atlanta or London or nowhere."

Moore's was a scrupulous spirit, an "unaffected, witty, colloquial sort of spirit." He had gone over Moore's syllabic-verse poem "The Fish," noting the subtlety of the rhymes embedded in her fastidious prose-like lines: a rhyming couplet, for instance, that ran "all/external," and a second rhyming couplet which followed just after: "marks of abuse are present on this / defiant edifice." What she produced out of her catalogues of things were poems which were "simple, radiant with imagination, contemporaneous, displaying everywhere her sensitive handling," and revealing that she—like himself—was a real romantic. Moreover she knew how to hybridize things so that they generated a new and imaginative reality. The old sense of the romantic had meant filling one's lines with "garden furniture or colonial lingerie." Hers, on the other hand, revealed "an uncommon intelligence," which, in a time of violent feelings like the present, could respond with "equally violent feelings." The truth was that she was after the same things he was, which was to think hard "about people and about poetry, and the truth," and this she had done "with all the energy of an intense mind and imagination."

That July Latimer published *Ideas of Order* in a limited edition of 165 copies, each signed by Stevens. It cost $7.50 a copy (about $130 in today's dollars). A number of notices and reviews were enthusiastic, happy that Stevens was writing again. Then there was the *New Masses*, the official news medium for the American Communist Party. Latimer, himself a strong Leftist if not a member of the Party, had sent the *New Masses* a copy, and the young Stanley Burnshaw had been assigned the job of reviewing it. Initially Stevens—a Hoover Republican—was intrigued by the idea, telling Latimer that "merely finding myself in that *milieu* was an extraordinarily stimulating thing."

But it was not a good match. "To many readers it is something of a miracle that Stevens has at all bothered to give us his *Ideas of Order*," Burnshaw began. "When *Harmonium* appeared a dozen years ago Stevens was at once set down as an incomparable verbal musician." But, then, nobody had ever asked if Stevens actually had any ideas, Burnshaw believed. Only one idea wove its way through the book, which was this: that "the one reality / In this imagined world" was the imagination itself.

Ideas of Order was actually nothing more than "the record of a man who, having lost his footing, now scrambles to stand up and keep his balance," a man desperately in search of escaping from the current political and economic realities of the world. But trying to escape from the realities Marx had revealed was in itself a bitter irony. What Stevens did was two-faced, speculating one moment "on the wisdom of turning inward," and in the next blaming mankind for being "the guilty bungler of harmonious life" in this, his "peanut parody for a peanut people." What was needed now, according to Burnshaw, was "a valid Idea of Order," and that would mean nothing less than Stevens' remaking himself to address the issues of the times.

So there it was, the thing Stevens feared most: being called out as the most inept because he was the most outdated of romantics. Burnshaw's review held a benzene-bright lamp steadily on Stevens's more vulnerable public side, a side he preferred to keep as private as he could. The upshot was that he would spend the following months dismissing Burnshaw, even as he searched more deeply into the political and social realities Burnshaw had pointed out.

In fact Stevens was already working on a twenty-five-page poem meant to address some of the problems of the present, which he would call "Owl's Clover." To the poem he now added a new section, called "Mr. Burnshaw and the Statue," with Burnshaw representing the appeal to politics and the Statue standing in for art. Stevens's argument, essentially, was that all movements, political and aesthetic, either destroyed themselves or were destroyed. Among the images which reveal how much Stevens overreacted to Burnshaw and the Communists—those faux romantic prophets—was his take on Keats's solitary urn morphed into "a trash can at the end of the world," where "the dead / Give up dead things and the living turn away."

Years before, another new romantic, the late Hart Crane, had used Charlie Chaplin's image of a moonlit trash can with a helpless kitten in it as a modern image for the Holy Grail. But Stevens's image provides one with a sense of hopelessness in the face of a world suffering from depression. "I hope I am headed left," Stevens wrote Latimer defensively, "but there are lefts and lefts, and certainly I am not headed for the ghastly left of *Masses*." After all, were the well-off really so well off as Burnshaw painted them? Conversely, were the poor really as poor as he made them out to be? What whiners the *Masses* crew were!

On the other hand, Stevens had to admit that he had come to see his earlier poetry as merely decorative, a time when imagism and "pure poetry" did appeal to him. He still liked that sort of thing, but we lived in a different time now, and actual life was a good deal more important than it had seemed to him then. Once he had thought that literature meant the most, and in some ways it still did. But he had also come to see that life itself was "the essential part of literature." Here in Hartford people spoke of his poems as the work of an esthete, a term he disliked as much as "decorative" and "formal." But he was certain that he never did the same thing for long, and it was ridiculous to speak of his poems as not having ideas. Still, people were going to have it their way no matter what he said. The truth was that "the real world seen by an imaginative man" might "very well seem like an imaginative construction."

If Burnshaw insisted on viewing *Ideas of Order* through a Communist lens, Stevens countered by offering the point of view of the poet to the world order proposed by Communism. After all, Stevens was a poet first, concerned with writing poems, not ideological tracts. The other night he'd read a poem by Sir James Frazer, author of *The Golden Bough*, in which Frazer had called Mussolini "a dirty dog." What Frazer, who was certainly no poet, had written was merely your "typical poem of ideas." And though he himself was pro-Mussolini, he could understand why a philosopher like Frazer would want to try his hand at a poetic condemnation of Mussolini. Perhaps it was the poet as philosopher who could best represent the idea of what the poet should be. The trouble was that his own ideas were never "permanently fixed," so that even his idea of what a poet should be and do was constantly changing and growing. That was the problem of adequately writing about a figure like Mussolini, who was also evolving. As for Mussolini's invasion of Ethiopia, he was all for it, because Italian culture was far superior to the culture of Ethiopia. "The Italians," he added with a racist, straight-faced irony, had "as much right to take Ethiopia from the coons as the coons had to take it from the boa-constrictors."

What then was the place of the poet in society? Poetry should be understood as an activity of the mind equal to and even greater than philosophy, Stevens argued, because poetry could offer the keenest minds and most searching spirits something only it could give. A dozen years before, *The Comedian as the Letter C* had attempted to address the basic questions of how to live and what to do, but that poem had moved, finally, into the realm of silence. With a poem like "Mozart, 1935," he had returned to those earlier questions, though he admitted he had made only modest inroads. In "Owl's Clover" he hoped to address the larger philosophical and political issues more fully, and to do that he would have to address the issue of what the figure of the new romantic poet should look like. That meant Shelley redux, armed to the teeth with poetic insights to confront a world in which so many Americans were without work and where Communism, Fascism, Nazism, and the imperial aggrandizements of Japan were among the serpents hiding in the bushes of one's reimagined Eden.

He'd recently read an essay by Howard Baker in the *Southern Quarterly* on what his, Stevens's, poetry had to offer and found it the best analysis he'd yet found. But even Baker had missed the point. "If I could create an actuality," Stevens confessed, "it would be quite a different world . . . from the world about us." But trying to explain this would mean killing the idea itself, because it would involve different egos in the argument, and all egos made a point of being antipathetic. For the world he envisioned, the poet would have to serve as the "Metropolitan Rabbi." The truth was that what he believed the world could finally yield was nothing less than a freshening of life itself, and that vision had not even begun to be realized.

"I took a look at *Ideas of Order* the other night," he wrote Latimer in mid-November, "to see whether there was any single poem in it that I preferred to all the others." If there was, it seemed to be "How to Live, What to Do," because it so definitely represented his way of thinking. Crispin, finally, had turned out to be little more than a "profitless philosopher" who had picked "his way in a haphazard manner through a mass of irrelevancies." Life for Crispin had been a mere throw of the dice, a matter of chance, so that all he could hope for was to make his life as pleasant as he could in the time he had left. That definition best described the Stevens of 1922. But 1935 was an entirely different time and in "The Idea of Order at Key West" life had "ceased to be a matter of chance." The question now—as everyone from Franco to Mussolini to Hitler to FDR was discovering or imagining—was what shape the new order should take.

In spite of what the critics said, he had never believed that life was a mass of irrelevancies, nor did he believe that everyone could introduce his own order as part of a general order. The question rather was what the poet could offer that the public would be willing to accept. One way to do that would be to sift through his own poetry to see if he could find an idea of order in that. Were we really nothing more than "biological mechanisms," predetermined to feel and act and think according to our material makeup only? Possibly. If so, that would mean returning to his origins to discover who he really was.

"We give our good qualities to God, or to various gods," Stevens explained in yet another letter to Latimer. But the truth was that those qualities came from within us, so that, "instead of crying for help to God or to one of the gods, we should look to ourselves for help." Better to exalt human nature than abase it, he insisted, which was why the instinct for joy was at the heart of the matter. If that was true in life, it was "infinitely more true in poetry and painting, and much more easy to realize there." What was it that defined our earliest sense of ourselves? "For me," he explained, "it means my surroundings, not necessarily natural surroundings." Take Crispin, for example. It had been hard "to say what would have happened to Crispin in contact with men and women, not to speak of the present-day unemployed," but it probably would have resulted in catastrophe. After all, life should be understood as "an affair of people not of places." But for Stevens, it had been "an affair of places and that [was] the problem."

Which brought him back to what he'd said about Mussolini and Ethiopia. For while he'd "spoken sympathetically of Mussolini," he explained, "all of my sympathies are the other way: with the coons and the boa-constrictors." Should he "have sympathized with the Indians as against the Colonists in this country? A man would have to be very thick-skinned not to be conscious of the pathos of Ethiopia or [the Japanese invasion of] China, or one of these days, if we are not careful, of this country. But that Mussolini is right, practically, has certainly a great deal to be said for it." Still, Fascism itself was merely one more form of political disillusionment like everything else these days. It was certainly not a necessary "stage in the evolution of the state," but merely one more "transitional phase." And yet, he believed, Mussolini's Italy and Franco's Spain would be suffering vastly more now under any other political system he could think of.

The real trouble with poetry was that not even poets had any idea just how important it was for living a fuller life, for "life without poetry" was, "in effect, life without a sanction." What made a poem successful was its "accuracy of conception or of expression," both of which were subject to change. Poetry was like the stock market, in that both were subject to innumerable influences. Still, there was no reason why the poet "should not exist now, notwithstanding the complexity of contemporary life." Consider Milton's "extraordinary existence" in a time of political upheaval.

If the author of *Paradise Lost* could do it, why not the poet of today? The major difference now, of course, would be that, "instead of going off on a myth," the poet "would stick to the facts."

As for order, he was always "orderly about my room, my office, and so on." But that was not the same thing as the various orders spoken of in *Ideas of Order.* Or was it? Take the Dutch painters and the predominance of the square in their work, what one scholar had "attributed to the flatness of the country and its linear effect." Was that really such a farfetched idea? Dutch painting did seem to be based on squares, just as Italian painting seemed to be "based on circles, or, at least, on something else than squares." But then, just recently, he'd come across the phrase "man's passionate disorder," and now he was as much interested in that idea as he had earlier been in the idea of order.

Did he contradict himself? Very well then, he contradicted himself. If just now mankind was interested in eliminating the old political and social orders, those were going to have to be replaced by other orders, whether those were purely military, as in Japan, or messy, as in New York. Whatever the future held, there would have to be an order of some kind if we were to survive. "One of the first things I do when I get home at night is to make people take things off the radiator tops," he told Latimer. On the other hand, his thirteen-year-old daughter seemed to favor disorder, which was evident from the magazines she read, the stamps in her collection, and her correspondence "with unknown people about unknown things." When the mail came, she would tear the wrappers off, discarding the scraps wherever she happened to be standing. Of course all sorts of people did things like that and had ideas which were just as messy. But enough theorizing: what was needed just now was a little applejack. And with that he signed off.

Latimer peppered him with questions. Why did Stevens prefer a Latinate to a Teutonic vocabulary? Stevens didn't know, really, though he wasn't about to fast at Christmastime in order to find out. In any event, the language of poetry was never Teutonic, not even, if one thought about it, the language of German poetry itself.

Was art meant to teach as well as give pleasure? There were those who considered his poems didactic, Stevens confessed, though he had not meant them to be. But he did have a penchant for abstraction, which could look didactic. His own early forays into imagism had been a mild rebellion against the didacticism of Victorian poetry. But did one now abandon images in order to write the new didactic poetry demanded by the times? Was it really necessary to choose one over the other? Poetry needed images—sensuous images, really—but there must also be a certain amount of didacticism as well. The issue was complicated, otherwise "life and poetry and everything else would be a bore." In any event you did not end a poem by adding a phrase "meant to be the last word in a job of seduction." In fact unpalatable endings were often the most palatable.

• • •

THREE WEEKS BEFORE LEAVING for Key West in mid-February 1936, Stevens wrote Phil May in Jacksonville to tell him that his doctor had put him on a strict diet, which meant that he would not be drinking down there. It also meant that, when he passed through Jacksonville on his way home, his newfound sobriety would put out of the question those theological issues which always arose after a couple of Scotches. In fact the reason he'd lately become a tea aficionado was that Elsie had forbade his drinking at home, especially now that their daughter was a teenager.

Yes, he supposed his sobriety would make him look like some pathetic cripple, which meant no more "hell raising," something that was going to be harder on Judge Powell than on May, since he and the Judge would be spending two weeks at the Casa Marina together. "The trouble is," he confessed, "that every time I go down to Florida with Judge Powell, while I never do anything particularly devilish, nevertheless I invariably do a good many things that I ought not do," so that by the time he was heading home again he felt like "a flagellant." He was a vice president at the Hartford now and had to be doubly careful. Besides, what he really wanted to do in Key West was to "get the sea and the sun and to loaf" and be himself "as much in Florida as I am anywhere else."

By February 16 Stevens had settled in his rooms at the Casa Marina, ready to enjoy the sun without drinking. The Judge explained that his own doctor had told him he could have only one drink a day and that he made up for that by enjoying an illimitable number of half-drinks all day and night. So it was just a matter of hours before Stevens, likewise recalibrating, was enjoying his martinis once more. For the hell of it, the Judge had also put together a book called *The Ordeals of Ida*, a send-up of *Ideas of Order*, "illustrated with copies of drawings from the *New Yorker*." Ida's principal ordeal had been "that she had to walk home." Fortunately there was only one copy of the book "in existence, and even that one was probably no longer in existence."

The weather in Key West that February turned to a mix of rain and more rain, so much so that it had kept the well-tanned, physically fit, six-foot, thirty-six-year-old novelist and resident Ernest Hemingway from venturing out in *Pilar*, the thirty-eight-foot wooden fishing boat he'd named in honor of his wife, Pauline. It boasted a 75-horsepower diesel engine for getting out into the deep, and an auxiliary 40 horsepower engine for trolling and cranking in the swordfish and marlin he loved hunting. Noble beasts, he liked to say, unlike most humans, and ripe for the killing. He'd already landed the largest marlin ever recorded in the Keys, to the dismay of many local fishermen. Mustachioed, grinning, muscular, he kept up his spirits by drinking at Sloppy Joe's, as well as by boxing, hiring black stevedores to spar with him down on the wharves.

Stevens, it turned out, already had something of a reputation with "the Mob," as Hemingway's friends in Key West dubbed themselves. He had already been to the forty-year-old John Dos Passos's rented bungalow on Waddell and Alberta just north of the Casa Marina. There he'd told the author of *Manhattan Transfer* that, based on his writing, he'd assumed that Dos Passos was a cripple. Moreover, Stevens was outraged (and no doubt fascinated) to see that several women socializing at the bungalow were wearing what looked to him like thinly clad pajamas.

Probably on the evening of February 19, Stevens and the Judge stumbled over to another of Dos Passos's cocktail parties, by which time Stevens was back to his old behavior of joking and bantering with that dismissive edge of his. The parlor was full of guests, among whom was Hemingway's sister, Ursula, who at one point overheard Stevens insulting her brother. When she objected, Stevens turned on her and called her brother a sap and no real man. He seemed suicidally itching for a fight. Since his own contact with the Reality which he'd tried to address in *Owl's Clover* had turned out to be a failure, he may well have seen Hemingway's alternative approach to Reality as something to be confronted and silenced with a good right to the jaw.

Shaken by Stevens's dismissal of her brother, Ursula left the party and hurried through the wet streets in the evening twilight to her brother's home on Whitehall Street. It was the third time, Hemingway would tell Sara Murphy a week later, that Stevens—that personification of a cholera descending on his pristine Key West—had disparaged him, which was three times too many. When his sister in tears told her brother what Stevens had done, the two hurried over to Dos Passos's, just as Stevens, accompanied by the Judge, was leaving, having shouted that, by God, he wished he had Hemingway here now so he could knock him out with a single punch.

And behold, directly in front of Stevens was the very nemesis of his Imagination—the antipoet poet, the poet of extraordinary reality, as Stevens would later call him, which put him in the same category as that other antipoet, William Carlos Williams, except that Hemingway was fifteen years younger and much faster than Williams, and far less friendly. So it began, with Stevens swinging at the bespectacled Hemingway, who seemed to weave like a shark, and Papa hitting him one-two and Stevens going down "spectacularly," as Hemingway would remember it, into a puddle of fresh rainwater.

At which point the Judge called a halt. He wanted a fair fight, Hem, a fair fight, and insisted on Hemingway taking off his glasses. Just as Hemingway obliged, a staggering Stevens swung his best Sunday punch, bam, flush into Hemingway's jaw, only to break his right fist in two places. Hemingway shook off the punch, sized up Stevens—was that the best shot he had?—then knocked him down again and again until Stevens could no longer get up. After which the Judge helped Stevens back to his rooms at the Casa Marina, where he remained for the next five days, while a doctor and a nurse tended to his bruised and blackened eyes and his broken right hand.

• • •

A WEEK LATER, ON February 25, a sober and chastened Stevens walked over to Hemingway's to apologize profusely to him and Ursula, asking him to tell no one about the drunken brawl. Too much booze, he explained, something he'd told himself he was going to stay away from. It would have serious ramifications, he explained, if word got back to the offices of the Hartford Indemnity Insurance Company. Or—worse—his wife. Except for crowing over the whole matter in a letter to Sara Murphy, published by Hemingway's biographer Carlos Baker after both Stevens and Papa were gone, Hemingway kept his side of the promise. He'd managed to land the largest poet in America—the six-two 225-pound Wallace Stevens, twenty years his elder—far easier than any marlin or swordfish. Let the story be that Stevens had fallen down a flight of stairs, Stevens suggested, and Hemingway agreed. Let it be the Key West lighthouse stairs visible from his study, for all Papa cared.

On the evening of the 25th there was a farewell cocktail party for the Judge, who would be leaving Key West early the next morning, the same day Stevens headed for Cross Creek, nearly five hundred miles north of Key West. On the evening of March 4 Stevens telephoned Phil May from the train terminal in Jacksonville as he was leaving, only to learn that May was out for the evening. A few minutes later Stevens spotted him "squiring a damsel" across the railroad terminal. He called out, but then, with his eyes and face still puffy and his right hand in a cast, decided he looked too "shaggy and unbathed" to see May, by which time the couple had disappeared into the crowd. His time in Key West, he reassured May when he was back in Hartford, had been uneventful, and he and the Judge had done "little of anything except sit in the sun."

Stevens had just left Key West and "gone up to Pirates Cove to rest his face for another week before going north," Hemingway told Sara Murphy. But he couldn't let a story as delicious as that simply float away. The man was certainly no matador, just "one of those mirror fighters who swells his muscles and practices lethal punches in the bathroom while he hates his betters," though having said that, he admitted he might be wrong about Stevens after all. The day after the fight he'd told Powell to tell Stevens that he was "a damned fine poet but that he couldn't fight." Oh, the Judge had retorted, but Hem was wrong there. Stevens was actually a very good fighter. Why, he'd once seen Stevens hit a man and knock him the length of the room. Had he caught the man's name, Papa asked. No, the Judge had to admit, but he thought he was a waiter. Well, Hemingway ended, he just hoped Stevens would forget the whole matter and not take up archery or machine gunnery and get back to his poetry.

What came to matter far more for Stevens was what he made of Hemingway the poet as he analyzed his prose for what it revealed of Hemingway. Two years before the Key West fight, Stevens had upset Williams by calling him an antipoet. He'd meant it as high praise, of course, though Williams did not see it that way. What Stevens had meant was that Williams had the ability to actualize a world in his poems, the cold bare facts of the matter shimmering brightly among his syllables. Here, for example, was Williams's take on two sunbathers on a Depression-bound New Jersey morning, a poem composed at about the time Stevens wrote "The Idea of Order at Key West":

A tramp thawing out
on a doorstep
against an east wall
Nov. 1, 1933:

a young man begrimed
and in an old
army coat
wriggling and scratching

while a fat negress
in a yellow-house window
nearby
leans out and yawns

into the fine weather

Six years after his encounter with Hemingway, Stevens wrote Henry Church, who was interested in putting together a series of talks on the "terrifying" subject of the actual, that the best man for that job was Hemingway, who encapsulated the poetry of the "extraordinary actuality of things" in words embodying the thing itself, apart from the dance of the self-conscious imagination. "Most people don't think of Hemingway as a poet," Stevens wrote, but in fact he was "the most significant of living poets, so far as the subject of EXTRAORDINARY ACTUALITY" was concerned. And that was what real poets were after, finally: words which somehow caught the reality of the thing itself.

A passage from *Farewell to Arms* may explain what Stevens found in Hemingway. It is a description like and unlike that in Stevens's "The Snow Man," the scene set not in Connecticut but on the Italian front along the Piave in the last months of World War I, presented here in the free verse embedded in Hemingway's prose:

> [*The cloud*] *came on very fast*
> *and the sun went a dull yellow*
> *and then everything was gray*
> *and the sky was covered*
> *and the cloud came on down the mountain*
> *and suddenly we were in it and it was snow.*
> *The snow slanted across the wind,*
> *the bare ground was covered,*
> *the stumps of trees projected,*
> *there was snow on the guns*
> *and there were paths in the snow*
> *going back to the latrines behind the trenches.*

That would seem to capture the reality of things seen through the lens of an eyewitness on the front lines and therefore fully aware of the transitoriness of nature and of life itself.

But in 1936 this was not yet Stevens's fully realized sense of what the poem could do, even as he wrestled with the events of history and the news of the day in *Owl's Clover*, much of which he left out of his *Collected Poems*. Try as he might, reality was not about to conform to his imagination, at least not yet. *Pace* Emerson and the transcendentalists, nature, even the sea, remained inhuman, its constant cry teasing the poet of reality into creating a cry coequal with the sea. And yet, in singing, Stevens had come to realize, the poet must do everything he can to shape reality to thought even as he realizes the impossibility of the task, even as something of the elusive real is smeared like the sun across the poet's words. But is even this "reality" any more solid, finally, than a flapping of the gums or a heaving of the summer air?

One thing was sure: he was finished with Key West, at least the Key West of Arthur Powell and the Good Ol' Boys. Which may explain why, when he published *Ideas of Order* with Knopf later that year, he added a new overture to the book. He was going to have to leave the Circe of Key West behind and return for good to the North and his solitary Penelope. But the loss of Florida, his venereal soil, a place he found "violently affective," perhaps with a nod to Hemingway, would mean leaving behind a world that had become his beloved. "Go on, high ship," "Farewell to Florida" begins, continuing in yet another vein with Crispin sailing the seas Ulysses-like, "since now, upon the shore, / The snake has left its skin upon the floor." The times have changed, and with them his Key West, receding now in the distance. No longer will the mind of his beloved South speak to him again. "I am free," he tells himself, though neither he nor we believe him, really. The romantic poet will have to sail elsewhere and take on a newer, darker, more northern reality from now on.

He has come to see that, like a Circe, "her mind had bound me round." Even her palms, her hands as well as those swaying palm trees, had been hot for this northerner, too hot, in fact,

As if I lived in ashen ground, as if
The leaves in which the wind kept up its sound
From my North of cold whistled in a sepulchral South,
Her South of pine and coral and coraline sea,
Her home, not mine, in the ever-freshened Keys.

Stevens's pain is almost too much for him, as he recalls "her days, her oceanic nights, calling / For music, for whisperings from the reefs." But it is a different time now, and we are in the middle of it: a world in which the poet must rise to the cry of the occasion as he has been challenged to do.

Now he will have to learn to hate "the sea floor and the wilderness / Of waving weeds," hate too those "vivid blooms / Curled over the shadowless hut, the rust and bones," and

> *stand here on the deck in the dark and say*
> *Farewell and to know that that land is forever gone*
> *And that she will not follow in any word*
> *Or look, nor ever again in thought, except*
> *That I loved her once.*

Now he will have to leave that world behind and return to a leafless North that lies "in a wintry slime / Both of men and clouds, a slime of men in crowds," where the crowds move with the currents, this way and that as the currents will, "cloven by sullen swells / Against your sides, then shoving and slithering, / The darkness shattered, turbulent with foam." Ah, to be free of that land of the Lotus Eaters and "return to the North, to "the violent mind / That is their mind, these men, and that will bind" him round, like the snake that bound Laocoön. Go on, then, "carry me, misty deck, carry me / To the cold, go on, high ship, go on, plunge on."

1

Stevens's parents, Garrett Barcalow Stevens and Margaretha Catharine Zeller Stevens.

2

Stevens's first home, a three-story brick row house at 323 North Fifth Street, Reading, Pennsylvania, a place and a town he was haunted by all his life.

3

The Stevens children. From left: Elizabeth, Garrett, Catherine, Wallace, and John. Photograph taken about 1894.

4

Wallace Stevens at Harvard, spring 1900.

5

The elusive Donald Evans, 1914. Of all the New York avant-garde, it was Evans who would have the greatest impact on the thirty-five-year-old Stevens. Unrecognized today, Evans offered his audience erotic poems liberally laced with the exotic.

6

Walter and Louise Arensberg's New York City apartment at 33 West Sixty-Seventh Street, with Duchamp's *Nude Descending a Staircase* displayed prominently. This was the Arensbergs' home and salon from 1915 until 1921. Photo taken by the artist Charles Sheeler, 1919.

7

The *Others* group, a photograph taken on the lawn of William Carlos Williams's home at 9 Ridge Road, Rutherford, New Jersey. Back row, from left: Jean Crotti, Marcel Duchamp, Walter Arensberg, Man Ray, W. A. Sanborn, Maxwell Bodenheim. Front row, from left: Alanson Hartpence, Alfred Kreymborg, William Carlos Williams, Skipwith Cannel. Wallace Stevens, then on the road beginning his new job at the surety division of the Hartford Accident and Indemnity Insurance Company, is conspicuously missing.

Mercury Liberty dime (1916–1946) for which Elsie's sculpted profile served as a model.

8

9

10

Elsie and Wallace Stevens in the summer of 1921 in Elizabeth Park in Hartford. Stevens has taken Elsie's photo, and Elsie has taken his. The unintended irony is that Elsie's dark shadow appears to dominate her husband.

11

Long Key Compound, January 1922, as shown on a postcard to Elsie. During the Category 5 Labor Day Hurricane of 1935, the mid-Keys suffered widespread destruction and the loss of hundreds of lives, which was one reason Stevens and Arthur Powell vacationed on Key West and the posh Casa Marina.

12

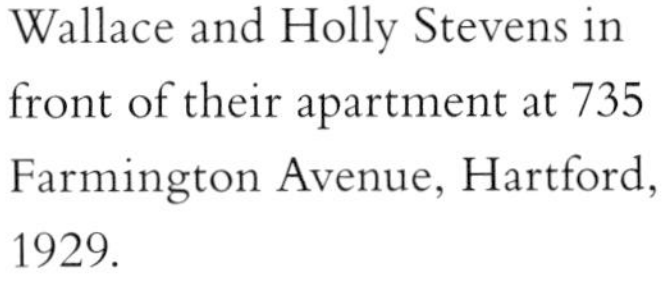

Wallace and Holly Stevens in front of their apartment at 735 Farmington Avenue, Hartford, 1929.

13

The Hartford Accident and Indemnity Insurance Building at 690 Asylum Avenue, Hartford, where Stevens worked for nearly forty years, rising to VP of the surety division.

14

The house at 118 Westerly Terrace, Hartford. It was the only home the Stevenses ever owned. Stevens bought it with cash at the height of the Depression in 1932.

15

RIGHT: The nattily dressed Wallace and Elsie, wearing clothes thirty years out of fashion, standing apart in front of their home at 118 Westerly Terrace, Hartford.

BELOW: Judge Arthur Powell of Atlanta with Stevens in February 1940, the last time the two would be in Key West together. It was Powell who introduced Stevens to the "land of the lemon trees," Long Key and Key West, to which Stevens would return each winter for fourteen years, until drinking and a fist-fight with Ernest Hemingway put an end to his bachelor visits.

16

17

Wallace Stevens and Robert Frost sitting in the inner arcade of the Casa Marina Hotel in Key West, February 1940. Stevens: "Your poems are too academic." Frost: "Your poems are too executive." Stevens: "The trouble with you, Robert, is that you write about subjects." Frost: "The trouble with you, Wallace, is that you write about bric-a-brac."

18

Portrait of Wallace Stevens taken by Sylvia Salmi, 1948.

19

Group portrait of the 1955 Bollingen committee. Standing, left to right: Wallace Stevens, Randall Jarrell, and Allen Tate. Seated: Marianne Moore (in her signature tricornered hat) and Muriel Rukeyser.

20

Stevens with his seven-year-old grandson, Peter, in Hartford in 1953. He delighted in the boy's rambunctious energy, which must have reminded him of himself growing up in a world that had long since disappeared.

12

The Man with the Blue Guitar: 1936–1937

Children picking up our bones
Will never know that these were once
As quick as foxes on the hill . . .
And least will guess that with our bones
We left much more, left what still is
The look of things, left what we felt
At what we saw.

"A POSTCARD FROM THE VOLCANO"

My expedition is over and I am at home again," Stevens wrote Phil May on Monday, March 9, 1936, his first day back in the office. After saying good-bye to the Judge, he'd gone up to Pirate's Cove and from there made a trip with May out to Cross Creek to have dinner with the novelist Marjorie Kinnan Rawlings at her farmhouse and orange grove. Stevens had found her to be "a very remarkable woman in her own right as distinct from her literary right," though May would remember it differently. Because Stevens had made it known that he was on a diet, Rawlings had served him a special meal of Boston sherried pot roast, salad greens, and fruit. But when he saw that everyone else was enjoying the baked-in-sherry ham she'd prepared, Stevens, who had been drinking again, explained that he'd been dieting not on doctor's orders but merely to lose weight (though in fact, at 235 pounds and with high blood pressure, he'd been ordered to shed twenty pounds). Rawlings had gone to much trouble to prepare that beef, and when Stevens went for the ham, she took the beef and tossed it on the hearth, where her pointer devoured it.

His discussions with Latimer likewise resumed. "There are people who think *Ideas of Order* is not only bad but rotten," Stevens wrote. Geoffrey Grigson, writing for *New Verse*, had called it "a stuffed goldfinch," and Stevens had shot back that Grigson was nothing more than a propagandist, part of a group searching for a social revolution, "if a social revolution may be said to be going on." For his own part, while he believed in reform, he did not want to see what was happening in Russia and Germany and Italy happen here in the States. Of course, from the point of view of social revolution, *Ideas of Order* must reek "of the most otiose prettiness," he admitted. But he was a poet first, and not a propagandist. "Conceding that the social situation is the most absorbing thing in the world today, and that those phases of it that you and I regret as merely violent have a strong chance of prevailing in the long run," he told Latimer, he was not going "to take the point of view of a poet just out of school." Let the innocence of the young attend to the young. He was too seasoned, too mature a poet to fall for that sort of benign nonsense.

By mid-May he'd completed *Owl's Clover*, and Latimer was given permission by Knopf to publish a version in a limited edition of 105 copies. Stevens liked his quirky title because, "in spite of the owlishness of the poems," there was "enough poetry in them to justify" it. They were poems in which he had tried to deal with the day's news, at the same time offering his readers the pleasure of poetry, "if not exactly the pleasure of thought." Combining poetry and the complexities of philosophical thought was one of the tasks that still lay ahead for him.

In early October, Morton Zabel wrote Stevens with the sad news that Stevens's longtime champion Harriet Monroe had died at the age of seventy-five while on a trip to Peru. "It is hard to realize that Miss Monroe is gone," Stevens wrote back. He'd been "very fond of her." He enclosed a short homage which *Poetry* would publish in December, underscoring just how much her friendship had meant to him from the start. Her job, he began, had brought her "into contact with the most ferocious egoists," which was a way, really, of describing most poets. But she knew how to adapt herself to her visitors and made everyone feel that she "liked them personally, as she usually did." One evening years before, she'd invited him to her home for dinner, after which she had produced "a small bottle of whiskey which she said was something like ninety years old, almost colonial, as if stored up for that particular winter's night." It was that sense of generosity that she had likewise managed to bring to *Poetry* by welcoming all sorts of voices. That quality stood out all the more for him, because he knew it was not something he himself possessed.

That December he wrote Latimer, thanking him for sending along two early reviews of *Owl's Clover.* He'd already read the one in the *New York Herald-Tribune* by the New Left critic Ruth Lechlitner, who had written that "at a time when politics shall rule a poet's world" his poems showed that he had refused to join the masses, and that left him open to attack by the Left. Now, he joked with Latimer, he was expecting his house to be "burned down almost any moment." The *New York Times* had been a bit kinder, noting that Stevens had at least tried to deal with the role of the poet in a world struggling with serious political issues, though he still had a long way to go. Perhaps the poems he had yet to write would be his political salvation. It was a sentiment echoed by Ben Belitt in the *Nation.* The real problem with Stevens, Belitt noted, was that, while he'd decided on a more formal mode of discourse in his search for order, he had yet to discover that discourse. Nor, he added, did Stevens seem to have the temperament necessary for such a method of discourse if he did find it. Stevens wrote Belitt thanking him for his careful attention, admitting that finding the precise method of address was indeed a problem he struggled with constantly.

On December 8 he was at Harvard to deliver an address he titled "The Irrational Element in Poetry." He was fifty-seven and it was the first time he'd ever addressed an academic audience, and that one his alma mater, and he'd looked forward to delivering it "the way one must look forward to one's first baby." By the irrational, he told his audience, he did not mean what Salvador Dali meant by the term. What he meant was "the transaction between reality and the sensibility of the poet from which poetry springs."

He meant to speak about reality not as a philosopher—for that he was not—but as a poet. Two weeks earlier, he told his audience, there had been a light snowfall back home. "It melted a little by day and then froze again at night, forming a thin, bright crust over the grass," and there had been a nearly full moon as well. Once he'd been awakened before dawn, hearing "the steps of a cat running over the snow under my window almost inaudibly." That sound, he said, had left him with an idea for a poem.

Why poetry? Because that was the form a poet would naturally give it. Poets were born, not made, he explained. Otherwise they would long ago have become extinct. On the other hand, they might just as well "have changed life from what it is today into one of those transformations in which they delight," and in the process "greatly multiplied themselves there." Moreover, this being the age of Freud, it was much easier to accept the idea of the irrational, which meant there was no accounting for what a poet might write about.

Then too there was the pressure of contemporary reality to consider. Recently he'd "dropped into a gallery" in New York, only to find that nothing there held the slightest interest for him, because these days the very air seemed "charged with anxieties and tensions," so that looking at those paintings was like playing the piano in Madrid while the bombs dropped about one. In "The Old Woman and the Statue" from *Owl's Clover*—which he read to his audience that same afternoon—he had tried to apply himself to the "perfectly matter-of-fact." The poem had turned out to be what he'd wanted "without knowing before it was written what I wanted it to be, even though I knew before it was written what I wanted to do." Indeed that was one of the hallmarks of poetry: that one's subject had to be constantly renewing itself just as much as one's rhythm and diction and style.

A poet wrote poetry because he had to and because one grew "tired of the monotony of one's imagination" and had to continually refresh it. Some believed that the poet wrote poetry to find God, real poetry being both mystical and irrational. But one might also write poetry to find the good—that which was both harmonious and orderly—something which, for Plato at least, was synonymous with God. And *that* sense of the good might be discovered just as well "in a duck in a pond or in the wind on a winter night." If one found in poetry a sense of "momentary existence on an exquisite plane," was it also necessary to ask the poem what it meant?

No one who had lived through the Great War could possibly be living now in some "happy oblivion." In fact the world in which he'd grown up was like some stage set long since "taken down and trucked away." Nazi Germany and Communist Russia: those were two of the world's present-day realities, so that, as one looked "from an uncertain present toward a more uncertain future," one felt "the desire to collect oneself against all this in poetry as well as in politics," because "the greater the pressure of the contemporaneous, the greater the resistance" to that pressure. He did not mean by this an escape from "an ominous and destructive" reality but rather a way of learning how to fortify oneself against the pressure of that reality by converting it into "an amenable circumstance." Wasn't it true, after all, that the poet who sought "to contemplate the good in the midst of confusion" was "like the mystic who wishes to contemplate God in the midst of evil"?

The artist who best represented someone willing to wrestle with the pressures of contemporary reality was Picasso, because the man was obsessed with the idea of freedom. So with the poet, who was free to use whatever language or rhythm or meter he liked, as long as he understood that his freedom had to be "consonant with the freedom of others." Take the question of sound. One might tintinnabulate all one wanted; others were "equally free to put their hands over their ears." To be a successful poet meant knowing the exact sound appropriate for the time, which, as it turned out, one somehow knew "without knowing how." The poet was always searching for the new, and when that new poetry came, it came in a flash. That was why poets were constantly purging "themselves before reality" in "saintly exercises," for it was the unknown that most intrigued them. The true poet was always "extraordinarily alive" to change: a figure of continual "gaiety and youth" who made most poetry look obsolete.

Milton and Shelley, then, reimagined for Depression America. The park with its marble horses rising on Pegasian wings "in the midst of a circle of trees, from which the leaves / Raced with the horses in bright hurricanes." Mussorgsky, say, a symphony with strings, drums, and trumpets, facing the approaching Götterdämmerung, the autumn sky "above the plaza widening," the marble of the statues "leaping in the storms of light."

Stevens the poet approaching sixty, reawakening as from a dream as the mob milled outside his bedroom or office, the rattle of rotten leaves swirling as in an apocalypse among the pillared columns of the Hartford, while the horses of the imagination struggled to free themselves of their marble casts and soar, "white forelegs taut . . . for the vivid plunge," their haunches "contorted, staggering from the thrust against / The earth as the bodies rose on feathery wings." Wrong from the start, such poetry, perhaps, but with no other way to go, the shadows of those great poet philosophers with their marble edifices weighing him down.

And she, the old woman, witch-like phantom with "the bitter mind / In a flapping cloak," unable to hope, unable to imagine a better time, tortured by a "fear too naked for her shadow's shape," a doomsayer predicting the worst, unwilling or unable to reimagine a world for the better, with a mood so fixed it had become "a manner of the mind, a mind in a night / That was whatever the mind might make of it." And yet, as dark as things were, the poet's task was to imagine a world where the imagination might begin to recover because both must: that moment when the imagination found a clearing in the darkness, and a new synthesis might be created from the destruction of the old orders. It was then that

the horses would rise again,
Yet hardly to be seen and again the legs
Would flash in air, and the muscular bodies thrust
Hoofs grinding against the stubborn earth, until
The light wings lifted through the crystal space
Of night. How clearly that would be defined!

He pointedly called the following section of *Owl's Clover* "Mr. Burnshaw and the Statue," though when he published the poem in *The Man with the Blue Guitar* he changed the title to "The Statue at the World's End," expunging Burnshaw's name altogether to concentrate instead on the end time as some "trash can at the end of the world," where the masses would be victorious, and the buzzard would

eat the bellies of the rich,
Fat with a thousand butters, and the crows
Sip the wild honey of the poor man's life,
The blood of his bitter brain.

In his replay of the French Reign of Terror, "majestic, marble heads" would lie "severed and tumbled into seedless grass, / Motionless, knowing neither dew nor frost," where the eyeless heads would pile up in the total destruction of the old, and where, somehow, out of that destruction, a better world would take shape, a happier world, where even

The colorless light in which this wreckage lies
Has faint, portentous lustres, shades and shapes
Of rose, or what will once more rise to rose,
When younger bodies, because they are younger, rise
And chant the rose-points of their birth, and when
For a little time, again, rose-breasted birds
Sing rose-beliefs.

Change: the one constant we can depend upon. What matters, then, is not to lament the past or worry over an imagined future. No, it is "enough / To live incessantly in change." Take solace in those imagined halcyon moments of summer while you can,

when the leaves
Appear to sleep within a sleeping air,
They suddenly fall and the leafless sound of the wind
Is no longer a sound of summer. So great a change
Is constant. The time you call serene descends
Through a moving chaos that never ends.

Consider the bankruptcy of Europe now, crowned with its empty Marxist heaven. Yes, "there was / A heaven once. . . . The spirit's episcopate, hallowed and high, / To which the spirit ascended": a time when "each man, / Through long cloud-cloister-porches, walked alone," when "the mind / Acquired transparence and beheld itself / And beheld the source from which transparence came," and where "meanings made / Into a music never touched to sound." Shelley's pure-white domes, "the temple of the altar where each man / Beheld the truth and knew it to be true." Such was the world of the Benedictines and Cistercians, the world of Dante and Aquinas.

But that world had never reflected any heaven the African knew, because Africa "had/No heaven, had death without a heaven." For Stevens the god of Africa would be a serpent god, "quick-eyed, / Rising from indolent coils," whereas the classical horses atop the Acropolis or on the arches of Berlin, Paris, London, and Rome belonged to a European imagination, "too starkly pallid for the jaguar's light." Africa, instead, was Stevens's version of "the black sublime," where "glittering serpents climb, / Dark-skinned and sinuous, winding upwardly / . . . Darting envenomed eyes about, like fangs, / Hissing, across the silence, puissant sounds." Africa was home to the "dirges of fallen forest-men," an ancient world, without a single "gill of sweet." Here, then, was Stevens's imagination, fed on Hollywood images of King Kong mixed with stereotypes of Uncle Remus: Africa seen in the purple light of Hartford.

• • •

STEVENS'S FIRST ATTEMPTS AT a political poetry date to the fall of 1935, when the Second Italo-Abyssinian War was launched against Ethiopia from Italian Somaliland under the generalship of Rodolfo Graziani, and concluded the following June, when the region became part of Italian East Africa, with Mussolini building schools, ports, bridges, hospitals, railways, and new roads between Mogadishu and Addis Ababa. In what must be a send-up, Stevens presents Italian fighter planes over Ethiopia, like European seraphim "armed, gloriously to slay / The black and ruin his sepulchral throne," their "wings spread and whirling over jaguar-men," machine guns blazing. The mock-epic language here recalls Milton's winged demons in Pandemonium. It is a new kind of war, with "filleted angels . . . / Combatting bushmen for a patch of gourds," before returning victoriously "with belts / And beads and bangles of gold and trumpets raised, / Racking the world with clarion puffs," a "masquerade . . . of military things," an "imagination flashed with irony."

But can Europe's marble statues stand on solid ground in Africa? Those statues were built for a northern clime, "to stand, not in a tumbling green" to make "a visible wreath" in a world of "endless elegies." No, the colonial experiment has failed, Stevens sees, for the Pax Britannica or Pax Americana or Pax Italiana could never take root in a soil so foreign as Africa (or, years on, in the Middle East or Indochina). In Africa, Stevens says, "the memory moves on leopards' feet" or on beaked wings which are

Wildly curvetted, color-scarred, so beaked
With tongues unclipped and throats so stuffed with thorns,
So clawed, so sopped with sun, that in these things
The message is half-borne.

Why? Because for Africa the final god is Fate, Ananke, blind Necessity, and no amount of European or American enculturation will ever change the way things are, short of a time that would dwarf all visionaries and certainly all statesmen. There are revolutions and then there are revolutions, each giving way to another in an endless cycle. It is a matter of the subman within each of us coming to terms with the rational man. Whatever future the extreme Left or extreme Right might envision, "the future must bear within it every past, / Not least the pasts destroyed." Not only a chicken in every pot, then, as Hoover's administration had promised, but more: a duck for dinner, one of the happy forms where the future will contain the past because that is how things go in the great return, "priestly in severity, / Yet lord, a mask of flame."

"The trees / Are full of fanfares of farewell," "A Duck for Dinner" concludes, rounding back on Elizabeth Park in Hartford, even as night comes on again. That is when "the statue stands / In hum-drum space, farewell, farewell," and spring returns as spring has always returned. Exhausted by his failed attempt to lift his marble-winged horses from their pediments, the poet must finally admit that even the imagination has an end.

"To feel again / The reconciliation, the rapture of a time / Without imagination, without past / And without future." To feel again "a present time," a passion "merely to be / For the gaudium of being," to be merely

The medium man among other medium men,
The cloak to be clipped, the night to be redesigned,
Its land-breath to be stifled, its color changed,
Night and the imagination being one.

Clipped: the word with which he'd ended his first failed attempt at the summative poem, *The Comedian*, fourteen years earlier. He has done what he could, has brought all his rhetorical guns to bear—his learning, his humor, his wisdom, cloaked in a mock-Miltonic verse, not knowing where the authorial voice begins and the mock-authorial ends—brought to bear on the politics of the day, the Fascist and the Komintern. Here is the poet-philosopher who would reconcile the real and the imagination, incorporating the individual among the masses. He will revise the poem, shortening it, winding up not creating a new style but merely composing a failed modest manifesto of his own, before abandoning the project to begin again, not with a symphony on center stage this time but assuming the role of shearsman singing the green real as he strums along on his Tennessean blue guitar his private version of the American sublime.

• • •

BY THE CLOSE OF 1936 Stevens had already assumed a striking new voice with his poem *The Man with the Blue Guitar.* "During the winter I have written something like 35 or 40 short pieces, of which about 25 seem to be coming through," he wrote Latimer on March 17, 1937. These new pieces, he confided to his closest literary confidant at the moment, dealt with "the relation or balance between imagined things and real things," which had been such a "constant source of trouble" for him. But at least these new pieces dealt head-on with the "painter's problem of realization," of seeing the real world "as an imaginative man sees it."

The thirty-three-part poem would in fact constitute a breakthrough for Stevens by indicating a new direction: proposing that poetry itself is the supreme fiction toward which the poet should strive. At last he had triumphed over his own literary anxieties in trying to adapt the epic voice of Milton and Shelley. Now he turned instead to the figure of Everyman, the hidalgo strumming a guitar.

That October Stevens's poem "The Men That Are Falling," appeared in the *Nation* and won the *Nation's* Prize Poem for the year. Stevens would state flatly years later that it was the deaths of so many Spanish Republicans he'd had in mind when he composed his poem. If the setting is his bedroom, it is Madrid that is on his mind. It is late summer, midnight, with the moon "rising in the heat / And crickets loud again in the grass." His bedroom is dark and his windows open so that he can feel the wind blowing over him as he lies there alone. Still, only the living can feel this wind, as only the living can feel desire. He is restless, thinking, staring out at the moon which "burns in the mind on lost remembrances." What he feels now is not sleep but desire, as he stares at his "pillow that is black / In the catastrophic room . . . beyond despair."

But what he is staring at is death: a disembodied head upon the pillow in the dark next to him, a covering that is "more than sudarium," and from which a head speaks

> *the speech*
> *Of absolutes, bodiless, a head*
> *Thick-lipped from riot and rebellious cries.*

What he sees there on the pillow is an image of the sudarium, the Shroud of Oviedo, kept in the Cámara Santa of the Cathedral of San Salvador in Oviedo, Spain. *Sudarium*, the Latin word for "sweat cloth," the cloth believed to be the one wrapped around the head of Jesus after his death in accordance with Jewish custom, the cloth mentioned in the Gospel of John which the eyewitness found in the empty tomb on that first Easter Sunday. King Alfonso II of Asturias built the ninth-century chapel to honor this cloth, brought from a cave near the monastery of St. Mark near

Jerusalem in the seventh century to keep it from falling into the hands of the Sassanid Persians advancing on Jerusalem. It is displayed only three times each year, twice in September for the Feast of the Triumph of the Cross and its octave. The head covering of the dead Jesus in Spain, then, to represent the head of just one of the many thousands of Spanish Republicans who perished in the opening weeks of Spain's civil war, placed "upon the pillow to repose and speak . . . / the immaculate syllables / That he spoke only by doing what he did." Not the words, poet, but the deed, the willingness of a man prepared to die for something he believes in.

"Taste of the blood upon his martyred lips," Stevens writes, accusing the rest of us—demagogues and those at the service of demagogues—who go on living in our pensioned worlds while the human costs mount. He knows, as we do, that the face on the pillow no longer feels, no longer loves or desires or wishes for anything, and that the death of this man, one among many who gave his life for a belief and was "turned to stone," was someone who "loved earth, not heaven, enough to die." Now the "night wind blows upon the dreamer," who cannot rest because these men are dead, among them another poet, Federico García Lorca, taken out and shot, a man much like himself who in the inescapable darkness "bent / Over words that are life's valuable utterance."

• • •

THE POET, THEN, BENT over the words upon his desk as he begins not an aria this time but a long *tink-a-tunk* serenade. Not an epic with trombone crescendo, but the poet with guitar, a shearsman of sort, a tailor sewing together from various patches of text or textile a new sort of poem, this one in four-beat lines with anapestic variations, with an extra stress as needed. A man who "shares" with us his own history and genetic makeup and poetic proclivities, summoned now by an audience he does not know, can never know, to sing for them a song for their time which will at the same time enlarge them and make of the moment a heroic time. A man who will sing a green reality on the strings of his imagination, his blue guitar, his contemporary lyre and cithern and psaltery all in one, and yet sing for the ages, Hartford's Virgil redux:

The man bent over his guitar,
A shearsman of sorts. The day was green.

They said, "You have a blue guitar,
You do not play things as they are."

The man replied, "Things as they are
Are changed upon the blue guitar."

And they said then, "But play you must,
A tune beyond us, yet ourselves,

A tune upon the blue guitar
Of things exactly as they are."

But can he? Can any poet, even a philosopher-poet, ever make this eccentric world go round? Can he ever compose it, patch it up, in a way to satisfy everyone—Left, Right, Center? Like Virgil, *Arma virumque cano*, "I sing a hero's head, large eye / And bearded bronze," but not a man,

Although I patch him as I can
And reach through him almost to man.

If to serenade almost to man
Is to miss, by that, things as they are,

Say that it is the serenade
Of a man that plays a blue guitar.

He has tried the epic, or at least the mock-epic, and failed. Very well, then, he will sing on his old guitar as he did as a young man, before he had the wherewithal to buy his baby grand.

Despite his repeatedly denying it, Stevens does seem to have a particular painting in mind here: Picasso's 1903 *The Old Guitarist*, which portrays an old man with white hair and beard sitting distorted and cross-legged as he plays his guitar. If Picasso attempted to portray the world of poverty and abject misery, it was because that had been his own plight as a struggling young artist in Barcelona, where he painted many pictures, including this one, of the poor. The painting is almost entirely done in monochromatic blues and blue-blacks, except for the guitar itself, which is painted in a slightly warmer brown. The man is blind but, no longer seeing the world around him, he sees more deeply into the reality within.

Stevens's frustration with the whole project, including asking the poet to do what cannot be done and play "man number one," creates a jarring counterpoint. To play such a man would mean killing him first, as Audubon had killed many birds in order to better paint them. Or kill a hawk or crow and nail its carcass, wings outspread, bang!, on the barn door, as they did in Reading years ago, as a sign to the other birds what fate awaited them if they stayed around. Or to bang one's living thought out of "a savage blue / Jangling the metal of the strings" and play "a million people on one string?" Really?

And all their manner in the thing.
And all their manner, right and wrong,
And all their manner, weak and strong?

Such buzzing of the blue guitar, then, would come to sound "like a buzzing of flies in autumn air," an incessant sound to drive us mad if we ever tried to craft such music, which, the poet knows, would be dealing with one's feelings dishonestly, "craftily," and turn the artist into the Sleight-of-Hand Man.

Let the trombones blare, heralding the politicos, statesmen, con men. Let the charade roll down the street, bearing with it the Public Man—Hitler, Mussolini, Stalin, Hirohito, yes, even FDR—as once Caesar was saluted, and all kaisers and all czars since: the public man whom "none believes" and yet "whom all believe that all believe, / A pagan in a varnished car," even as we suffer our present misery, confronting an adversary who must someday fall. In 1935 Picasso had told Christian Zervos in an interview in *Cahiers d'art*, that in the past, pictures were created by stages and thus amounted to a sum of additions. But for him a picture was a hoard of destructions. "I make a picture—then I destroy it. In the end, though, nothing is lost; the red I removed from one place turns up somewhere else." As with painting, so with poetry and society, those other hoards of destruction. And so, at the eccentric center of his poem, it is as if Stevens calls upon Picasso to lead the way.

It is 1937 and strains of that old chestnut "Shine on, Harvest Moon" from 1908—the words altered here to "Good-bye, Good-bye, Harvest Moon"—echo in his room tonight. *Ain't had no lovin'*, the lyrics go,

> *Since April, January, June or July.*
> *Snow time ain't no time to stay*
> *Outdoors and spoon;*
> *So shine on, shine on, harvest moon,*
> *For me and my gal.*

Is this an allusion to those evenings in Reading when he courted Elsie, a time when this very song was in the air, the sort of thing one might strum on one's guitar? To catch at "good-bye, harvest moon, / Without seeing the harvest or the moon"? But things "as they are," God knows, "have been destroyed." Has he been destroyed along with them? Is he "a man that is dead / At a table on which the food is cold?" How, in the face of so much chaos—chaos without, chaos within—shall one "reduce the monster to / Myself" and be myself "in face of the monster, be more than part / Of it," to be "the lion in the lute" and play a music equal to the pressure of Reality, cold Ananke, that "lion locked in stone."

To what shall the poet compare his search? Is the poem not like "a missal found / In the mud," a sacred text discovered amid the quotidian, the scholar "hungriest for that book, / The very book"? To see into the essence of things and not flinch, but rejoice in what one finds. To think, but to give the imagination room to play as well. To think of oneself as some circus magician singing in his Pennsylvania Dutch ai-yi-yi, as he spins the world "upon his nose," flinging it this way and that, as he pleases.

The poet as philosopher: "Copernicus, Columbus, Professor Whitehead, myself, yourself," he would later explain, the one who sees the world as one imagines it:

And that-a-way he twirled the thing. . . .

And the world had worlds, ai, this-a-way:
The grass turned green and the grass turned gray.

And the nose is eternal, that-a-way.
Things as they were, things as they are,

Things as they will be by and by . . .
A fat thumb beats out ai-yi-yi.

Yes, "the shapes are wrong and the sounds are false," and the bells in the cathedral "are the bellowing of bulls," papal bulls explaining to the faithful things as they are. And yet, here in the cathedral, reading his missal, Franciscan don that he imagines himself to be in the silence and peace of that interior space, it is not dogma that centers him but the mystery of things, the realization that he is "never more / Himself than in this fertile glass." "I imagine that I chose a Franciscan," he would explain to his Italian translator years later, half-joking, "because of the quality of liberality and of being part of the world that goes with the Franciscan as distinguished, say, from a Jesuit."

Behold: the sun rises gloriously each morning, not to orisons but to yet another day of interminable class warfare, where "employer and employee contend, / Combat," then, weeks or months later, "compose their droll affair." And through it all the sun will bubble up again, and "spring sparkle and the cock-bird shriek," and again "the employer and employee will hear" the cry "and continue their affair." As in Babylon or Rome or Paris or London or Shanghai, so here in Hartford, so that we will not hear the lark but only the shriek of the cock who claws at our sleep each night, and we will turn our mornings merely into a "posture of the nerves, / As if a blunted player clutched / The nuances of the blue guitar." And when we have blotted out the sun, will the poet then play what a blind-deaf audience demands, "the rhapsody of things as they are"? What shall we do then? What say? "Throw away the lights, the definitions," the poet tells us,

And say of what you see in the dark
That it is this or that it is that,
But do not use the rotted names.

We must begin again, imagining a time before there were words: Adam in the garden standing in wonder before creation, before there were words by which we might name or misname things in order to have power over them. The night is not empty. Rather it is filled with energy, filled with possibility, and to know it is to know "its jocular procreations." A hoard of destructions, Picasso had said. Very well, then, a hoard of destructions, but a hoard opening onto the eighth day of creation to see oneself at last.

And shall our "generation's dream" lie "aviled / In the mud, in Monday's dirty light"? Alas, that it should be "the only dream they knew," Stevens sighs. Now, like the priest at the consecration of the host, the poet extends his hands and offers us "the bread of time to come." It is like the stone at Bethel on which Jacob rested his head and slept, only to witness angels ascending and descending. The bread of time will come to be our bread, and the stone our bed, Stevens ends, offering us a covenant with the imagination, a place where "we shall sleep by night" and forget "by day," except for those moments when we choose to play on the strings of the blue guitar: the green of a new reality in harmony with the imagination's blue: "The imagined pine, the imagined jay."

• • •

IN MAY 1937 LATIMER wrote Stevens to tell him that he was thinking of giving up the Alcestis Press. The project had given him a great deal of pleasure, but the costs associated with it were just too demanding. Better to move on, perhaps to Mexico. The news saddened Stevens, but he understood and offered the young man he had never met and never would some practical advice: "A good many years ago, when I really was a poet in the sense that I was all imagination . . . I deliberately gave up writing poetry because, much as I loved it, there were too many other things I wanted not to make an effort to have them." He'd imagined living in "a village in France, in a hut in Morocco, or in a piano box at Key West." But he didn't want to have to be thinking about money all the time, and he "didn't for a moment like the idea of poverty, so I went to work like anybody else and kept at it for a good many years."

Working at a job and saving your money would be only a temporary matter of "the next twenty-five years" or so, he added, during which Latimer might "have a thoroughly good time" and then come back to the world of art and bookmaking and be "all the better for your life away from it." True, he "would not be the same person," but he would be "pretty much the same person," as Stevens himself had learned. Now, when he went upstairs each evening, he entered a world he kept reinventing to please himself: new artifacts, new paintings, periodically rearranging the furniture to give his room a new look. Each night, as he looked out his windows, he studied the trees. Just now there was a rabbit outside digging up his flower bulbs. But he was fifty-seven and had earned the luxury of no longer having to listen to the radio to find out what was going on in the world. Now, finally, he could afford to "spend the time worrying about the rabbit and wondering what particular thing he is having for breakfast." To arrive at such a state: *that* was what made life worth living.

In mid-June, with his favorite couple expecting their second baby, Stevens wrote Jim Powers to say that, while having a second child in the house might be difficult, how grand it would be "to have someone to knock round with Jim, Junior." And while there was nothing he would have liked more than having a second baby, he'd been afraid to make that a reality. Nearing sixty, and with a "fairly substantial income," he still had trouble saving money—"real hunks" of it—against an unsettled and unsettling future. His father's money failures followed by his breakdown still haunted him after all this time.

Jim Kearney, who had engineered the takeover of the Hartford Accident and Indemnity Company three years earlier and who had made Stevens one of his VPs, was blind now. "When one calls on him," Stevens told Powers, "he is cheerful enough and no longer sleeps through one's visits, but he really says nothing except hello when one comes and goodbye when one goes." It was Mrs. Kearney who carried on the conversation when Stevens visited now. "One feels the same old affection for him," he confessed, and felt "the deepest sympathy for a man in such a dreadful hole." On the other hand, business was booming and the general feeling at the office was "high and optimistic." One could feel the wheels "going round more neatly . . . an immense thing in a world in which most of the wheels are scraping and squalling."

Christmas came and went. There were the usual gifts of oranges for Holly from the Mays down in Jacksonville, and packages from Ceylon sent by Leonard van Geyzel, a gentleman planter whom Stevens had asked months earlier to gather local artifacts which only Ceylon could offer. It was "difficult for anyone on this side of the earth to realize . . . just what Ceylon is like," he wrote him on New Year's Eve, but Van Geyzel's package and letter certainly helped. Besides the woodapple jelly and the local teas which he breakfasted on each morning, he had placed his new sitting Buddha in his room. "At night, when my windows are open and the air is like ice," that Buddha probably wished Stevens would "put a postage stamp on him and send him back to Colombo."

That October Knopf had published *The Man with the Blue Guitar & Other Poems* in an edition of one thousand. "Owl's Clover" appeared in a shortened version following the title poem, and two longish pieces filled out the book: "A Thought Revolved" and "The Men That Are Falling." The colophon page included a statement about the typography's "unusual blank spaces and extra-wide spacing of certain crucial words," by which "the author wishes to indicate a desirable pause or emphasis suggested by the sense." But Stevens was having none of it. All he'd done was suggest to the printer that he adjust certain spaces to give a more uniform look to the text. The colophon statement was pure nonsense. The truth was that he had "a horror of poetry pretending to be contemporaneous because of typographical queerness." That was Cummings's domain, or Williams's, not his. But it would take seventeen years before the oddity was corrected.

"The story is that Stevens has turned of late definitely to the left," Williams astutely noted in his review of *The Man with the Blue Guitar* in the *New Republic* six weeks after the book appeared. "I should say not, from anything in this book. He's merely older and as an artist infinitely more accomplished. Passion he has, too often muted, but not flagrantly for the underdog," so it was "no use looking for Stevens there." The title poem was one of his best and had everything "we know as Stevens." Still, here in these pages was "a troubled man who sings well, somewhat covertly, somewhat overfussily at times, a little stiffly but well," at his best "thrumming in four-beat time." But that had not been enough for Stevens, who had felt he needed "to make a defense of the poet . . . facing his world." And though *Owl's Clover* had "its old woman very effectively balanced against the heroic plunging of sculptured horses," Williams felt strongly that the poem had failed to get under way.

The trouble lay in Stevens's use of the blank-verse line, which had a "strange effect on a modern poet" because it made a poet think he had to think. The result was a "turgidity, dullness and a language" no one "alive today could ever recognize—lit by flashes, of course," because Stevens was "always a distinguished artist." But this time he had let the meter run the language. "Fortunately" there were five shorter pieces at the book's close, the last of which, "The Men That Are Falling," was "the most passionate and altogether the best work in the book," in fact "one of the best poems of the day," because there Stevens had allowed himself to show through the poem. For once those five-beat lines had worked. Then too there was that disfigured, disembodied head that spoke the immaculate syllables of truth. Behold the man who gave his life for something he believed in. That was something of which our literature could be proud. That, Williams saw, was "a lesson for us all."

13

The Noble Rider and the Sound of Words: 1938–1941

The actor is
A metaphysician in the dark, twanging
An instrument, twanging a wiry string that gives
Sounds passing through sudden rightnesses, wholly
Containing the mind, below which it cannot descend,
Beyond which it has no will to rise.

"OF MODERN POETRY"

By the fall of 1936 Stevens's older brother, the affable, gregarious Garrett Barcalow Stevens Jr., had become so ill he could no longer work. He'd spent his early years as a lawyer, first in Reading before moving to Baltimore, and, when those ventures failed, in New York from 1910 until 1912, though Wallace had no time when Garrett called on him and Elsie. Now Garrett was fifty-eight, with a wife and children to support, having difficulty breathing, and with heart troubles to boot. John, the youngest of the three brothers, asked Wallace to help support their brother and his family by sending monthly checks, as he was doing, and Wallace agreed.

Stevens understood that his brother needed his help, and sending a monthly check was a relatively painless way to do that. But he did not plan on visiting Garrett in Cleveland. Garrett had not attended Wallace and Elsie's wedding back in 1909, and though Stevens knew his father had been right about his marriage to the girl from across the tracks, he had neither forgiven nor forgotten Garrett's refusal to stick by him. When, on November 3, 1938, Garrett finally succumbed to heart failure at the age of sixty, John's family, along with some two hundred well-wishers, were there for the funeral. Wallace sent his condolences, explaining that he would not be able to attend, though he did continue to send checks to Garrett's widow, Sarah. The Stevens siblings were now down to three: John in Reading, Elizabeth in Philadelphia, and Wallace (now fifty-nine) in Hartford. With the passage of time, the loss of his brother would strike Wallace deeper than he had at first been willing to acknowledge.

• • •

AT THE BEGINNING OF 1938, Latimer wrote Stevens that, in spite of having earlier said he meant to quit publishing, he now wanted to publish another volume of his poems, or, barring that, a deluxe edition of Stevens's *Collected Poems* limited to one hundred copies. Stevens wrote back to say it was too early to be thinking of yet another book after publishing two in two years' time. If he was "shilly-shallying at the moment," he explained, it was because "the force of a book" depended necessarily "on the force of the idea about which it is organized, and ideas of real force don't occur to one every day." He wanted his poems "to grow out of something more important than my inkwell."

But Latimer was unsure about the future as well. Four months later Stevens was surprised to learn that Latimer had still not paid Knopf the $75 he'd asked for as a permissions fee. When Latimer told Stevens he'd finally abandoned his plans for bringing out a *Collected* because it would cost over $3,000 to produce those hundred copies, Stevens was relieved. He knew Latimer did not have that kind of money, and Stevens wasn't ready to publish such a volume. Poetry these days had become "an affair of weekends and holidays, a matter of walking to and from the office," and he needed leisure if he was ever going to put together such a book. It was like the long time he was "going to live somewhere" where he didn't live now. And with that the correspondence ended. That summer the elusive

Latimer disappeared for good, off to Mexico or Ceylon or someplace else, under another alias, and the Alcestis Press ceased to exist.

But even as Latimer disappeared, his place was filled by another Stevens admirer. Hi Simons of Chicago was a literary critic and president of Year Book Publishers, which specialized in medical texts. Simons had written Stevens in the fall of 1937 to say he wanted to put together a bibliography of Stevens's publications. Like Latimer's, Simons's politics veered to the Left. Twenty years earlier Simons had been arrested for urging others to avoid the draft, claiming that as an anarchist conscientious objector his obligations were to the people and not to the capitalists. Sentenced to seven years of hard labor, he spent a year in Leavenworth before being released. A friend of Emma Goldman, Simons returned to Chicago and worked as an instructor at the Workers Institute, at the same time serving as Goldman's go-between while she was in prison. His prison poems were published in 1922 as *Orioles and Blackbirds.* Later he became a literary critic with close ties to *Poetry*, whose associate editor, Eunice Tietjens, was his wife's sister-in-law. After Latimer's disappearance, Simons would become Stevens's confidant in matters of poetry, though that too would take time. When, for example, Simons sent Stevens a list of questions about the first publication of Stevens's poems, it took Stevens eight months to reply. But when he did, he sent a large parcel containing many of the little magazines in which his work had appeared.

In 1938 new poems continued to pour from Stevens's office and study, many composed during his walks to and from work. For the fall issue of the *Southern Review*, he published a group of twelve poems he titled *Canonica.* Among them were "The Poems of Our Climate," "Study of Two Pears," "The Man on the Dump," and "The Latest Freed Man," all dealing brilliantly with the idea of the truth, evoking—slantwise—Christ's words in the Gospel of St. John, "I am the Truth, the Way, and the Life."

"The Man on the Dump" evokes a nameless Russian who had built a makeshift shelter on the public dump just north of the Stevenses' home. Stevens presents the garbage dump as poetic catalogue, among whose detritus the poet searches for what might sustain him—and us. "Day creeps down. The moon is creeping up," the poet begins, as the romantic imagination, under the influence of the moon Blanche, seizes on the bits of dead history that pile up each day. "The dump is full / Of images," and the days pass one after the other like newspapers rolling off the press. Beautiful things like bouquets and corbeils of flowers end up on the dump. But then everything ends up here, even the "janitor's poems / Of every day." The catalogue of garbage is as full as anything by William Carlos Williams, though the garbage is a bit more chic in Hartford than in Paterson. Here we have "the wrapper on the can of pears, / The cat in the paper-bag, the corset, the box / From Esthonia," and even "the tiger chest, for tea."

It is here of all places that the freshness of night returns, as it did back in the time of Cornelius Nepos. It is not a name on everyone's tongue, but that is precisely the point. If the Roman historian of the first century B.C.E. was once an illustrious figure, his works have settled on the dump like the historian himself, just as the poet fears his work will wind up there. The breeze puffs and it puffs, the way newspaper and magazine and radio ads puff up the latest fads before they are inevitably tossed on the dump. One wants the freshness of things, Stevens acknowledges: "the dew in the green" smacking "like fresh water in a can, like the sea / On a cocoanut," until "one grows to hate these things except on the dump," where one comes to discard even the names we give things.

Ah, but to see the thing in itself, when "the moon comes up as the moon" and you see "as a man," and "you see the moon rise in the empty sky." Is it the nightingale—that quintessential romantic image—Stevens asks, that tortures the ear and packs the heart and scratches the mind? Is it the truth one wants? Or peace? Is it "the philosopher's honeymoon, one finds / On the dump?" Shall we too sit among the discarded "mattresses of the dead" and the "bottles, pots, shoes, and grass and murmur *aptest eve*"? And is the aptest eve the finest, freshest evening we can imagine? Or is this that aptest Eve that Adam the wordman, weary with the naming of things, needed to fulfill him? "Is it to hear the blatter of grackles and say," yes, just here we have a reality which might suffice, and to which we might cry out "invisible priest"? Or is it "to pull / The day to pieces," to get at the impossible center of things," to utter the words which should suffice "and cry" stanza my stone"? The man. The moon. The sun. The dump. The bouquets. The papers. The janitor's poems. The wrapper. The can. The cat in the paper bag. The corset. The box from Estonia.

The tiger chest. The truth. "Where was it one first heard of the truth?," reduced now to the mere predicate of substance. Live with that, poet, if you can. Live with the the.

"It was when I said, / Words are not forms of a single word," the poet concludes in "On the Road Home," rejecting the idea that all words and all things are part of a greater whole, a single Entity. Better to return to the fragmented parts of a world, where "the silence was largest / And longest" and "the night was roundest" and "the fragrance of the autumn warmest, / Closest and strongest."

In "The Latest Freedman," the poet rises at six to sit on the edge of his bed and think with relief. If Thomas Aquinas, Doctor of the Church, provided a map for understanding the world, the poet is having none of that:

I suppose there is
A doctrine to this landscape. Yet, having just
Escaped from the truth, the morning is color and mist.

Call it "being without description," where "everything is more real" and he finds himself now "at the center of reality," seeing "everything bulging and blazing and big" in itself: "The blue of the rug, the portrait of Vidal, / *Qui fait fi des joliesses banales*, the chairs."

"We are at a time of the year when winter is over," Stevens wrote Van Geyzel in Ceylon in April 1939, when "everything is washed out and colorless." This would tell him just how welcome were the brilliant colors of the saris Van Geyzel had sent and how beautiful they would look adorning the seats in his garden come summer. Ceylon had taken hold in his imagination, and the saris helped him "visualize the people in the streets." The day before, he'd received a copy of Lord Angus Holden's *Ceylon*. It contained the best photographs of the country he knew of, especially those of the giant statues of the reclining Buddha. "Somehow or other, with so much of Hitler and Mussolini so drastically on one's nerves, constantly," it was hard sometimes "to get round to Buddha," but the Buddha was what was needed now.

Earlier that year Stevens had received a letter from Henry Church, an American expatriate living in Paris with his wife, Barbara. Church, the editor and cofounder with Jean Paulhan of the French magazine *Mesures*, had written Stevens asking permission to have a number of poems from *Harmonium* translated for a forthcoming American issue of the magazine. Stevens was happy to agree. In late April he wrote Church a second time. He had thought Church was an Englishman but learned that Church's mother hailed from Hartford, and he saw now that it was the American quality of his poems which his French translators were interested in. That July five of his poems appeared in translation in *Mesures*, including "Thirteen Ways of Looking at a Blackbird" "Disillusionment of Ten O'Clock," and "The Emperor of Ice-Cream." But, he told Church, the ideas in *Harmonium* belonged to an earlier world. What he was interested in these days was how the poet could assist the artist "in restoring to the imagination what it is losing at such a catastrophic pace, and in supporting what it has gained." More important, though, Stevens realized that he'd found in Church, as later he would find in Church's German-born wife, someone who understood French culture intimately. How often he'd dreamed of being part of that particular world. And so began what he thought of as his most important literary friendship.

Requests for poems kept coming in. Allen Tate, twenty years Stevens's junior, formalist poet, essayist, critic, friend of John Crowe Ransom, Hart Crane, and T. S. Eliot, and a member of the Southern Fugitives and the conservative Agrarians, and now writer-in-residence at Princeton, wrote Stevens asking if he might be interested in publishing an inexpensive edition of his poems with the University of North Carolina Press. As much as he liked the idea, Stevens wrote back, Knopf would want them for his next book of poems. He was sorry to have to disappoint Tate, especially since this was his first contact with the poet. But contact had been made and would continue.

"It depresses me to think that I don't see more of you," he wrote Pitts Sanborn that June, but he got to New York much less often now. He'd been there with Mrs. Stevens and Holly to visit the World's Fair in Flushing Meadows and felt he could now "describe it in the dark," but had had no time to see Sanborn. And soon he and his family would be heading to the aptly named Holly Inn at Christmas Cove in Maine for a few weeks. Then they meant to spend two weeks near but not too near Reading, because his relatives still lived there and it was "embarrassing to be asked to stop at people's houses when we are so much more comfortable at hotels."

Still, how he wished he might spend an evening with his old friend again. Sanborn's pamphlet on Beethoven's symphonies, written for the New York Philharmonic-Symphony Society, was still on his table at home, and he liked picking it up to hear Sanborn's voice again. But time was running out for Sanborn, who would soon die of a heart attack, alone in his Greenwich Village apartment, composing a review of a performance he'd attended that same evening at the Metropolitan Opera House. The date was March 7, 1941, and Sanborn was just sixty-one. His papers, including Stevens's many letters to him, would be destroyed by Sanborn's landlord, eager to get the apartment ready for its new renters. Ironically the Holly Inn would burn to the ground in 1940. It was the third inn on that site, but this one would not be rebuilt.

In December 1939 Stevens thanked Hi Simons for his analysis of *The Comedian*, just published in the *Southern Review.* His focus now was on "the primordial importance of spiritual values in time of war," but, he felt, his early long poem did deserve the kind of attention Simons had given it. So far, eight interpretations had been proposed, all of them "mutually contradictory," and Simons had set about to rectify that situation. Recently the *Harvard Advocate* had published its homage to T. S. Eliot, in which Robert Penn Warren maintained that, had Stevens's poem been as attentively regarded as *The Waste Land*, Stevens would now be acknowledged as significant a poet as Eliot.

The Comedian, Simons explained, was an allegory of how a representative modern poet had "tried to change from a romanticist to a realist" by adapting to his social environment. Stevens had moved from a "juvenile romantic subjectivism" to a position of stark realism, moved on to a mode of sensuousness, then to a mode of realism based on the acceptance of the world on its own terms. By the poem's conclusion Crispin had discovered "the beauty in the commonplace" as the basis for "an honest American poetry." *The Comedian*, in fact, had done for poetry what Joyce's *Ulysses* had done for prose, pointing to the skepticism and fatalism one found in Stevens's more recent poetry. Moreover Stevens was interested in "questions of political and social order," as well as "with the incessant conjunctions between things as they are and things imagined," and "many of his seemingly precious and whimsical short poems" gained in significance if read in that light. Stevens's politics had always been to the Right, from his bland conservatism of two decades before to the starkness of the question he had posed just three years earlier, asking if Picasso's "hoard / Of destructions" was after all "a picture of ourselves."

Stevens was intrigued by what Simons had discovered, especially the notion of how one determined what was real and then made contact with it. Suppose, Stevens suggested, "one happened to be playing checkers somewhere under the Maginot Line, subject to a call at any moment to do some job that might be one's last job." (Was this his take on Marcel Duchamp, who had long ago given up art to play chess?) And what if one was about to take a bullet? Wouldn't one "spend a good deal of time thinking in order to make the situation seem reasonable, inevitable and free from question"? That was the kind of thinking that mattered now.

During Stevens's time with Elsie and Holly at Christmas Cove that July, his muse had been both serious and playful despite the distant rumblings of war. All about him seagulls were mewing and "flying / In light blue air over dark blue sea." It was the first of twenty notes struck in his "Variations on a Summer Day." Once again he listened for what the ocean might be telling him in

A music more than a breath, but less
Than the wind, sub-music like sub-speech,
A repetition of unconscious things,
Letters of rock and water, words
Of the visible elements and of ours.

Then too there was the strange metamorphosis of "the rocks of the cliffs" resembling "the heads of dogs / That turn into fishes and leap / Into the sea." And the lighthouse out on Monhegan Island shining at night like an Atlantic star, seeming to drift in the darkness like everything else, "one of the portents of the will that was." Who were we, if not mere leaves shaken by the sea, though once, perhaps, "there was a tree that was a father," a God, a principal, beneath which we sang our songs? Were we not worth more than a thousand sparrows, and was not "one sparrow . . . worth a thousand gulls, / When it sings"? Like Hitler, the "gull sits on chimney-tops" and mocks the guinea—the guinea hen but the blustering Mussolini as well—and "challenges the crow"—that even darker nemesis, Hitler—"inciting various modes." In spite of which the sparrow, by singing, "requites one, without intent."

Ah, to be free of the cares of the world, to "escape from the body" even for a moment, and feel "those feelings that the body balks, / The feelings of the natures round us here," or as "a boat feels when it cuts blue water." To note the timothy at the lighthouse at Maine's Pemaquid Point, "silver-tipped / And cold." Or the moon which seems to follow "the sun like a French / Translation of a Russian poet," softening the landscape with its softer sounds, even as "the spruce trees bury soldiers," like "Hugh March, a sergeant, a redcoat, killed, / With his men, beyond the barbican."

On September 9, 1695, a squadron of English colonial redcoats rounding a rocky point near their outpost at Pemaquid had been fired on by Abenakis. In the ensuing battle six soldiers were wounded and four killed, including March. Stevens had probably picked up a copy of John Henry Cartland's *Ten Years at Pemaquid*, where he would have learned of the fate of March, who was just twenty-two when he died. In the 1880s Cartland had found a remnant of March's slate gravestone, which had been defaced long before. By the time Stevens visited the area March's burial site was gone. But what of it? Everywhere spruce trees were burying soldiers as they buried the past. As it was then, so it will be, even as British soldiers faced new enemies, *per omnia saecula saeculorum:* forever and ever and ever.

The sound of the bell buoy tolls on and on like the sea itself, like bells in a cathedral by the sea, where "pine-figures" go on pining, pining, until they bring on sleep. Then a moment of lightness, as "low tide, flat water, sultry sun" roll on in a place called Damariscotta, empty Dadaist syllables by which to define a place against the eternal skies and waters: "Damariscotta, da da doo." A boy swims under a small boat turned upside down while another boy sits on top, as Stevens did on the Schuylkill fifty years before. And other boats, like Mussolini's warships sail out of Naples into the Mediterranean. Meanwhile, a sailboat glides through the waters off the Atlantic coast, the beads of water on the boat's brass railings grasping at transparence. A momentary thing, yes, but real for that moment.

• • •

ON SEPTEMBER 1, 1939, the war so many had feared began when the German Wehrmacht marched into Poland. Less than forty-eight hours later, France, England, New Zealand, and Australia would all declare war on Germany, with Canada soon to follow, while the United States declared its neutrality. When the war broke out, Stevens was on vacation in Williamsburg, Virginia, with his family, where, as he told Van Geyzel afterward, though he was horrified by the war, and while American sympathies were strongly with the British and French, he shared the nation's feeling about staying out of the war this time around.

It was "a habit of mind" with him, he told Hi Simons, always "to be thinking of some substitute for religion." While he believed in the Church as an institution that provided an order of sorts, he no longer believed "in the sort of God in Whom we were all brought up to believe." Humanism might have seemed to be a natural substitute for religion, but the more he saw of it, the less he liked it. Perhaps the best substitute for religion would be enjoying "a baseball game with all the beer signs and coca cola signs." At least for most people. As for him, a strong spirit stood by its own strength.

But even strong spirits needed support, in which case they would have to rely on the imagination of the strong poet. People, he believed, should enjoy poetry as naturally as "a child likes snow & they would if poets wrote it" using noble images. "Tell me more of the eagle, Cotton," he had written in "Some Friends from Pascagoula," bidding two shepherd-like figures to describe the "sovereign sight" of a god-like bird descending from the heavens above:

See how his heavy wings,
Spread on the sun-bronzed air,
Turned tip and tip away . . .

Dropping in sovereign rings
Out of his fiery lair.
Speak of the dazzling wings.

Ideas ran in cycles, he told Simons, from "romanticism to realism, to fatalism and then to indifferentism." Once that had exhausted itself, the cycle began all over again with a new romanticism. Just now—as the 1930s unwound—the world he knew was passing from fatalism to indifferentism, and the feeling was one of helplessness. But as the world was far more vigorous than the people in it, "what the world looks forward to is a new romanticism, a new belief."

Until recently it looked as if Communism would prevail. And while he believed "in any number of things that the so-called social revolutionists believe in," he didn't believe in calling himself a revolutionist simply because he believed "in doing everything practically possible to improve the condition of the workers." He did believe in education as the basis of gaining freedom and power, and he wanted to see the working class "live decently and in security and to educate their children and to have pleasant homes, etc." But one could have all those things without the United States becoming a Communist state. Right and Left meant many things, but if the Right meant what he thought it meant, then the Left wasn't anything he was interested in. Still, talking about the Right and the Left was ridiculous. What he was really interested in doing was telling someone like the archbishop of Canterbury—for Stevens an image of an altogether outmoded order—to "go jump off the end of the dock."

• • •

IN FEBRUARY 1940 STEVENS was back at the Casa Marina, this time with Elsie and Holly, along with Judge Powell and his wife, and it would prove his final, tame farewell to the land of swaying palms. They'd flown down this time, to Miami, because Holly wanted the experience of flying, though Elsie would suffer another bout of motion sickness, as she had on their cruise through the Panama Canal seventeen years earlier. Any ride in a car lasting more than half an hour seemed to cause her motion sickness. Now, with the war looming ever closer to home, the United States was in the process of requisitioning the Casa Marina for naval officers' quarters. By then, in fact, Key West had become "furiously literary," what with the annual presence of Frost, accompanied now by Lawrance Thompson, his official biographer. One of the younger poets in Key West that winter was twenty-five-year-old Elizabeth Bishop, who confessed to riding her bike down to the fancy hotel there, hoping to catch a glimpse of Stevens through her binoculars.

On one occasion Frost and Stevens sat together by the inner arcade of the Casa Marina to have their photo taken. Both were tanned and white-haired, Frost in a suit and tie, Stevens in light trousers, jacket, matching vest, and a tie as well. Thompson would capture one of their exchanges for posterity. Stevens had opened the volley by telling Frost that he was "too academic," to which Frost had answered that Stevens was "too executive." Then Round 2: "The trouble with you," Stevens retorted, was that Frost wrote about subjects. To which Frost retorted, "The trouble with you, Wallace, is that you write about—bric-a-brac." All of this said, of course, good-naturedly, with just the slightest edge.

Why wasn't there more of an exchange between these two giant contenders in the field of Modern American Poetry? If their poetry is different in terms of its accessibility, if Frost was the poet of the everyday, the poet of practical wisdom, the poet of narratives, the New England farmer-teacher poet who had caught the American idiom in his traditional meters, but with an ironic smile that left you wondering how he had managed to cut your legs out from under you as you walked away from one of his poems, wondering what he had said and not said at the same time, Stevens—at least the Stevens of *Harmonium*, the mandarin poet, the Frenchified dandy, the lawyer-poet of the inscrutable edifice, the poet of abstractions—seemed to live in another world altogether. That they were, finally, after the same thing—discovering by dint of hard work and genius a language which could speak convincingly and deeply to the mind and heart of those ready to listen—would have to be left to others to discover and confirm. In the meantime both men would steam ahead into the uncharted world of language, pretending not to notice the other's wake, swallowing many smaller boats as the two giants sailed on.

• • •

THAT MAY STEVENS SENT Van Geyzel a copy of Rimbaud's *A Season in Hell*, which the young poet Delmore Schwartz had just translated, though Stevens thought it sophomoric in places, along with a copy of *Poetry* with a note on another translation of Rimbaud, this one by Philip Rice. Rice's was perhaps the more accurate translation, Stevens said, but Schwartz was a poet well worth watching. And when it came to translation, Stevens would choose a poet over a scholar or philosopher any day.

Early in July he was in Reading, this time for the funeral of his brother John, former judge and Democratic Party boss of Berks County, who had died from ulcer complications. This funeral felt surprisingly different, as Uncle Wallace mingled with his nephews and nieces. One in particular, his sister Elizabeth's twenty-one-year-old daughter, Jane, delighted him. He had never before met Jane, or John's two children, or any of the grandchildren, for that matter, but if there was ever going to be a time to reunite with his family, that time was now. Elizabeth had been unable to attend the funeral because of her health, so Stevens decided to accompany Jane back to Philadelphia and see Elizabeth for the first time in twenty-five years. When they arrived, Stevens greeted his sister—a six-two, 250-pound woman—with the words, "My God, Elizabeth, you've put it on!" Elizabeth shot back her own riposte, and the ice was broken. From that moment on, confessed Jane, whose father had abandoned the family years before, Uncle Wallace replaced her Uncle John. In fact in time Stevens would become the father she never had.

A year later John Stevens Jr. and his bride, Anna May, would visit Uncle Wallace on their way to Lake George for their honeymoon. Stevens had attended their wedding in Reading the week before and had insisted on their stopping off at the house for lunch. When they got there, John was met at the front door by "a little woman in a brown cardigan" who told him that she was Mrs. Stevens. "I almost fell out of the car," Anna May remembered. So this was Aunt Elsie, "a church mouse" without a sense of humor. Was this the same woman whose profile adorned so many millions of dimes? Elsie's hair was pulled straight back and she was wearing a "terrible brown long . . . housedress and nondescript shoes." She had carefully prepared "a divine filet mignon with asparagus hollandaise," which she served without joining them. After dinner Stevens took them upstairs and showed them "the men's quarters and the women's quarters." His was the right side, including the study and a "Spartan bedroom," while Elsie's and Holly's smaller bedrooms occupied the left side of the house. It was a "very well appointed house" with everything in its place," Anna May remembered, but with "very little warmth or personality." How different all this was from Stevens's warmth when he'd let himself go at their wedding, drinking abundant martinis and joking with his newfound family.

• • •

"THIS HAS NOT BEEN a good summer," Stevens wrote Henry Church in late August 1940. "My only brother died a month or two ago, and last week my wife's mother was killed in an automobile accident. This sort of thing . . . added to the [damnable] grind at the office, makes me feel pretty much as a man must feel in a shelter waiting for the bombing to start." The climate was changing, and it seemed "pretty clearly to be becoming less and less a climate of literature." By then the Churches had left France and were living in an enclave in the shadow of Princeton University. Church had written Stevens about finding a new home for *Mesures* there, and Stevens had replied that it might be time to give up the magazine for now, much as Eliot had done with *The Criterion*. Why not instead underwrite a chair of poetry at Harvard to study "the history of poetic thought and of the theory of poetry"?

When he tried to explain to Hi Simons what he'd said in *Ideas of Order* about the "difficulty of imposing the imagination on those that do not share it," the subject came around once more to the idea of God, which, Stevens insisted, was necessarily "a thing of the imagination," and that meant turning to the idea of the Prime Mover: Poetry in its purest essence. Poetry was "the highest objective of the poet," a concept "as great as the idea of God," in fact greater, when one realized that the idea of God was "only one of the things of the imagination."

Of course one would have to be Poet Number One to "produce a poem equivalent to the idea of God," except that such a poet would be as concerned "with a knowledge of man as people are now concerned with a knowledge of God." And to know man, one needed to understand the idea of good and evil. If Europe held one idea of God and Africa another, those differences would have to be reconciled in a universally held idea of poetry, which only the imagination could provide. And since the idea of heaven in Europe was now empty, it might be the time "to recognize Ananke," or Fate. In any event, some idea would have to take the place of God since people had to believe in something.

Logically, such a mind as his ought to believe in what he called the "essential imagination," but such an abstraction presented its own difficulties. It was much "easier to believe in a thing created by the imagination," and the search for that thing was what he was looking for now in his poems. Back in the mid-1930s, when he was trying to name that thing, he'd called it Fate, or Ananke—an import from Italy which seemed for the moment to fill the necessary gap. But now, in 1940, he'd come to believe that "one's final belief" had to be found "in a fiction." In fact the history of belief, he pointed out, had always manifested itself in a fiction, as paradoxical as such a statement might seem. This was what a new poem, called "Asides on the Oboe," was about. It began this way:

The prologues are over. It is a question, now,
Of final belief. So, say that final belief
Must be in a fiction. It is time to choose.

There were obsolete fictions enough, the poem explained. Like those mythy gods the painter Boucher had killed by turning them into eighteenth-century royal figures. Then too, there were all those statues, "metal heroes that time granulates." But now the major man, the philosopher's man, Myth Man Number One, had to take the place of those gods and walk alone in the dew, in a world realized only in the moment of the poem's unfolding, as one muttered "milky lines / Concerning an immaculate imagery." If nothing and no one could actually stand in as God, still there was

The impossible possible philosophers' man,
The man who has had the time to think enough,

The central man, the human globe, responsive
As a mirror with a voice, the man of glass,
Who in a million diamonds sums us up.

Such a figure, who would replace the Incarnate Christ, would represent "the transparence of the place in which / He is," the figure who, once realized, would bestow peace on us with the very words of his poems, who could say, "Thou art not August unless I make thee so." But even such a poet, Stevens deflated his own heady balloon, would then have to go door to door with his pie: his pi—a synthesis, yes—but a pi that was finally just one more pie in the sky.

Where then was the new Garden of Eden to be found, the *hortus inclusus*, the fabled jasmine island (or was jasmine but another word for Gethsemane?) where such peace reigned? Were not those jasmine islands filled now with Japanese soldiers and "bloody martyrdoms"? If what we found now was "the central evil," then, by contrast, we might also find its opposite: "the central good." Which was why "we buried the fallen without jasmine crowns for there was nothing he did not suffer, no; nor we." In accepting death as part of life, the world turned to a transparency like man himself, and "we and the diamond globe at last were one." We had always "been partly one." But now, as the people harkened to the poet, they might finally hear him "chanting for those buried in their blood," there, "in the jasmine haunted forests," and know ourselves at last, "without external reference," no longer crying out to a God no longer there. And if the message was too much for us to bear, then the music, the waverings on the oboe, might be enough to comfort us.

• • •

OUT OF THE DARK, then, and back into the dark. Consciousness, Stevens understood, was both preceded and followed by the unconscious, and the unconscious was but another name for the imagination. To recognize consciousness was like recognizing a force pushing through the ocean that contained the wave. In the presence of the things of the imagination, the rationalist seemed to live in an ever-changing world. But there were realities like summer nights which so closely resembled the way we imagined summer nights to be "that in their presence, the realist and the man of imagination" became one.

Thus when he'd composed *Ideas of Order*, he, like so many others, had felt the presence of an evil which only later, with the outbreak of World War II, was actualized. What we felt was fear, because we saw the evil of the First World War replaying itself in a larger hall. By way of a counterbalance, we hungered for words in which we could believe, like a statue "brimming white in a perspective of trees as black as crows." In the "hum-drum space by night" it was still possible to feel "the rapture of a time" when time seemed to fulfill itself, when one night might mirror another, and "all the nights that ever were."

• • •

IT WAS TIME, THEN for "the essential poets" to be recognized as "spiritual figures," he told Henry Church that October. The one who should be awarded his proposed chair of poetry would have to be a strong figure who could discover step by step what was needed. Someone like his mentor, George Santayana, though there "the religious and the philosophic" had played too dominant a role. Eliot had the necessary character, but then he was too negative a force. In any event, it was "an odd civilization" where poetry was not recognized as the equal of philosophy. And if poetry was made up of exceptional individuals, that was because it had no other choice.

That December Church told Stevens he was going to speak with Dean Christian Gauss and Allen Tate about his arranging for four lectures on poetry each year at Princeton. Among the subjects to be included would be semantics, language, theory, and the metaphysical foundations of poetry. When Tate suggested that Stevens should give a lecture, Stevens was at first reluctant, then agreed. Of all the subjects mentioned, he liked "theory of poetry" best, because it covered the widest ground and would "attempt to disclose the truth about poetry." Tate, he thought, might introduce the speakers and at the same time "round out and connect the several phases of the subject."

He wanted to do everything he could to make his talk work, he wrote Church in early January 1941, for it was not every day one was invited to speak at Princeton. He planned to call it "The Noble Rider and the

Sound of Words," and it would "trace the idea of nobility" through "the disaster of reality, and particularly the reality of words." This description, he admitted, sounded "rather stupid" and would take a "good deal of thinking and a good deal of reading" before he got it right. If Stevens's talk, delivered that May, seemed long and convoluted, it was also brilliant, serious, and comic by turns—though how many caught his wit when he delivered it with his poker-face demeanor is uncertain.

He began by comparing a number of images representing the spirit of man as noble rider, beginning with Plato's figure in the *Phaedrus* of two winged horses, one of them of noble breeding which attempts to soar upward, and the other of ignoble origin, which keeps pulling the chariot downward to earth, while the charioteer tries to control the mismatched team. If Plato distrusted poets, the image itself, Stevens pointed out, was pure poetry, though admittedly "antiquated and rustic," because the soul as Plato portrayed it—with chariot and charioteer—was a fiction even for Plato. Still, the underlying idea of the noble, Stevens underscored, was real then and was real now. After all, even if we did not accept the image of the plunging horses themselves, we were moved by the clearness and fluency of Plato's poetic instinct. Of course the idea of nobility, like everything else, had its vicissitudes, changing as the mind had changed over the past 2,500 years, and the imagination in turn lost its vitality as it ceased to adhere to the real. If, then, the modern mind could understand what Plato had tried to convey, it could not participate in his myth because it saw through to its unreality.

Stevens had considered passing from Plato's winged horses to the idealism of Don Quixote, the tragicomic knight on horseback. But standing in the way was Verrocchio's equestrian figure of the *condottiero* Bartolomeo Colleoni in the Piazza di San Marco in Venice. Here was the figure of the noble warrior, the indomitable one, the figure of rhetorical passion, Mussolini's prototype. But the mind rejected this figure as well, because it was too magnificent. Had not Cervantes tried to "right the balance between the imagination and reality"? Nobility for the Spaniard was not merely a thing of the imagination, but something so true and yet so misunderstood that it was now in danger of disappearing forever.

So much, then, for Europe. Now he evoked an image of the American

Sublime figured in another equestrian statue, this one Clark Mills's rendering of General Andrew Jackson at the victory of New Orleans. Erected in Washington's Lafayette Square and facing the White House in the years leading up to the Civil War, the statue portrayed Jackson "riding a horse with one of the most beautiful tails in the world" and "raising his hat in a gay gesture, saluting the ladies of his generation." But what if Verrocchio had sculpted Jackson instead? Would not "the whole American outlook today" be far more imperial? If what Mills had created was a thing of pure fancy, at least it helped us understand how Americans had viewed themselves a century earlier.

Finally, in a glorious send-up, Stevens evoked one more equestrian image: a contemporary painting by Reginald Marsh called *Wooden Horses*. Marsh depicts a merry-go-round, such as one found at Coney Island, in which one of the horses seems to be prancing, while the others seem to be going "lickety-split." In the center of the painting is a yellow horse with "two riders, one a man, dressed in a carnival costume" and "seated in the saddle," the other "a blonde . . . seated well up the horse's neck." The man has "his arms under the girl's arms" and holds himself stiffly "to keep his cigar out of the girl's hair." Her feet are "in a second and shorter set of stirrups," and she has "the legs of a hammer-thrower." It is clear too that the couple likes riding wooden horses together. What Marsh had created in fact was "a picture of ribald and hilarious reality . . . wholly favorable to what is real."

But if one followed Marsh's image, nobility seemed to exist in art today "only in degenerate forms or in a much diminished state," because that was now the nature of the real. For the poet too "a variation between the sound of words in one age and the sound of words in another" was itself "an instance of the pressure of reality." Locke and Hobbes had denounced the seventeenth century for its connotative use of language, and that had resulted in an era of urbane, witty poetic diction, with Pope and Swift as its chief proponents. Then, at the start of the nineteenth century, Wordsworth had opted for a poetry which employed "a selection of the real language of man in a state of vivid sensation," with the result that the poem had swung back to its earlier connotative phase. Painting and music had likewise shifted, thanks to Freud, toward the subconscious and the surreal. Freud had also suggested that religion seemed less credible now, so that the human race had had to venture into a more hostile world, leaving poetry behind.

In fact the spirit of negation was so dominant now that one wondered if "our salvation, if the way out," was not the romantic, especially in a time when "all the great things have been denied" and we lived in a time of incoherent and self-contradicting mythologies. On top of which there now seemed to be an "absence of any authority except force." And with the absence of a more reasoned authority had come "the disparagement of reason" itself.

Social discourse was at a nadir everywhere. Turn on the radio and you heard comedians getting a laugh by simply using a word made up of more than two syllables. Hadn't Kierkegaard insisted that poetry was unjust because only a relative few could enjoy it? Education provided everyone with a little learning, which in turn meant a growing middle class who preferred material satisfactions to intellectual pursuits. Moreover there was no discreet distance between people anymore. "We are intimate with people we have never seen," Stevens lamented, and they are intimate with us. Once Democritus had plucked his eye out because he could not look at a woman without lusting after her. Had he "read a few of our novels, he would have torn himself to pieces." People lived now simply to make money. As for the worker, what was he but a mere Marxist abstraction?

What could the poet offer in a time like the present? For ten years now the news had been asking if the world would one day be "all-English, all-German, all-Russian, all-Japanese, or all-American." Now, with Hitler's victories in Europe and Russia, Americans were facing "a set of events . . . beyond our power to reduce them and metamorphose them," except to react to them with a commensurate violence. But what was needed now was resistance to that external pressure with the countervailing pressure of the man of extraordinary imagination. In other words: the poet.

And what would such a poet look like? First, he would have to have lived the "last two thousand years, and longer," instructing himself as he went along. That meant understanding Virgil, Dante, Shakespeare, and Milton within the contexts of their times. It would mean being able to abstract himself and likewise abstract reality by giving himself over to "the musical and creative powers of words." Like Don Quixote, he would have to understand that the ideal imagination and reality were partners: equal and interdependent.

Stevens had grown up with the vital reality of the world of "twenty or thirty years ago." Then, ten years ago, reality had turned violent. If not violent for Americans, certainly "for millions of our friends and for still more millions of our enemies and spiritually violent . . . for everyone alive." In the long run the poet owed nothing to the political and moral exigencies of the time because poetry was about life itself, and it was the poet's task to make his imagination a light for the minds of others and thus help them live. Moreover, the poet had every right to address the elite. In fact there wasn't a living poet who did not do just that. And because the poet offered that elite (or elect) what it needed, it would repay him by doing what he could not do for himself: receive his poetry. It was the poet who gave life savor, who gave us "the world to which we turn incessantly and without knowing it." We needed the poet's words to express our thoughts and feelings, because they were all the truth we were ever going to experience. Moreover, it was the poet who made us love words and search them "for a finality, a perfection, an unalterable vibration." And it was the nobility of poetry which gave us "our spiritual height and depth," though, like the idea of God, the idea of the noble would go on resolving itself "into an enormous number of vibrations, movements, changes," for to try to fix the idea of the noble would be "to put an end to it."

Finally, Stevens turned to the flower paintings of Jacob Epstein. These, he pointed out, made "no pretence to fragility." They shouted, they exploded "all over the picture space," opposing "the rage of the world with such a rage of form and colour as no flower in nature or pigment has done since Van Gogh." If the noble was absent from contemporary poetry, still, there was no element that poets sought after "more curiously and more piously, certain of its obscure existence." Nobility was a "violence from within that protects us from a violence without." It was "the imagination pressing back against the pressure of reality," the very sounds of its words helping us to live our lives. The noble writer, then, and the sound of words.

No one, he told Simons that July, would ever have guessed from his talk "what a lot of serious reading" had been required. What he did not tell Simons was that he'd acted boorishly at the dinner following his speech, when he'd asked Caroline Gordon, Allen Tate's wife, to change seats with the wife of Christian Gauss because Mrs. Gauss knew people he knew. That was Stevens. When Richard Bissell, president of the Hartford Insurance Company, died that summer, Stevens wrote a brief portrait of him for the *Hartford Agent.* Afterward one of his fellow vice presidents had stopped by Stevens's office to say he'd found the tribute a "very nice piece." Stevens, without raising his head, had replied, "I hope I can do the same for you someday."

For months afterward he worried that he'd lost Church's friendship over his behavior at the Princeton dinner. In fact eight months would pass before he heard from Church again, but mainly because Church had suffered a severe case of angina and was now in Tucson for his health. "I love to hear from you," Stevens wrote him, relieved. "You have so thoroughly lived the life that I should have been glad to live, and you are so much more intricate a personality than any half dozen people that I can think of put together, that I felt that I had lost a good deal more than one would ordinarily lose." Even nobility, after all, had its human face.

14

The Son Restores the Father: 1941–1945

It has a clear, a single, a solid form,
That of the son who bears upon his back
The father that he loves, and bears him from
The ruins of the past, out of nothing left,
Made noble by the honor he receives.

"TRADITION"

Who was he, really? A Pennsylvania Dutchman with roots going back to the original settlement of New Amsterdam, whose ancestors had moved to Philadelphia and then westward to Reading via farming communities like Feasterville? Having attended Harvard and written poetry with Santayana and then gone on to law school and become in time a vice president of one of the most successful insurance companies in America, how had those Pennsylvania Dutch roots shaped him? Now that the Zeller and Stevens siblings had been reduced to just two, he and Elizabeth, the pressure to find out who those figures in the old oval portraits on the walls of his house really were had become an imperative, a way of discovering what forces had shaped him before he too passed beyond the brackets of his own birth and death. In the summer of 1941 he began his genealogical research in earnest. Though he had once pooh-poohed his mother's keen interest in becoming a Daughter of the American Revolution, he now wrote to the DAR to ascertain what had been discovered there. What also helped spur him on was Elsie's interest in her own background, knowing that her ancestors included a number of prominent members at least as important as the Stevenses, that is, before economic hard times had quashed all that.

Only Elizabeth—whom he would lose soon enough—and Garrett's and John's widows remained from his own generation: ghostly reminders of an imaginary Booth Tarkington, Currier and Ives youth that loomed larger and larger in the dark solitude of his study. When he was a boy he had visited his father's parents, Benjamin Stevens and Elizabeth Barcalow, in Feasterville. That was where his father had grown up, farming and fishing, so that his grandparents had long ago become "figures in an idyll" to him. It was their world, morphed by memory and the imagination, which now led him to exhume his long-dead ancestors and give them a living name.

How important it was for Elsie to prove her own worth. In the summer of 1931 she had attended a session at Vassar's Institute in Euthenics (a program which strove to bring the techniques and disciplines of the arts, sciences, and social sciences to bear on the life experiences and relationships of women, especially on how to properly raise one's children). She'd brought seven-year-old Holly with her, and Elsie—who had had to drop out of school in the ninth grade—would later tell visitors that she'd gone to Vassar, just as years later she would tell a professor from Smith that she had once won an award for composition (though that had been in the third grade).

Now, in the fall of 1941, seventeen-year-old Holly was more or less forced to enroll in Vassar. Which was fine with her father, who insisted that she attend an all-woman's college and one not too far from home. Vassar seemed ideal, being a mere hour and a half to the west, a distance Holly might easily traverse in her brand-new red convertible.

But Holly hated Vassar from the start. She'd wanted to attend a coed school farther from home to be on her own for the first time in her life. At the close of her first semester, Pearl Harbor was bombed and the United States was in a war with Japan and Germany. She made it through her first year, and then—against her wishes—returned to begin her sophomore year in the fall of 1942. But when she returned home for a visit that October, she insisted that she wasn't going back, though she did return for a few more weeks before dropping out, saying she meant to find a job and do her part for the war effort. "I felt like a perfect ninny sitting by the Hudson River as an English major with a war going on," she later explained, though the real war for her was one for independence from her parents. When she had left to begin her sophomore year, her father had avoided any contact with her as a way of paying her back for her distant behavior toward him and Elsie. Of course he could not keep up this silent charade with his daughter; within days of her leaving he had written her explaining why he'd been upset with her, increasing her allowance to try to undo any damage he might have caused. It was his way of apologizing for not having bidden her a proper good-bye.

In early October Holly sent her father a birthday card for his sixty-third birthday, along with a list of grievances against him and her mother and—having now reached the legal age of eighteen—demanding her independence. "For a long time our situation at home has made me unhappy," she wrote. "When I am at home Mother always bustles around wanting to open windows, turn on lights, etc. I am often occupied and resent these interruptions: I know enough about windows and lights to look after them myself." As for her father, he let her know his displeasure "in a way that makes me feel I must choose either to stay in every night, or to go out every night." Really, what was wrong with staying overnight with one of her girlfriends or making up her own mind about things? "I am not arguing with you now," she made clear, "but the next time you so outrageously say 'Don't argue with me' I certainly shall, feeling every right in so doing." The letter was, "in a nutshell," a call for "freedom from criticism" and a greater share of independence, which meant a place of her own.

Stevens wrote back in his own scrawl; after all, he explained, this was not the sort of letter one dictated at the office. He knew her mother had already responded to Holly's letter, but what she had said he'd not been privy to. "For my own part," he told her, "I think you already have the independence you desire. No parents could be less authoritarian than we have been." In fact Holly had always been free as far as he could see. "That your parents," like anyone's parents, had their imperfections was "nothing to brood on," for they also had their good qualities, and Holly's mother—tough as she was—had them "to an exquisite degree." Yes, he knew Holly had witnessed tensions between her parents, but they were merely "blow-ups of the nerves," and "when they are over they are over." As for his own "stubbornnesses and taciturn eras," they came "straight out of Holland," and he could no more change them than he could take off his skin. Still—and this was true—he never hesitated "to seek to undo any damage" he might have done. After all, they both loved her and wanted "only to help you and part of yr education is to get on with us and part of ours to get on with you." He signed it, "Love, Dad."

Two weeks later Stevens wrote Professor Ruth Wheeler, a member of the Vassar faculty and the person who had directed the Institute of Euthenics in the summer of 1931. "You may remember," he wrote, "that ten years or so ago Mrs. Stevens and Holly were members of the Institute." Well, Holly was now a sophomore at Vassar. She had returned home two weeks earlier, determined to leave college, or at least take a leave until the following fall. The news had been a great shock to his wife and to him, because he had wanted to provide his daughter with "the best education possible, first with the idea that it would at least give her a strong and clear mind, which would be about as much as I could expect to give her now-a-days," and then "because a college education would at least fit her to go farther if by the time she finished college she was disposed to go farther." She'd returned to Vassar unwillingly, and would no doubt bring up the matter with them at Christmas, because "she was bored by her subjects and . . . wanted to get a job," perhaps—he added sardonically—"as a copy boy on one of the local papers." But there was no need for Holly to work because he could provide everything she wanted. That Holly wanted her independence was a puzzle to him, because he and his wife had always "been the least authoritarian parents." Then too there was that irresponsible crowd she ran around with in Hartford.

Perhaps Miss Wheeler might "find some girl of intelligence and tact who would make friends with Holly" and get her through this crisis? True, Holly was not "a brilliant scholar," but there was so much to be gained by the "regularity and discipline" which Vassar could provide. He was even "willing to pay anyone whose assistance" Miss Wheeler thought might help. He knew that if Holly made up her mind at Christmas not to return, he and his wife would "have to acquiesce" in her decision and "watch helplessly as she went her own way." Holly was too young to understand "how much in later life she will be dependent on spiritual values, all the more so if she happened to have no others." On the other hand, he had no idea what his daughter was really thinking. In any event, she must never learn that he had written Wheeler for advice.

Three days later he wrote Holly again, pleading with her to stay in school. Giving oneself to something, as he had learned long ago, in time became "a source of unfailing happiness." Her girlfriends would merely go from one job to another and that would be the end of it. "Learn to live the good in your heart," he ended, a sincere Polonius, "and devote your life to it." But despite her father's pleas and his last-minute trip to Vassar to hold a conference with the dean, Holly withdrew in mid-November and, with the help of her father, found a clerical job at the Aetna insurance company, close to her father's office, where in time she would become a fire underwriter. It was while working there that she would meet an office equipment serviceman whom she would marry a year and a half later.

Disappointed by his daughter, Stevens turned to her surrogate, his niece Jane. In the midst of his crisis with Holly, Elizabeth wrote him to say Jane was serious about marrying a soldier, and asking his advice. But he hadn't "the faintest idea what to say about Jane," he told her, "even though I know that there is nothing closer to your heart than her welfare." If Jane did marry her GI, she might well have twins within a year "and be the wife of a soldier with one leg and possibly with none." On the other hand, if she didn't marry now "for the obvious prudential reasons, the same reasons would prevent her from marrying as long as the war goes on, and it may go on for a long time so that she may wind up as an old maid, and Jane was never meant to be an old maid." True, if it were Holly, he admitted, "I shouldn't much like the idea, but I should feel that I had very little choice about it . . . and certainly not oppose it, if the boy was, in himself, a sound, healthy, real person." That was the real issue: Would the young man make "a desirable husband," by which he meant someone physically fit and with a decent temperament, "reasonable intelligence, will and character"? That was all any girl could ever ask for, "for every girl takes a chance on her husband's future."

That Holly had failed to write Jane about her recent engagement had not really come as a surprise, he explained, because his family meant nothing to his daughter. "The lovely country round Reading and all the interesting people and places that you and I have known and which we might well think that she would enjoy, just don't exist for her." For one thing, Elsie never spoke of Reading "except to mention one or two of her aunts occasionally," on top of which he knew Holly had drifted more and more from her mother. Yet there was nothing he or Elsie could do about it. "But then," he admitted, he'd felt exactly the same way when he was eighteen in taking his own family for granted.

When Jane married her GI that December, it was Uncle Wallace whom she asked to walk her down the aisle. Stevens made the wedding even more special by sending Jane a generous sum of money that allowed her to buy a wedding gown she could not otherwise have afforded. "She was positively radiant when she saw the check," Elizabeth wrote her brother, "and hugged me saying, 'Mother he doesn't know what he's done. He's made it all possible now.' "

• • •

IT WAS ONE OF the last letters he had from his sister. Four months later, on February 19, 1943, Elizabeth succumbed to encephalitis at the age of fifty-seven. "You lost your brother at about the same time that I lost my sister, the last member of my family, so that we are in a position to exchange sympathy," he wrote Henry Church. She had died "within less than 24 hours after being taken to the hospital." As distressed as he was, he coped with the loss of his last sibling by trying to think "about it as if it was something that had happened long ago." What helped was going back to Reading after the funeral with two of his nieces, both young and "pretty and robust, and living in an atmosphere of children." Jane of course was one of those nieces. The other was Anna May, the wife of John Jr., who had been serving with the Army Tank Corps in Hawaii for the past year and who had yet to see his baby daughter. During that time, Stevens added, Anna May had "completely transformed the house," so that, like Ulysses, if his nephew "were to come back tomorrow and put away his uniform, he would forget all about his experiences of the last year in ten minutes."

It was Jane who had telephoned her uncle with the news of his sister's death. Stevens arrived in Philadelphia the following morning to make all the arrangements for the funeral. After the service he suggested he and Jane get some exercise. "We walked along the Parkway and . . . Walnut Street, downtown Philadelphia," Jane would remember. There was a bakery there, and when her uncle spotted a delightful whiskey cake in the window, he ordered two: one for her, the other to be sent up to Hartford. Remember, he told her, she was not alone as long as he was still around.

Long disappointed in what his own marriage had become, and deeply disappointed in the direction Holly's life had taken, dating an office-equipment repairman named John Hanchak—a *Roussian*, he called him dismissively, a "Polack" and a Communist—with none of the credentials Stevens wanted for his daughter (shudders of history repeating itself with a vengeance), it was Jane who represented his family now. She and the ancestral ghosts of the Stevens, Barcalow, and Zeller lines. But if the dead were beyond betraying one, the living were not. In the months following Jane's wedding, she and Stevens exchanged long, comforting letters. After all, here was a young woman who had just lost a mother to whom she had been devoted, and now she was separated from a man fighting for his country. No wonder, then, that when Jane wrote Uncle Wallace in April 1944 to say that she was getting a divorce, Stevens was so upset he stopped writing her altogether.

That was the one time she felt his strong disapproval, Jane would remember. Up to that moment she and her uncle had written each other "just about every week." In spite of Stevens's silence, she continued to write because, as she told him, she loved him, and whether he loved her or not made no difference. She'd gone to Miami to facilitate her divorce, expecting to stay there for three months at most, and had taken "a bookkeeping job in a tire shop." But she decided to stay in Miami, so she found a job as a reservationist with Eastern Airlines. When she wrote Stevens telling him what she'd done, he finally broke his silence. "At least," he wrote back, that was "better than working in a recap shop!" The truth was that he admired Jane's pluck and resolve, for in his research into his past it was the women he'd come most to admire, and Jane was a living example of what he took to be their character and strength. "Everyone in the family is precious to me," he would tell his nephew, John, "and it is the easiest thing in the world for us to drift apart instead of clinging to each other as we should."

• • •

STILL, IT WAS BETTER to concentrate on the dead, who seemed far more capable of being shaped according to one's imagination. "Who could ever have imagined that, after three or four years, I should still be at work" on genealogical research, he wrote a cousin he'd recently discovered. That was in 1945, and the interest would continue for another five years as he searched for the inhabitants of his imaginary Eden. In time there would be 2,500 genealogical letters and documents, as well as his multivolume genealogical work in progress, even as he continued to head up the fidelity and surety claims department at the Hartford and compose more poems, some greater than he'd ever written.

He joked that "after muddling round" with genealogy for so long, he would be happy just to find among his ancestors some decent "carpenter, or a really robust blacksmith, or a woman capable of having eleven sons and of weaving their clothes and the blankets under which they slept." That would be as fulfilling as learning that he had royalty running through his veins. Yet he was deeply disappointed to learn that he did not qualify for membership in the Holland Society of New York, open only to direct descendents of those Dutch who had settled in the New World from the beginning. He'd found "horse thieves and all kinds of people back there," Stevens told his niece Eleanor's husband, John Sauer, over a fine French dinner in New York's upper Seventies, but then some "bastard from Danzig" had shown up, and that had ruined his whole Dutch line and kept him from being admitted to the Society.

However, he was invited to join New York's Saint Nicholas Society. In his poem "Recitation after Dinner," composed for the Society's annual black-tie dinner in September 1945, the year after he joined, he spoke of what had really motivated him to spend so much money and time imagining what his ancestors must have been like. "A poem about tradition could easily be / A windy thing," he acknowledged. But it was the sense of filial piety that had moved him to write as he did now. Tradition, he'd discovered,

> *has a clear, a single, a solid form,*
> *That of the son who bears upon his back*
> *The father that he loves, and bears him from*
> *The ruins of the past, out of nothing left,*
> *Made noble by the honor he receives,*
> *As if in a golden cloud. The son restores*
> *The father.*

The son's devotion to the father: an attempt to redeem what he had lost by his falling out with his own father and then his siblings. There was the heart of it. In March 1942 he published *Five Grotesque Pieces* in *Trend*, one of which was called "Outside of Wedlock." Here he did not boast of pedigree or apotheosize his forbears. Instead he commanded the winter wind, that bleakest sound in his work, to sing a dirge, as if it spoke with the keening voice of two ancestors, his Dutch Adam and Eve: Grandfather Benjamin Stevens and Great-Great-Grandmother Blandina Janse van Woggelum Stevens. "Sing for her the seventy-fold Amen," the poem begins. Not the traditional sevenfold Amen he remembered from his boyhood, but an Amen ten times that size:

> *White February wind,*
> *Through banks and banks of voices,*
> *In the cathedral-shanty,*
> *To the sound of the concertina,*
> *Like the voice of all our ancestors,*
> *The père Benjamin, the mère Blandenah,*
> *Saying we have forgot them, they never lived.*

A man approaching old age himself now, he is as much the father Anchises as he is the son Aeneas who carries his father on his back, escaping from the ashes of his ruined city. The names of ancestors he never knew must serve here as surrogates and, in attempting to rescue them from oblivion, the poet finds a momentary comfort in his song. Family ties, after all, are lifelines that reach out from the present to the past, then return upon themselves from the past into the present.

When Stevens visited Reading in May 1943, he learned from the minister of the local Dutch church the name of his mother's grandfather. It was John Zeller Jr., which meant that his great-grandfather had to have been called John Zeller Sr., or "Old John Zeller," who, it turned out, had sired nine children. For another year that was all Stevens could find out about the man. Then, in May 1944, his genealogist came across a reference to John Zeller's grave in the churchyard of St. Paul's Evangelical and Reformed Church in Amityville, twelve miles east of Reading. The headstone lay buried under bramble, the name half-erased. Stevens lost no time in having the site restored and the stone reset.

In the fall of 1944, Stevens wrote his nephew, U.S. Army Captain John Stevens Jr., home on leave, that genealogy had become a "substitute for the reading of detective stories." Old John Zeller, it turned out, had been born during the Revolutionary War and had spent his boyhood on a farm in the Tulpehocken area of Berks County, where his own great-grandfather, the original Zeller immigrant, had first settled in the 1720s, years after fleeing the Palatinate in order to avoid persecution by the Catholics. After Old John had married, he and his wife, Katherine, had left the farm and moved to Philadelphia, where he'd made his living as a shoemaker before moving to the Valley of Oley, where he died at seventy-nine in 1858. The shoemaker's trade John would pass on to his son, John Jr., which was something within living memory for Stevens, who remembered how his mother, with all her anxieties about social respectability, had insisted that her father had not been some ordinary shoemaker but rather a maker of fine boots.

What could one take away from all this? What, really, did he know about his mother's grandfather, though he was flesh of his flesh and bone of his bone, besides birth and death dates, names of places where Old John had lived, and the location of an abandoned grave in a churchyard a dozen miles from where he'd grown up? What indeed beyond a "structure of ideas" composed of the "ghostly sequences / Of the mind"? But then, what did any of us know about ourselves? In trying to uncover the past, it seemed, all one accomplished, really, was to add to the disorder of one's mind and the inevitable disaster of trying to recover a living presence from the dust. Easy enough to wish it otherwise,

to wish for another structure
Of ideas and to say as usual that there must be
Other ghostly sequences and, it would be, luminous
Sequences, thought of among spheres in the old peak of night.

Wasn't that what his genealogical venture had turned out to be: "a habit of wishing, as if one's grandfather lay / In one's heart and wished as he"—both the poet and the old man—"had always wished," and yet "unable / To sleep in that bed for its disorder"? What difference was there, finally, between the imagined bed of Old John Zeller, tossing in his grave, unable to sleep even in death unless he could communicate something of himself to his great-grandson, and the great-grandson at sixty-five, tossing in his own bed in Hartford, likewise "talking of ghostly / Sequences that would be sleep and ting-tang tossing," until both "might slowly forget" everything and finally rest in peace? At least Old John would have been content to accept the world as it was for him—a world composed of shoe leather, taxes, his children's teeth, church services, the cold coming in under the door—rather than preoccupy himself as his twentieth-century offspring had to do with his metaphysical concerns about the structure of ideas, when, after all, all structures inevitably blended into the oblivion of death.

One thing Stevens wanted to believe about the Zellers, because he had seen this quality manifest itself in his own mother, was that they seemed "to have been both poor and pious." He was sure, though, that the Zellers had been "fanatics," filled with religious fervor, unlike the Dutch on his father's side. "Unlike the Puritans of Massachusetts and the Catholics in Maryland," he knew, "the Dutch did not come to this country for political and religious freedom." The Stevenses had emigrated to the New World to make money and "better their condition in life." They had not come to be "alone with their maker."

That Christmas Stevens returned to Reading to visit his nephew John Jr., then on furlough. It was John and Anna May who took him to visit the grave of Old John Zeller. Over the weekend the three of them visited the various cemeteries where the Stevenses lay interred. Stevens, who had planned the trip, took the opportunity to reminisce with some of his old Reading friends. "We were with him and we had a ball," Anna May recalled. Stevens talked about growing up in Reading and told the story of seeing his brother Garrett on the street in Cleveland twenty-five years earlier and—not having anything to say to him—crossing the street and continuing on. That visit—which coincided with the Battle of the Bulge—turned out to be one of his last to Reading. By then, solitary that he was, he had gleaned what he could from the younger generation about his ancestry, and events had shown him that even the best of the Stevenses were as vulnerable as anyone to the misfortunes of ignoble choice.

In September 1946 he spent a leisurely month at the Hotel Hershey, an hour west of Reading, with Elsie and Judge Powell and his wife, during which time he crisscrossed the area with a local genealogist. This time his nephews and nieces were not included. Once again he found Reading "unbearable," so that he left without seeing anyone there. "When one has left home the place naturally changes," he wrote Powell afterward. "What I had not realized is that it keeps changing until a point is reached at which the old familiar life of it is dead and gone."

• • •

"WHEN A POET MAKES his imagination the imagination of other people," Stevens wrote Simons in February 1942, "he does so by making them see the world through his eyes." To achieve this, one first had to strip the paint from the world and then repaint it according to one's own perceptions. But "powerful integrations of the imagination" were "difficult to get away from," so we saw the world not through our own eyes but through the eyes of those with the strongest imaginations. Because poetry allowed us to escape from the numbing sameness of the world around us, it was a benign illusion, like the idea of God. And because poetry was an imaginative construct, it had no obligation to attach itself to *any* political reality.

Consider, for example, a poem he'd published two years earlier in the *Nation*, called "On an Old Horn." If the poem seemed obscure, that was not what he had intended. If he had succeeded in saying what he had to say, the reader would get it. "He may not get it at once," Stevens explained, "but, if he is sufficiently interested, he invariably gets it." A difficult or complex thing must be allowed to remain difficult, because to explain it destroyed it as a poem. As here, where "the bird kept saying that birds had once been men":

Then the bird from his ruddy belly blew
A trumpet round the trees. . . .
In the little of his voice, or the like,
Or less, he found a man, or more, against
Calamity, proclaimed himself, was proclaimed.
II
If the stars that move together as one, disband,
Flying like insects of fire in a cavern of night,
Pipperoo, pippera, pipperum . . . The rest is rot.

In other words, what if we erased our normal way of seeing for a moment and saw ourselves in an entirely new light? What if we turned Darwin's evolutionary process on its head, so that the end to which man seemed to be evolving turned out to be a bird rather than the other way around, and we saw ourselves as birds looking at humans as strange variations of themselves? Then suppose we started all over again as birds, say, and saw reflections of ourselves in men, where bird babies became human babies, "with some unexpected transitional features," such as a rat's tail dangling from the human baby as the feathers molted. As we evolved from birds into men and began "to think the thoughts of men," wouldn't there be "survivals of the thinking of our primitive state"? Wouldn't "the things of which birds sing" be subject to change, just as men's thoughts changed, so that, whether bird or man, one had only one's horn on which to toot? Following that sort of surrealist logic, our composing of songs and poems would become a version of our own "fester Burg," the equivalent of Luther's *Ein feste Burg ist unser Gott:* "A Mighty Fortress Is Our God." After all, a bird sings and a man contrives an order out of words to keep from being overwhelmed by chaos.

Why not, then, let the imagination create its own chaos? The stars would leave their places and move about outwardly, aimlessly, and the constant peep-peep-peep of the bird, even if its syntax were to be expanded with genitives and ablatives and the rest, would revolve only along that unalterable linguistic grid, the bird's lexical spectrum expanding merely to *pipperoo, pippera, pipperum.* It would all stem from that elemental peep hurled against the chaos of a world exploding once more into fragments, as the stars broke apart, zigzagging through the universe, like fireflies lighting the dark randomly on a summer night.

In the end all that matters was the cry, the poem, something sounding on an old horn to give us a momentary sense of comfort, like those lights from the boats blinking in the dark harbor at Key West, where "the order of the spirit is the only music of the spheres: or, rather, the only music." If birds "rely on their voices as chief encourager," he told Simons, "it follows that a lion roaring in a desert and a boy whistling in the dark are alike, playing . . . an old horn." He picked up the image of a sibylline chaos a week later in a letter to Barbara Church: "They are building a new house not far from where we live. Odds and ends have blown over the neighborhood: pieces of tar paper, cement bags, etc." Such random bits of chaos, contained within the window of the mind, looked exciting, covered as they were with frost each morning. Especially on these "early war mornings" when houses all over Europe were being blown to hell.

• • •

BACK IN DECEMBER 1941 Stevens had received a letter from Katharine Frazier of the Cummington Press in Cummington, Massachusetts, asking if she could publish a small book of his poems. At the moment, he explained, he was still rounding out his next book, *Parts of a World,* and had nothing to offer her. In the meantime he asked her to send him copies of some of the books the press had already printed, and was delighted with what she sent him. "Your package looks like the packages that used to come from [Yeats's] Cuala Press," he wrote her, so she could count on his sending her something by late June. That "something" turned out to be his long poem *Notes toward a Supreme Fiction.* After all, late winter and early spring were the ideal times for composing a long serenade. "Weather by Franz Hals, / Brushed up by brushy winds in brush clouds." On Westerly Terrace that March "the gay forsythia / And yellow, yellow thins the Northern blue." Even the exterior of his house seemed to have "changed a little" in the returning sun. And "the fragrance of the magnolias comes close, / False flick, false form, but falseness close to kin." An abstraction of the sun, then, "a seeing and unseeing in the eye." The weather, and the idea of the weather, "the mere weather, the mere air: / An abstraction blooded, as a man by thought."

A perambulation yet again through Elizabeth Park by this Thoreau redivivus, the poet as philosopher, as Adam, as Descartes, around the lake,

A composing as the body tires, a stop
To see hepatica, a stop to watch
A definition growing certain and

A wait within that certainty, a rest
In the swags of pine-trees bordering the lake.

Call the present moment "a kind of Swiss perfection," "a balance that happens, / As a man and woman meet and love forthwith." Call it a moment "of awakening, / Extreme, fortuitous, personal," where we "sit on the edge of sleep, / As on an elevation," a realization which makes even the vaulted academies of the mind mere "structures in a mist."

It was part of the 651-line meditation he composed that spring of 1942 on his daily walks about Hartford. *Notes toward a Supreme Fiction*; not the whole harmonium, but more realistically parts of a world. And not the Supreme Fiction Realized, but, far more modestly, Notes *toward* a Supreme Fiction. The poem has three parts, each composed of ten cantos, each canto composed of seven three-line stanzas, each verse a variation on the blank-verse line, Stevens's version of what he called his "Virgilian cadences, up down, / Up down." Six hundred thirty lines, with a wartime coda consisting of a final canto in the same form as the others, addressed to GIs who might read his lines "in a book in a barrack" or somewhere in Malay, gaining sustenance, Stevens hoped, from the words wrested from the poet's war with the dark angel of chaos, where the abstract "fictive hero becomes the real" and where, with the proper words offered up by the poet-priest, the soldier "dies, / If he must, or lives on the bread of faithful speech."

"Dear Miss Frazier," he wrote on May 19, "I am now approaching the end of NOTES etc., and have, in fact, only one more poem to do, although I am thinking of doing a few lines as a sort of epilogue." He had used a pentameter line, though it ran "over and under now and then." He was eager that the printed edition avoid overruns and wanted one poem printed per page; if, when she came to set up the book, she found "a line or two a little hard to handle," he would be happy to rewrite it. A poet's order, to be discovered in a world which found itself in a violent disorder.

A month later he wrote her again, asking to dedicate the poem to Henry Church. He'd already written Church, explaining that he wanted to dedicate the poem to him simply because he wanted to. The thing about Church was that he had "a way of saying in a scrawl more than most people say in a much more domesticated hand." Theirs, he told Church, was a friendship like that between Erasmus and Thomas More, accentuated by Erasmus's chic and More's civility. *Notes*, he explained to Church on September 8—the day the book was published (273 copies, each bound in yellow oasis goat leather, with gold tooling on the binding)—at least had "the merit of delineating an important subject, even though it does not go very far beyond the subject itself."

But then how could it, without taking the poem out of the realm of poetry altogether? Now that his fourth collection, *Parts of a World*, was out there as well for the world to see, he was waiting to be assassinated "by some aggressive critic" in the next month or two. He preferred what had just happened when a classics instructor at Yale writing for the *Nation* had visited Stevens about the book. "We had a good time," Stevens noted, because they had never once mentioned the book itself. That was the way Stevens liked his interviews to go. The interviewer was Frank Jones, and his careful review, entitled "The Sorcerer as Elegist," appeared on November 7. Stevens, Jones wrote there, reminded him of a toucan, "perky and pensive by turns," eyes flashing with delight, and yet skeptical, having swallowed the "magical world" of *Harmonium* forever and now hoping to fly like an eagle.

It was Yeats, now three years gone, who had actually been the eagle, "at ease on the heights" to which Stevens now aspired. In time, of course, Stevens too might become an eagle, for he had certainly mastered the art of the poem over the past two decades. In *Harmonium* he'd created "an enchanted country, uniquely rounded, wholly credible," but which yearned "for a more perfect imagined universe." Then had come *Ideas of Order* and *The Man with the Blue Guitar*, where the poet's longings kept butting against an increasingly cruel world. But the search, Jones believed, had ended again and again in defeat. How difficult to dwell, as Stevens had, in what Henry James called "the great glazed tank of art," where "strange silent subjects float," and where one had to separate oneself from the real world for long periods of time. But how was Stevens ever going "to set his art right with the world" if all he had to work with was a mythology of the self?

Hadn't Yeats finally banished his romanticism, his "heroic mother moon" to stare instead upon "the timid sun"? Where Yeats had built towers, though, Stevens had thus far only proclaimed that he meant to renounce his "bastard chateaux and smokey demoiselles" and "build towers of my own, / There to behold . . . the naked man in a state of fact, / As acutest virtue and ascetic trove." If instead of creating merely the "concept of the hero as a redeeming, radiant force inherent in humanity," Stevens could give us the actual man "capable / Of his brave quickening," what an achievement that would be. The trouble was that his longer pieces, for all their beauty, lacked the light and music that had made the world of *Harmonium* so alive. Only in some of the shorter, more personal poems could Jones find a language married to a "contemplative yet quickening love of the sensible world."

Jones also believed that Stevens himself was unhappy with the turn his poems had taken. With the world at war, the poet had come to see that a new sense of reality had to take the place of his earlier imaginative constructs. But then Stevens himself did not yet seem to believe he possessed "the invincible imagination of the supreme poet" that Yeats had achieved in the end. Was the reason for Stevens's not yet reaching that mastery that his imagination had ripened into "a willed detachment" from the peopled world, whereas Yeats's imagination had matured "in a willed togetherness" with his country? If Stevens was to become a poet on the level of Yeats, he would have to incorporate the world around him and the people who inhabited its houses.

Elizabeth Drew, in a short review in the November *Atlantic Monthly*, summed up Stevens in this way: "His intricately subtle mind spins his webs of verbal tracery round and round the central puzzle of reality and illusion, but the result is a poetry so objective and elusive, and so removed from the experience of the average reader, that the majority of the poems remain, as perhaps Mr. Stevens intended that they should, beautifully phrased and cadenced enigmas." This snow man, this no man who seemed to speak to and for no one.

Worse, Stevens only reinforced this sense of detachment in his responses to Simons, who had asked him to explain a number of his images. Who, for example, was that Arabian in Stevens's room, the one "with his damned hoobla-hoobla-hoobla-how," who inscribed "a primitive astronomy / Across the unscrawled fores the future casts" and threw "his stars around the floor"? That, Stevens explained, was simply the moon, whose light seemed to draw an "undecipherable vagueness" across his bedroom floor. Of course that was not something the reader could possibly know, but then he hadn't thought that was necessary for the reader to know.

Or that elephant a dozen lines on, the one that breached "the darkness of Ceylon with blares," and who shook "the glitter-goes on surfaces of tanks, / Shattering velvetest far-way." Those tanks would, he explained, "be obscure to anyone not familiar with the use of that word in Ceylon." Still, he argued, it had not been an affectation on his part to leave the word unexplained. After all, he *had* mentioned Ceylon a line or two above. In Ceylon a tank was "a basin which may have been an ancient bath or the excavation for an ancient building." "Glitter-goes" was merely another way of speaking of "vibrancies of light"; the "velvetest far-away," of course, was merely a paraphrase for a "very remote distance."

More important was for the reader to discover an order for oneself rather than have the poet impose that order on one. What he desired more than anything was just that:

To discover an order as of
A season, to discover summer and know it,
To discover winter and know it well, to find,
Not to impose, not to have reasoned at all,
Out of nothing to have come on major weather.

That, he believed, underscoring the word four times, "had to be possible, possible, possible. It must / Be possible." In time the Real would "from its rude compounding come," even if at first it seemed dreamlike, strange, otherworldly, something perhaps akin to that rough beast birthed in Yeats's "Second Coming": "a beast disgorged, unlike, / Warmed by a desperate milk." What he wanted was "to find the real," to "be stripped of every fiction except one": the Supreme Fiction, "the fiction of an absolute," with himself a luminous Angel silent in his "luminous cloud," who heard "the luminous melody of proper sound." Stevens, the twentieth-century scholar monk in his monk-like bedroom study, furnished with fresh flowers and gay wallpaper and a contemporary French painting or two to appease his storming spirit.

True, the abstract as such, *pace* Plato, did not exist. But it was certainly a thing alive and immanent "in the mind of the poet," as much so as the idea of God was "immanent in the mind of the theologian." Wasn't that why he wrote poetry: to wrestle "with the inaccessibility of the abstract" before turning again to the weather outside, simply because that was "not inaccessible and is not abstract"? Back and forth, then, between the abstract and the world, his lines reaching to and fro, the abstractions of the poem continually renewing themselves with Hartford's weather: its rain, mist, sun, and moon. In a very real sense there was "no such thing as life," only "a style of life" by which we learned to live.

He was also aware, he admitted to Simons, that he had not defined his Supreme Fiction. The astute reader, he believed, would no doubt identify the Supreme Fiction with Poetry itself. But Stevens was not willing to make that leap. He confessed that he did not yet know what he meant, so that he would have to learn "to be a little more precise about this enigma." The trouble was that when he did try to explain what he meant, he was in danger of losing "the poetry of the idea." Still, he had settled on "certain characteristics" which the Supreme Fiction would have to contain. It must be abstract. It must change. It must give pleasure. No doubt the subject might "occupy a school of rabbis for the next few generations," for in "trying to create something as valid as the idea of God has been" and continued to be, the first necessity was breadth. And yet the Supreme Fiction would never amount to much until that breadth had come to a focus, a point. What that omega point was he was not yet prepared to say.

But wasn't the idea of the Supreme Fiction synonymous finally with the idea of God? Hadn't he described that fiction by evoking Exodus, as when he had spoken of "a lasting visage in a lasting bush"? An ancient face, like a Greek or Mayan visage of the deity, a face

of stone in an unending red,
Red-emerald, red-slitted blue, a face of slate,
An ancient forehead hung with heavy hair,
The channel slots of rain, the red-rose-red
And weathered and the ruby-water-worn.

Or was it the face of Christ, a face the same and different, repeated a million times in art: that "dead shepherd" who had harrowed the underworld and "brought tremendous chords from hell / And bade the sheep carouse"? But if the Supreme Fiction was not Poetry, he was not yet willing to call it God. "Let us think about it," he told Simons, "and not say that our abstraction is this, that or the other."

After all, since "the first thing one sees of any deity is the face," it followed that the "elementary idea of God" was a face, "a lasting visage in a lasting bush." But when the compulsion he had felt as a boy for the sacred had all but disappeared, the face of God had disappeared with it. As for the face of the dead shepherd, he equivocated, he'd had no one specifically in mind. It had merely been "an improvisation," made necessary by the image of the face in the burning bush, because what the human spirit desired or needed, it created, "even if it has to do so in a fiction."

One danger in making the Supreme Fiction an abstraction, of course, was that it was a way of escaping reality altogether. True, one might escape from fact, but then one "would only arrive at another nothingness, another nakedness, the limitation of thought." Thus the figure of Canon Aspirin in his search for the abstract there in his cell, ending up where Satan, Milton's dark intelligence, had ended up, facing the frigid null, the Void, the ultimate black hole. For if one tried "to elude human pathos, and fact," one would have to "go straight to the utmost crown of night" to try to find a way "through the imagination or perhaps to the imagination." In other words, the abstract had to become thought enfleshed: thought made human because it was we who thought and felt.

Would the reader "get it," though? To look at the reviews of his work, Stevens explained, one would think not. But wasn't the real value of the reviews that they brought with them a degree of acceptance? People read poetry nervously, afraid that something would "go wrong with the sentence after next." Still, wouldn't it be nice to hear that someone had actually received pleasure in reading his poems? Possibly, he sighed, "one never has more than a very few readers who pick up the feelings that one puts into one's poems." Reviewers usually underestimated the poet until the time came when he was accepted, and then they tended to overestimate him. But then people did not have the time to "put someone under the microscope." If acceptance was ever to come, it would be because there were those who were willing to point out what the poet had achieved.

One evening a student from Trinity College had walked home with him, and Stevens had told him that the modern mind had now "reached a point at which we could no longer really believe in anything unless we recognized that it was a fiction." The student had demurred, saying such a stance was impossible, because no one could believe "in something that one knew was not true." But, Stevens countered, didn't people do that all the time? Wasn't that what Coleridge had meant when he spoke of the suspension of disbelief, something we did when we read a poem? After all, there were plenty of people who believed in Heaven. Yet was the idea of

Heaven anything more than "an extension of reality"? In the long run the Supreme Fiction might turn out to be poetry, after all, since "the essence of poetry is change and the essence of change is that it gives pleasure."

The articulations between the sections of *Notes* were not the articulations one found in a philosophical tract. In fact he had begun writing the poem with the idea of stripping the imagination of all existing fictions in order to get back to the clarity of the First Idea. But, he discovered, if he'd stuck to such a logical development, he would have lost all of the qualities he wanted to get into his poem, in the end producing something that was not poetry. If only he had all the time in the world to pursue his idea. But of course he did not. Each morning the idea of the supreme fiction crawled over him, but at the office he would have to put the poem aside. After all, he confessed, "I like Rhine wine, blue grapes, good cheese, endive and lots of books . . . as much as I like supreme fiction." Then too, didn't even the most brilliant new idea always end up amounting to nothing?

• • •

IN JULY 1942 THE critic Harvey Breit wrote Stevens asking to interview him for *Harper's Bazaar* in his dual roles of poet and insurance executive. Breit added the carrot that Williams had already signed on to be interviewed in his dual roles of poet and physician. Williams himself wrote Stevens, asking him to come on board, but Stevens balked. He'd been through this before, when he'd allowed himself to be interviewed by the young poet Charles Henri Ford for a piece in *View.* That had been in the summer of 1940, and Stevens was so angry with what Ford had done that he promised himself never to repeat the ordeal.

Ford had called his review "Verlaine in Hartford," and from its opening lines it was cavalier and dismissive. "Has the mystery man of modern poetry really another self?" Ford had asked. And was this "reputable" insurance executive and poet as "disreputable" as Verlaine had been? If Stevens had once described his poetry as a "secret vice," at least Verlaine had had a God to confess to. But who could Stevens confess to? To the God of Poetry? But then wouldn't Stevens's vice and God be one? To most of Hartford's citizens, Stevens was a successful lawyer and not a poet. Nor did Stevens "talk poetry with his associates—because they would not be interested." Surely James Thrall Soby, a serious art collector and Hartford neighbor, would know about Stevens's poetry and would even know Stevens by sight, so that, if he saw Stevens walking home from his office, Soby would think he was looking at "Verlaine after his third absinthe!" Not that Mr. Stevens drank, of course.

When he'd visited Stevens on a Sunday afternoon that summer, Ford had seen a hefty man "with a deep soft voice, pink skin, curly gray hair—and, of all things, smiling!" They'd gone into the garden to recline on some rustic chairs under the shade of some trees. Before long Stevens was lecturing Ford, telling Ford that he wasn't serious enough, that he lived far too fantastic a life and hobnobbed with too many people. It was not of course what Ford had wanted to hear from Stevens. He did learn that Stevens was of Pennsylvania Dutch stock and had once had a friend from Reading who would recite poetry to Stevens after a bottle or two of claret.

At Harvard Stevens had written a bit of verse, but he'd been more interested in becoming a lawyer and making money so that he could afford a wife, a home, and all the comforts therein. Later, in New York, he'd met up with some of his Harvard classmates as well as with Carl Van Vechten at a time when "Greenwich Village was budding, blooming," and "one poem after another was written down," eventually resulting in a collection called *Harmonium.* Then he had put poetry aside while he turned himself into a successful corporate lawyer, until, after a decade, the poems had returned, "in spite of himself." Now, however, with the passage of the years, he had become "more jealous of the demands business makes" and wanted to devote all of his time "to the study and writing of poetry."

Perhaps Ford himself had an imaginative mind, Stevens queried. Back in February Stevens and Elsie had flown down to Miami on the same plane with Eleanor Roosevelt, and he'd noticed that the first lady had waited until everyone else had disembarked to make her exit, a ploy which had disgusted him by its theatricality. He talked too about Holly being "allowed to buy each week one book and two pieces of music of her own selection" and how he'd once tended to the flowers until Elsie had taken over.

As a special treat, he invited Ford up to his study to see his collection of paintings by "obscure Frenchmen, mostly impressionist in style." Naturally, Stevens added, a serious collector like Ford's friend James Thrall

Soby "would probably be contemptuous of these paintings," to which Ford, whose partner for the past six years had been the renowned Russian painter Pavel Tchelitchew, had remarked to himself that, yes, that was true, what with Soby's collection of De Chiricos and Tchelitchews. Of course, Stevens had added, with money one could duplicate Soby's collection fifteen times over, whereas his own collection was far more original in its choices. When the interview was over Stevens had quipped, "Make me look romantic in those photographs" Ford had taken. At the door he introduced Ford to his blond, blue-eyed Holly, "who paints, and writes poetry, which the man with the blue guitar," Ford fired off with his parting shot, "never discusses with her."

Clearly Stevens had managed to offend the edgy Ford, and in return Ford had revealed that not only was Hartford's Mystery Man no Verlaine, but he had shown himself to be little more than a hale and successful bourgeois with mediocre tastes in painting. No wonder, then, that Stevens was delighted when, six years later, a young Cuban friend of his pooh-poohed Ford. "I like to hear you say 'Pooh!' when you speak of Charles Henri Ford," Stevens replied. As far as he was concerned, Ford didn't know much about anything. Still, he was clever enough to have created for himself "a sphere in which everything approves of him and is as he wants it to be." But he was "as untamed a snob as ever breathed," and *View Magazine* nothing more than a monument to "the snobbery of the young man who knows a little more about painting than his neighbor, in the sense that he knows an artist or two." Amazing, he added, how God could be so "gracious to some very peculiar people."

No more interviews, thank you. Was Harvey Breit intent on dispelling some myth about the poet being either "an idler, a man without clothes, a drunk, a 'fantast',"—or on the other hand . . . "an untouchable, a seer"? Most people did not think of the poet in that way. Was Whitman really the image of the American poet? Didn't he belong instead "in the same category of eccentrics to which queer looking actors belong"? A poet in 1940 was simply someone who wrote poetry and looked "like anyone else, acts like anyone else, wears the same kind of clothes, and certainly is not an incompetent." If only Americans "could get rid of all the caricatures . . . we should only be seeing what we see every day," which, of course, was "not so easy after all."

• • •

"THE BELIEF IN POETRY is a magnificent fury, or it is nothing," Stevens wrote Henry Church. It was the message he meant to deliver to the French philosophers who would gather at Mount Holyoke that August for Les Entretiens de Pontigny, which, because of the war raging in Europe, had had to relocate to western Massachusetts. That April he told Jean Wahl, who was teaching at Princeton, that he would give a paper he called "The Figure of the Youth as Virile Poet," because it would allow him to think about poetry and hear his ideas discussed. Many of those attending the conference would be Frenchmen forced into exile because of the war. Because public conferences made him uncomfortable, he would be driven to the campus, deliver his paper, and then return home.

One wrote poetry, he once told Simons, out of an all-consuming passion and not out of mere habit. But it was a passion that had to nourish itself on reality because that was its only source. The imagination, after all, did not create reality ex nihilo. Rather, it transformed the real that is found all around one. Ultimately reality was coequal with the imagination, and by extension—in what amounted to a Trinitarian metaphor—reality, the imagination, and pure poetry were ultimately one. Now, in the summer of 1943, it was his task to tell the *philosophes* who would gather on the plains of Mount Holyoke that not only did poetry add to philosophy, but the fully realized poem was superior even to the finest philosophical tract because it illuminated reality and made it human, allowing the mind and heart to give their full consent to the real, just as in the final pages of *Notes toward a Supreme Fiction* the great captain, Poet Number One, had married the maiden Bawda, each taking the other "as sign, short sign / To stop the whirlwind, balk the elements," and find for the moment, the peace that had eluded him until then. The two had married "well because the marriage-place / Was what they loved. It was neither heaven nor hell." It was Catawba, a native place with a native name. Bawdy, yes, but with a euphony bestowed upon it by this mystic marriage: the bread of ordinary life transformed by the high priest of the imagination.

• • •

HE WAS EAGER TO have the Churches attend his talk, as they would be a great support for him. Afterward they could return to Hartford with him and drink good wine and share a meal prepared by Elsie. The second week of the 1943 Les Entretiens de Pontigny met on the grounds of Mount Holyoke from August 9 to 15, with mornings devoted to poetry and afternoons to politics. Poets, philosophers, economists, political theoreticians, musicians, and artists were invited to commingle and argue their points of view late into the night. Of course Stevens was having none of that. He meant to speak on the roles of poetry and philosophy as a culmination of the talks he'd had with the Churches about establishing a chair in poetry to counter the many chairs in philosophy at many of America's elite campuses. But if he carried his talk in one hand, he carried a grenade in the other. Like Duchamp thirty years before, he would address the *philosophes*, drop his grenade, and let the conference pick up the pieces after his departure.

"It appears," he began under the shade of the maples outside Mount Holyoke's Porter Hall, "that what is central to philosophy is its least valuable part." He followed with what he called scraps culled from three letters. The first was something the philosopher Henry Bradley had confessed to the late poet laureate Robert Bridges. "My own attitude towards all philosophies old and new, is very skeptical," Bradley had said, for the universe was "too vast to be comprehended even by the greatest of the sons of Adam." Philosophers did sometimes have glimpses of reality's real problems and even of their real solutions, but they had "always substituted illusory problems for the real ones."

Stevens followed up with a comment by the poet Paul Valéry, who had called the philosopher Henri Bergson "perhaps one of the last men to have given himself to thinking exclusively." But Bergson belonged now to the past. Finally, Stevens quoted the philosopher William James, who had praised a philosophical essay of Bergson's by comparing its style and tone to the style of *Madame Bovary*. So, it appeared, philosophy was simply one more form of literature, and—as literature—paled in comparison to poetry. If philosophical truth was the official view of Being, then wasn't poetry the unofficial view? And if truth changed because philosophers lived and died, wasn't the same true of poetry?

For the past forty years Coleridge as both poet and philosopher had been one of Stevens's mainstays, especially his *Biographia Literaria.* Once, Stevens told his audience of *philosophes*, on a boat on his way to Germany Coleridge was asked to join a party of Danes and had been treated to wine and grapes. The Danes had christened him Doctor Teology, Coleridge wrote. "Dressed as I was all in black, with large shoes and black worsted stockings, I might certainly have passed very well for a Methodist missionary." But he had demurred; certainly he was no philosopher. But then the Danes told him that everyone was a philosopher, after all, he'd acquiesced, and they'd all drunk and talked and sung and then danced on the deck.

Coleridge the poet as dancing philosopher, dressed in black, and Stevens the poet, dressed in a pearl-gray three-piece suit accented by a red tie, imagining himself drinking and talking and singing and dancing among the philosophers, poet who had spent years trying to say just what poetry was. Of course a new definition of poetry and reality would now have to be forged. If the philosopher approached truth through reason, and the poet through the imagination, were not these merely statements of convenience? Didn't skeptics of both philosophy and poetry have every right to their skepticism, since rational ideas no more satisfied the reason than imaginative ideas satisfied the imagination? If an idea could satisfy "both the reason and the imagination," as with the traditional idea of God, such an idea would be enough to "establish a divine beginning and end for us," where the reason merely proposed and on which the imagination merely meditated.

It was left to the poet, then, to create a poetry that would satisfy both the reason *and* the imagination. Where the philosopher ended in despair, however, the poet ended in fulfillment, since the poet could find a sanction for life in a poetry that satisfied the imagination. And yet there still did not exist an adequate definition of poetry. Aristotle had never given us one, nor had Horace. Even Shelley had offered only an approximation, calling it the "imperial faculty whose throne is curtained within the invisible nature of man." Yet we knew when we were in the presence of real poetry. As with definitions of God, definitions of the Supreme Fiction—because they used words—remained peripheral.

Was there a center, a logos, possible to discover, after which the definition would no longer be subject to chance? For Stevens the answer was no. An adequate definition of the Supreme Fiction would have to be accounted for, not in some exterior reality, but from within, created by the personality of the strong poet, for it was the force of the poet's imagination that made poetry a living thing. Simply put, poetry had to be abstract, it had to be continually changing, and it must always provide the intense pleasure that accompanied the new and surprising. Just as the mind of the sculptor revealed itself in the forms his sculptures took, and the painter revealed himself in what Cézanne called "psychological landscapes," so it was the poet who wrote the truly heroic poem who would ultimately "satisfy all there is of us and all of us in time to come" through his reason, imagination, and distinctive individuality. In the process the poet would share "in the transformation . . . accomplished by the poem," teasing the reader with a mystical "*vis* or *noeud vital*, which struck one's very nerve center." After all, there was nothing rare about this sense of aspiration, for if the saints felt it, so did young men and women who had written a few poems and could see in themselves traces of a long line of poets who had gone before.

What was needed now, therefore, was the figure of the poet as virile youth, "half-beast and somehow more than human," possessing the imagination and intelligence and accurate speech of the son who carried on his shoulders "the antique imagination of the father." The poet, then, as the new Aeneas, bearing his father on his shoulders because he loved him. Now was as good a time as any, in spite of the ever-changing nature of things, to discover the credible and believe in that. So too the fully realized poem would be a "moment of victory over the incredible."

Politics to the right of one. Politics to the left. And yet, mercifully, life was possible apart from politics. That was what the youth as virile poet, alive "in a kind of radiant and productive atmosphere," had to discover: the pleasure of one's imagination in harmony "with the radiant and productive world in which one lived." It was the world Mallarmé had found in the sound of "le vierge, le vivace et le bel aujourd'hui" and that Hopkins had found in the color of "the thunder-purple seabeach plumèd purple-of-thunder." Only there, in the poem itself, could one approach the Supreme Fiction, in an "incandescence of the intelligence." The everyday world, enhanced by the imagination's fire, until the everyday world ceased to turn, except in crystal.

Marianne Moore was in the audience when Stevens delivered his paper. She was scheduled to give her own talk the following day, on "feeling and precision" in poetry, but had taken the train to Mount Holyoke with her mother a day early in order to hear Stevens and meet him for the first time. She sat with the Churches and had a warm conversation with them, and she probably exchanged a few words with Stevens before he left to return to Hartford with the Churches. "Wallace Stevens is beyond fathoming," she confided to Williams a year later. She'd been reading and reviewing his poetry for twenty years now and still she found him "so strange . . . as if he had a morbid secret he would rather perish than disclose and just as he tells it out in his sleep"—by which she meant his poems—"he changes into an uncontradictable judiciary with a gown and a gavel and you are embarrassed to have heard anything." She quoted three lines from Stevens's *Esthétique du Mal* to make her point. Wasn't Stevens talking about his own poems when he called them those "firm stanzas" that hung

like hives in hell
Or what hell was, since now both heaven and hell
Are one, and here, O terra infidel?

When, a year later, "The Figure of the Youth as Virile Poet" appeared in the *Sewanee Review*, Paul Weiss, a professor of philosophy at Bryn Mawr who had participated in the Entretiens proceedings but had missed Stevens's talk, read what Stevens had to say about the relative positioning of philosophy and poetry and wrote Stevens to say Stevens had gotten it wrong because Stevens hadn't taken into account what contemporary philosophy had to add to the question. "A man with your [last] name,"

Stevens wrote Theodore Weiss, editor of the Yale-based *Quarterly Review*, had written him "objecting to my founding my view of philosophy on James and Bergson," suggesting that what Stevens should have done was "grapple with a philosopher full-sized." When Stevens had written back, asking him "whom he had in mind," Weiss had mentioned Plato, Aristotle, Kant, and Hegel, and then, "as a relief from these divinities of the Styx, suggested Whitehead, Bradley and Peirce." The trouble with all this, Stevens felt, was that most modern philosophers were too academic. Paul Weiss would continue to write Stevens over the next several years, hoping to educate the poet on the deeper nature of philosophical inquiry, but Stevens was having no part of that. He had had his say and had since moved on to other things.

• • •

THE SON RESTORES THE father. "My father wasn't a man given to pushing his way," he wrote his niece Jane soon after giving his paper at the Entretiens. "He needed what all of us need, and what most of us don't get . . . discreet affection." He saw now that he was like his father in being "incapable of lifting a hand to attract any of us, so that, while we loved him . . . we also were afraid of him, at least to the extent of holding off. The result was that he lived alone." He was glad to have the photograph of his father she'd found, for it showed his father at a time when he still had hope. Looking now at the pictures of his brothers and sisters was like watching people "come into the world, live for a while and then go out of it again." Well, he meant "to think well of everyone in my family" and forget the unfortunate things that had happened. When he thought of his father now, "and of all the anxiety that he must have felt, and then look at this last picture of him in which he seems so completely defeated, the feeling isn't anything that I want to renew." Perhaps now he understood his father better than his father had ever understood himself. "Had he been more selfish than he was," he summed up, "instead of working so hard to see his children succeed, no doubt things might have been different."

15

Farewell to an Idea: 1944–1947

Farewell to an idea . . . The mother's face,
The purpose of the poem, fills the room
They are together, here, and it is warm,
With nothing of the prescience of oncoming dreams.
It is evening. The house is evening, half dissolved.

AURORAS OF AUTUMN

March 18, 1944: a squadron of twin-engine B-25 medium-range bombers crosses over an erupting Mount Vesuvius, its black plume billowing like some hell flower higher than the bombers themselves, hell-bent on bombing the monastery of Monte Cassino and environs, as they have for the past month now. Here is man's destruction dwarfed for the moment by nature's age-old destroyer of Naples, Herculaneum, and Pompeii. Here too are centuries-old buildings caving in under the flow of red-hot lava, while other buildings turn to dust under the incessant Allied bombings.

Stevens picks up a copy of the spring 1944 *Kenyon Review* to read an essay by John Crowe Ransom. It is called "Artists, Soldiers, Positivists," and it is part of an ongoing discussion of the purpose of poetry in a time of war, underlining especially those recurring "moral difficulties . . . which art encounters when it begins to manifest its curious luxuriance." If, Ransom asks, "the time scarcely comes when there is enough of dedicated public service to fight the evil in the world, and improve the lot of the citizens," then "when is there a time for art?" What public service does art render "that it should hope for reputation and favor?" In the same issue a letter from a soldier overseas asks what it is we are after in poetry, especially now, when the "commandos of contemporary literature are having little to do with Eliot and even poets of charming distemper like Wallace Stevens (for whom we all developed considerable passion)." For himself, "the question of poetry as in life (and in the Army) is one of survival, simply," and it is the younger poets—like Karl Shapiro and John Berryman and Delmore Schwartz—who are showing the way and transcending "the aesthetic of poetry—thank God!" But the poetry in the *Kenyon Review* is cut off from the soldiers' pain and the agony of civilians dying day after day. What poetry must provide the living with now is "an overwhelming desire to go on."

"What particularly interested me was the letter from one of your correspondents about the relation between poetry and what he called pain," Stevens wrote Ransom in mid-June. Whatever that soldier meant, "it might be interesting to try to do an *Esthétique du Mal.* It is the kind of idea that it is difficult to shake off." The psychogenetic irritant provided Stevens with the idea for his next long poem, aptly called *Esthétique du Mal*, which he composed over the next six weeks. "I hope you will like it," he told Ransom in late July. While the title was "not quite right in the sense that anything of that sort seems to be not quite right now-a-days," it was better than any alternative he could think of. As for the poem's concluding lines, he was aware that a question mark was in order, but instead he ended with a period as his way of signaling that he was abandoning the question. Then, in late August, with Paris back in the hands of the Allies, he wrote Henry Church to say he'd finished the poem and that, while "I think of something that I said in the course of it that I wish I hadn't said," it no longer mattered.

The Aesthetics of Evil. First, evil as a real force in the world, and poetry as a response to that force. That was the problem that confronted Stevens in the summer of 1944, even as the main force of the war shifted from Naples and Rome to Normandy and Paris. He began by imagining a soldier very much like the soldier who had written Ransom, someone at the raging edge of the war just south of the stalemate at Monte Casino which had pinned the Allies down for nearly half a year now, a man "writing letters home" in a café in Naples, and, "between letters, reading paragraphs on the sublime." But whose sublime? Longinus's surely. And Kant's and perhaps Edmund Burke's, while in the distance "Vesuvius had groaned / For a month," preparing to unleash its fire and brimstone as it had back in AD 79, burying the city of Pompeii, which would remain swallowed for a millennium and a half before being resurrected, and which now stood in the path of yet another death. From the soldier's vantage there in Naples Vesuvius appears as a *son et lumière* show where "the sultriest fulgurations, flickering, / cast corners in the glass" off the windows and mirrors, reflecting too off a decent bottle of Montepulciano.

Here, in the spring of 1944, the sound of Vesuvius rumbling might almost be contained because it has been described so often, including what that grand classicist, Pliny the Younger, had to report as an eyewitness of the eruption. At this remove, and the even greater remove of the poet back in Hartford, one must roll the pain of the event across one's tongue to taste the "pain / Audible at noon, pain torturing itself, / Pain killing pain on the very point of pain," Vesuvius trembling "in another ether, / As the body trembles at the end of life." Pain until one is beyond pain, and the body folds into death.

Then the first rumblings of hunger as the soldier realizes it is "almost time for lunch." If pain is human, if it needs a human being to be conscious of its presence and consider what meaning it might have, so too with the pangs of hunger, however mild. To study the Sublime abstractly in the pages of the book open before you is one thing. To feel the actual terror and awe of standing in the path of Vesuvius's lava flow is another. Yet "except for us, Vesuvius might consume / In solid fire the utmost earth and know / No pain," because there would be no consciousness to register it. In fact "the total past felt nothing when destroyed," for what besides human consciousness is even aware of a concept like the past?

Evil as the experience of pain; evil as a human catastrophe; evil as a natural catastrophe, like a volcano erupting, or a tsunami, or a raging wildfire; evil as a moral issue. A nameless man—another stand-in for the poet—notices the moon rising and figures that into his calculations. But what if we reversed our perspective? If, that is, the moon is oblivious to our pain, so too our pain remains oblivious to the moon or to the beauty of yellow acacias blooming in the fields. The indifference of the universe toward our pain is what, ironically, might save us in the end.

The problem began with Christianity, Stevens says, and was exacerbated by one of the great poets of all time: Dante. The fault, that is, lies with Christ, "an over-human god," who took on human flesh and in doing so complicated matters by taking on our human pain as well. "If only he would not pity us so much," the poet sighs, thus accepting one's fate. For what is this Christ figure if not "a too, too human god," born of our human self-pity? The ancients had it right, Stevens suggests, following Santayana's meditation on Longinus, for would not "the health of the world . . . be enough," knowing that there is a time to live and love and kill if need be, just as there is a time to die? Would not the pleasure we experienced in "the honey of common summer" be enough, when death was seen simply as the last act of one's life and when pain itself, "no longer satanic mimicry, / Could be borne" and we might be "sure to find our way"?

"The genius of misfortune," Stevens notes axiomatically, "is not a sentimentalist": he is "that evil in the self" from which "fault / Falls out on everything." When things go wrong for us, how easy it is to blame our misfortune on some other, whether Satan or God or Fate. But such blame would be "wrong and wrong," a spending of our strength merely on "the false engagements of the mind." Because pain is universal and inescapable, it would be better to eschew "the sob / Beyond invention" and focus instead on "the actual, the warm, the near," the things that tie us to each other: family, the familiar, the "brother even in the father's eye" or "half-spoken in the mother's throat." To "willingly forfeit the ai-ai" (the I-I of self-pity's sorrow) in the long parades that constitute the human generations, those "obscurer selvages," which puns on the *selva oscura* which opens Dante's journey. How good to be able to say, "Be near me, come closer, touch my hand, phrases / Compounded of dear relation."

Even the sun in its "clownish yellow . . . / Brings the day to perfection and then fails," for it too is subject to time, that "big bird" that incessantly "pecks at him / For food." So must each man one day die. In that high mannerist mode of his, Stevens imagines all the chest wounds and head shots and amputated limbs as some vast red rose, "the soldier of time grown deathless in great size," seen against the flow of hot red lava. Better to imagine a ring of men, summoned again around their dying comrade, whose "wound is good because life was," and for whom the woman waits in vain, smoothing "her forehead with her hand," while the dying soldier, thinking of his beloved, "lies calm beneath that stroke."

We speak of the death of God, but the death of Satan was as much "a tragedy / For the imagination." For if the good of God is denied, so too is the evil ascribed to Satan, so that it follows that filial redemption is no longer necessary, for there is no Son of Man to redeem a fallen nature if it never fell. "How cold the vacancy," then, "when the phantoms are gone and the shaken realist / First sees reality." Even in the face of the moon there is the look of panic now, because, if the face of God has been erased, the moon too has no face, reduced now to a "comic ugliness / Or a lustred nothingness," where at night the "indifferent crickets chant / Through our indifferent crises."

Consider the image of paratroopers falling at dawn, "and as they fall / They mow the lawn." Falling from the skies, they often fall to their deaths. And as they fall they "mow the lawn," a pastoral image, until one remembers that they mow the ground with machine guns. There's the old pun here on *coup de grâce*—to cut the grass—to deliver or receive the fatal blow. The newspapers speak of victories and losses in abstract terms, and the uninspired imagination, defeated, retreats so that when ships are destroyed sailors wave adieu before they perish, and tufts of violets "spring up from buried houses / Of poor, dishonest people" to the sound of church bells ringing out farewell, farewell. And yet the pain might also be washed under by the "gaiety of language," our one Seigneur.

But there is also the human need to love and be loved. Must we wind up reliving the same nightmares our fathers did? Better to retire to one's study after dinner, where one might surround oneself with "a zone of blue and orange / Versicolorings," or gaze upon the fire-feinting sea and call it good, as the God of Genesis did when he created the world, and so accept what is because it is. If it is heaven we desire, consider this: that heaven will be but a shadow of what we have now, and that

After death, the non-physical people, in paradise,
Itself non-physical, may, by chance, observe
The green corn gleaming and experience
The minor of what we feel.

To live fully, then, in a present world: *this* is "the thesis scrivened in delight, / The reverberating psalm, the right chorale." In a long and beautifully rounded final question without a question mark, Stevens's magic wand has managed to create out of the scintillant dust of language

So many selves, so many sensuous worlds,
As if the air, the mid-day air, was swarming
With the metaphysical changes that occur
Merely in living as and where we live.

A shout—a howl of pain almost—down the long corridors on the main floor of the Hartford Insurance Company one July afternoon in 1944. Nineteen-year-old blue-eyed, blond Holly has brought her fiancé, John Hanchak, to her father's office to tell him that they are going to be married. There is that stubborn look in her eye as if to tell her father, "Okay I'll show you!," and now Stevens has lost his self-control. From the beginning he has forbidden Holly to bring Hanchak to the house, but now, here they are: Holly and the "Roussian." Manning Heard, Stevens's friend and associate, has heard the commotion and hurried into Stevens's office to see what the matter is. In all the years he has known Stevens, it is the only time he has ever seen Stevens this upset.

When Holly and John Hanchak married on August 5, 1944, neither Stevens nor Elsie was present. Holly did continue to see her mother, but only when her father was at the office. But if Stevens was furious, Elsie, seeing her own past repeated in her daughter, as if to spite her husband and his family, seemed "very glad for Holly's happiness." Twenty months later Holly would give birth to a son and name him Peter, soon after initiating divorce proceedings against her husband on grounds of extreme cruelty. Stevens, who wanted his daughter back, did what he could to see that the marriage ended as quickly as possible.

• • •

BY DECEMBER 1944 STEVENS, looking ahead to the Allies' eventual victory, viewed the war as "no longer anything except an overwhelming grind." The issue now was the resurgence of Communism and a New Left here in the States. Roosevelt's New Deal "to improve the condition of labor" had in fact "created in the labor movement a force quite as great as the force of war." Worse, it was a problem that was going to survive the war itself. Stevens lamented "the rattle and bang on the left and in the labor movement," he told Allen Tate. But with the surprise attack by German troops in the Ardennes, and Iwo Jima and Okinawa and Hiroshima looming ahead, there was—*Esthétique du Mal* or no—still a good deal of red blood to be spilled.

Then word came from his old friend and associate at the Hartford from before the war, Henri Amiot, who was alive and living in Paris. "What a curious world it is in which one has to go for so long without knowing even that," he wrote Amiot, "and then to have to find out by way of a postcard!" The last he'd heard, Amiot was with the French Army at Nancy, and, "since the Germans made very short work of Nancy when they were on the way in, it was always possible either that you had been put out of business or that you were a prisoner." But Amiot had managed to survive both the First and now the Second World War. Did he know if Anatole Vidal, Stevens's book dealer who lived on the rue de Tournon, was still alive? Stevens knew that Vidal had a daughter, Paule, "a highly nervous creature," according to Jim Powers, who had met her before the war. He wanted to know, so that he could begin sending for books and French paintings once again. As for business at the Hartford, most of the officers Amiot had known in the 1920s had moved on or retired or died, while he continued to do "exactly the same thing day after day," and was happy to be doing it. In fact the Hartford had "made prodigious strides all during the war, and done a tremendous amount of business" and was now "by far the largest company of the kind in the country."

It was not until March 1945 that he learned that Anatole Vidal had died the previous year. On the 20th he wrote Paule to say how much the news had saddened him. "I had hoped that, when the war was over, we could go on as before," he told her, acknowledging her father's "willingness to take pains" in procuring books for him. He would write to Vidal in English, and Vidal would answer in French, "which enabled both of us to say exactly what we had in mind, without awkwardness." Now he hoped he and Miss Vidal might continue to do business in the same manner. Since it had been Paule who had written most of her father's letters to Stevens, it was easy enough to pick up the correspondence once again, Paule reporting on the political situation in France, and Stevens on the situation in the United States.

"You ask about Truman," he wrote her a year later, his Republican sensibilities evident. "He is very much of a politician and, while he seems to be a man of sincerity and of sufficient ability, I think most people who are not themselves politicians feel diffident about him." He'd noted a piece in the *Samedi-Soir* to the effect that the United States was going "to go without hot biscuits in order to feed the world." That, he said, was merely a political statement and untrue. The truth was that half his income went to paying taxes, much of it to help Europe recover. So, while he had "a taste for Braque," whose palette had a certain severity, dryness, and asceticism about it—much like his own poems—he could afford only a Bombois for his light, cheerful paintings. Above all, what he wanted in a painting (as in his own poetry) was "something real but saturated with the feeling and the imagination of the artist."

• • •

A TWENTY-FOUR-YEAR-OLD CUBAN ARTIST, writer, and Harvard alum (class of 1943), José Rodríguez Feo, wrote asking Stevens if he might translate the *Esthétique du Mal* for *Orígenes*, a magazine he copublished with José Lezama Lima in Havana, to be illustrated by the artist Mariano. Stevens was delighted. Just after New Year's 1945, he'd spent an evening engrossed in the copies of *Orígenes* Feo had sent him and had been particularly struck by Mariano's "happy little drawings." There in Havana the war seemed absent and the world of *alegría* and *felicidad* everywhere. He wished he was better versed in Spanish so that he might read the poems, for in poetry language was everything. Yes, he had known Santayana at Harvard, but all that was "forty years ago, when I was a boy and when he was not yet in mid-life."

When Feo sent him two paintings by Mariano, one with pineapples, he immediately hung them in his bedroom, because he found them "as bright and cheerful a thing as there is in the house," something he sorely needed to counter the daily news of the war. Both paintings, he thought, were "a good deal more Cuban" than Feo probably realized and brought with them a sense of an unfamiliar place. Cuba: that was what he needed just now. "One grows tired of the familiar figures," he wrote, "and to be able to find a fresh mind in a Mexican critic, or in the many writers in South America, and elsewhere in the Spanish-speaking countries, for which one would feel an instinctive respect would be a real excitement."

In late February he wrote Feo that he'd just written a poem he'd titled "A Word with José Rodríguez-Feo," which addressed the question of the grotesque, not as a part of the surreal but as part of reality itself. As terrifying as the images of one's nightmares might be, he and Feo, being poets and therefore honorary "secretaries of the moon," both understood that the moon presided over the lunatic, the imbecile, and the poet. If the night made everything grotesque, wasn't that because man's interior world was also dominated by darkness? How strange Feo's world seemed to Stevens, and yet how alluring, where even the image of an "old man selling oranges" and snoring by his basket, his bloated breath bursting at intervals, was troubled by his dreams. But then such an image was merely the minor of the grand grotesque, *pace* the Freuds—Sigmund and Lucien—*pace* Dali, De Chirico, and Tanguy. The grotesque came down to the strange, the unsettling, the unexplained, part "of that simplified geography, in which / The sun comes up like news from Africa."

A few weeks later he wrote Feo again, this time about a young poet named Robert Lowell, who was all the rage just now, especially "from the Catholic point of view," though he'd avoided reading him since it was "the easiest thing in the world to pick up something unintentionally." When he'd visited his old friend Walter Pach in his Washington Square apartment, Stevens, cautious as ever, was relieved to hear Pach speak of

Feo in the "most friendly way," which made Feo "all right." Pach's studio had "a touch of Paris," or Dresden or Mexico City, but in the end the place was merely "a dreary old hole," so that, as one's taxi started uptown for Grand Central Terminal and home, one felt a sense of relief. Who needed more of old Paris these days? Better, he advised Feo, not to become too eclectic in what *Orígenes* published, for they were "putting together a world": an actual Cuba.

On April 4 Hi Simons, who for the past eight years had devoted himself to writing a critical study of Stevens, died suddenly of a heart attack in Chicago. He was fifty-nine. When Stevens learned of Simons's death from his widow, he wrote to tell her that the news had devastated him. In the beginning, he admitted, he had held off from becoming too friendly. But as "time passed, and as we grew accustomed to exchange letters, I felt much freer and had it been possible for us to see one another more often we should soon have had something much heartier in common." At first death terrified, then in time it "overwhelmed us with its solitude," but now she would always have her husband's personality there to console her. Now too Feo's letters would have to help fill the void created by Simons's loss.

Six weeks later he wrote of the war again in a letter to James Guthrie, editor of the Pear Tree Press in England. Where, he wondered, was the nation headed as it faced such determined Japanese resistance? "What bothers me isn't so much the mere growing old," he admitted, as it was his growing sense of obsolescence. Here in Hartford, except for the lines of men registering for the draft, the war seemed far away. Back in 1942 the news that someone one knew had been lost had come as a shock. In time, though, even that news had become part of the everyday as the numbers of dead mounted. Most Americans, it seemed, had no real interest in what was happening in the Orient, including Japan. After all, America had "never been on the make." But now it would have to establish military bases even in the East to make sure what had happened never happened again.

Undoubtedly a general change in how the United States viewed the world was part of the new reality. Up to the present, "conspiracy and greed and gall" had dominated the world. Regardless of how Americans were viewed abroad, they had been essentially a happy people, content to live "among elm trees and farms." Now the war had changed all that, and what the country had to look forward to was a sense "of profound . . . bewilderment" about the future. To Church in mid-July he again wrote about the "benumbing effect of the war" on everyone. Gas rationing had kept him and Elsie pretty much housebound all summer. Besides, he was beginning to feel his age. No longer could he walk "ten or fifteen miles before lunch and as much again after lunch and feel the better for it." He'd considered visiting Reading again, but to what purpose? To visit "the haunts of unimportant ghosts whom I could not understand, since they would be certain to talk to us in Pennsylvania Dutch"? And what would they have to talk about anyway? The damage the rain had done to the wheat and hay?

• • •

ON JUNE 27, 1945, Stevens delivered the Phi Beta Kappa poem at Harvard. On the podium with him that day was Sumner Welles, Roosevelt's former undersecretary of state, a strong proponent for the United Nations. Welles's speech, "Vision of a World at Peace," asked Americans to move beyond their earlier isolationism, at the same time recognizing that the country would now have to contend with a belligerent Soviet Union, though America had made it repeatedly clear that it had no interest in either "territorial or material gain." The graduating class Welles was addressing would have to realize that, as the new leaders in world affairs, they would be making decisions which would affect the world for decades to come. Soon Communism would flood into Estonia, Lithuania, Poland, Czechoslovakia, Bulgaria, Latvia, Romania, East Germany, and Greece. And though these were places with little or no reality for many Americans, these were the new political and economic realities they would have to contend with.

Ironically Stevens addressed the same issues that day through the denser lens of the historical imagination. His poem, which he called "Description without Place," began with the captain of reality, the sun itself, which, for all its presence, was "something seeming and it is." At the same time, the imagination, with her ever-green mind, was primarily interested in making "the world around her green," something ever fresh, ever beginning as each day dawned. We looked to the past, and there was the sun. We looked forward and imagined the sun would be there too. An age might be red with raw reality or green with the promise of spring. But did an age exist apart from the name we gave it? Was there really ever an age of the Reformation or the Enlightenment or the new age of Communism. What, for instance, might Feo's mule, Pompilio—blank realist that he was—think about the current regime in Havana, the world in which the animal lived and breathed each day? What of the "potential seemings turbulent in the death of a soldier," the "commonplace of blood," which "gushed upward and was gone," as on the beaches of Iwo Jima and Okinawa, where the world shrank in that instant to something we did not "need to understand, complete / Without secret arrangements of it in the mind"?

Consider the world as a Museo Olympico, an Olympian Museum containing, among others, Calvin in Geneva, Queen Anne in England, Pablo Neruda as ambassador to Ceylon, Nietzsche in Basel, and Lenin by a lake. Imagine Nietzsche's reveries beside a pool, deep and reverberating with shimmering color, where Nietzsche gilded the waters with his own reflections and "swarm-like manias." Might he not stand in for the modern German imagination which had given rise to the Nazis, just as Lenin might stand in for the Russian Revolution and the Communist state, a man "on a bench beside a lake," disturbing the swans? Lenin, in his proletarian shoes and hat, a modern Moses imagining the chariots of the enemy drowned and a new order where the regal swans fled, pursued by Lenin's "apocalyptic legions."

"If God made a progress through the streets of Moscow in a carriage drawn by twelve horses, ornamented with red pom-poms, and preceded by the massed bands of the Red Army," Stevens had told Henry Church back in 1943, "I don't believe that he would cut any more ice than Stalin would," In fact Stalin would probably attract more notice than God. But then God didn't need all that livery, while one could never really be sure of Stalin as the new savior until after he was dead. For the foreseeable future, it looked like Soviet Russia would create the new postwar reality, a place without description embedded deeply in the imagination, which Stevens, like everyone else, would be dealing with for the rest of their lives. Better instead to imagine "the seeming of a summer's day," another "description without place," a "column in the desert" leading the Hebrews through the desert for forty years, the column on which the dove—the Spirit of

God—had descended. A description without place, then, was different from what the eye could see. It was a future, "an expectation, a desire, / A palm that rises up beyond the sea," and so "different from reality," the difference being that we should witness and remember such "sprinklings of bright particulars" descending from the sky.

In fact a description of what the world might be, could still be, with the right imagination, was something "intenser than any actual life could be," nothing less than "the book of reconciliation," a "canon central in itself," like the Book of Revelation. The imagination, then, as a "word for those / For whom the word is the making of the world," a world made up not of things but of words and of men who "make themselves their speech." A better, richer, fuller world, not shaped by the false promises of Communism. A promised land made up of brilliant sounds, a world "alive with its own seemings" and wedded to the real, a future "like rubies reddened by rubies reddening."

• • •

WHEN WILLIAM CARLOS WILLIAMS read "Description without Place" in that year's autumn issue of *Sewanee Review*, he saw it as a personal affront to his own poetry, which had so often begun with something he'd seen or heard on the streets of New York City—where he and Stevens used to meet thirty years before—or Rutherford (his hometown), or something he'd recorded in his epic of the New World called *Paterson*, the first part of which had been published in May 1946, the same month Stevens was finishing his poem (though Stevens was careful to say he had not read *Paterson*). Who the hell had Stevens been pointing to when he spoke of how men made themselves by their speech? Who else might that "hard hidalgo" be whom Stevens had spoken of, who had shaped, as much as Stevens had, "a style of life" and the "invention of a nation in a phrase"? That November Williams confessed to another Reading poet, Byron Vazakas, that he had not liked Stevens's poem at all.

In fact he was so irked by Stevens's seeming dismissal of place that he wrote his own poetic rebuttal, calling it "A Place (Any Place) to Transcend All Places," which the *Kenyon Review* printed that winter. "In New York, it is said, / they do meet," the poem begins, recalling his time with

Stevens there. Yes, part of New York was Walter Arensberg's place on West Sixty-seventh Street, where he'd listened to Stevens and Arensberg and Duchamp banter in French at those evening soirees. But it was also "a museum of looks / across a breakfast table," made up of "subways of dreams" and "towers of divisions / from thin pay envelopes." It was a city composed of hundreds of miles of sewer lines draining into the Hudson and East Rivers, of "sweatshops / and railroad yards at dusk." It was a place where the southerner Allen Tate now flourished, his Southern Agrarianism retrofitted to speak to a new generation of "foreign writers."

But this had all happened before, hadn't it, Wallace, back then, when all the talk was about Duchamp and "Le Futur"? He bade Stevens remember, for instance, the Baroness Elsa von Freytag Loringhoven, murdered by her boyfriend in Berlin when he'd turned on the gas in the kitchen and walked out. Or how Stevens had once seen her down in the Village, dressed in one of her outrageous outfits, sardine cans hanging from her earlobes and breasts, half her face painted purple, half white, and Stevens applauding her until she'd taken off after him and he'd turned and fled uptown, refusing to venture below Fourteenth Street for years after. Was *that* a place without definition, their New York, "obscene and / abstract as excrement," and fit only for nourishing lettuce? So much for abstraction.

Actually, resistance to the direction Stevens's poetry had assumed had been on Williams's mind for a long time now. He missed that "lamb-like urban talent" he'd found in Stevens's *Harmonium*, long since gone, that "metropolitan softness of tone, a social poetry that Chaucer had long ago [brought] to such perfection," he told Marianne Moore. Back in early 1943 Williams had written James Laughlin at New Directions about the long poem he was cobbling together called *Paterson*. If Stevens could speak of "Parts of a World," he said, *Paterson* would consist of " 'Parts of a Greater World'—a looser, wider world where 'order' is a servant not a master." After all, order was something "discovered after the fact" of composing, and not some "little piss pot for us all to urinate into—and call ourselves satisfied." Another war, then, this one undeclared, and carried on between two poets now in their sixties, one living along the Passaic and the other along the Connecticut: two currents which would refresh and trouble the American landscape long after both men were gone. "You know," Williams had told Stevens in July 1944, "it makes me think that we do begin to have an elder group who are, in fact, in themselves, a critique & a *vade me cum* of an art that is slowly acquiring reality here in our God forsaken territory." He was even coming to believe that he and Stevens might yet "generate an assembly who will make the history."

• • •

"WHAT IS GOING ON in the world now," Stevens wrote a correspondent in October 1945, with the war finally over, "is an extraordinary manipulation of the masses." Just who or what these manipulating forces consisted of he did not yet know. But it was not the politicians who were behind this upheaval. If it was anyone, it was the masses themselves, who were able to carry out general strikes and bring things to an abrupt halt. And yet he had to believe that it would turn out all right in the end, at least for Americans, who had "never exploited workers as they have been exploited elsewhere," and where "the man at the very bottom" still felt he had a chance to become "the man at the top."

The following month Charles Norman, editor of the daily newspaper *PM*, wrote Stevens asking him to take part in a symposium on the current situation of Ezra Pound, who was about to be transferred to Washington, D.C., after having been held for the past six months in an American detention center outside Pisa, charged with treason for his wartime radio broadcasts from Rome in defense of Mussolini. Among those who had signed on were Williams, E. E. Cummings, Karl Shapiro, F. O. Matthiessen, Louis Untermeyer, and Conrad Aiken. Characteristically Stevens refused to join. He would explain why, but did not want "to be quoted or referred to in any way."

First of all, Stevens did not for a moment doubt that Pound had done what the government accused him of doing. That the man was a genius was no excuse, since we were all "subject to the common disciplines." Of course, the "acts of propagandists" were not to be thought in the same category with spying. After all, for all the daily propaganda in the United States, he did not smoke Camels, eat Wheaties, or use Sweetheart soap. That Pound was a poet mattered no more than the fact that Tokyo Rose sang and wisecracked. If Pound wanted help and could show he was entitled to help, Stevens would do whatever he could, "in a practical way." Nor did his attitude toward Pound soften with time. Two years later, when Theodore Weiss, editor of the *Quarterly Review*, asked Stevens to contribute to a symposium on Pound, Stevens refused. He would have to saturate himself with Pound's work for that, and he did not have the time. Besides, "there would be the special difficulty that he is as persnickety as all hell." A friend had just written him from France "speaking of 'My pink Persian cat in front of me, looking up just now with his reproachful amber eyes. He does not like to be molested even by thoughts or looks.' " That, he said, was Pound.

• • •

"THE MISERY OF EUROPE, which was greater six months ago than it is now," Stevens wrote Feo at the beginning of March 1946, "seems not to have been so real to us then as it is now; and the more real it becomes the more sharply" one felt that the poetry now being written was too academic and unreal. Perhaps the critics who pointed to this problem were right. The life of a poet was "just as difficult and as unpredictable as the life of a speculator in Wall Street." If conditions now were confusing for everyone, no matter. The poet had to find a way to break through and speak to the present because "to live exclusively in reality is as intolerable as it is incomprehensible." On the other hand, he told one interviewer, the poet could not "allow himself to be absorbed as the politician was" in the moment, for to do so would sabotage the poet's freedom to write anything of real significance. If poetry was ever to make a significant contribution to the fundamental satisfactions of humanity, it would have to find for itself an even greater "intellectual scope and power" because "we never understood the world less than we do now nor, as we understand it, liked it less." Yes, the way a poet spoke was important, but what was just as important was what the poet had to say.

• • •

NINETEEN-FORTY-SIX, AT LEAST IN the States, was like a midsummer's interlude after the years of war, a gift, something to be believed in, "the inaccessible jewel" of the normal for a moment caught in the difficult pursuit of it. Out of this momentary interlude came a poem composed of ten equal parts, each consisting of three five-line stanzas in Stevens's signature iambic pentameter. He called his new poem *Credences of Summer*, and it was a kind of description *with* place, that place being the Reading of an old man's youth, a place much changed, but unchanged in the amber light of memory's imagination.

"Now," the poem begins, "in midsummer come and all fools slaughtered"—April Fool's, signaling spring, but those fools Hitler and Mussolini gone as well. A time too for sitting in one's garden, with young broods of birds in the grass and Elsie's well-tended roses giving off their scent, a time when the mind might lay by its troubles: "the last day of a certain year / Beyond which there is nothing left of time." Call it the real and the imagined for the moment married, when the ghosts of one's parents for a moment return, and two lovers walk hand in hand in the summer fields outside Oley as it was forty years ago, when one was happy and picnicked in the dry grass humming with its summer crickets.

This was not a time for analyzing, for pulling apart the dream to get at the quotidian reality. Postpone that for now and live in the moment, observing the thing itself and nothing else. No more metaphors, just now, no more similes, no more *as ifs*. Time instead to see the gold sun as it was and tell yourself that "this is the centre that I seek." Fix that moment "in an eternal foliage / And fill the foliage with arrested peace," and taste the "joy of such permanence." Not desire for the dream, then, but the dream achieved.

This, then, is the end, the climax, when the intensest and yet most peaceful moment at last arrives: high noon, the Metaphysician's apex, which, alas, we know must also fall away. How many poets have desired this moment, what Williams called this grasshopper transcendence, or Frost's understanding that "nothing gold can stay"? The eternal dilemma: to want to hold on to what we cannot. And so back to the Reading of his courtship years and the seven-story pagoda atop Mount Penn, visible for miles,

> *the natural tower of all the world . . .*
> *A point of survey squatting like a throne,*
> *Axis of everything, green's apogee*
> *And happiest folk-land, mostly marriage-hymns.*

A place where the mind might dwell at its ease, as in a bedroom in Hartford, a "refuge that the end creates." But what end? The natural end of all one's thinking? A world at rest where a man dreams, recalling his lost youth, who stands on a tower and reads no book? A Large Red Man from Reading, who has read and read, but whose eyes tire easily now, so that he spends his time looking out on the world about him, absorbing "the ruddy summer," so that he is "appeased, / By an understanding that fulfils his age, / By a feeling capable of nothing more," because there is nothing more that he desires?

A picnic with Elsie, the two of them resting side by side on a midsummer's day in the countryside of Oley, the piled mows, an echo, perhaps, of Elsie and Wallace moaning with delight in each other? It is a "land too ripe for enigmas, too serene," too distant in time even for the poet's clairvoyant eye: a world that was but no longer is, "the secondary senses of the ear" swarming not with the sounds of cicadas and orioles, crickets and bluebirds, but with choirs, the "last choirs, last sounds / With nothing else compounded, carried full."

Call it a "pure rhetoric of a language without words," a pure music within the mind, where words are no longer necessary. Faust's moment realized, then, so that "things stop in that direction and since they stop / The direction stops and we accept that is / As good." It is the day, the abstracted day at last realized, the day which "enriches the year," a day "stripped of remembrance," the thing itself for a moment realized, here, now: "the vital son, the heroic power."

It is half green reality, half abstraction realized, this moment, insubstantial air become substantial rock. This is not something such as one man alone feels. Nor is it a symbol only. It is a reality, something that we too, as readers, can see and hear, the poet as Sleight-of-Hand Man assures us. It is—because it must be—the final

rock of summer, the extreme,
A mountain luminous half-way in bloom
And then halfway in the extremest light
Of sapphires flashing from the central sky,
As if twelve princes sat before a king.

Sing a fable of summer, when "far in the woods they sang their unreal songs" of "summer in the common fields," a song of deep desire realized, the woman won.

And—like that—the music changes as the thing desired slips away, and the mind struggles to hold on to what it knows it cannot hold. "Three times," Stevens writes, evoking Jacob's wrestling with the angel, or Virgil, or Milton:

Three times the concentred self takes hold, three times
The thrice concentred self, having possessed
The object, grips it in savage scrutiny,
Once to make captive, once to subjugate
Or yield to subjugation, once to proclaim
The meaning of the capture, this hard prize,
Fully made, fully apparent, fully found.

Now the trumpet blows, announcing the visible, "the more than visible, the more / Than sharp, illustrious scene." It is the mind itself, "aware of division, aware / Of its cry as clarion," the central mind among a multitude of minds, the poet who speaks our deepest desires, "a personage in a multitude," who realizes that what has grown venerable is also, finally, unreal.

And so the dream of summer's credences begins at once to unravel. The "cock bright" settles on a bean pole and waits for warmth, one eye on the willow summoning death and loss, where the thing that would harm us in our enclosed garden, the "gardener's cat," is dead, and even the gardener who designed the garden—God, the great designer, the Imagination which set the scene—is gone, and what remains of the great design is merely a field full now of "salacious weeds." Now another moan, but this one a sound of despair, coming from outside the reality one summoned, a sound "not part of the listener's own sense."

This is the "inhuman author," evoking a world populated by the "personae of summer" in a world long vanished—if in fact that world ever existed except in the imagination—and the day gone with it, leaving behind an old man to meditate on "gold bugs, in blue meadows, late at night." A man who suddenly realizes that he cannot make out what his characters are saying and sees them as in some midsummer night's dream, "mottled, in the moodiest costumes" of forty years ago, "the manner of the time, / Part of the mottled mood of summer's whole." If the figures in the dream speak, it is "because they want / To speak," these "roseate characters" full of life's hale, safe for a moment

> *from malice and sudden cry,*
> *Completed in a completed scene, speaking*
> *Their parts as in a youthful happiness.*

"New York seems to go from a low level to a still lower," he wrote Henry Church that August, so that he wondered if it could "go any lower." What he missed most here in Hartford was the absence of things European as a result of the devastation of the war. But what worried him even more was the growing sense in America "of the increasing strength of the powers at work to promote interests other than our own." Such powers, of course, were always at work, but they had not always been as strong as they seemed now. Still, given the devastations of the war, he could understand why Europe should ask for America's help.

What was harder to understand was just what game the Russians were playing. One English weekly had just accused the United States of making a large loan to England because it feared Russia. But, Stevens rejoined, the United States wasn't afraid of Russia. True, the Soviets' "aggressive attitude" toward the United States seemed to show that they were making progress toward their goals faster than the United States was making toward theirs. For many, Communism did seem a way out of poverty, and maybe it was. And, yes, there was poverty here in the States as well. But there were also many "happy, hopeful and ambitious people who expect to make something of themselves and of the world in which they live." Was that why, he wondered, Russia was so antagonistic toward the American system of free enterprise?

On August 30 the Stevenses left by rail for Pennsylvania to vacation at the posh Hotel Hershey with Judge Powell and his wife for three weeks. It was, Stevens would remember, one of the happiest times he and Elsie had ever spent together. It was on this trip too that he found the final resting places of two of the Zellers attached to churches: Trinity Tulpehocken and Christ Lutheran, both just off the pike that ran from Harrisburg to Reading. Over the door of the old Zeller house he also discovered an architectural cartouche made up of a cross and palm branches meant to indicate that its inhabitants had consecrated themselves to the glory of God.

The Zellers, his mother's family, he'd learned, had been religious refugees who had emigrated to America in 1709, living "for some fifteen or twenty years in the Schoharie region in New York," before going down to the Susquehanna Valley and Tulpehocken, twenty miles west of Reading, where they'd built this very house, from whose doorway, he believed, they had looked upon the hills framing their valley, happy in their work and their faith, reality for them consisting "of both the visible and the invisible."

On another occasion a "stout old Lutheran" had accompanied him when he'd visited Christ Lutheran Church outside Stouchsburg. The old man, he thought, seemed to feel "very much as the Irish are said to feel about God," where "God is a member of the family." Back on the turnpike again, the two had met a friend of the old man, "who had been leader of the choir in Trinity Tulpehocken Reformed Church for more than a generation" and who accompanied them to that church's graveyard. The wall about the square-acre graveyard had been built of limestone and was "about four feet high, weather-beaten, barren, bald," with "eight or ten sheep, the color of the wall and of many of the gravestones . . . bleached and silvery in the hard sunlight." He remembered a few cedars here and there, which only "accentuated the sense of abandonment and destitution, the sense that, after all, the vast mausoleum of human memory is emptier than one had supposed." There was about the place a desolate reality "that penetrated one like something final."

Back in New York, visiting an exhibition of books at the Morgan Library with their bright pages of tales, poetry, and folklore from Poland, France, and Finland, he recalled the "barren reality that I had just experienced in that graveyard suddenly taking color" and morphing into "many things and people, vivid, active, intently trying out a thousand characters and illuminations." The stark reality of his Pennsylvania past then, but transformed by the brilliant colors with which his imagination might paint that past and make it live once more.

That December he sent the typographer who had designed Stevens's Cummington Press editions, Victor Hammer, a photograph of a stone he'd found set in the west wall of Trinity Tulpehocken Church. He asked that the inscription be reproduced so that it could serve as his personal bookplate, the words reproduced "in the exact form in which they are used and including the old form of Wol" rather than Wohl. The inscription was "WER GOTT BERTRAUT HAT WOL ERBAUT G.Z. 1772." *Who trusts in God has built well.* G.Z. was George Zeller, one of his maternal ancestors, a people renowned, if for nothing else, for their piety. Piety: that was the thing he realized he shared with the Zellers, but his own form of piety. "I write poetry," he had once told Hi Simons, "because it is part of my piety: because, for me, it is the good of life, and I don't intend to lift a finger to advance my interest, because I don't want to think of poetry that way." Who trusted in the imagination, therefore, also built well.

• • •

THAT DECEMBER HE WROTE Feo again, this time explaining some of the images he'd embedded in his dark poem "Attempt to Discover Life," which began:

At San Miguel de los Baños,
The waitress heaped up black Hermosas
In the magnificence of a volcano.

That volcano again, nightmare image of death and annihilation, into which all the beauty of roses was juxtaposed to a cadaverous woman, a strange duenna, bearing in her mantilla "a woman brilliant and pallid-skinned." She stood beside the man—the figure of the poet himself—watching the beauty of the world suddenly decay into "yellowing fomentations of effulgence, / Among fomentations of black bloom and of white bloom," and then the man and the brilliant woman and the cadaverous one all disappeared, leaving on the table dos centavos. Feo's San Miguel de los Baños in Cuba, a lovely spa and "a spiritual place," Stevens called it, a dream not unlike the Hotel Hershey for luxuriance, with roses of all sorts, such as Elsie grew. Was that, then, the life of Crispin/Stevens and his blonde revisited twenty-five years on? The question "prompted by that poem," he told Feo, expecting that the answer would stay with him and not make its way back to Hartford, was this: Was life "in the end worth much more than those tuppence, those dos centavos?"

Shortly before Christmas he was in New York to see the "infallible Dr. [Alfred D.] Mittendorf about blobs" in his left eye. "Happily," he wrote Church, "these have largely disappeared since then. But I am left with one more eye medicine, in addition to the three that I have been using for the last twenty years." He'd been told to cut down on his reading, especially at night (which was the only time he could read), and not drink coffee or alcohol, the first of which he never touched, and the second, he believed, he touched only on rare occasions. As for postwar New York, it still seemed threadbare and without the freshness and variety of the New York of thirty years before, he lamented, and had as much real panache as "an Indian with diamond ear-rings."

• • •

IN FEBRUARY 1947 HE gave a lecture at Harvard he called "Three Academic Pieces." It was composed of a section of abstract prose followed by two long abstract poems, the first titled "Someone Puts a Pineapple Together," the second titled "Of Ideal Time and Choice." This time he would quote nobody. "Taking a new and rather quackish subject and developing it without the support of others is not quite the easiest thing in the world to do," he admitted to Feo. But if he got "nowhere with it," he could "always abandon it and do something else." An accurate theory of poetry, his lecture began, demanded that the poet begin by examining the structure of reality. Reality therefore was a mental structure, of which one of the significant components was metaphor, which was continually changing the relationship between the things compared, and therefore our sense of the real as well. With metaphor, or the creation of resemblance by the imagination, the resemblance might be "between two or more parts of reality," or "between something real and something imagined," or between two imagined things, "as when one said that God is good." And because Nature was constantly creating something new without ever reproducing itself exactly, so too must one's metaphors constantly surprise with the freshness of their comparisons, for what the imagination provided was a sense of *vif*: a vitality, life refreshed at every turn.

Nature, of course, could outshine even the most powerful imagination. Thus "a strand of a child's hair" might bring back the whole child, as with a locket or a grandfather's high beaver hat, for these "intimations of immortality" were as real in the mind as the objects themselves. And weren't these private resemblances to be preferred to, say, "the resemblance of the profile of a mountain to the profile of General Washington"? If we did not write the text of life, we all read from it, and the disclosures of our meditations were "no less a part of the structure of reality" than things themselves. What a ghastly situation it would be, he suggested, "if the world of the dead was actually different from the world of the living and if, as life ends, instead of passing to a former Victorian sphere, we passed into a land in which none of our problems had been solved . . . and nothing resembled anything we have ever known." Who among us hoped that after we said farewell to the world, we should find ourselves "in a Jerusalem of pure surrealism"? Better oblivion than that!

Seeing resemblances between things gave us pleasure. But even more, resemblance allowed us to enhance our sense of reality, so that what two dissimilar things shared in common could shine through more brilliantly. If the resemblance was between two things of adequate dignity, both might be transfigured by the comparison. Was not the glory "of the idea of any future state a relation between a present and a future glory"? And wasn't it earth's brilliance that gave paradise its brilliance? Similarly a catalogue of images from Ecclesiastes—*Or ever the silver cord be loosed, or the golden bowl be broken, or the pitcher be broken at the fountain, or the wheel broken at the cistern*—gave us a heightened sense of reality, as well as the pleasure associated with a sense of solemnity, because each object was in harmony with the other.

If, then, one's "desire for resemblance" was "the desire to enjoy reality," perhaps what we really hungered for was to enjoy reality in a world where the song of larks in a Viennese wood might displace an atomic bomb with its grotesque volcano and plume. Among so many naysayers and skeptics, one needed more than ever a poetry which could provide us with a sense of pleasure and peace. If we could look into the chaos of the sea and see there "some extraordinary transfiguration of ourselves," wouldn't that be worthwhile? And if the "structure of poetry and the structure of reality" were one, it followed that poetry and reality were also one. Or ought to be.

If what he had just proposed was mere hypothesis, so be it. After all, "hypotheses relating to poetry," even when they appeared to be distant illuminations, might also be the fires of fate, "if rhetoric ever meant anything." If this meant first ascending through the realm of illusion, it meant penetrating at last to its underlying reality. And if metaphor contained within it something of the ideal, it must not be dismissed merely because our civilization had outlived the ideal, for we were constantly outliving our idea of the ideal, "and yet the ideal itself remains alive with an enormous life."

• • •

"I SAW A PHOTOGRAPH of the *America* in a very rough sea and I thought that it might take you a few days to pull yourself together after that sort of thing," Stevens wrote Henry Church the following month, as the Churches returned to New York after wintering in a Paris still recovering from the war. He was going to be in New York on business the following day for the annual meeting of the Hartford Live Stock Insurance Company, of which he'd been a director for the past thirty years, and he was finally going to meet José Rodríguez Feo, his young Cuban friend, at the Ritz Tower on Fifty-seventh and Park for a cocktail, then have dinner with him afterward if Feo turned out to be more than "all teeth and no ears."

In fact Stevens found Feo quite likable, and they decided to meet again on Easter Monday, April 7, 1947, in the same location, inviting Allen Tate as well. Back in February, Karl Shapiro, then serving as poetry consultant at the Library of Congress, had written Stevens asking him to make a recording for the Library, and Tate had tried to persuade him to do it. But,

Stevens told Tate, that was exactly the sort of thing he'd refused to do at Harvard. Robert Penn Warren had also asked him to make a recording a while back, and he'd refused him as well, and the same with Columbia University. Some years back they'd "put in a dictaphone system here at the office," he explained to Shapiro, whereby "you dictated your letters down a pipe . . . and when you turned the machine so that it read back what you had dictated, it sounded very much like a leak somewhere in the house in the middle of the night."

But Stevens canceled the meeting with Feo and Tate when Ananke—Fate—intervened. On Good Friday, April 4, Henry Church died suddenly of a heart attack in his apartment at 875 Park Avenue. He was sixty-eight. That Easter Monday Stevens attended Church's funeral at St. Bartholomew's Church on Park and Fifty-first. When he'd last seen Church two weeks earlier, Stevens noticed that he seemed much thinner and tenser, but had attributed that to the Churches' storm-tossed trip back to the States. At the funeral Barbara Church had looked "so completely crushed," he told her in a letter, that he'd wanted very much "to come to see you and yet feared to do so." Only time was going to heal this wound. Better that Henry had gone first since he could not well have carried on without her. What Henry had wanted more than anything, he added, was making "a contribution to the ideal welfare of his fellows," and Stevens was ready to help her in any way he could.

Five months later he wrote her again. In the interval, he explained, he'd written a long poem called *The Owl in the Sarcophagus* by way of homage to her husband. "Two forms move among the dead," the elegy began. One of those forms was "high sleep / Who by his highness quiets them"; the other was "high peace, / Upon whose shoulders even the heavens rest." Two brothers, Stevens called them. And a third form: "she that says / Good-by in the darkness, speaking quietly there, / To those that cannot say good-by themselves." It was death herself who spoke now, but "without a voice, inventions of farewell." Death, "the mother of us all," who in the brief "syllable between life / And death cries quickly, in a flash of voice, / Keep you, keep you, I am gone, oh keep you as / My memory."

Once there was a man who walked "among the forms of thought," a man who conceived his passage—his journey, yes, but his passing as well—

"as into a time / That of itself stood still," less "time than place, less place than thought of place," a place like and unlike the earth he had inhabited, akin to the underworld of the ancient Greeks, like that afterworld he'd evoked in "Sunday Morning" and those early poems for a dead French soldier: a flowing mass of whiteness, where all agitations come to rest, as "water of an afternoon in the wind" does, "after the wind has passed."

And peace: the peace death brings realized at last, where in our last blood we make out in the darkness a figure "stationed at our end," a figure we imagine because we must, a figure who will watch over us as we descend into a strange summer like none we have ever known, where peace, bright peace, like a "candle by our beds" will guard us when we stand on oblivion's edge. This is the "mythology of modern death," and these figures—sleep, peace, and death—"the monsters of elegy . . . of pity made," are death's "own supremest images." What *The Owl in the Sarcophagus* offers us are words humming in the troubled mind, like a child who "sings itself to sleep," comforting itself with the fictions "that it makes" by which one lives and dies.

When Barbara Church returned to France that June, Stevens wrote her that it might turn out to be "an exquisite happiness" to be back in a place where she had always been happy. As for himself, the roses in his garden were "thick with big buds" and only needed "two or three days of the bright, warm, humid weather that roses like." The evening before, "after all the noisy Katzenjammer children in the neighborhood were upstairs saying their prayers," he'd strolled about, "without politics or philosophy." It was just the sort of peace and quiet that answered so many questions.

Later he sent her the poem he'd written for her husband, which would be translated into French by Pierre Leyris as "Portrait" for *Mesures* the following April. When he'd last seen Henry, he told her that November, Church had seemed as eager as ever to make friends because friendship was precious to him. He was a simple man interested in complex ideas, a plain man "who lived in a certain luxury which he ignored," a man for whom ideas "were the bread of life" and who might spend "half the night in reflection recovering himself and almost willing to chatter, almost but not quite." No wonder, then, that Henry's death left a hollowness in Stevens nothing could fill.

• • •

WHEN HIS NEXT VOLUME of poems, *Transport to Summer*, was published in late February 1947, it received its share of reviews and qualified accolades. F. O. Matthiessen, reviewing it for the *New York Times*, wrote that Stevens continued "to exhibit the fecundity which has made the last decade more prolific for him than all the rest of his previous career." In the past eleven years Stevens had published *Ideas of Order, The Man with the Blue Guitar, Parts of a World*, and now *Transport to Summer.* At sixty-seven his subject had indeed become—as it had with the later Yeats—"increasingly the imagination itself." There were poems here which suggested that Stevens was more the "critical esthetician than poet." But then there were "full-bodied sensuous poems" as well.

Notes toward a Supreme Fiction, Matthiessen thought, was too much of a set piece, unlike his more successful *The Man with the Blue Guitar.* In fact it was with his shorter poems that Stevens had been most successful. There was a gaiety of language about these, spilling over with freshness, lightness, ebullience, and those nonsensical grotesqueries breaking "through the restrictions of the fixed and dry rational." Even in a time of violent disorder like the present, Stevens had shown how a man might "recreate afresh his world out of the unfailing utilization of his inner resources." Of course, in "expressing such truths with the mellowness and tang of a late-summer wine," Stevens had snagged "about one reader to every hundred of the latest best-seller." Yet it was Stevens who would come to be recognized more and more as belonging "in the company of Henry Adams and Henry James, with that small body of important American artists who have ripened as they matured." For while many poets fall away from their earlier promise as they approach late middle age, Stevens was one of those who kept maturing and revitalizing himself in his poetry up to the very last.

• • •

MOREOVER, STEVENS WAS FAR from finished with what he proposed to do for poetry. In the fall of that year he composed what many consider his capstone poem: "The Auroras of Autumn." "This is where the serpent lives, the bodiless," the poem begins, with Stevens looking up at the grand spectacle of the Northern Lights, by which any of us must feel dwarfed to insignificance: "His head is air. Beneath his tip at night / Eyes open and fix on us in every sky." These "fields, these hills, these tinted distances" surrounding him: these were the serpent's nest, these "and the pines above and along and beside the sea," all of these constituted "form gulping after formlessness." Crispin/Stevens, the comedian as the letter C revisited. Again the mind is overwhelmed by what it sees: the thing itself, Fate, Ananke, the serpent of Time shedding its skin over and over, the sublime majesty and terror washing away every color but the bleak blackness and bleached white of some ever-vanishing, insistent Omega.

And there is that other terrible Sublime to try to comprehend, this one invented by our own species and now unleashed on us: the Bomb, the ultimate light and sound spectacle, a cloud expanding like a flower, the light like ten thousand suns, annihilating everyone who at the last moment will stop and turn upon the sand to stare into the bomb's terrible, formless, and still-forming face. The bomb, still in the hands of the United States alone, but with Russia clearly closing in: the second country which would summon its own monster two years hence, in the summer of 1949.

The end of innocence, then, if ever there was a time or place for innocence except in the hungering mind. Farewell to such an idea, and with it a world imagined or at least cobbled together, where "a cabin stands, / Deserted, on a beach, a white cabin . . . according to / An ancestral theme," where the flowers too

against the wall
Are white, a little dried, a kind of mark

Reminding, trying to remind, of a white
That was different, something else, last year.

A cold wind blows across the floor and "chills the beach . . . / And the whiteness grows less vivid on the wall," and a solitary man "turns blankly on the sand" to observe

how the north is always enlarging the change,
With its frigid brilliances, its blue-red sweeps
And gusts of great enkindlings, its polar green,
The color of ice and fire and solitude.

A deserted cabin on the beach: one more empty house among Stevens's houses, whether his family's home growing up in Reading, or his half-empty house in Hartford, filled with so many regrets and silences.

Farewell too to the idea of "the mother's face, / The purpose of the poem," the mother and the son together for a moment here, with evening coming on, and the house of his youth "half dissolved," a memory only, like the memory of she who made "that gentler that can gentle be," before she too dissolves, her necklace now a mere carving set on a dresser to look at, and "not a kiss." Farewell to the mother who used to read to him and his siblings and tuck them in, whispering to each "good-night, good-night."

For just a moment the upstairs bedroom windows light up, not from within this time but from without, ablaze with the terrifying light of the aurora borealis, an apocalyptic light, signaling the end, the way the wind bangs against the door here in Hartford like a rifle butt, like soldiers rounding up suspects door to door, when the "wind will command them with invincible sound." The mother who made their house a home, gone now, except for the half-remembered memories of a woman singing to the accompaniment of an accordion, as Stevens self-protectively mocks even that memory before letting it go as something illusive and irretrievable, an irritant to get rid of so that unencumbered he may face the unflinching polar North and the serpent-like Aurora.

Then the lost father conjured up to bid farewell to: the God figure, the patriarch, fetching "negresses" to dance among the children in some madcap mock antebellum scene from *Gone With the Wind*, with Atlanta in the background burning. What are we, after all, he wonders, but figures in a masque, a play, except that "there is no play," acting out our improvised scripts "merely by being here." No progression, no denouement, no trombone crescendo ending. No lone, lingering cello note.

No, the play is elsewhere, and not with us, he sees. For it is the monstrous cloud that improvises the ultimate reality show:

A theatre floating through the clouds,
Itself a cloud, although of misted rock
And mountains running like water, wave on wave
Through waves of light.

Waves of light, like the cold light of the aurora borealis. Like the light and heat of the Bomb. As in an abstract expressionist painting, say, by Jackson Pollock. A force field, an energy, a cosmic serpent shedding its skin again and again and again, the world gone over to formlessness, except in the propensity of the imagination to make form out of formlessness. Call it a force field spreading across the northern reaches of our planet, or a serpent, at once terrifying and yet innocent of any design on the minuscule beholder of the ever-changing shapeless shape there in the arctic dark.

Can the imagination contain such a force, the thing we name that remains nameless? Can we really ever tame it? Or tame our own mocking, reverent, questioning, relentless minds? Our little houses, we like to imagine, will protect us. But even they are helpless against the rifle butt that knocks against our door:

He opens the door of his house
On flames. The scholar of one candle sees
An Arctic effulgence flaring on the frame
Of everything he is. And he feels afraid.

How tentative and terrified the solitary poet is by the thought of the imminent obliteration of all he is and knows. And yet only the imagination is real, Stevens insists, so that, while everything will be reduced to whatever ash the world's wildfire leaves behind, some "shivering residue," what must remain is the imagination's "crown and mystical cabala." And yet even the imagination has its limitations, the curse of an insistent self-consciousness for one, so that even the imagination "dare not leap by chance in its own dark." To do so would be to instantly morph from one's grand "destiny to slight caprice," with everything turned on its head by a clap of the hands or some comic punch line uttered at the wrong moment, "a flippant communication under the moon."

And yet and yet and yet surely there must have been, there had to be a time of innocence. Or at least the idea of a time and a place where innocence played once, or what's a childhood for? Once upon a time, this modern-day Hamlet laments,

We were Danes in Denmark all day long
And knew each other well, hale-hearted landsmen,
For whom the outlandish was another day
Of the week, queerer than Sunday.

In that world whose other name was Reading "we thought alike / And that made brothers of us in a home / In which we fed on being brothers." But that was then. Now that home is no more, and his brothers like his sisters are all gone. He has dreamed his life away, stuck in the honey of sleep, aware more and more now of the inevitable, in which only two are real: himself and his imagination, boon companion, mother of his poems.

But how can he be sure even of his imagination? Or, for that matter, even of himself? Winter is coming on once more, and he can see Orion putting on his glittering belt in the long nights of late autumn. Still, it might come, that final rendezvous, it might, it might. It just might come tomorrow, say,

In the simplest word,
Almost as part of innocence, almost,
Almost as the tenderest and the truest part.

He understands that the auroras in and of themselves have no more design on us than Shelley's Mont Blanc had on the poet, or even that terrible iceberg which married the *Titanic* in Hardy's "The Convergence of the Twain." After all, ice and snow and polar lights mean us no harm, because they do not mean. It is we, the poet tells us, who must therefore make our necessary adjustments, "contriving balance to contrive a whole," as if Emerson's New England Poet had to undergo a new stock-tallying of his central position as all-seeing eye, taking in "the full of fortune and the full of fate / As if he lived all lives."

What is there to see, finally, other than the wind shaking one's house here in the "hall harridan"? It is by such lights that one comes to experience the momentary "blaze of summer straw" as an illusion in the vast mind of winter's dark. It is Stevens's elegy to the world, a world which just might disappear in the fires of human hatred or, just as terrible, human indifference: the ineffable text of an imagined world dissolved at last to a "thing of ether that exists." In this unhappy world with its unhappy folk, what is left for the poet but to try to conjure up a whole:

The full of fortune and the full of fate,
As if he lived all lives, that he might know,
In hall harridan, not hushful paradise,
To a haggling of wind and weather, by these lights
Like a blaze of summer straw, in winter's nick.

The poet at forty and now the poet at seventy, meeting once more across the intervening years: the poet of the *Auroras* waving to the poet of the *Comedian*, who once made "gulped portions from obstreperous drops," until finally he proved that what was proved is nothing. Now the old man nods to the young man, even as the young man bows in return, each acknowledging that, in the end, the relation of each man must be, as Stevens ended *The Comedian*, clipped by the Fates and, of course, by death itself.

16

The Eye's Plain Version: 1948–1949

There were those that returned to hear him read from the
poetry of life,
Of the pans above the stove, the pots on the table, the tulips
among them.
There were those that would have wept to step barefoot into
reality.

"LARGE RED MAN READING"

January 1948: the French Connection. Stevens has been reading Jean Paulhan's recently published *Letters to the Comité national des écrivains*, carrying the book back and forth with him between his office and home half a dozen times. Paulhan, the Churches' old friend and editor of the *Nouvelle Revue Française* for nearly two decades, arrested by the Gestapo for his activities with the French Resistance, had continued to keep tabs on his compatriots. The French Purge, *Pépuration légale*, which had followed the collapse of the Vichy government, had begun in late 1944 and would continue for some time to come. Some 300,000 cases of collaboration with the Vichy would be investigated, with more than 6,700 people sentenced to death (nearly 4,000 of them in absentia) for treason, of which 791 executions would be carried out. In addition, some 50,000 French citizens would be officially disgraced and lose their civil rights.

The Purge, Stevens confessed to Barbara Church, was something he'd not been able "to follow very attentively," though Paulhan's letters did bring the issues into sharper focus. That is, except for the complexities of the postwar trials, which had soared beyond his ability to grasp even as a lawyer. Pétain was a case in point. From Stevens's point of view, the marshal had been treated "quite badly." After all, someone had had "to stand for France" and carry on with Germany, "unless the whole country was to be directly subject to the German police," and Pétain had "acted depending on his own loyalty and honesty to shield him," so that he deserved to "receive the funeral of a marshal of France." Had Pétain really given the enemy anything "they could not and would not have taken if he had not given it to them"? So, while he was not privy to all the complexities of the case, his sympathies were strongly with Paulhan "that those who are purifying might themselves" stand to be purified as well. More broadly, however, the correspondence demonstrated the sort of left-wing free thinking that was destroying free thought itself.

Take art, for instance. All art that was not modern in the best modern sense was being dismissed now as merely antique, and most modern art enjoyed "the completest possible prestige merely because it is modern." If he went into an art gallery "containing the work of a dunce," he was sure to find that dunce defended. And if he tore his hair at the dunce's ineffectiveness, the dealer would no doubt think him "illiterate and insensitive." Free thought, like free art and free poetry, had all conspired to produce this tyranny, Stevens complained. What had actually happened, he explained after he'd calmed down, was this: he'd been jarred by the work of a young surrealist and abstract expressionist by the name of William Baziotes, and then learned that the Museum of Modern Art had actually "bought one of his filthy things." The problem with modern art (as with modern poetry) was that one had to acquire a technical interest in its development in order to understand how to see it. That was the kind of understanding experts had acquired. All he knew, on the other hand, was that some artists were "more intelligent, more sensitive, more practiced" than others. "But, of course," he added wearily, he had to be in the wrong, for "in the modern alphabet soup all the letters are A."

Come mid-March, he told Barbara Church, he would be giving "another one of those lectures which I do so badly," this one at Yale, which would "require a lot of sitting around and looking out the window, making notes and so on." The talk, which he titled "Effects of Analogy," was not coming easily, he confessed to Feo a month before he had to deliver it. "After I have walked home when I would ordinarily have a glass of water and a few cookies and sit down in an easy chair with the evening paper," he sighed, "I go upstairs . . . and work over my chore like one of the holy fathers working over his prayers."

He began his talk by quoting from two seventeenth-century sources: John Bunyan's *Pilgrim's Progress* and La Fontaine's fable "The Fox and the Crow." Bunyan, he explained, overwhelmed his readers with strict allegorical personifications which left nothing to the imagination. One read the story either for the story itself or for the meaning behind the story. What was needed, however, was a reading where both the story and the meaning interacted to produce "an effect similar to . . . the prismatic formations that occur about us in nature in the case of reflections and refractions."

A passage in St. Matthew provided the sort of image and feeling that worked for him. It was the passage where Jesus, seeing the multitudes, "was moved with compassion on them, because they . . . were scattered abroad, as sheep having no shepherd." This was not, Stevens insisted, merely "an emotional analogy," but one in which Matthew had made an imaginative choice based on the degree of the rightness of the image, and where object and image had fused. Such rightness came only with discipline, and the strongest poets, poets like Paul Valéry, understood the imagination as not just one's own but something much larger, which it was the poet's duty to make one's own.

Most poets, like the surrealists, lived on the edge of consciousness, writing poetry that was marginal and subliminal. But the strong poet understood the imagination as a power which could provide such insights into reality as made it possible for him to be at the "very center of consciousness," and thus create nothing less than a central poetry. What these strong poets were after was "the poetry of the present," a thing of "incalculable difficulty" and something rarely achieved by anyone. For if these poets were "mystics to begin with," they were continually pushing away from the mystical and back "toward that ultimate good sense which we term civilization." That was the sort of poet St. Matthew had shown himself to be in comparing the masses to sheep without a shepherd. To be successful, poetry had to move with lightning speed from the poet's imagination to the reader's and do this through analogies.

Then too there was the poet's personality to consider, and that came down to the poet's sense of the world. A man's sense of the world was something he was born with and which stayed with him, which meant that for each poet certain subjects were congenital while others were not. The difference between a strong painter like Picasso and his followers, for example, was that, while Picasso pursued a subject, his followers merely pursued *his* subject. And what was the poet's subject if not his sense of the world? It was a subject that was inevitable, inexhaustible, and "autobiographical in spite of every subterfuge." The poet needed his so-called ivory tower because, like anyone, "he could do nothing without concentration . . . and because, there, he could most effectively struggle to get at his subject," even when his subject was other people.

Stevens turned now to the music of poetry. Poetry, he explained, had changed character at the same time that painting began to change character. To make his point, he quoted a passage from T. S. Eliot's "Rhapsody on a Windy Night," with its irregularly spaced rhymes and cadences. Until recently the music of poetry had meant "metrical poetry with regular rhyme schemes repeated stanza after stanza." Yet Eliot's poetry, while it did not follow the older music, was still music. When we listened to the music of "one of the great narrative musicians," we learned to move quickly when the music moved quickly, and slowly when the music moved slowly. Listening to a successful long poem, in fact, was like listening to an emotional recital. Analogies, Stevens concluded, were by their very nature elusive. Consider the man for whom reality had been enough, returning at the end of his life to the place where he had grown up, where everything he'd cherished was tangible and visible now, a world "full of the obvious analogies of happiness or unhappiness, innocence or tragedy, thoughtlessness or the heaviness of the mind." That was what poetry was: "a transcendent analogue composed of the particulars of reality," but a reality created by the poet's sense of the world.

As usual, Stevens felt his presentation had gone badly. "The other day I read a paper somewhere," he confessed to Allen Tate afterward. "As we walked down the aisle to get on the platform, I felt more like an elephant at every step. When we had taken our seats . . . I noticed that the reading desk was low and said that that would make it necessary for me to stoop as I read." Then the fellow "went over to the reading desk and began to screw something in the pedestal to elevate the desk to a decent height," which for some reason made everyone laugh. Would Stevens give a public reading for Tate now? To which Stevens answered point blank, "Not on your life."

Another thing that troubled him for a long time was a conversation he'd had with Cleanth Brooks and his wife after his presentation. "Either the cocktails were too good or too many," he told Tate, so that he'd mentioned to Brooks, a southerner, that Louisiana "was not a part of the United States at the time of the Revolution." Worse, he thought he'd acted disrespectfully toward Mrs. Brooks. If Tate happened to run into Brooks, perhaps he could explain that he'd meant no harm by his remarks and hoped the Brookses might forgive him. Yes, it was true that, after a few drinks, the shy, inaudible Stevens had morphed into a "relaxed, easy, joking, talkative, delightful companion," Brooks would remember twenty years later. But given their lively repartee, Brooks was dismayed to learn that Stevens thought he'd acted badly. The whole thing had merely been "a full-grown chimera," Brooks explained, and existed only in Stevens's imagination." That Stevens had been so troubled by an imaginary slight only reinforced Brooks's sense of the gentleman Stevens was.

A repetition of sorts occurred three years later, when, after he'd read a paper at the 92nd Street YMHA, he'd let himself unwind afterward. "A few weeks ago I wrote a note to Cleanth Brooks and hope that I purged myself of all evil in his sight," he confided to Norman Holmes Pearson. Brooks "could not have been more decent about it, so that I feel quite relieved." That is, until he made yet "another bugaboo" three years later, this one at "a little party at which I was to meet a number of people whom I was much interested in meeting. After three cocktails I asked them if they had ever heard the story of the man who. . . . After making quite sure that they all wanted to hear it, I told it. It is the funniest story in the world, but, curiously, I was the only person that really laughed and I have been worried to death ever since, that is . . . until recently, when I said the hell with it."

• • •

IN APRIL 1948 HE received a letter from the poet Thomas McGreevy of Dublin, an old friend of the Churches, asking if it was true that Stevens had once praised his poems to Henry Church. Yes, Stevens, wrote back, he had. But, he added, "I also said that it was extraordinary that a man should wait year after year to be able to ask was it true." Ireland, with its *nostalgie du divin*, was much on his mind these days, but it was an Ireland "much more modern and vigorous" than the Ireland he'd imagined as a boy. McGreevy's poems, he wrote McGreevy that May, were like "memorabilia of someone I might have known and they create for me something of his world and of himself," something which was central for Stevens. In turn, Stevens sent him several of his own books of poetry, noting that American poetry was "at its worst in England and, possibly in Ireland or in any other land where English is spoken and whose inhabitants feel that somehow our English is a vulgar imitation." The two men were opposites in many ways, the fifty-four-year-old McGreevy being outgoing and outspoken, especially about his Catholicism—"God bless this" and "God bless that"—and quick to establish intimacies, but they hit it off at once, and the correspondence continued until Stevens's death, with McGreevy's Ireland the inspiration for a number of Stevens's late poems about place.

"I have a new correspondent, a citizen of Dublin, a fellow of great piety but otherwise of impeccable taste," he wrote Feo. "It seems that troupes of singers of operas fly from Paris to Dublin, fill the night air with *Melisande*, then go to a party and fly back to Paris, all in a single circuit of the clock. What a dazzling diversion." One was never bored in Dublin "because with all the saints they know, and know of there, there is always company of a kind and in Dublin saints are the best company in the world." Dublin—at least his mental construct of it—was like something out of a novel, he wrote Barbara Church that August, "not one of those frightful continental novels in ten volumes, all psychology and no fresh air, but a novel full of the smell of ale and horses and noisy with people living in flats, playing the piano, and telephoning and with the sound of drunks in the street at night."

By contrast, there were no saints in Hartford. If there had been, he told

Feo that same month, the meaning of life "would come to one without trouble like a revelation and it would ripen and take on color." By life he meant the sort of thing one picked up "on beaches and in the presence of one-piece bathing suits," the footing "from which we leap after what we do not have and on which everything depends." One wrote poetry, he told McGreevy, because it was one of life's sanctions, a "very serious thing to say" so early in the morning, he added. He seemed to be weaving one long ars poetica across a warp and woof which included all of his correspondents.

Real things, "without the interventions or excitements of metaphor" (this to Barbara Church): Wasn't the whole effort behind modern art "about the attachment to real things"? Were not the cubists attempting to get not at the invisible but the visible, where behind the reality of a particular painting "lay a more prismatic one of many facets"? And in "deviating from reality," weren't the real painters actually trying to get at it? So with his own poems. Of course all thinking tended toward the abstract, but the abstractions of the poet were even "abstracter than the abstractions of the painter."

On June 22 a book on the Jesuit Church at Luzern arrived at his office. Looking through it, he wondered—a bit abstractly, of course—why one would "rather be in that church at Luzern" than in one's own garden in Hartford. The *why* of the question was not very difficult to see, even if one stripped the church of every sanction except its physical aspect. If it was merely a matter of the physical aspects of the two, then the church and the garden came down pretty much to the same thing. So what *was* the real difference between that Jesuit Church in Switzerland and his garden? Perhaps one's relation to what one saw from one's bedroom window, "without any effort to see to the bottom of things," might someday actually "disclose a force capable of destroying nihilism." Then, realizing how serious he was becoming, he added, "How in the world the full moon of these nights can go on looking as if nothing had happened gets me."

Summer mornings and afternoons he spent strolling through his beloved Elizabeth Park. Until recently, he told Barbara Church in mid-August, a group of nuns had come there "each morning to paint water colors especially of the water lilies." There was a chasteness there "like the chasteness of the girl in Oscar Wilde who spent her time looking at photographs of the Alps." But this morning even those "exquisite creatures were no longer there and in addition the tops of the ferns were dry and there were acorns on the path."

His poem "Nuns Painting Water-Lilies" speaks of this occasion. "These pods are part of the growth of life within life" and are "part of the unpredictable sproutings, as of / The youngest, the still fuzz-eyed, odd fleurettes," sweet peas in summer's apogee, unraveling a "ruddier summer, a birth that fetched along / The supernatural of its origin." Here was a day on which he watched those nuns mumbling "the words / Of saints not heard of until now, unnamed, / In aureoles that are over-dazzling crests." Stevens at sixty-eight, looking up to behold the nuns in their "queer chapeaux," seeming to chant the names of saints. That and the park and the water lilies. It was all part of a *fraîcheur*, a freshness there and then just as quickly not there, these angels of reality, "inaccessible / Or accessible only in the most furtive fiction."

"Sweet peas I love," he confessed to his old friend and former colleague, Wilson Taylor, and when "on a soft summer evening" he walks through Elizabeth Park "where there are sweet peas, or, better still, a place where there is woodbine, I feel that I have laid off all my Aryan habits and that I am a big fat colored person: and I am able to hum again and make plans on how I shall spend the next dollar that I get and feel good because I have only fifteen cents to go." In real life, however, he took "a hundred dollars to New York," spent the day, and came back broke that night "with nothing to show for the trip except a swell shoe shine." Big, fat, successful Stevens, missing these days more than anything else the thrill he'd felt once in everything, like a man in a grocery store who is "sick and tired of raisins and oyster crackers and who nevertheless is overwhelmed by appetite."

• • •

"IT WOULD NOT SURPRISE me if in time we came to be much better friends with the Irish in Eire than we have ever been with the English in England," he wrote McGreevy that August. Consider the recent death of the Englishman Talbot de Malahide, "Admiral of Malahide and of the

Adjacent Seas, or something resembling that," he joked. Was that a real title, or simply a satirical one? In any event, it was "the sort of thing" that both the Irish and the Yankees had suffered from "for so long at the hands of the English." He thought of Tommy Collins, "a poor thing at home when I was a boy, who rode around town in gorgeous costumes. The people in the livery stable used to lend him a white horse. . . . What a cry would go up when children saw him in the distance coming their way and dressed up say like the Admiral of the Schuylkill and its Convivial Streams." McGreevy's reminiscences of Ireland had a way of making him think of his own half-mythical Reading, with its Schuylkill, named by the Dutch, its "deep slightly sulphurous blue . . . succeeded by piles of coal dust . . . washed down from the coal regions in the Spring floods." Or the Swatara, with its Indian name, "a country stream," he explained, "that empties into the Susquehanna above Harrisburg."

In "Our Stars Come from Ireland" Stevens would create a palimpsest, combining McGreevy's memories of his birthplace in Tarbert on the River Shannon with the Swatara and Schuylkill rivers of his own Reading, merging McGreevy's image of the Bank of Ireland with his own Hartford offices:

Over the top of the Bank of Ireland,
The wind blows quaintly
Its thin-stringed music,
As he heard it in Tarbert.

These things were made of him
And out of myself.
He stayed in Kerry, died there.
I live in Pennsylvania. . . .

The stars are washing up from Ireland
And through and over the puddles of Swatara
And Schuylkill. The sound of him
Comes from a great distance and is heard.

Ah, the freshness of McGreevy's (and by extension, Yeats's) Ireland, its rinsed airs moving toward Hartford over the great Ocean in what he called "the Westwardness of Everything," those "Gaeled and fitful-tangled darknesses" made suddenly luminous, as if

There was an end at which in a final change,
When the whole habit of the mind was changed,
The ocean breathed out morning in one breath.

When Norman Holmes Pearson invited him to address the English Institute at Columbia University on September 10, Stevens wrote back that, as long as he could choose his own topic, he was game. He was interested because he'd been thinking of "at least making notes on the subject of the imagination as value," which in fact became the title of his talk. For three days, he wrote Barbara Church, "various professors will be reading papers and then on Friday evening I shall get up before this group, which by that time will be thoroughly flabbergasted by all that they have heard, and try to set them on fire." If only he could take with him that bottle of Jameson whiskey she'd mentioned in a letter. Then he would "really get somewhere."

He began his talk by evoking Pascal, who had once dismissed the imagination as "the mistress of error and duplicity." Yet how was it that vast populations could be "brought to live peacefully in their homes and to lie down at night with a sense of security and to get up in the morning confident," merely because they imagined they were safe, unless the imagination also served a positive function? Even Pascal, as he lay dying, had desired nothing more than the Catholic sacraments. It was Pascal's sister who'd written that, when Pascal had finally "received the sacred wafer and extreme unction with feelings so tender," he had "poured out tears." Was it not Pascal's own imagination, his belief in the efficacy of those sacraments, which had brought him such consolation at the end? It was precisely because the imagination had the power to shape reality that Stevens had become so interested in it. After all, the true poem was "not the work of the individual artist" but of the universe itself, the mind shaping matter and evolving an ever deeper sense of the Real as it moved toward "the one work of art which is forever perfecting itself." Or think of that Jesuit church at Lucerne, he added, where one passed from the real to the visionary "without consciousness of change."

Of course one had to purge the imagination of its false romanticism, for the real imagination was nothing less than the mind's final freedom. And if the imagination with its fictions was not yet perceived as the ultimate clue to reality, might it not become so in time? To live in the mind, after all, was to live in the imagination. If the great poems of heaven and hell had been written, "the great poem of the earth" had yet to be. Here in America, what passed for the greatest imaginative construct was the political, and in particular Communism, that "grubby faith" that promised "a practicable earthly paradise." If only poetry could "address itself to the same needs and aspirations, the same hopes and fears, to which the Bible addresses itself," he explained, "it might rival it." But then, the biblical imagination and the Church's ceremonies of innocence were one thing, the poetic imagination something else altogether.

Consider Santayana, whose very life had been lived in the imagination. The old philosopher, now in his eighties, dwelling in a convent in Rome, in the company of nuns and familiar saints, both of which made "any convent an appropriate refuge for a generous and human philosopher." But, then, don't we all live in a world shaped by our imaginations? Didn't we leave our offices behind to enter the world of opera, say? Wasn't it the imagination which allowed us to "import the unreal into what is real"? And wasn't it through the imagination that we projected "the idea of God into the idea of man" and found "the normal in the abnormal"?

The imagination, that "miracle of logic," whose "exquisite divinations [were] calculations beyond analysis," just as the conclusions of reason were "calculations wholly within analysis." In the end the portal of the imagination should open onto "a scene of normal love and normal beauty," which would be, after all, "a feat of great imagination." The chief problem for the artist, really, was to actualize the normal, and to solve that problem the poet needed "everything the imagination has to give." A real poetry would be a poetry divested of the poetic, and the very idea of such a poetic made "everything else seem false and verbose and even ugly."

• • •

"ONE GOES TO THE Canoe Club," he wrote Feo that October, "and has a couple of Martinis and a pork chop and looks down the spaces of the [Connecticut River] and participates in the disintegration, the decomposition, the rapt finale." And yet one had "a sense that the world was never less new than now, never more an affair of routine, never more mechanical and lacking in any potency of fineness." It was "as if modern art, modern letters, modern politics had at last demonstrated that they were merely diversions, merely things to be abandoned when the time came to pick up the ancient burden again and carry it on." What was needed now was "getting rid of all our horrid fiction and getting back to the realities of mankind." What music had he heard that had not simply been "the music of an orchestra of parrots"? What books had he read "that were not written for money"?

How many "men of ardent spirit and star-scimitar mind" had he met in the past year? Not one, he sighed. "Not a goddam one." No longer did the world seem to be moving forward. There was "no music because the only music tolerated is modern music . . . no painting because the only painting permitted is painting derived from Picasso or Matisse." Just so, when he went into a fruit store nowadays, he could find nothing "but the fruits du jour: apples, pears, oranges," all of which he felt like hurling at the Greek proprietor. Where were the exotic things of life? The things that gave life sparkle? Where were the "sapodillas and South Shore bananas and pineapples a foot high with spines fit to stick in the helmet of a wild chieftain"? They were certainly not to be found in Hartford and rarely ever even in New York.

He was sixty-nine now and felt more than ever like a man wandering in a desert. He read less and less because literature nowadays was "largely about nothing by nobodies." He and Elsie had spent several days in New York, but this time around he hadn't even bothered to call on Barbara Church. He'd even torn up his Christmas shopping list, did not even care what had happened to a batch of poems he'd sent to an editor. Even the ninety-foot-high blazing Christmas tree he'd watched going up in Rockefeller Center had failed to stir him. And when he'd dropped into his old familiar bookshops, he'd found nothing of interest. The one exception had been the exhibition at the Wadsworth Atheneum, with Thomas Cole's century-old paintings and their biblical allegories. Only that had managed to touch him.

• • •

THEN THERE WAS POLITICS. In spite of the pundits' predictions that Dewey would win the election that November, Truman had carried the day, and about Truman he was "of two minds." Truman, being a Democrat, kept himself in office "by taxing a small class for the benefit of a large class," he complained to Paule Vidal. On the other hand, he understood the hard truth "that the vast altruism of the Truman party was probably "the greatest single force for good in the world today," and while he regretted that he would once again "have to think twice about buying pictures, still one could not enjoy books and pictures in a world menaced by poverty and enemies." By enemies, he explained, he meant the Russians. That is, "assuming that they are enemies. One never knows." Perhaps they were merely undertakers.

• • •

ONE SATURDAY AFTERNOON IN late January 1949 Stevens spent an hour viewing the sculptures of Jean Arp at Curt Valentin's gallery on East Fifty-seventh Street. He'd been afraid of inadvertently knocking one of the sculptures over, especially in such a small gallery, "when one has more elbows than usual." He thought he would like the show because Arp's abstracts seemed to morph into poetry. There was one foot-long abstract gray-white marble form whose title, Stevens noted, was "full of the transformation that a gesture creates." *Owl's Dream*, another abstract in black, he found "equally full of the disintegration of reality in the imagination."

He could see that Arp's conceptions occurred to him "in moments of aesthetic intensity" and that there was an exquisiteness to his work, but the man's imagination lacked strength, lacked the "sense of violence" necessary to the serious artist so that "the human spirit" did not need to fear him. But it was "nonsense to speak of Arp's integrity as an abstractionist in the same breath with . . . Mondrian." For Mondrian the abstract truly *was* the abstract. After all, what validated so much of modern art was not its results but "its intentions and purposes." But what he'd liked much better than the Arp display was the Piranesi exhibit at the Morgan, complemented by a dozen oysters in that hole down at Grand Central, and Manganaro's over on Ninth between Thirty-seventh and Thirty-eighth streets, where he'd bought "some Dago things, including grated Parmesan cheese." After so much Arp, what better way to fix himself "with the greatest firmness back on the ground" than to take in the "odor of cheese, fish and Dagos."

"Somehow modern art is coming to seem much less modern than used to be the case," he wrote Tom McGreevy that same day. "One feels that a good many people are practicing modernism and therefore that it no longer remains valid." How quickly the experimental became routine. Moreover it required "so much effort" and even then seemed unsuccessful. But then the New York galleries were not the places "by which to judge how alive modern painting or modern art" were. What New York had come to mean for him these days was not so much books and pictures, as "getting a decent haircut and . . . seeing a few decent looking girls." If Hartford was "the best place in the world" for him on a daily basis, the occasional trip to New York was like taking "a trip in a balloon."

• • •

FIVE MONTHS LATER HE took another balloon trip down to the city. "When I was in New York," he wrote Barbara Church, "I bought a lot of fruit in the place on 58th Street. One likes to look at fruit as well as to eat it and that is precisely the right spot to find fruit to look at." Afterward he'd "bought a chocolate cake" simply because Saturday and cakes were part of the same thing." Holly had brought his grandson, Peter, now twenty-six months old, with her and, "as the top of the cake had some sugar on it: a couple of roses, sprays of leaves, we put Peter in a chair and placed the cake in front of him and let him go to it to see what he would do," and soon "he had it all over the place." It was "a good way to get rid of it because I am afraid that cakes, too, ought merely to be looked at."

It was one sign that life at home was getting better once more. Holly was at last separated from her husband and had custody of Peter, which was, of course, a great relief for Stevens. Each evening, after dinner, he and Elsie each went upstairs to their own rooms. He would shut the door, open his window, and in the silence watch the fireflies in the garden below. Really, what could be a finer way to pass the book of hours, remembering what it had been like growing up in Reading all those years ago? A good night's rest, followed in the morning by a walk down to Elizabeth Park, after which he could catch the bus and get downtown to his office "in quite normal time."

• • •

"WE SEEM TO BE coming closer to the Italians," he wrote Barbara Church that August, by which he meant "the generation of young Italians in this country which is now growing up" and whom he found to be "an extraordinary fine group of people and certainly . . . the healthiest looking people in the world." Once a week the *Hartford Times* published photographs of the local brides, many of whom were of Italian extraction and, though most were "far from good looking," they all looked "strong and cheerful and worthwhile and I must say that I am for them."

"I am glad that you share my interest in Tal Coat," Stevens had written Paule Vidal back in May. Already one French critic had noted that Pierre Tal-Coat was "one of the few young painters from whom it seems possible to expect a new reality." When, in late September, the Tal-Coat still life he'd ordered from Vidal arrived, he'd found it to his surprise "so much cooler and richer and fresher" than he'd expected. He loved "the strong blue lines and the high point of the black line in the central foreground" around which the objects seemed to gather themselves. Soon enough the picture was hanging in his room, adjusting itself to his bed, mirror, and desk. He'd even renamed the painting *Angel Surrounded by Peasants.* The angel was "the Venetian glass bowl on the left with the little spray of leaves in it," he explained, while the peasants were "the terrines, bottles and the glasses that surround it." The title alone, he added, tamed Tal-Coat's violence the way "a lump of sugar might tame a lion." While he noted "the absence of mandolins, oranges, apples, copies of *Le Journal* and similar fashionable commodities," such as one found in the Braque and Gris paintings of forty years ago, all of Tal-Coat's objects had a "solidity, burliness, [and] aggressiveness" about them. And that was what he looked for in poems as well as paintings.

"I am the angel of reality, / Seen for the moment standing in the door," Stevens writes in "Angel Surrounded by Paysans." Not the angel as he is usually portrayed, with "ashen wing" and "tepid aureole," but rather an angel that looks like any of us, through whom one might actually see the earth again:

A figure half seen, or seen for a moment, a man
Of the mind, an apparition apparelled in

Apparels of such lightest look that a turn
Of my shoulder and quickly, too quickly, I am gone . . .

The bright quotidian: reality glimpsed in its transfigurative splendor, "cleared of its stiff and stubborn, man-locked set," in which we hear again earth's "tragic drone / Rise liquidly in liquid lingerings," and where meanings might be gathered in the "repetitions of half-meanings."

• • •

"EVERY FRESH BEGINNING IS a beginning over," Stevens told Barbara Church that June, so that one was "always beginning." Which was why it was so important to devote "one's whole life to poetry in the same way that people devote their whole lives to music or painting," because it brought with it "a sense of moving forward." Or so he believed. In any event, he had "just finished one long thing" and was ready now to move on. The long thing was *An Ordinary Evening in New Haven*, a poem which he read on November 4 in New Haven for the Connecticut Academy of Arts and Sciences.

New Haven then and New Haven now. The New Haven of the city's founders as a new haven in a new world, and the New Haven of 1949, with its buildings, its inhabitants. "The eye's plain version," the "vulgate of experience," a thing set apart in its holiness as in its plain reality, a reality shared by everyone: the vulgar, the polis, the people. A poem like a house composed of the sun, the primal reality out of which all creation was nourished and grew, and the poet among a multitude of poems, "words, lines, not meanings, not communications." Williams's Paterson and Stevens's New Haven: two nondescript American cities, two long poems, in which it would be the poet's task to kill the first giant of the epic imagination with a second giant, a more "recent imagining of reality," like and unlike what Williams had called in *Paterson* "the Delineaments of the Giant," the spent waters of the Passaic Falls "forming the outline of his back," and Stevens's giant of a poem with its river of consciousness

> *Down-pouring, up-springing and inevitable,*
> *A larger poem for a larger audience,*
>
> *As if the crude collops came together as one,*
> *A mythological form, a festival sphere,*
> *A great bosom, beard and being, alive with age.*

A crude collops of thirty-one parts, each composed of six three-line stanzas (i.e., rooms), each of which in turn is made up of blank-verse lines, 558 of them, composed in going to and from work each day, between March and June of that year. An imagined city, like and unlike what the visionaries who settled this new heaven-haven imagined, houses "composed of ourselves" become "an impalpable town, full of / Impalpable bells" heard only within the mind, whether one imagined a seventeenth-century Connecticut or its twentieth-century kin. This city held together in the mind, a reality made up of "confused illuminations and sonorities," and yet a reality "so much ourselves." In short, the force that revealed to the mind a new, sun-drenched reality, where the idea of God and the imagination might fire-fuse into one.

It is such a compound, complex serenade, this poem, that volumes might be written, (alas, hooray) in the attempt to unpack its riches. It is in fact Stevens's Book of Revelation, where the poet doubles for the author of the Book of Revelation, and where the "ancientest saint ablaze with ancientest truth" might at last celebrate the poem of earth. It is that space where "the point of vision and desire are the same" and where the poet's will to attain to the holiness of his vision should at last find that "celestial ease in the heart" he has for so long desired. Not the thing possessed, then, because for Stevens it could never be fully possessed, but the thing desired, "set deep in the eye, / Behind all actual seeing, in the actual scene," the ineffable, the mystery, glimpsed now "in the street, in a room, on a carpet or a wall, / Always in emptiness that would be filled." A porcelain jar of inestimable beauty, but necessarily reconfigured in the fragments one finds in one's life.

Reality is "the beginning not the end." It is "naked Alpha, not the hierophant Omega," clothed in the "dense investiture" the imagination offers. Was he thinking of Williams here as the Aristotle to his Plato, where "for one it is enough; for one it is not," both appointing themselves the custodian "of the glory of the scene, / The immaculate interpreters of life"? Williams as Alpha, with his mantra always to begin again, Stevens as Omega, "refreshed at every end," both "rigid realists" and both, because they were human, "impoverished architects" becoming, even in their desire to touch the hem of reality, "much richer, more fecund, sportive and alive," even in their searches, displaying "the truth about themselves," because they had lost "that power to conceal they had as men." In any case it is the poet's function to seek "conceptions of new mornings of new worlds" until at last "that which was incredible becomes, / In misted contours, credible day again."

Eight cantos in by way of prolegomena, "Part I: Metaphysical Overture." No matter how high the imagination soars, we find ourselves "coming back and coming back / To the real," to a hotel room in New Haven, say, seeking "the poem of pure reality, untouched / By trope or deviation, straight to the word" and therefore "straight to the transfixing object . . . / At the exactest point at which it is itself." As in "a view of New Haven, say, through the certain eye . . . with the sight / Of simple seeing, without reflection," without compounding thought. In the end we should seek "nothing beyond reality." And yet within those bounds we seek everything, including the alchemy which the spirit provides.

It must change, Stevens had said of the Supreme Fiction. So here, now, where our spirit "resides / In a permanence composed of impermanence," where "the poem is the cry of its occasion, / Part of the res itself and not about it," the poem as a "reverberation / Of a windy night as it is," where even the marble statues flicker "like newspapers blown by the wind," and where what is and what was are like "leaves burnished in autumnal burnished trees" such as Moses saw, the leaves here, now, "in whirlings in the gutters," like thought itself, as if,

In the end, in the whole psychology, the self,
The town, the weather, in a casual litter,
Together, said words of the world are the life of the world.

The poet then as disciple, like Stevens "solitary in his walk," skipping the "journalism of subjects," to find instead "the perquisites of sanctity," the strong mind "in a weak neighborhood," the "serious man without the serious," the poet as "neither priest nor proctor at low eve," defining "a fresh spiritual" like a blast of cold, fresh air "in a long, too-constant warmth." Ah, to behold in the streets of New Haven "the actual landscape with its actual horns" (not the celestial horns only, but the horns of delivery trucks, say) "of baker and butcher blowing, as if to hear, / Hear hard, gets at an essential integrity."

"The dry eucalyptus seeks god in the rainy cloud," but "Professor Eucalyptus of New Haven seeks him / In New Haven," and seeks him "with an eye that does not look / Beyond the object." Like the monk-like scholar Stevens, the anti-Apocalyptic, hidden-from-the-world (*eu-kalyptos*) Professor Eucalyptus (of Yale?) "sits in his room, beside / The window, close to the ramshackle spout "in which / The rain falls with a ramshackle sound." It is in that sound that he "seeks / God in the object itself, without much choice," the "commodious adjective," the description which makes a thing larger than itself," a "reality grimly seen," but "spoken in paradisal parlance new," which is never grim because the ramshackle tink-tonk sound "of the rain in the spout is not a substitute" for reality but rather "of the essence" of what he seeks, though "not yet well perceived."

Professor Eucalyptus "preserves himself against the repugnant rain" by the imagination's evocation of its opposite: a rainless land, where the self might find itself. For the "instinct for heaven" has its counterpart in the "instinct for earth." Not a new heaven but rather a New Haven, this hotel room, "the gay tournamonde as of a single world / In which he is and as and is are one." Call it a world in which "the oldest-newest day is the newest alone," and where the sun—that "Oklahoman"—wakes from its "youthful sleep" over the sea as it has each morning for billions of years, almost able to erase the whimper of "death's poverty." And yet the poet knows that reality is something greater than the comic and the tragic both, that there is a zenlike "dominant blank" at the center of things, where the "commonplace" abides, as in an ordinary evening in New Haven.

To paint what one sees outside one's window or as one walks to work: to paint "in the present state of painting and not the state / Of thirty years ago," to paint what one sees at seventy rather than what one thought one saw at forty. "The life and death of this carpenter," Stevens writes—for is he not a carpenter, cobbling together these rooms and houses one by one until a city has been "slapped up like a chest of tools," a wood model that might serve for those future generations of "astral apprentices," because we all depend finally on what beauty we can find, whether it be "a fuchsia in a can" to say that one was here and wrote these poems, these "iridescences / Of petals that will never be realized"? Here is Crispin revived: the would-be colonizer picking up the challenge he threw down thirty years before, Crispin envisioning a new haven, "this present colony of a colony / Of colonies" in the "changing sense / Of things." Except that Crispin the dandy has become "a figure like Ecclesiast, / Rugged and luminous," the poet at seventy chanting "in the dark / A text that is an answer, although obscure."

But who is he, really? And what has he achieved in abstracting New Haven until it is no more than "a residuum, / A neuter shedding shapes in an absolute." Yes, the poems about reality he has written remain as imaginative blue shapes, retaining "the shapes that it took in feeling, the persons that / It became, the nameless, flitting characters" of his poems, verbal actors who "still walk in a twilight muttering lines" while the poet "sits thinking in the corners of a room," where the abstract poem, "the pure sphere," escapes the impure, but only because "the thinker himself escapes." But what has he accomplished in evading the world and its inhabitants? What has he done but leave himself "a naked being with a naked will / And everything to make"? Let him evade, evade, evade, until he evades "even his own will and in his nakedness" ends up inhabiting not a city but merely a self-delusion, the mere "hypnosis of that sphere."

But this he may not do: "not evade his will, / Nor the wills of other men," who will see what he has tried to do by this sleight of hand. Nor can he evade his own fate, "the will of necessity, the will of wills," the very reality he has sought for all these years. Shall he settle for some escapist pastoral, some "romanza out of the black shepherd's isle," with its constant humming of some nostalgic past, some amniotic sea? Or shall he seek "the opposite of Cythère," with its island isolation at its center, a world of mere surfaces: "the windows, the walls, / The bricks grown brittle in time's poverty"? No, for when all is said and done, the celestial mode must remain paramount for him. Two romanzas, then: "the distant and the near," composed of "a single voice in the boo-ha of the wind."

But if New Haven "is half sun"—the daily round of things—it is also half night, a world lighted by the stars, by a single space and future "big over those that sleep," containing for this Prospero its own comforting sound, "a kind of cozening and coaxing sound," a mother's sound, the day's fragments come together now as one, dream songs, where "disembodiments / Still keep occurring" and where "desire prolongs its adventure to create / Forms of farewell, furtive among green ferns." A desire for what? For the God of his youth? That idea belonged to "the neurosis of winter," which with the return of "the genius of summer . . . blew up / The statue of Jove among the boomy clouds."

But if the disappearance of God brought with it a clamor, "it took all day to quieten the sky / And then to refill its emptiness again" with something new. But what? "An escape from repetition," at least, the idea of a new haven "poised at the horizon's dip," an idea urged on by Life itself, fixing the poet "with its attentive eyes" watching hawk-like that he not give in to the "unfaithful thought" of some false romance. Someone like that man with the blue guitar, some hidalgo with his "shawl across one shoulder and the hat," a combination of Picasso and Williams, watching him closely for any false note "to keep him from forgetting, without a word, / A note or two disclosing who it was," until even the real, the commonplace, become unreal again, while the hidalgo sits there across from him, something "permanent, abstract, / A hatching that stared and demanded an answering look."

Rain crossing Long Island Sound just to the south, and the sound of waves, of reality, in perpetuity. And the scholar, among his axioms and adagia and notes on life, leaving behind a book of notes, such as this: "The Ruler of Reality, / If more unreal than New Haven, is not / A real ruler, but rules what is unreal." The one who thought it all out, "as he has been and is and, with the Queen / Of Fact, lies at his ease beside the sea." The real joined to the imagination, "New Haven / Before and after one arrives." Like those cities and places he will never know except from the postcards sent by those who ventured there: Bergamo, Rome, Sweden, Salzburg, Paris—"the theory of poetry, / As the life of poetry." Is it merely simile, an *as* or *as if*? Isn't it, rather, that "the theory / Of poetry" *is* "the theory of life," life as it is, and yet life "in the intricate evasions of as, / In things seen and unseen, created from nothingness, / The heavens, the hells, the worlds, the longed-for lands"?

"Kennst du das Land, wo die Zitronen blühn?" Goethe's Mignon asks, the German dreaming of the warmth of Italy, and beyond that—Eden. *Know you the land, where the lemon trees bloom?* The search, then, for an earthly paradise, the Key West of a quarter century before remembered, that "land of the lemon trees," where

yellow and yellow were
Yellow-blue, yellow-green, pungent with citron-sap,
Dangling and spangling, the mic-mac of mocking birds.

And, by contrast, Hartford and environs. *Go on, high ship*, the mariner had sung in his farewell to Florida twenty years before—returning to his North, "leafless" and lying "in a wintry slime / Both of men and clouds, a slime of men in crowds." Hello Connecticut, "land of the elm trees," where "wandering mariners / Looked on big women" and dreamed in the autumn of their lives. There, in the South, on a sailboat, say, with the boys from Georgia, down in the land of the citrons, "they rolled their r's," whereas here in Hartford "the words they spoke / Were mere brown clods, mere catching weeds of talk." When the mariners, Stevens among them, "came to the land of the lemon trees, / At last, in that blond atmosphere, bronzed hard," they could say they were "back once more in the land of the elm trees, / But folded over, turned round." New Haven and

Florida, part of the same reality, "except for the adjectives, an alteration / Of words that was a change of nature, more / Than the difference that clouds make over a town." Eden in a postlapsarian world, where Connecticut's "dark-colored words" would have to redescribe the citrons.

But Florida is a land he knows he will never return to. And this is New Haven on a rainy November evening, where "the last leaf that is going to fall has fallen" and "the robins have left, là-bas," and the squirrels "huddle together in the knowledge of squirrels." A winter wind blows over New Haven now, a wind which "has blown the silence of summer away," and hidden it, as in Elizabeth Park, beneath the "mud under ponds, where the sky used to be reflected." For once the mind is cleared of its illusions, and "the barrenness that appears is an exposing," a "coming on and a coming forth," where "the pines that were fans and fragrances emerge, / Staked solidly in a gusty grappling with rocks."

A wintry clearness at last come back again, a new "visibility of thought, / In which," thanks to the central poet who speaks for us, "hundreds of eyes, in one mind," see at once. What are we left with in the end? "The less legible meanings of sounds"? Those "little reds" in a landscape or painting "not often realized"? Those "lighter words / In the heavy drum of speech"? Those little "sheets of music / In the strokes of thunder" like "dead candles at the window / When day comes"? What are these flickings if not

the edgings and inchings of final form,
The swarming activities of the formulae
Of statement, directly and indirectly getting at,

Like an evening evoking the spectrum of violet,
A philosopher practicing scales on his piano,
A woman writing a note and tearing it up?

An insolid billowing, then. Reality seen for what it is: a shade traversing a dust, a force traversing a shade.

17

The Obscurity of an Order: 1950–1951

It is a kind of total grandeur at the end,
With every visible thing enlarged and yet
No more than a bed, a chair and moving nuns,
The immensest theatre, the pillared porch,
The book and candle in your ambered room.

"TO AN OLD PHILOSOPHER IN ROME"

January 1950: the midcentury mark, beginning with "the longest and dreariest month" he could remember. A shabby winter made worse when he slipped on the ice climbing the steps of the Hartford and had to stay home for several weeks, followed by "bad walking since," which had so unnerved him that he now took taxis to the office, leaving him "frantic for fresh air and exercise." In that time he'd been able neither to read nor to think. It took "a squalid interval like this to realize the opportunities of low spirits and the ravages they make on one's pride and ambition." At least Elsie had been there for him, "true angel" that she was, and being at home with her had—perhaps surprisingly—made it a happy interval. Enough self-pity. No, he was feeling "perfectly fit," he told Barbara Church now, and was pining because he could not "ride a wild horse around the block."

It had been "a winter of mist and rain and now, suddenly," in late February, as the season began to come to an end, "more snow from a single day's storm than we seem to have had since last autumn." There was the time, he told McGreevy, when he used to go south, "staying until there was at least a touch of spring at home." But something had spoiled that, whether "the cold war, or the iron curtain, or the bamboo curtain." Now his next book, *The Auroras of Autumn* (his last before a collected poems would be printed), was due out in a few months. Confidentially, he confessed, he felt it was "something of an improvisation and not at all" what he would have liked it to be.

Still, at seventy-one he could not be expected to move "in the circles of spaciousness in quite the grand way that one moved a generation ago." If even Beethoven "could look back on what he had accomplished and say that it was a collection of crumbs compared to what he had hoped to accomplish," where would he himself "ever find a figure of speech adequate to size up the little that I have done compared to that which I had once hoped to do"? The truth was that he had "not even begun to touch the spheres within spheres that might have been possible if, instead of devoting the principal amount of my time to making a living, I had devoted it to thought and poetry." And yet suppose he had given everything to his poems. Might he not "now be looking back not with a mere sense of regret but at some actual devastation"? At least he was "now in the happy position of being able to say" he didn't know what would have happened if he had been given more time, which was "very much better than to have had all the time in the world and have found oneself inadequate."

When Barbara Church wrote him from Princeton with the news that Allen Tate's wife, the novelist Caroline Gordon, had become a Catholic like herself, Stevens wrote to say how odd that seemed because Gordon did not seem to have "a Catholic spirit," and because—if one was going to settle down in Princeton, that citadel of Presbyterians—why become "a Catholic or anything else, for that matter, except a Presbyterian"? Perhaps the answer was that "most women have Catholic spirits and that if you are going to settle down in the citadel of the Presbyterians you have to do something about it to make life possible."

Two months later he would write Tom McGreevy, then living in Rome as Ireland's representative to the Vatican. To be in Roma and

Venezia and so many other Italian towns and cities, he joked, meeting "so many tall black-haired girls . . . and giving them a whirl all over the place." That, and "the lovely propriety" with which it had all come about: "the peace-giving memories of the Pope, and of his glorious church and the happiness of feeling both sanctified and everything else all at the same time, as if you had been on an airplane trip through several of the more celebrated planets with two days of heaven thrown in." What a blessed creature McGreevy was, "sustained by a habit of almost medieval faith," whose "God bless yous" with which he ended his letters Stevens found "so extraordinary all around."

In late March James T. Babb, head librarian at Yale and chairman of the Bollingen committee, telephoned to say that Stevens had just been awarded the 1949 Bollingen Prize in Poetry. The prize had been established in 1948 by Paul Mellon and funded by a $10,000 grant from the Bollingen Foundation to the Library of Congress. To date the only other recipient had been Ezra Pound, now incarcerated at St. Elizabeths Hospital for the Criminally Insane in Washington, D.C., chosen by a jury of Fellows in American Letters of the Library of Congress for his *Pisan Cantos*. Though it was undoubtedly the most accomplished book of poems to be published that year, the choice to give the award to a U.S. citizen who had broadcast for Radio Rome during the war had infuriated many Americans, with the result that Congress immediately ended the Library's involvement with the prize. It was at this point that the Bollingen Foundation picked up the program, under the aegis of the Yale University Library. When the committee met to award the honor to a second American poet, they chose the conservative Stevens, who certainly deserved the award.

"I suppose that in reality the most important thing about the Bollingen Prize is not the excitement nor the money but the fact that it induces people from whom you have not heard for years to write to you," he wrote his niece Eleanor Stevens Sauer a week later. Her letter had in fact been the only word he'd had from Reading in a long time. "When you are young you look back to returning home," he told her. "But when you become my age and go home you don't know anybody any longer." On top of which you had "nothing but trouble at the hotel and the only person that takes any interest in you is the superintendent of the cemetery." Even the last of Elsie's Reading aunts had died a few months before.

A month later William Van O'Connor's New Critical reading, *The Shaping Spirit: A Study of Wallace Stevens*, arrived at Stevens's office. Before reading the book, Stevens wrote Feo, describing Professor O'Connor as "intelligent and hard-working and, I believe, friendly enough, since otherwise he would not have interested himself in writing the thing." As it turned out, O'Connor was the first critic to succeed Hi Simons, who had once "made a most elaborate study of everything and who died, unhappily, before he got around to doing his book." O'Connor's study, however, would probably not be "much more than just a book by a youngish critic looking around for a subject not too hackneyed."

While he was pleased to have O'Connor "do the job," he knew how self-conscious it was going to make him feel when he read it. If O'Connor typecast him, there would be a "disposition to act up to the type," which would of course "be a complete fraud" on his part. But after he'd read several chapters, he wrote O'Connor to say that the book had proved a charming gift, though reading the first chapter, on Stevens's background, had felt rather like "looking over a batch of negatives from a photographer." Later, after the first reviews of O'Connor's book had appeared, Stevens confessed to Barbara Church that it had not, after all, "set the Hudson River on fire," though it had managed to antagonize most of the reviewers.

By late April the alarms of war were blaring in Asia, which was the reason he listened now only to comedians on the radio like Groucho Marx and Jack Benny. He was certainly not looking forward to another war, when "so many that we have known have disappeared, almost as if they had never been real." One became "too deeply engaged with life to have it disappear like that." Take his "dear old boy" Judge Powell of Atlanta, who was now a spry seventy-seven. He'd just invited Stevens to come down to Georgia for a picnic. But then, the Judge was "an extrovert and extroverts live only in the present." Still, when Stevens went to New York for Barbara Church's annual going-away-to-France party, he was going to be sure "to be highly extrovert."

On June 10, 1950, chauffeured by "one of the colored boys from the office," Stevens rode the Merritt Parkway down to New York and crossed the George Washington Bridge on the way to East Orange, where he could order several suits from Spencer Lofquist, the son of Alex Lofquist, who had been making Stevens's suits since 1905. Then it was back to New York, where he bought "a load of mangoes, fresh apricots," some "out-sized cherries," and "a little Chablis and a little Meursault," the "coldest thing in the world on a hot day," when he dined in his garden while the neighbors were away. By three he and his driver were on the road again, heading home.

Mr. Stevens, "he was the king," Naaman Corn, his main driver (who would make an appearance in one of Stevens's poems) recalled years later. "Sometimes, he would want to go on some back roads, go up on top of Avon Mountain and take a look. Then he'd go right down the mountain to Farmington, just dirt roads all the way down there." They'd ride around on Saturday afternoons, and then Stevens would ask him to pull into a gas station to have the tank filled. "He never would sponge on the company," Corn added, and "he would pay for my services. At that time we didn't have no such thing as overtime, [but] he was very generous."

• • •

JULY 1950: ANOTHER SUNDAY morning in Elizabeth Park, while Stevens pretends "that everything in nature is artificial and that everything artificial is natural," and that the roses have been placed there "daily by some lover of mankind." An interesting perspective, no doubt, but with its own difficulties as the conflict in Korea heats up. On a practical level, for instance, will this mean another "New Deal and war controls and a fresh generation of parasites"? Truman's desire for money and power alarms him, and the UN isn't going to get them out of this mess. "Obviously," he tells Barbara Church, "this could be a moment in the history of the world, if all the nations offended by Russia, and intended to be offended by her, rallied to American support." But no one is really going to do anything, which will leave America "to do the fighting and bear the expense; and, when it is all over, the U.N. will only be one more burden to us and a joke to all the world." Only if and when the North Koreans begin to lose will Russia step in and "put a stop to what is going on." Worse, religion itself, with its abstract Index of Good and Evil, was part of the problem as much as Russia, a country that was "making a fortune out of life's poverty" while providing "a fury of belief and a fury of hope in return."

If he was grumpy, so be it. Where, for example, did Chopin fit into all of this? Would the Soviets have given him a Marxist visa? At least one could still "listen to his grieving and nostalgia with the windows open" there in France, he told Paule Vidal. At least it was still possible to be oneself in France, and—for that matter—even in Hartford, "provided one isolates oneself a little" by turning off the radio news and gazing into the air. In fact he had just sent off six poems to a Harvard-based magazine called *Wake*, including lines such as one might make from gazing out one's window, lines like "Another sunlight might make another world" and "In the first inch of night, the stellar summering / At three-quarters gone, the morning's prescience." How blessed he was to have Barbara Church and Paule Vidal and José and Tom McGreevy and the Sweeney brothers for friends, because they made "life exciting and precious."

It had not been "a particularly pleasant summer," he wrote Feo, "except in Korea where it is possible to shoot Communists." On the brighter side, people could still "lunch on the terraces of Paris and drink Chablis," travel in Spain, and listen to the little steamers on the blue lakes of Switzerland go "toot-toot-toot (in Swiss)." He had no desire to go to New York to wade through an exhibit of Edvard Munch's paintings at the Museum of Modern Art. Munch after all, was "a repulsive painter," an example of what New York offered these days under the guise of culture: a stew of the "violently new" and "criminally unpleasant." In a similar vein he even found Delmore Schwartz's new collection of poems overly fascinated by the idea of evil. Why not be fascinated instead by the idea of the good? Wasn't a bird singing in the sun at least equal to a dog barking in the dark?

It had been nine months since he had slipped on ice on the steps of the Hartford. "A year ago I used to feel that I was as good as I was at 28 or 30," he wrote his cousin Emma Jobbins that October. But since his fall he had not been quite himself, the main trouble being his left ankle. He couldn't walk like he used to and he constantly felt the need for exercise and fresh air. For the most part, though, he was well, was constantly busy at the office, and had "a never-ending pile of new books to read." As for Elsie, she could be found in the garden every decent day.

• • •

ON JANUARY 15, 1951, he presented a paper called "The Relations between Poetry and Painting" at the Museum of Modern Art. To make his point that there was in fact an identity between poetry in words and poetry in paint, he offered a number of examples, not by such American abstract expressionist painters as Robert Motherwell, but by those French painters and poets more familiar to him, noting that what painters said about their work could be equally applied to poetic practice. Picasso's comment, for example, that a picture was "a horde of destructions" could equally describe the poem. Or there was Braque's comment that, though the senses deformed, the mind formed. Shortly before he'd begun writing his paper, he'd stopped in at the Louis Carré Gallery on Fifth Avenue to look over some paintings by Jacques Villon, Marcel Duchamp's older brother. There was, he found, an intelligence in all Villon's work, whether it was "a woman lying in a hammock" transformed into "a complex of planes and tones, radiant, vaporous, exact," or a teapot and a cup or two taking their place in a reality composed wholly of things unreal. That was what modern art sought to do: see everything as new, everything as uncompromising and at the same time plausible. How surprising, Picasso had said, that people should ask what his pictures meant, when in fact he did not intend them to have meanings. In any event there was no way to judge their work, except in relation to what other modernist painters were doing.

And so with modern poetry, which Stevens divided into two classes: the modern in respect to what a poem said, and the modern in respect to how a thing was said. The first—which was the line he followed—accepted the "banality of form as incidental to its language." Thus one employed blank-verse lines because it was the subject of the poem that mattered. As for the second group, concerned as they were with the way the poem appeared on the page, one had only to look at Mallarmé's *Un Coup de Des*, where one found the "use of small letters for capitals, eccentric line-endings," and "too little or too much punctuation." But such things were mere aberrations and had nothing to do with the life of the poem. And yet both classes of poets had in common a search for the truth.

He understood that he'd been asked to address the question of modern poetry and modern painting. But there were deeper issues at stake here, issues which were difficult to see clearly because we were still in the midst of their influence. We lived in an age "in which disbelief is so profoundly prevalent or, if not disbelief, indifference to questions of belief, poetry and painting," that poetry and painting had become "a compensation for what has been lost." If, then, people felt that the imagination was "the next greatest power to faith," it was because all that remained was a "vital self-assertion in a world in which nothing but the self remains, if that remains." His was a generation which, in spite of its material good fortune, was experiencing a profound poverty of spirit. What mattered, then, was that the mind sought a new and greater sense of reality and the excitement attendant upon that search, so that the spirit might continue to enlarge itself as it could. It was a time, in fact, "in which the search for the supreme truth" was really a search for a supreme fiction they could believe in. That was what gave validity and dignity to the human race: its constant search for wisdom and understanding. And that meant acknowledging our dependence on the arts, which could show us who and what we are.

• • •

TEN DAYS LATER HE was back in New York to give a reading at the 92nd Street YMHA. Once again the stalwart Marianne Moore, though "feather-headed" with a cold, was in the audience. It was a unique evening, Moore wrote Elizabeth Bishop the following day, which began with an orderly series from *Harmonium* on through Stevens's other books, ending with a manuscript poem and a translation from La Fargue. He'd read "Bantams in Pine Woods" "with the acme of pith," and as funny as it was, did not once glance out at the audience or "change the position of his feet, or so much as smile." Instead he had read "deliberately, slowly and with eloquent pauses, was in evening dress," and—as always—very "neat." She'd had no trouble hearing him, but then she'd been in the third row. When James Sweeney went up to him afterward and asked him why he hadn't laughed now and then, he answered, with that poker face of his, that he "thought that was for the audience to do." When he'd recited the third section of "Certain Phenomena of Sound," written ten years earlier, she had found it "a perfect pearl of persuasive effectiveness," so that all she could murmur to him afterward was that she didn't see how he had done what he had: "achieve an effect of tranquility—without monotony." In those lines he had addressed Eulalia, "sister and nun," the beauty of language bodied forth in perfect sound. "You were created of your name," he had all but whispered, as if speaking to himself,

There is no life except in the word of it. . . .
I am and have a being and play a part.
You are that white Eulalia of the name.

Afterward, when Stevens had finished autographing copies of his books with bad pens for half an hour, Barbara Church invited "a very small committee" composed of Moore and the Sweeneys and Marcel Duchamp ("an old friend & intimate apparently," Moore noted) back to her Park Avenue apartment to talk with him. Then the car took Stevens to the Drake Hotel, where he stayed while in New York, Duchamp to Fourteenth Street, and Moore to her Brooklyn apartment. "I had a perfect time," she summed the evening up, "& sick or well was grateful I was in motion sufficiently to go."

For Stevens the awards and kudos kept coming. In late February Alfred Knopf wrote to congratulate him on winning the National Book Award for *The Auroras of Autumn*. "I had not the slightest expectation of winning the award," Stevens replied. He was back in Manhattan to accept the award on March 6. "I thought it best to isolate myself in New York," he wrote Barbara Church afterward, "at least until the business of that day was over." Instead of seeing her he'd walked about the city to calm himself before delivering his acceptance speech that evening. After his remarks a news reporter asked him why he didn't write "on the level of intelligence in the literal sense," to which Stevens responded that to write "on a literal level one was not writing poetry."

After the ceremony Moore, the critic Lloyd Frankenberg, and his wife, the painter Loren MacIver, returned with him to the Drake Hotel for a quiet dinner together. It helped that he was "well-disposed toward a reasonable amount of drinking" (three or four martinis) because lately New York seemed "saturated in alcohol," so that he "should have to become a temperance agitator if I lived there." Of all the people he'd met that evening, Lionel Trilling most appealed to him. Here was "a man of real power," who was also affable and pleasant. Still, Stevens was happy to be home again, where he could open his windows at night and take in the cold air. The snow was gone now, and when the sun filled his room the following morning it made him "happy to be alive." No. "Happy again to be alive still," and he walked halfway to the office before getting on the bus, only to find "the usual result of several days absence" piled on his desk.

"There has been entirely too much activity for me recently," he confessed to the teacher-critic, Sister Bernetta Quinn, O.S.F., three weeks later, "and I am beginning to feel that publicity is definitely a thing that degrades one. I should like to forget all about all this, at least for a while, and spend the time quietly doing what I want to do, as you are spending your time." Still, there were obligations to fulfill, and shortly he was back in New York to take the train up to Bard College for a literary weekend and receive yet another honorary degree. On March 30, amid thunder and the loud patter of rain on the tin roof of the gymnasium—the only building on campus large enough to hold the event—he delivered a short address. As usual he made no effort to make himself heard beyond the first few rows of faces he could see straining to hear what he said, which made no difference to him. He would read as he would read.

A year earlier William Carlos Williams had received the same award and had been scheduled to give a talk about modern poetry on this literary weekend. Instead, he lay in the intensive care unit at Passaic General Hospital, capable of no more than a weak stutter, having suffered a severe stroke two days earlier. Still, he'd insisted on talking on the telephone to Ted Weiss, the organizer of the event, trying to explain why it would not be possible for him to be there to greet Stevens. Hemorrhage . . . cerebral accident . . . eyes unfocused . . . slurring . . . listed as critical . . . stroke. So Stevens had managed to outlast Williams, Stevens crowed, though he was four years Williams's senior. And here he was, receiving a standing ovation while the rain rapped on the roof and the applause rolled on and on. As Stevens turned from the lectern, he caught Weiss's eye. "Well," he said, "we didn't need the old man after all, did we?"

Three weeks later, feeling his usual remorse for his initial actions, he wrote Williams. The Bard College affair he'd found extremely pleasant, though the news of Williams's illness had "saddened and disturbed everyone." Williams had worked too hard getting to the top to be deprived now of a leisurely old age. Then he caught himself. "As the older of the two of us; I resent those words more than you do. If a man is as young as he feels, you are, no doubt, actually twenty-five and I am say twenty-eight. . . . I still come to the office regularly because I like to do so and have use for the money, and I never had any other reasons for doing so." He wished he could see Williams when he was in New York, but his day always seemed to be taken up with errands to run—buying shoes, socks, and so on—so that there was "rarely time to meet people." Stevens's poetry, of course, had already told Williams as much.

As soon as he felt strong enough, Williams wrote back. It was the first letter he'd been able to peck out on his typewriter since his stroke, and he told Stevens he was thrilled to be writing at all, especially to a friend he'd known for close to forty years. The stroke, he admitted, had caught him by surprise, "for though I know I am far from invulnerable I didn't expect THAT! . . . It seems to have resulted from trying to write a book in three months while carrying on a practice of medicine. Just couldn't bring it off," though he'd almost "had the book finished at that." At least now he was back at work finishing up his *Autobiography*, And, yes, either of them might "croak at any moment," but they weren't old. He was even looking forward to a whole "new way of life," hoping to "hobnob" with his few real friends, among whom he counted Stevens. What he could not know was that the two would not meet again, at least this side of Dante's circle of philosophers.

"One grows accustomed to the larger colleges and takes them for granted," Stevens wrote Ted Weiss. The honorary degrees from such prestigious universities and colleges had made a big splash at the office. But after so much publicity lately, he hoped "to retire to the first desert I come across and then try to recover myself." In fact he'd been too lost in his job "to do any writing now for some months," he confessed to McGreevy a week later, and was hoping to get some writing done and get away from the incessant chatter about the war in Korea and the political scene. If only he could "emigrate to some region where there are no radios, newspapers etc. and where the natural man can be himself, saying his prayers in the dark without fear of being slugged."

Instead, in late April he was back at Mount Holyoke to give yet another talk. This one he called, simply, "Two or Three Ideas." His first idea was this: that the style of a poem and the poem itself were one. To explain his idea, he evoked a line from Baudelaire's *Les Fleurs du Mal*, which he translated as "I lived, for long, under huge porticoes." Translated this way, it was as if "we had stepped into a ruin and were startled by a flight of birds that rose as we entered." By a simple turn of phrase, the familiar had been made unfamiliar, so that now, whenever we thought of that scene, we would remember "how we held our breath and how the hungry doves of another world rose out of nothingness and whistled away." What the right words in the right order could do, he believed, was re-create "a remembered habitation" of old dwelling-places: "abodes of the imagination," of "memories of places that never existed," encounters which had the ability to pierce and dazzle us. Perhaps, in time, "the poets who seemed to have little or nothing to say would actually be the poets that mattered. Plain English of itself came to nothing. Why, for instance, should Anglo-Saxon (thank you, Bill Williams) "have the right to higgle and haggle all over the page, contesting the right of other words?" If a poem required a hierophantic phrase, so be it. Style should not be limited but enlarged, not impoverished but enriched and therefore liberated.

In a time of disbelief like the present, it was the duty of the poet "to see the gods dispelled in mid-air and dissolve like clouds" by supplying in their place the satisfactions of belief, in the poet's unique measure and style. There remained the problem, of course, that when we had succeeded in at last killing off the gods, it was we who were left orphaned, so that we would have to learn to fend for ourselves and find divinity within. And who was the true priest of the new Apollo if not the poet who composed Apollo's hymns? And who but the people would sing those hymns, speaking of the gods and listening for their replies? If it was the imagination that created "a new style and thus a new reality," was it not possible that the poem and the gods were one? Or that the style of the gods and the style of men were one? It was time, now, to equate the poem with both the gods and men. True, we did not create in light and warmth only, but in darkness and coldness as well. And yet here it was, spring in New England, a time of warmth and promise. While the poetry of the future would most likely consist of the antipoetic, even the most intense cynicism could never eliminate the need for the Romantic, for the Romantic had a way of renewing itself just as mankind inevitably had a need to renew itself.

• • •

THAT JUNE STEVENS CELEBRATED his fiftieth reunion at Harvard with the class of 1901. Jack Sweeney, head librarian at Harvard, held a special exhibit of Stevens's work in the Poetry Room there, including several of the books which Stevens had had specially bound in Paris and New York. Even better, his alma mater presented him with yet another honorary degree and that in the presence of his classmates. Few of them had actually shown up for the event, because there had been a "tremendous blow-out the night before" at the Isabella Stewart Gardner Museum. But later that afternoon, standing on the steps of Widener Library, he spotted many of them when the classes marched by in review. "When my own class marched by," he beamed, "I borrowed the top hat of one of my neighbors and saluted them, very greatly to their satisfaction and without any real loss of dignity on my part."

• • •

THAT SEPTEMBER HE WROTE his niece Eleanor to say that Holly was in the process of finally getting her divorce from her husband. They'd been separated for the past several years, and—though Hanchak had decided to contest the divorce "for the hell of it"—Stevens knew Holly was never going back. For the past several years Holly and Peter had lived in a "very pleasant little apartment" Stevens had rented for them, often stopping by to see them on his way home from work. He also provided Holly with a monthly allowance so she could stay home with Peter, who was four now and would start preschool shortly. Every other Saturday afternoon the two of them came to the house to visit. The last time Peter had taken "a ride on the doors of the ice-box when nobody was looking" and had been "in Dutch ever since." He was fond of the boy, and only wished he could see more of him. On his seventy-second birthday he wrote Barbara Church to say that Holly had her divorce and was going to celebrate with a filet mignon and treat Peter to a "double-chocolate ice cream for dinner," then take him to the Bronx Zoo so he could have another "chat with his friends, the elephants."

For Stevens, New York had become by this time a place to buy three cases of wine and have his driver store them in the cellar without Elsie catching on. He had privileges at the all-male Century Association club at Fifth and Forty-third Street—his kind of club, he called it—though he'd been there only once in the past six months. Nor did he care anymore for "vacations as they are practiced in this country." Back when he was at Harvard, going home felt like "going back to mother earth," so that he would return to Cambridge "not only invigorated . . . but rather furiously set up and independent." But he doubted that a vacation could do that for him anymore. Those winter vacations in Key West, when he and Judge Powell, who had just died, used to lounge about, enjoying "breakfast on a porch, usually with a warm wind fluttering the leaves of the palms": where were they now, when he needed them? Powell would "order so much for breakfast that the waiter would have to bring it on a special tray," he remembered: "fruit, eggs, kippered herrings, lamb chops and hot cakes." Then he would eat "a little of the scrambled eggs, perhaps one of the hot cakes and . . . light a cigar." *That* was "what holidays a la mode came to, an enormous panorama of things . . . at one's command," which one could then choose to simply ignore.

• • •

THE PREVIOUS DECEMBER HE'D sent the *Hudson Review* a short poem called "Final Soliloquy of the Interior Paramour." He'd intended to write a long poem, but had "got no farther than the statement that God and the imagination are one." The poem is one of Stevens's strongest from his last phase, offering a space in which the poet and the reader might collect themselves, an attempt to comfort us in our essential poverty. An old man with a shawl wrapped about him sits alone in his room in the evening light to collect his thoughts, the mind for once at peace with itself, feeling "the obscurity of an order" beyond himself and yet part of himself, a place where God seems to dwell and where for once we are at peace.

Light the first light of evening, as in a room
In which we rest and, for small reason, think
The world imagined is the ultimate good.

This is, therefore, the intensest rendezvous.
It is in that thought that we collect ourselves,
Out of all the indifferences, into one thing:

Within a single thing, a single shawl
Wrapped tightly round us, since we are poor, a warmth,
A light, a power, the miraculous influence.

Here, now, we forget each other and ourselves.
We feel the obscurity of an order, a whole,
A knowledge, that which arranged the rendezvous.

Within its vital boundary, in the mind.
We say God and the imagination are one . . .
How high that highest candle lights the dark.

Out of this same light, out of the central mind,
We make a dwelling in the evening air,
In which being there together is enough.

He was still thinking about the subject when he delivered the Moody Lecture in November 1951 at the University of Chicago. He called it "A Collect of Philosophy," and he managed to include two of the Churches' closest associates in it: Jean Wahl and Jean Paulhan. He also managed to get Longinus, Pascal, Schopenhauer, and Max Planck in there as well. At first he was excited by what he had written, but going back over it now, it seemed slight, and his chief deduction—"that poetry is supreme over philosophy because we owe the idea of God to poetry and not to philosophy"—no longer resonated for him, reduced as it was to a maxim.

After all were not God and the imagination finally one and the same? Philosophers, after all, did not make discoveries but rather offered hypotheses, which were in themselves poetic. What the poetic imagination provided were the words and images essential to furthering scientific knowledge. If the philosopher probed the universe, making sure of his every step by logic and deduction, the poet moved far more swiftly and light-footedly, returning over and over to the actual world. "To say that philosophers are poets," he told Barbara Church, "does them no harm and at the same time somehow magnifies poetry, so that one comes to see [poetry] in all its greatness and power, in spite of all the bad or silly poetry." Civilization was to be measured, then, by how far poetry could go in imagining the idea of God. After all, was not the very concept of some final knowledge, some Omega point, an idea poetic in itself?

No, he was not an atheist, he told Sister Bernetta that Christmas, though he did "not believe to-day in the same God in whom I believed when I was a boy." But, then, to talk to her about God was "like explaining French to a Frenchman." What he really liked doing on cold winter nights was watching the saintly moonlight through his bedroom windows, which he kept open to the winter air. When he went up to his room after dinner and closed the door, he told Feo, it was like "shutting out something crude and lacking in all feeling and delicacy." Perhaps it was selfish to think that way, but that was how he liked composing his world: just a man alone with his thoughts.

18

A New Knowledge of Reality: 1952–1954

At the earliest ending of winter,
In March, a scrawny cry from outside
Seemed like a sound in his mind . . .

NOT IDEAS ABOUT THE THING BUT THE THING ITSELF

With time, and except for the evidence of his own late poems, Stevens seemed to grow more distant from William Carlos Williams, not so much because of Williams's insistence on the American idiom and "beginning again" and "making it new" and "no ideas but in things," but because for Stevens such avant-garde stylistic notions had long ceased to matter. For years now Stevens had felt a closer kinship to Marianne Moore, sensing her Victorian modesty and privacy as belonging "to an older and much more personal world" more akin to his own. A world, he told Yale professor Norman Holmes Pearson at the beginning of 1952, "of closer, human intimacies which existed when you and I were young."

To actually try to "confront fact in its total bleakness"—as he himself had once done—was "for any poet a completely baffling experience," because reality was not a thing, but only an aspect of a thing. What Moore had managed to do in her poetry, as he'd said years before, was defamiliarize her subjects and thus release the poet's (and the reader's) energy. In making the world strange again, she had "freshened it, added sunlight, as it were, and made us see it as if she were Eve in the garden," giving her readers a sense of contact with an external reality, not something which simply dissolved "itself into the conceptions of our own minds."

And yet, like Williams and Moore, with both of whom he had traveled the uncharted roads of high modernism for forty years now, he knew that it was only in foregrounding "the individual and particular" aspects of things that we might see reality renewed. When most people read a poem they tried to extract a meaning, which they then appraised in terms of its "moral or religious truth." But what resonated for him was the *way* Moore said a thing that revealed the reality radiating from the words themselves. It did not have to reveal a major reality, but simply some aspect of the real. In this pursuit art and religion formed a common bond, for both had "to mediate for us a reality not ourselves," a reality "adequate to the profound necessities of life today," which the poet would have to offer with humility.

No wonder, then, that he supported Moore's nomination for the 1951 Bollingen Prize for her *Collected Poems* at a meeting of the committee in late December 1950. It was a volume for which she would also win the National Book Award and the Pulitzer Prize. But it was the dignity with which Moore dealt with the profound loss of her mother that winter that impressed him most. "It is easy to say that Marianne, the human being, does not concern us," he wrote Pearson afterward, but, "mon Dieu, it is what concerns us most." Here, he'd confided to Barbara Church, was "a woman of natural goodness, sympathy, consideration for others, which people may not always notice in the face of her prowess in other respects." She was "the true connoisseur, who expertises everything she does," and it was her womanly "willingness to make friends" which he felt, especially after being locked in several cigar smoke–filled conference rooms with his male business associates for three days. It was then that he understood why one would want to become an assassin. He would not be able to come to New York when Moore was presented with the National Book Award, but he did send her a telegram, which read:

I knock this morning at your door
To bow and say Forever! Moore!

• • •

AT SEVENTY-TWO HE NO longer felt like his old self, he told Feo that February. Nor was he having "a particularly good time" these days, especially since in the old days he would have been sunning himself and sipping a dry martini on the veranda of the Casa Marina in Key West. Winter in Hartford was not a bad time, really, but it was "a dull time, with a lot to do and a loss of interest in things in general." Tomorrow he would be going down to New York, but he knew "almost no one there anymore, so that I am like a ghost in a cemetery reading epitaphs." He would see a bookbinder about binding some of his books, go to Brooks Brothers to buy a pair of pajamas, procure a copy of the December issue of the *Revue de Paris* because it contained an essay on the French philosopher Alain—the pseudonym of Émile-Auguste Chartier—then "visit a baker, a fruit dealer and, as it may be, a barber." A day like that did more for him than most days now. After all, wasn't "the bread of life . . . better than any soufflé"?

At least his grandson continued to delight him, sitting on his lap while he made up elephant stories, including one about an elephant that had "two trunks, one tenor, one bass." The winter had been hard, but now there were crocuses and robins under the trees. What "a joy to hear them in the early morning and again in the evening as I walk home," he told Barbara Church. Red robins made him think about *Rosenkavalier* and the presentation of the Silver Rose; the glancing chords of that piece, he explained, "haunt me and sometimes I try to reproduce the effect of them in words."

That same week he sent the *Hudson Review* five new poems, among them "To an Old Philosopher in Rome." "On the threshold of heaven," Stevens begins his homage to his mentor, Santayana, now eighty-eight and hovering between two worlds, tended to by an English order of Roman Catholic nuns living and working in the shadow of the Forum. It is an imagined world Stevens himself has grown more familiar with, where

the figures in the street
Become the figures of heaven, the majestic movement
Of men growing small in the distances of space,

> *Singing, with smaller and still smaller sound,*
> *Unintelligible absolution and an end.*

Rome, the eternal city, and that other, "more merciful Rome / Beyond," the two merging now, "alike in the make of the mind," as if "in a human dignity / Two parallels become one." Here, on this threshold, the "blown banners change to wings," where the news of the day, the "newsboys' muttering," becomes "another murmuring" in the presence of the great reality hovering before one, where "the bed, the books, the chair, the moving nuns, / The candle as it evades the sight" all become "sources of happiness in the shape of Rome," and the "light on the candle tearing against the wick" prefigures the soul waiting to be released from the body to become "part only of that which / Fire is the symbol: the celestial possible." Now the poet bids the philosopher, "Speak to your pillow as if it was yourself," an orator "with an accurate tongue" and yet "without eloquence," in the half-sleep of dying, in the pity of it, here in this room—Rome or Hartford, what matter?—where "each of us / Beholds himself in you," an old man "dozing in the depths of wakefulness, impenitent and yet most penitent," a man "impatient for the grandeur that you need / In so much misery."

But in the end it was only "poverty's speech that seeks us out the most," a speech "older than the oldest speech of Rome." And it was Santayana who spoke that language, not with words but by example, "the one invulnerable man among" the "crude captains" who speak of that of which they know nothing. "A kind of total grandeur at the end," Stevens called it, where "every visible thing" has been enlarged and yet is what it is: the bed that is "no more than a bed, a chair and moving nuns," a theater and a pillared porch, as in that other Asylum at 690, where he had worked these thirty-odd years, and this "ambered room," this study, with its book and its candle, gilt-edged, a "total grandeur of a total edifice, / Chosen by an inquisitor of structures / For himself," this Catholic in all but a final belief, who stops now "upon this threshold," where what one imagines and what is merge into one, "as if the design of all his words takes form / And frame from thinking and is realized."

"I grieve to hear of the death of George Santayana in Rome," he wrote

Barbara Church on September 29, 1952, three days after his mentor died. "Fifty years ago I knew him well, in Cambridge, where he often asked me to come to see him. This was before he had definitely decided not to be a poet." But it was "difficult for a man whose whole life is thought to continue as a poet," because reason was such a "jealous mistress." Still, it was Santayana's noble example which had shaped all these years. Once, back in 1949, Feo had told Stevens that he'd just received a letter from Santayana in which the old philosopher said that he had "always bowed, however sadly, to expediency or fate." For weeks after, Stevens found himself repeating that sentence over and over to himself.

• • •

ON MAY 1 STEVENS read his poems at Harvard, later to learn that someone had taped the reading, which—given his obsession for privacy—left him feeling uneasy, so that for a time he vowed to give no more readings. There were two more honorary degrees that spring: one from Mount Holyoke and the other from Columbia. Then the Faber edition of his *Selected Poems* was published in England. He asked Moore to make the selection for him, but she declined, saying that he would know better than anyone what to include in such a volume. He was happy to receive that honorary degree from Mount Holyoke, especially as the colorful PhD cowl they would give him could be counted as one more scalp to show Elsie, though he declined the offer to give the commencement address.

"Notwithstanding all the talk of war and all the difficulties of politics, something fundamentally gay and beautiful still survives," he wrote Paule Vidal that same month. "I continue to remain well and active at the office just as if I was not almost 73." He had no plans for another book of poems, and things were too busy at the office to think about such a project anyway. "Usually, at my age," he added, "a poet starts to write a long poem chiefly because he persuades himself that it is necessary to have a long poem among his works." But then the French had a saying that long poems were written "by people who cannot write short ones." From now on he meant to write only short ones.

He'd read that bus drivers in Havana, he joked with Feo, were wrecking buses now "in order to procure more pay." Maybe it would help matters simply to shoot the people "who own the buses" or "stand along the sidewalk and shoot the passengers." That scenario, however, was still a few years off. Worse for him personally were summer nights at home in the stifling heat. "I suppose that if there is ever a war with Russia, I shall look back on July 1952 and consider [the month the] worse," he wrote Barbara Church. "The heat has been ungodly—except that, when one went upstairs at night, it was ungodlier." August, with its dog days, which felt like another foreign oppressor, left him "low-spirited and blank." Most of his neighbors were away at the shore or the mountains, but he and Elsie preferred Hartford. And yet how deep the need for people to be with other people. On top of which was the stark fact that Holly was now twenty-eight, which certainly made him feel old. It was as if he stood ghost-like, "outside the destiny common to people," merely observing them.

"Over here the presidential election, so far as the New Deal is concerned, is based on the idea that the poorer people were never so well off as they are now," he wrote Barbara Church that September, who was back in France. But how well off they were remained to be seen, with bankruptcy facing France unless things changed. But all that was the world of politics and money. His *Selected Poems* would be published in London shortly: a slight book, really, small and—worse—"unbelievably irrelevant to our actual world." But then all poetry was like that and probably always would be. After all, "the close approach to reality" had always been "the supreme difficulty of any art," its communication of an actuality seeming not only impossible but not even worth the trouble because the reality of the moment lost its identity as the event itself passed. For that reason nothing in the world was "deader than yesterday's political . . . poetry."

A postcard arrived from Jack Sweeney featuring the Irish Cliffs of Moher, "towering up over the Atlantic," and out of that image came a meditation on the passage of time evoking one's father "in this world, in this house, / At the spirit's base," the "parent before thought, before speech," the first father at the "head of the past," the father summoned by those ageless "cliffs of Moher rising out of the mist, / Above the real." It was a landscape "rising out of present time and place, above / The wet, green grass." But these moss-bearded cliffs seemed something more, something deeper even than the landscape, something "full of the somnambulations / Of poetry / And the sea." They were in fact his true father, or his bearded father as he once was, "a likeness, one of the race of fathers: earth / And sea and air." The sense of the father, then, in the necessary, welcome return to "the spacious, solitary world in which we used to exist."

• • •

MONDAY EVENING, SEPTEMBER 29, 1952: "To-day there is a light as of the end of the boulevards—the extra hour of lateness and the sense of autumn," he wrote. The day before Elsie had spent hours in the garden, planting new peony roots, while he had lunched "with a little *Corton* (1929, *Tete de Cuvee*) and tried to feel as one ought to feel." And didn't a glass of Corton help one "appreciate sad weather" by accentuating it with its own sad flavors? And this morning, a neighbor's beagle, Bridget by name, lay nearby in a patch of sunlight, on the leaves, "the very essence of melancholy, her head on her paws," until Stevens had scraped the sidewalk with his shoe as he'd passed her, startling her out of her musings and back into the quotidian.

• • •

ELIAS MENGEL, A YOUNG teacher at the University of Connecticut in Hartford, became a close friend of Holly's soon after she began classes there in the fall of 1952 and was soon invited out to 118 Westerly Terrace for tea with the Stevenses. To Mengel's surprise, Stevens seemed "extremely kind, even cordial, courtly." Holly and Peter were there, but Elsie, who had prepared "a very good tea with wonderful cakes and cookies," remained in the shadows. How strange to be taking tea there, almost as strange as taking tea at the Palaz of Hoon. Holly had explained to Mengel that her mother had "psychological problems," and Mengel had to agree. She seemed distant from her mother, though she enjoyed her father's company, so that, as Holly explained, Elsie was "terribly jealous of her father" and—because she could not understand his poetry—felt inferior to him. For all that, though, from where Mengel sat on the chintz sofa, surrounded by the unexceptional paintings on the walls, he thought the Stevenses appeared to be a contented couple.

• • •

THAT OCTOBER STEVENS PUBLISHED a poem in *Poetry* called "St. Armorer's Church from the Outside." There is no church by that name, but there is a portal fronting the Episcopal Church of the Good Shepherd, which sits south of 690 Asylum Avenue and is known as the Armorer's Porch. The church lies near Samuel Colt's gun manufactory, close to the Connecticut River, and is easily recognizable by the sky-blue onion dome one sees even today driving south along Interstate 91. The church was built by Colt's widow, Elizabeth, just after the Civil War, thanks to the huge sums of money he earned for supplying the Union Army with thousands of repeating rifles and handguns, and it lies just a quarter mile west of the former factory in an open field with a large parking lot.

What is particularly odd about the church is that its architect, Edward Tuckerman Potter, decorated the friezes, columns, and even the crosses with revolver parts prominently or subtly displayed among the ivy carvings. It is, in fact, the only church in the world to feature handguns in its decorative structure. It is this church, and much of what it tells us of American culture, both spiritually and aesthetically, which Stevens compares—unfavorably—to the Chapel of the Rosary in Vence which Matisse, also in his seventies, designed between 1949 and 1951. Matisse had done this as a special favor to Monique Bourgeois, his nurse during a difficult time, who had gone on to become a Dominican nun, taking the name Sister Jacques-Marie.

"St. Armorer's was once an immense success," the poem begins, the language capturing the Madison Avenue advertising lingo of the 1950s, meant to mark one kind of success. Though when Stevens wrote his poem, the church was in need of repairs to its roof and bell tower, it had once "rose loftily and stood massively," and to own a plot and lie in its churchyard "fixed one for good in geranium-colored day." It was a symbol of the Protestant Christianity which had shaped his youth and with which he had quarreled for the past half century: a world and a world order that seemed to have

the foreign smell of plaster,
The closed-in smell of hay. A sumac grows
On the altar, growing toward the lights, inside.
Reverberations leak and lack among holes.

Yet there is something about Christianity, the poet concedes, that still lives and shines here, its chapel rising now not here, perhaps, but "from Terre Ensevelie," the buried earth,

An ember yes among its cindery noes
His own: a chapel of breath, an appearance made
For a sign of meaning in the meaningless,

No radiance of dead blaze, but something seen
In a mystic eye, no sign of life but life,
Itself, the presence of the intelligible
In that which is created as its symbol.

No symbol this, then, but the thing itself: light caught and cupped in one's hands, as at that chapel in Vence, "a new account of everything old," a new hallucination, a new fiction in which one might believe: the very thing Stevens's poems searched for. Vence and "a new-colored sun, say, that will soon change forms / And spread hallucinations on every leaf." Here is "a sacred syllable rising from sacked speech," like "the first car out of a tunnel en voyage" approaching

lands of ruddy-ruby fruits, achieved
Not merely desired, for sale, and market things
That press, strong peasants in a peasant world,
Their purports to a final seriousness.

Final for him, the acceptance of such prose,
Time's given perfections made to seem like less
Than the need of each generation to be itself,
The need to be actual and as it is.

The Christianity his poems had for so long rejected, from "Sunday Morning" on, and embodied here in the pride and individualism of his Pennsylvania background, has nothing of the present found in Matisse's Catholic chapel full of light, "this *vif,* this dizzle-dazzle of being new / And of becoming," embodied in the living light of this newly realized sacred space, the ever-fresh immanence of green reality merging with even as it maintains its own identity from the ever-refreshing blue imagination,

In an air of freshness, clearness, greenness, blueness,
That which is always beginning because it is part
Of that which is always beginning, over and over.

A *vif,* a light, a re-creation, which might rise from the buried foundations of St. Armorer's, and to which he might turn now for his own health's sake, standing

in a light, its natural light and day,
The origin and keep of its health and his own.
And there he walks and does as he lives and likes.

There are echoes in this poem of *The Waste Land* with its "reverberations," as well as of Hopkins's "blue-bleak embers," which "fall, gall themselves, and gash gold-vermilion," and which Stevens seems to allude to in that "ember yes among its cindery noes," having read and admired Hopkins years earlier. There is also a short piece of prose which seems to speak volumes to this poem: Stevens's appreciation of John Crowe Ransom in the *Sewanee Review,* which appeared four years earlier. "One turns with something like ferocity toward a land that one loves," Stevens wrote there, remembering his native Reading. Now the poet demands that that vital world "surrender, reveal, that in itself which one loves." This, he insists, is no mere nostalgia, "an affair of the heart (as it may be in one's first poems)," but rather "an affair of the whole being (as in one's last poems)," until "one's cry of O Jerusalem! becomes little by little a cry to something a little nearer and nearer until at last one cries out to a living name, a living place, a living thing, and in crying out confesses openly all the bitter secretions of experience." These things, trivial as they may appear, "often touch us intensely," he explained, so that "the sight of an old berry patch, a new growth in the woods in the spring, the particular things on display at a farmers' market, as, for example, the trays of poor apples, the few boxes of black-eyed peas, the bags of dried corn, have an emotional power over us that for a moment is more than we can control."

The poet as both outsider and insider. For, while the words of the poet or philosopher often appear to have the objectivity of the outsider, it is the insider who "remains as the base of his character, the essential person," and it is on that quotidian reality that "he lavishes his sense of the prodigious and the legendary, the material of his imagination."

Stevens has come to understand that the American poet in the high romantic tradition creates poems which "are not composed of the books he has read, of the academies he has seen, of the halls and columns and carvings on the columns, the stairs and towers and doorways and tombs, the wise old men and the weak young men of nowhere in particular, going nowhere at all." Rather the poet is made of the "hard stuff on which a mountain has been bearing down for a long time with such a weight that its impress on him has passed into everything he does and passes, through him, outward, a long distance." It is as if everything "which was native to one took on a special quality so that "the more closely he sought out its precise line and look, the more it became . . . the peculiar legend of things as they are when they are as we want them to be."

Was Stevens pointing to something more here, something final in a final seriousness in evoking this chapel imagined by the serious artist, where light itself takes on a new reality as it streams through the stained-glass windows, pooling on the floor and painting the walls with transitory hues? If even the light in which we walk and have our being is a fiction we imagine, so be it. After a lifetime of wrestling, the poet has come to terms with himself, so that standing in the chapel in Vence, bathed in the light of Matisse's imagination, would be enough. "At my age," he wrote McGreevy later that month, "it would be nice to be able to read more and think more and be myself more and to make up my mind about God, say, before it is too late, or at least before he makes up his mind about me."

• • •

IN ANOTHER TWENTY MONTHS he would turn seventy-five, and it was for that occasion that Knopf planned to publish his *Collected Poems*, for which Stevens was now busy composing the final section, which he planned to call simply "The Rock." "When I consider the excitement that is being caused by Carl Sandburg's 75th birthday," he wrote Bernard Heringman, then studying for his PhD at Columbia University, in January 1953, "I am embarrassed. They are having a big party for him in Chicago. Governor [Adlai] Stevenson has declared this week . . . to be Carl Sandburg Week. They are going to give him a gold medal shortly in New York and, with a shrewd eye to business, that becomes any poet, he has just issued the first volume of an autobiography which it appears can be added to indefinitely."

When his own seventy-fifth birthday arrived, no doubt he was going to be asked "down to Washington to address a joint session of Congress, while they mount guard day and night in front of my house here in Hartford." Sandburg, he'd heard, raised goats. Did that mean that he would have to start raising ducks now? But then Sandburg was an enormously popular figure. He remembered a time when the poet had visited him in Hartford with his guitar to sing for him and Elsie. As for himself, he had no intention of ever going on the poetry circuit, where you read the same things night after night, which was "a waste of time and money unless one makes a business of it." When Sandburg visited them, he "read in Hartford in the afternoon, in New Britain in the evening, and Meriden the next day . . . and enjoyed it and made a lot of money." But that was Sandburg. The only traveling Stevens planned to do was to take the train to New York to buy "handkerchiefs, socks, eye medicine [and] a Latin version of the *Imitation* [*of Christ*]." He was happy to have a job that kept him "well, cheerful, prosperous, overweight and sober."

"A young man in a new scene, a new man in a young scene, a young man in a young scene," he wrote José Feo in January 1953, echoing his own *Man with the Blue Guitar.* Here in Hartford these days his guitars were "stacked along the attic walls," probably for good. Now it was the everyday which gave him the most pleasure. The time was coming "when just to be will take in everything without the least doing since even the least doing is irrelevant to pure being." He was glad too that, after twenty years of Democrats, Eisenhower and the Republicans were back in office, because the Democrats had so altered the very idea of American life that "just to think of things as they were twenty-five years ago makes one feel like William Cullen Bryant's great, great grandfather."

The most respectable book published in 1952—not "a conspicuously good year for poetry" in the States—was Archibald MacLeish's *Collected Poems*, which won the Bollingen Prize. Williams had not published a book that year, though he certainly deserved the prize "because of his general value to poetry," which was why the committee had decided to award two prizes that year. Williams was in worse shape than Stevens had thought, having suffered not one but three strokes, which had left his right side paralyzed. Worse, though his old friend had been "invited to act as consultant in poetry to the Library of Congress" and had agreed to take the position, rumors had begun circulating that he was a Communist because he had contributed to several leftist magazines during the 1930s, so that—in this frigid cold war era—Washington had decided to play it safe and strip him of the honor.

Stevens had no idea whether or not Williams was a Communist. But since he'd always been on the cutting edge of things, chances were that he'd probably associated with Communists in the past. Of course, Stevens told Feo, Williams was "the least subversive man in the world." But what of the people he'd mingled with? The government must have discovered something to act as it had, which was really too bad, since Williams was one of the few people in the country who really cared about writing. Besides, how could Williams of all people throw bricks at the government after the way the United States had treated him? On the other hand, though Williams had been born in Rutherford, New Jersey, that had not been the case for either his Puerto Rican mother or his English-born father, and that was something to consider.

In late March 1953 Stevens went to New York again for another bon voyage party at Barbara Church's Park Avenue apartment and—thanks to the alcohol—was sure he'd acted the boor once more. "I was in rather a chaotic state when we separated the other evening," he apologized to Marianne Moore on the 27th, "and may have been dog-gone informal. Your note tells me, in effect, that you have no grudge." The most important and most delicate thing in the world was "the web of friendship between poets," and that was not something he was willing to damage in any way. That same day he wrote Barbara Church, promising that from now on he would stick to anchovies. He told Church that Moore resonated for him the way Jacques Maritain, the Catholic philosopher, did: as someone he found both fascinating and extraordinary.

In a month's time Smith College would be hosting a symposium on art and morals, to which he'd been invited. W. H. Auden, Allen Tate, and Lionel Trilling would all be speaking on the same evening, with Jacques Barzun and two others speaking the following evening, all of which fascinated him. But since it would mean having to be away overnight, he would not be attending.

• • •

THAT SUMMER HE SPENT several weekends with Jim and Margaret Powers and their daughter. They had bought a farm in Cornwall among the hills along the Connecticut border with New York, and Jim had steadfastly refused even to cut the grass. A power mower hunkered in the tall grass like a statue. What, Stevens asked Barbara Church that August, could be more comatose than that? "Last Friday," he would write in a poem he titled "Reality Is an Activity of the Most August Imagination," the pun on August intentional,

in the big light of last Friday night,
We drove home from Cornwall to Hartford, late.

It was not a night blown at a glassworks in Vienna
Or Venice, motionless, gathering time and dust.

Instead, as the car coursed along Route 202 heading east, he was aware of "a crush of strength in a grinding going round, / Under the front of the westward evening star." That, and the crush of time moving past at fifty-five miles an hour, the oncoming traffic lights like a time-lapse zodiac, everything silvered in the August moonlight, until the night seemed to transform itself into a veritable lake of moonlight, things emerging and moving and dissolving, as in

The visible transformations of summer night,

An argentine abstraction approaching form
And suddenly denying itself away.

There was an insolid billowing of the solid.
Night's moonlight lake was neither water nor air.

In mid-October 1953 he was in New York again to see Barbara Church, back from her summer in Europe. Holly accompanied him this time, and the two of them were back home at half past eleven, "after a cautious drive through a good deal of mist." He and his daughter had enjoyed themselves immensely, caught up by the "special spirit of it." It had been so long since he'd been to New York that he'd "almost forgotten the relaxation that is possible there," although he'd found the traffic in New York incredible. One of the things he and Church had talked about that evening was Williams's new step-down lines, lines like these:

Be patient that I address you in a poem,
there is no other
fit medium.
The mind
lives there. It is uncertain,
can trick us and leave us
agonized. But for resources
what can equal it?

If Williams's mobile-like lines were the things readers preferred now, what would the next generation favor? The bare page? "For that alone would be new," the equivalent to the bare canvas some of the New York School of painters preferred these days. He could only hope that someday there might really be a new world for the poem, and "not the mere variations of an old world," as there was now. The trouble with Williams, he told the poet Richard Eberhart that December, was that for him the poem was essentially "a structure of little blocks," where the idea of meaning had "only the slightest value."

The younger generation of poets was best caught in that roaring boy from Wales, Dylan Thomas, a figure antithetical to everything Stevens stood for. On this, his fourth reading tour in the United States, Thomas had drunk himself into a stupor at the White Horse Tavern in the Village on November 9 and died later that night at St. Vincent's Hospital. "Someone telephoned me yesterday," he told Barbara Church a week later, "to ask that I come down and speak at a memorial meeting for the poet." But *oraisons funèbres* were not his line. The truth was that he didn't like the idea of having to praise Thomas, who had proven himself "utterly improvident" toward his family. Nor did it sit well with him that Thomas had come to the States merely to hobnob with Charlie Chaplin and insult rich American industrialists. "Of course," Stevens added, "his death is a tragic misfortune, but, after all, if you are going to pronounce a man's funeral oration you do have to have some respect for him as a man."

Five days before Christmas he listened to someone on the radio go on about "the loss of all religious significance in respect to Christmas." It wasn't that he himself missed that aspect, he wrote Jim Powers, or for that matter the religious significance of any other time. But when someone got on the air and talked "about the Incarnation and its practical value for all of us," he wanted to clap his hands and stamp his feet and "say Bravo, Bravo!" Of course, he added, that only went "to show how queer you become if you remain in New England long enough."

He brought his cousin Emma up to date about the family. Peter was six now, and he and Holly lived in an apartment, mostly because his grandson was "too lively and requires too much attention to live with us at home." As for his Reading relatives, he was pretty much out of touch with them because they all belonged to a younger generation who no doubt regarded his generation "pretty much as they would regard the pictures on the wall." And as for himself, come October he would turn seventy-five and had every intention of staying "75 for some years after that."

• • •

JUST AFTER THE NEW Year, 1954, he went to Yale as a member of that year's Bollingen committee, which gave the prize to W. H. Auden. He sat through a performance of Eliot's *The Confidential Clerk*, then spent the evening talking with Randall Jarrell. He got "a tremendous kick" out of finally meeting Tom McGreevy, though not in Hartford, where McGreevy had given a talk (that would have been too close to home for Stevens's comfort), but at Barbara Church's apartment. He purchased another painting from Paule Vidal (his last, as it turned out): Jean Jules Cavaillès's 1931 marine scape of the Cote d' Azur, which Vidal had assured him was a *joie des yeux.* Cavaillès had titled his painting *Interior with Still Life*, but Stevens renamed it after one of his early poems, *Sea Surface Full of Clouds.* By early May the picture was hanging in his room, the colors like "melted candy." He went to New York on May 30 to view an exhibition of Vuillard at the Museum of Modern Art, featured, it seemed, merely because the painter knew the right people. Vuillard, after all, was merely a recorder, his small works trivial "and his large ones flops." Cavaillès, at least, had managed, however imperfectly, to create something new.

That March he went to the University of Massachusetts in Amherst to record some of his poems and did what he thought was a decent job. He was also invited to attend a celebration in honor of Robert Frost's eightieth birthday at Amherst the following week, but declined. True, Frost was "greatly admired by many people," but, he equivocated, he didn't know Frost's "work well enough to be either impressed or unimpressed," though the poems were "full (or said to be full) of humanity." It didn't help matters that years before he'd "visited the rare book library at Harvard" and had seen Frost's bust calling attention to itself in the entranceway.

"Your Easter message made me happy," he wrote Sister Bernetta, "as all your notes do, because they seem to come from something fundamental, something isolated from this ruthless present." Still, spring had returned to New England again, with robins hopping about the lawn and wild doves cooing at dawn. It was time to decide on a name for his collected poems. *The Whole Harmonium*, he suggested to Herbert Weinstock at Knopf's, and not his earlier choice, *Amber Umber*, which smacked too much of Hopkins. Instead, Knopf decided to go with *The Collected Poems of Wallace Stevens*, even though, as he told Knopf, it was "a machine-made title if there ever was one." This would no doubt be his last book, though he would try to "go on writing cheerful poems on good days and cheerless ones on bad days." He'd held off from a *Collected* for as long as he could, knowing it would mean the inevitable end to things. But he had now reached an age when he didn't have much choice in the matter. After all, it was only good housekeeping to see a book like that in print.

• • •

ON MAY 31 HE delivered *The Sail of Ulysses* as the Phi Beta Kappa poem at Columbia for the college's 200th anniversary. It had been hard for him to find a form for this assignment, because they'd asked him to write something on a theme they'd chosen: freedom and knowledge. It was to be his last long poem, and—except for the brilliant and profound breakthrough the poem managed at its conclusion—perhaps his least successful. At one point, in fact, he'd even thought of discarding it altogether. "Perhaps I shan't throw it away," he wrote the poet-critic Babette Deutsch two days after delivering his address. "But I shall certainly never use it in its present form nor allow anyone to see a copy of it." Ordinarily a Phi Beta Kappa poet chose his own subject, but he'd been asked "to write a poem which would have to do with one aspect of [the school's] birthday theme," and the great difficulty had been to read such an abstract poem "in such a way as not to create confusion." In fact he did not think he'd succeeded. He meant to work on the poem and "at least keep it without any thought of doing anything with it." But for him the project had been wrong from the start.

"Under the shape of his sail," the poem begins, "Ulysses, / Symbol of the seeker, crossing by night / The giant sea, read his own mind." He'd worked and reworked that theme for so long now, and considered so many outcomes, that it must have surprised him to find himself turning over the tiller to something even bigger than a major man like Ulysses.

"If knowledge and the thing known are one," Ulysses muses, "so that to know a man is to be / That man, to know a place is to be / That place," then it followed that knowledge was "the only life," the "deep comfort of the world and fate." But to know something was to isolate oneself from others.

Why? Because knowledge was the one "luminous companion," "the hand, / The fortifying arm, the profound / Response," the indispensible "aid of greatness." It was life's directing force, the radiant "joy of meaning in design / Wrenched out of chaos." Knowledge was—with a bow to Columbia—an "Eden conceived on Morningside," a "freedom at last from the mystical, / The beginning of a final order" that would place mankind at the center. But if knowledge underwrote our very freedom, it pointed to something else: another, deeper knowledge, "not an attainment of the will" but something "illogically received, / A divination."

For a moment he was back where he'd been a dozen years before in *Notes toward a Supreme Fiction*, where the world went around in "the crystal atmospheres of the mind," to a place where the mind might renew that world in a piece of music or a passage by the right philosopher. Wasn't it true that the credible idea seemed to spring from the incredible? What, then, was "the shape of the sibyl" who should speak the truth? Not, finally, even the Sybil abstracted, "the englistered woman, seated / In colorings harmonious, dewed and dashed / By them." No, it would have to be "the sibyl of the self, / The self as sibyl," created out of our own essential poverty and deepest need, the Sybil as "a woman looking down the road, / A child asleep in its own life," Sybil as "part of the inhuman more," and yet an "inhuman of our features," an abstraction we were sure we knew and yet would never know: Ulysses sailing "under clumped stars" which dangled their fire-featured brilliance all the way.

Afterward he kept coming back to the poem, trying to find for himself what it was he was after. "What there is left of *The Sail of Ulysses* which I read before Phi Beta Kappa last spring," he confessed to one critic four months later, "has just appeared in a supplement to the *London Times Literary Supplement* devoted to American literature." He'd changed even the title to reveal that it was not Ulysses, not the self, at the center of the journey, but rather the "Presence of an External Master of Knowledge."

The poem now was much shorter—cut from 176 lines to just 24—and represented but one aspect of the poem: that if Ulysses was free to read his own mind, what he read and felt there was a vast and overwhelming sense of "human loneliness," in which the knowledge of his own "world and fate," the inalienable "right within me and about me," was "joined in a triumphant vigor, / Like a direction" upon which he saw that he himself depended.

What Ulysses had discovered on his long sea journey was that a wind had always driven his sail, "a longer, deeper breath" even than his own that had sustained "this eloquence of right, since knowing / And being" were one. But what was he to call this central being, this Supreme Fiction, this great Omnium, descending on him "like an absolute out of this eloquence"? At which point the poet drew back to look at what he had said in this coda to his final soliloquy, where "the sharp sail of Ulysses seemed, / In the breathings of that soliloquy, / Alive with an enigma's flittering." Call the journey an enigma, then, call it a fluttering and a flittering, the oscillations of light from the aurora borealis, perhaps, a "bodying, and being there" the necessary spirit wind supporting his sail at every turn "as he moved, straightly, on and on, / Through clumped stars dangling all the way."

• • •

STEVENS SPENT A SUNDAY afternoon that June reading through a manuscript analyzing his comic spirit, which a young poet and doctoral student at Columbia named Robert Pack had sent him. In returning the manuscript, he complimented Pack on his "many pages of extraordinary analysis," and especially for going to the trouble of citing "so many poems to which other people have paid no attention." Why was it that critics always seemed to stop their analyses with *Harmonium*? True, the book had worn well and remained fresh even for him. "But, after all," it had been "written more than thirty years ago." There were, of course, many things which Pack—that young Ulysses—had said with which he disagreed, though that was "bound to be the case." To take but one example, style was not merely a mechanism but a way of getting at the heart of one's subject. But since Pack had avoided contentiousness in his manuscript, Stevens meant to avoid it in his letter.

Then too there was the larger world to think about, like that virus called McCarthyism which had hurt Williams so deeply. Senator Joe McCarthy's investigation of the U.S. Army for being soft on Communism was now entering its third month. On June 9, 1954, Joseph Welch, special counsel for the army, had lashed back at McCarthy during Senate hearings. No wonder that when Stevens wrote his old correspondent Leonard van Geyzel in Ceylon it was the Communists who were on his mind, "growling not only at your back door but all around the house," what with Korea winding down and Vietnam winding up for the United States.

Here in the States, he noted, the newspapers were saying that the response to Communism had grown "much less hysterical than it was." But as far as he was concerned, he really had no sense that, despite McCarthy, things had ever been hysterical. Long experience had taught him that the newspapers and the radio used words "about as inexactly as they possibly can be used." If Eisenhower was right in saying that the cold war might continue for another forty years, looking ahead forty years for an old man like himself was simply incomprehensible. He could imagine how things might look in a year or so, but certainly not how things would look at the close of the twentieth century.

The best way to proceed, then, was simply to take the day's news in stride. "I cannot say that there is any way to adapt myself to the idea that I am living in the Atomic Age," he confessed; in fact it was "nonsense to try to adapt oneself to such a thing." But this much seemed clear: that the continued exhaustion of Europe a decade after the end of the war was "a great menace both to Europe and ourselves." Nor was he looking forward to the publication of his *Collected Poems*: "A book that contains everything that one has done in a lifetime does not reassure one." And the fact that the publication would coincide with his seventy-fifth birthday was beginning "to seem like the most serious thing" that had ever happened to him.

• • •

IT WAS SUMMER AGAIN, "that heavenly time of year when there is no news," he wrote Barbara Church in late July, "except of murders which do not concern me." Yes, there was the slight inconvenience of men fixing his roof, but for all that he and Mrs. Stevens remained "quietly at home, engaged in meditation and prayer and thoughts of Paris." He and Jack Sweeney and the young poet Sam Morse had spent an afternoon relaxing on the porch of the Canoe Club, drinking martinis as they watched the Connecticut River flow by. Then too there was the satisfaction of sitting on a bench under the elms in Elizabeth Park. He even managed to write a few poems, which gave him a deep satisfaction, "as if one had fulfilled one's self and, in a general sort of way, done something important—important to one's self."

• • •

WHEN BARBARA CHURCH SENT him a series of postcards featuring the baroque Jesuit churches in Munich and Geneva that August, he wrote to say how "super-duper" they were: "Your boy opening his arms before the altar and singing some hymn of the German soul was expressing his experience of the glory of the church through which he had just conducted you." It was a gesture not only of elation but "of the highest truth on the part of the man who first thought of it," which, by the repetition of the gesture over the years, had become a ritual. Wasn't building "a great church in a meadow the same thing as having a vision during one's work"? His own people, for instance, those pious Pennsylvania Dutch forbears, how often they must have had visions. In fact wasn't it a vision that had prompted them to come to the New World in the first place? "How curious," he added, "that we don't have chapels in [our] factories or insurance offices." What a thing it would be, for instance, to find Matisse's Vence chapel among Detroit's Ford plants. But there was "too much sectarianism nowadays to make such a thing possible." Still, hadn't those religious visions given his ancestors as much satisfaction as, say, a group of New York businessmen found in bars on cruise ships?

Perhaps the shipping companies, he half-joked, "especially French and Italian ones," should advertise something like this: "Take a trip on the *Christoforo Colombo* and get a glimpse of the next world in its lounges and cafes. Forget the income tax in its bars. Enjoy the peace of three weeks without a single letter asking you to contribute to something that makes the world a better world. Lose yourself in the poetry of publicity." What a profound grace it was "to have a destiny no matter what it is, even the destiny of the postman going the rounds and of the bus driver driving the bus." The destiny of merely going around and around, the destiny of the wind, or even of the great clock in the hall outside his office, "which ordinarily tells the time so drearily that it would take twelve musicians to mark the true tediousness of it." What if even it rang "*sostenuto* something," its bells sounding "with all chiming gaiety"?

No doubt his office mates at the Hartford spent part of every Sunday reading the travel sections in the papers, mostly displaying "well built girls in bathing suits" along "with the ship's bars and bathing pools and dancing salons." Such images only made him feel like an old man who spilled tea on his waistcoat or who thought he'd "eaten too much for breakfast when I have hardly eaten anything." In three days he would turn seventy-five, which would mark the beginning of his final quarter on this planet, so that by the time he reached one hundred he wouldn't even "know what a birthday is." He'd yet to make the million he'd set out years before to make, but his health seemed to be holding out, and he could still sit at home and listen to Chopin and Mozart on the radio.

19

A Final Seriousness: 1954–1955

His self and the sun were one
And his poems, although makings of his self,
Were no less makings of the sun.

It was not important that they survive.
What mattered was that they should bear
Some lineament or character,

Some affluence, if only half-perceived,
In the poverty of their words,
Of the planet of which they were part.

THE PLANET ON THE TABLE

For his seventy-fifth birthday Stevens was interviewed at his office by Lewis Nichols, chief drama critic for the *New York Times.* It was "an imposing structure," Nichols wrote of the Hartford's main office. In fact all of its first-floor executive rooms were impressive, what with their "rugs, glass-topped desks and a silence suitable for those who deal with the subtleties of insurance." But midway down the corridor to the right was a room "from which booms a hearty laugh." This was Wallace Stevens's office, where as vice president of surety Stevens signed business papers, with the same signature he affixed to copies of his *Collected Poems*.

Stevens was a tall man, "heavy without being ponderous," who sported a "close-cropped gray crew cut," with a face "equally at home dressed with a Santa Claus beard and entertaining grandchildren, or, with professional sternness dressing down malingerers." He was amused by many things, expressed "whimsical conceits," and liked to laugh. Poetry and surety claims he took seriously, but he also seemed to know himself too well to take himself seriously. He wrote poetry when he felt like it, but best when he could concentrate on it, as when he walked, alone, to the office and back or strolled in Elizabeth Park. He carried slips of paper in his pocket "and put down ideas and notes," then handed the notes to Miss Flynn, who in turn typed them out from his almost indecipherable script. Then he placed them in a folder and forgot about them until it was time to go back to them and revise. Though, he added, he didn't revise much, because anything he'd finally gotten out, he was reluctant to change, such change not being good for the poem he had composed in the first place.

He didn't like being asked to write on particular subjects. The only value for him in writing a poem was that it rang true, poetry being "a very important sanction to life," especially in a time when traditional sanctions were fast disappearing. He liked painting, books, and poems and—in his younger days—had definitely liked girls. "But," he winked, "let's not stress that. I have a wife." He also liked lunching at the Canoe Club on Wednesdays. There was only a single canoe there, actually, and that was "a stuffed one, and hangs on the wall." Best, however, was the fact that only the disreputable frequented the place.

For his seventy-fifth birthday Knopf threw a party for him at the exclusive Harmonie Club at 4 East Sixtieth Street, a building designed half a century earlier by the Beaux-Arts architect Stanford White. Among those who had turned up for the event were W. H. Auden, Jacques Barzun, Harvey Breit, Norman Holmes Pearson, Irita Van Doren, Conrad Aiken, Delmore Schwartz, Louise Bogan, James Merrill, Marianne Moore, Lionel Trilling, and Carl Van Vechten, whom Stevens hadn't seen for years. Van Vechten was "a year younger than I am but," to Stevens's eye looked "ten or fifteen years older." But then, as a friend reminded him, "to live to be 75" these days was not, "after all, a conspicuous achievement." He'd been especially happy to see Delmore and the young James Merrill, but he'd enjoyed "everybody and everything," except when he'd had to stand up at Blanche Knopf's urging and say something.

Three weeks later he was in New York again, this time to speak at the Metropolitan Museum for the American Federation of Arts convention. He'd thought of calling his talk "Picturesque Platitudes" but instead decided on "The Whole Man: Perspectives, Horizons." He began forcefully, brilliantly, quoting Alfred North Whitehead, the mathematician turned philosopher, to the effect that, if the American universities had been "up to their job, they would be taking business in hand and teaching it ethics and professional standards." Whitehead was the model of the imaginative man addressing business from outside. Consider, Stevens suggested, the effect Whitehead might have had if he'd been made "a member of the board of directors of a corporation" or, for that matter, an executive member of a large union. In other words, the all-around man without any "actual technical business experience" but possessing "breadth of character and . . . diversity of faculties." After all, was the man who had an "aptitude for economic advancement" really superior to the humble man who also had his special aptitudes? And who was to say "that to live kindly and graciously and meet one's problems bravely from day to day is not a great art, or that those who can do it are not great artists"? Aesthetics was too often "understood in too restricted a sense."

He spoke of Peter Lee, "a young scholar, a Korean," who used to come to Hartford and sit with him on a bench by the pond in Elizabeth Park and talk about poetry. Though Korean-born, Lee spoke "in the most natural English." Now he was living in Fribourg, Switzerland, and had sent Stevens a letter "in the most natural French." In his letter Lee pointed out that seventy-five years was no great deal when one remembered that poets and philosophers in the Far East, "nourishing themselves only on the mist," had lived to be 100 and even 150. Some had even found a way to enter fairyland, something beyond the reach of most Westerners today. "By reducing themselves to skin and bones and by meditation prolonged year after year," these venerable men had found a "final harmony in what all the world would concede to be final form." These were our vertical men, living among the horizontals, who ought to be counted among "life's most magnificent" adventurers, true specialists, as opposed to all-around men like Whitehead.

Still, there was "an inevitable rapport between all men who seek the truth and who hope, thereby, to be made free and to remain free." Even the best technician, practical man that he was, was something of a theorist. But it was the theorist who made the world what it was, who conceived of the whole and told the rest of us about it. To build a bridge, you had to find a bridge builder. But it would be the all-around man who would have to ask why a bridge should be built in the first place. And so with modern painting, the topic he meant to address that evening, the analogy being that modern art itself would be affected more by what the all-around man, the thinker of the first idea, had to say than by what the painters themselves had to say about art.

What kept painting or poetry or music alive generation after generation was deep form, for that alone contained within it an "ever-youthful, ever-vital beauty." The vigor of art, the truly new, was an energy, and therefore in itself formless, so its embodiment would have to come from what developed from it over time. Of course to actually elevate life was a technical problem. A city the size of New York, for instance, could never exist without its technicians. Most people today were specialists in something. But what of the few like Whitehead in whom we might place our "profoundest confidence"? We all had to believe that we were governed by the truth. Wasn't the "key to an understanding of our times" faith in the idea that the truth was something we might attain, and that a civilization based on truth was "no less attainable"? Thus, by extension, the figure of the poet, Man Number One, who could give us a Supreme Fiction in which we might believe.

• • •

ON NOVEMBER 6 HE read from his poems at the 92nd Street Y, returning home with Holly and Elias Mengel. They took the Merritt Parkway, which gave him a sense of "living in the suburbs—as if one might possibly be able to make it on foot on a good day." Living in an objective world such as the Merritt Parkway provided was a blessing for him, whereas the "objective world of so many poets" seemed to consist merely of "a seat in the lounge on a cruise." That night the Poetry Center had been "filled up to the roof," he told Alfred Knopf afterward. Yet when it came to signing books, only ten or twelve had come forward with copies. No doubt, he added, the book, priced at $7.50, seemed expensive. He and Holly and Mengel had gone to Barbara Church's for a drink before the reading. Marianne Moore had been there, and Mengel would recall Moore and Stevens sitting on a sofa together, enjoying themselves, and talking about William Carlos Williams's friend, Robert McAlmon. Mengel was surprised to find himself deeply moved by Stevens's presence on the podium that evening. Here was "a monumental presence," poised and formidable who seemed to give everything he had that evening, so that, by the time they started back to Hartford, Stevens sat quietly, thinking. When they arrived at Westerly Terrace, Mengel offered to help him out of the backseat, but Stevens refused. After all, he was not Robert Frost, he said.

For the first time Stevens did not attend the Yale-Harvard football game that November. Instead he stayed home, listening to the rain with the windows open. Two weeks later he wrote Archibald MacLeish, declining his offer to become the Charles Eliot Norton professor at Harvard for 1955. The reason, he explained, was that the Hartford had a rule that fixed the mandatory retirement age at seventy, and while he was now well beyond that age and believed he could continue as long as he wanted, to take a year's sabbatical even for something as prestigious as the Norton professorship would no doubt precipitate his retirement. Even if he did somehow manage to return to work, he could not imagine "taking up the routine of the office again . . . after being away from it for a long period of time." He had no choice but to decline, though "with the greatest regret," because the chair would have made it possible for him to finally formulate a theory of poetry that would have made it a "normal, vital field of study for all comers." Now, however, someone else would have to do the job.

• • •

"EVERYTHING I'VE GOT GOES into the office," he confessed to Barbara Church early in 1955, so that by the time he got home he no longer had the energy for poetry. He was going to New Haven in a few days to help choose the winner of that year's Bollingen, which would be shared by Léonie Adams and Louise Bogan. "Mr. Babb, the librarian at Yale, gives a dinner," he added, "which will, no doubt, be pleasant. I am always surprised when people are friendly." As was José Feo's mother down in Cuba, "who loves her burro and asks José to tell me, for Xmas, that Pompilio is well. Saludos, Pompilio." That same day he wrote to thank Peter Lee for the delightful Korean scroll he'd sent. That was happiness, he told Lee: "to be able to grow old and fat and lie outdoors under the trees thinking about people," and of course "eat and drink and chase girls."

On the evening of January 25 he was driven to New York to receive his second National Book Award in four years, this time for his *Collected Poems.* William Carlos Williams and E. E. Cummings had also been finalists that year. Given that Williams had won the first-ever NBA back in 1950 for *Paterson*, many thought Cummings would take the prize for his *Poems 1923–1954.* But it was Stevens who won, as he would also win the Pulitzer later that year. On the stage with Stevens that evening was William Faulkner, who received the award for his novel *A Fable.*

"When a poet comes out of his cavern or wherever it is that he secretes himself," Stevens said that evening, "and suddenly finds himself confronted by a great crowd of people, the last thing in the world that enters his mind is to thank those who are responsible for his being there." This was "particularly true if the crowd" had come to catch a glimpse of some novelist who was usually "better known to it than any poet." And yet, he insisted, the crowd would be there on account of the poet too, because the poet exercised "a power over life, by expressing life, just as the novelist does." In fact, the poet exercised that power with at least as much perception as the novelist, and did so using the very "rhythms and tones of human feeling." It was imperative therefore that the poet call his audience to that fact and "address himself to what Rilke called the mighty burden of poetry" and "have the courage to say that . . . the significance of poetry is second to none."

Of course a "belief in the greatness of poetry" was "a vital part of its greatness." At seventy-five he could be forgiven for looking back one last time on what he had managed to achieve, as modest as that achievement might seem. That was what comforted him now. It was not what he had written, but rather what he "should like to have written that constitutes my true poems, the uncollected poems which I have not had the strength to realize." Awards and honors were peripheral to that, for the only true satisfaction for the poet lay in the making of poetry itself. Still, it was a nice touch when, three weeks later, he received a scroll from the State Senate and House of Representatives in Connecticut containing a copy of Joint Resolution No. 46, congratulating him on winning the National Book Award. "This resolution," he wrote back, thanking the appointed committee, "was as generous in act and in word as it was unusual," for it was as much as saying that in Connecticut poetry was "recognized as an element of the life of the community," which was all any poet could ask for.

But there were more serious concerns on Stevens's mind that winter. On January 14, 1955, Elsie suffered a stroke which left her incapacitated, so that a nurse had to be brought in each weekday until Stevens could get home from the office to take over. "Mrs. Stevens had a thrombosis about a month ago," he told Barbara Church in mid-February, but was making rapid progress now, coming downstairs every day and trying "to grow well by main force." Of course, given who Elsie was, it was "difficult to make her take it easy." Still, she remained "cheerful and courageous," so that within a few months he hoped she would "be fully or almost fully as she was before." He knew she would be upset knowing that he had spoken of her condition to anyone, and she had made up her mind "to exorcise the devil by not recognizing him or, rather, to expel him by turning her back on it." Well, he sighed, in another month winter would be "on its way to South America and down there the birds will be on their way to North America." Just now there weren't many signs, except that the sun was beginning "to seem a Christian," with daffodil tips breaking through the ground and people reporting snowdrops. Though he did not know it yet, that spring would be his last.

• • •

THERE WERE ALSO PROBLEMS at the office to contend with, over which he likewise had no control. The surety claims department which he'd headed for the past twenty years was in the process of being absorbed into other departments, until, he realized, it was now little more than a parenthesis. He made no secret of the fact that he was upset when the company turned the fidelity claims division of surety over to E. A. Cowie, as Cowie recalled twenty years later. "I can remember going down to talk to him one day" in that winter of 1955, "and he was seething. At first he refused to talk to me." They had "insulted him by taking his authority away." Then, just as quickly, he mellowed. He'd "been practically shaking; he was almost having a tantrum. I was prepared to leave his presence, but finally he softened and he said, 'I'm not blaming you.' "

It was Wilson Jainsen, president of the Hartford, who had decided to consolidate operations, turning over the merged division—along with some of Stevens's longtime staff—to Cowie. It was only a matter of time—with Stevens's retirement—before surety would follow. Stevens had grown far too independent, as far as Jainsen was concerned. There had been the time, Cowie remembered, when he'd had a problem in the Chicago branch of the bond claims department, and when he got back to Hartford, Jainsen had taken Cowie with him to talk to Stevens about it. But Stevens had simply shrugged the matter off, saying he "wouldn't know a thing about it." Jainsen had turned to Cowie and said, "Let's get out of here." For his part, Stevens avoided going into Jainsen's office, afraid that Jainsen was just waiting to ask him when he meant to retire.

• • •

SOME MONTHS EARLIER PROFESSOR Jackson Matthews had written Stevens to say that the Bollingen Foundation was bringing out a new translation of the complete works of Paul Valéry in fifteen volumes, and wondered if Stevens might be interested in writing an introduction to *Eupalinos* and *L'Ame et la Danse.* Though he knew the project would keep him busy for months, Stevens accepted because he'd always wanted to know Valéry better. Once under way, though, he found it hard to stick to the task, as it was almost impossible to place the two works in relation to Valéry's other writings. "Taken by itself," he told Barbara Church that February, while the *Eupalinos* had many values, as all nice books by civilized thinkers have," Valéry had not explained clearly what it was he was after. No wonder, then, that Stevens's introduction to the text consisted mostly of long quotations and vague generalities. In late March he sent what he had to Jackson, explaining that he'd highlighted those aspects of Valéry that had interested him but that he was going to have to let the project go.

He was back in New York for St. Patrick's Day, which he celebrated over a noisy, cheerful lunch with Marianne Moore and the Sweeneys at Barbara Church's apartment, then caught the 4:07 back to Hartford to avoid "the possibility that the evening train, full of the festive and good-natured Irish, might not be as tame as it usually is." He was anxious now to get back to writing "a poem or two, as the weather brightens." With Elsie still trying to recover from her stroke, the house was unusually "sleepy and full of sleep." But as the weather flowered, he was walking again, once for nearly two hours, "incredible as that seems."

That afternoon at Barbara Church's apartment, the Sweeneys had promised to send him a catalogue of early Irish Christian art, which arrived at his office a few days later. It still amazed him how "the identity of the Irish with their religion" was the same thing as their identity "with their lonely, misty, distant land, a Catholic country, breeding and fostering Catholic natures." Then, on the last Friday of the month he and Holly attended a performance of the Berlin Orchestra in Hartford, something he looked forward to because, "in a world so largely undisciplined, the music of this orchestra" would flow "from the very center of discipline" and order.

That same day, sitting in his office, he had confided to his old friend and colleague Anthony Sigmans that he'd not been feeling well lately. Maybe he should see a doctor, Sigmans suggested. "Oh, hell!" Stevens answered. "Go see a doctor, and he'll blab my business all over town." Well, Sigmans's doctor was a model of discretion. His name was James Moher, and Sigmans offered to accompany Stevens to an appointment. When he saw Moher the following Monday, Stevens told him he'd been seriously constipated for the past month, and for the past several weeks he'd also been experiencing severe stomach pains, especially after dinner, in spite of the fact that he had almost no appetite lately and had lost a lot of weight.

All of this, he thought, had been caused by his constant worrying over Elsie's health and because he'd been unable to get in much walking lately. An examination that day showed nothing out of the ordinary, nor did an X-ray and barium enema the following week.

"In spite of its solemnity," he wrote Peter Lee, Easter is "the most sparkling of all fetes since it brings back not only the sun but all the works of the sun, including those works of the spirit that are specifically what might be called Spring-works: the renewed force of the desire to live and to be part of life." By then the doves had "returned from Korea and some of them sit on our chimney before sunrise and tell each other how happy they are in the most melancholy tones."

His grandson certainly took "Easter and the rabbits very seriously," he wrote Barbara Church, though Peter also took the Bronx Zoo "and the lions and tigers there, and the circus with its forty or fifty baby elephants, with equal seriousness." Now that Elsie was up and around again, they'd let the nurse go and were trying to get back to normal. That same week he read and enjoyed Robert Pack's essays on his poetry, noting especially the one called "The Hero as the Final Abstraction of Character." But once again he felt he had to clarify some of the analyses. "Your use of the word nobility causes some difficulty," he wrote Pack in mid-April. In fact he'd written John Crowe Ransom to say that, while the word "nobility," which Ransom too had used was "essentially the right word, it was a most impolitic word to use" to describe his work.

Back in December he'd had to tell Pack that he took exception to his saying that he got nowhere in his poetry. "I hope you don't really feel that that is true," he'd told him, because he did "at least arrive at the end of my logic." Where that led, Pack would certainly know. A week later he'd written Pack again, trying to clarify what he'd said earlier: that a poem might remain indefinite and still lead somewhere. Thus in projecting a supreme fiction, nothing was "more fatal than to state it definitely and incautiously." Then he added that he'd been thinking "of adding other sections to the *Notes* and one in particular: It Must Be Human." But then, of course, the last thing in the world he wanted was "to formulate a system."

Farewell, then, to a mythology, a description with place. "Here / In Connecticut, we never lived in a time / When mythology was possible," he wrote that April. And yet that same month he managed to write something for the *This Is America* radio series, which he called "This is Connecticut," as well as two short poems: "A mythology reflects its region," which came out of his meditation on Connecticut, and another, called simply "Of Mere Being." "The thrift and frugality of the Connecticut Yankee were necessary to life in the Colony," his cold war script begins, "and still are." Those early settlers were proud of their strength of character, of their ingenuity, intelligence, and dignified style of living. Earlier that month, "when the weather was still bleak and everything still had the look of winter," he'd traveled by rail from Hartford to Boston. "Everything seemed gray," he wrote, "bleached and derelict," like Connecticut itself. "The soil everywhere seemed thin . . . and every cutting and open pit disclosed gravel and rocks, in which only the young pine trees seemed to do well. There were chicken farms, some of them abandoned, and cowbarns" and "orchards of apples and peaches." It was a landscape composed "of spare colors and thin lights," a watercolor, really, where "the dry grass on the thin surfaces would . . . change to a lime-like green and later to an emerald brilliant in a sunlight never too full."

This was Connecticut's true mythology, which one breathed in "with every breath," filled with "the joy of having ourselves been created by what has been endured and mastered in the past." Here in spring the mother revealed herself among her two million inhabitants, so many of whom, like himself, had come from elsewhere. But once you were here you were on your way to becoming a Connecticut Yankee. After forty years of living here, he felt very much like a native of this place, with its "small ports and harbors" along the Long Island Sound, and its towns "up and down the Connecticut River, the anchorages of the whalers." Once many Connecticut Yankees had made their living "in China or the Marquesas or Jamaica," using "the banks of the Connecticut River as the sites of their dwellings with gazebos in their gardens, in which they sat and planned and fostered the temples and universities and the many practical enterprises to which their imaginations were addicted."

Nothing gave one "the feel of Connecticut like coming home to it." He did not mean the thousands of commuters who came back to it every night from their jobs in New York. After all, the whole state formed a "single metropolis, highly industrial, with factories and mills and shops and schools and homes spread out everywhere, with a few major concentrations in Bridgeport, New Haven, Hartford, New London." That was what made Connecticut. That and "the salt-water of Noank and Stonington," the hills surrounding the Cornwalls and Pomfret, as well as "the special countries of the Housatonic and the Thames." Coming home to Connecticut, he had come to understand, was like coming home to one's American self: a return to one's origins, consisting of the primary virtues of "hardihood, good faith and good will."

And farewell to the poem. The final one he wrote was a short lyric, composed of four tercets, which he called "Of Mere Being." It evokes Long Key or Key West or paradise, perhaps, where "the palm at the end of the mind, / Beyond the last thought," rises "in the bronze décor," and "a gold-feathered bird" sings in the palm, sings now "without human meaning" sings even "without human feeling, a foreign song." It is a world both intensely familiar and yet strange, a place beyond fear, beyond anything human, where one knows that it is not reason that makes us happy or unhappy. There in that land beyond language a bird sings, its feathers shine, and

The palm stands on the edge of space.
The wind moves slowly in the branches.
The bird's fire-fangled feathers dangle down.

On April 19 he underwent a series of tests ordered by Dr. Moher, which revealed an obstruction preventing anything from passing through his stomach. Three days later he was admitted to St. Francis, the Catholic hospital in Hartford where Dr. Moher practiced, the grounds of which Stevens had passed each day for decades to and from work. On April 26, the day his grandson turned eight, he was operated on by Dr. Benedict Landry, the surgeon Moher had called into the case. The surgery found diverticulitis and a gallstone and—worse—cancer of the stomach.

He spent the next three weeks in St. Francis recovering. Landry had called in Holly to explain that he'd found a large cancer attached to the back wall of her father's stomach that was blocking the opening into the large intestine. It was too late to remove the cancer, but he had performed a gastroenterostomy above the cancer to allow food to pass out of the stomach. As was customary then, he urged Holly not to tell her father about the cancer, but to tell him he would, with time, recover. In the meantime Stevens's secretary visited him each day at the hospital, taking down his correspondence and signing his letters. Six days after his operation, he dictated one such letter to Barbara Church: "I expect to be able to leave the hospital towards the end of this week for several weeks of recuperation at home." The operation itself, he had been told, had been "a complete success," and he planned on being around "for a long time to come."

For the past nine years Father Arthur Hanley had served as chaplain at St. Francis. It was his ministry "to see all the patients in the hospital, especially Catholic patients," and it was Dr. Landry who suggested that he stop by to visit with Stevens. "He received me very well," Hanley remembered, "and he always said, 'Be sure and come back, Father. Be sure and come back.' " Which was what Hanley did, stopping each day for up to half an hour. They talked about a lot of things, including Stevens's poems. Hanley had taken classes in poetry at Boston College and at St. Bernard's Seminary and had even studied Chaucer. "He got quite a kick out of me when I gave off about five lines of Chaucer's *Canterbury Tales* in Old [Middle] English," Hanley remembered,

> so that he thought I was a real lover of poetry, but all the time in the back of my mind was, how can I get this man in the Church? He was very fond of Pope Pius X [who'd been canonized the year before]. He thought he was a very great man. He said that someday he was going to write a poem about the Pope. So I said, "Oh, what are you going to call the poem?" He said, "I was going to call it 'The Tailor,' or 'The Love of Poverty' or 'The Poor Tailor.' " And during that time I did get some of his poems and I read them so I would have something to talk about when I went into the room.

It didn't take Hanley long to sense that something was troubling Stevens's spirit. He wanted to talk, Hanley recalled, and he wanted to talk about God. Whenever Stevens went to New York, he told Hanley, he used to spend a couple of hours in St. Patrick's Cathedral, quietly meditating, because he found peace and enjoyment from doing that. "He had such a marvelous idea of what God was," Hanley recalled: that God was this absolute idea. Everything had been created, except for this one original uncreated concept, and that was God. Stevens's thinking was "unusual in this respect," Hanley told him. Then he added that, if Stevens was ever going to get into the fold, this was the time to do it. There was, however, one thing that bothered Stevens, and that was "how a just God could construct a place like hell," because "a merciful God, knowing the weakness of mankind, would not fashion a place like that to punish anyone—not even a dog." Hanley had heard that argument many times, so he explained that, whereas God was merciful, he was also just, "and in His justice, He must recognize that some people, no matter what grace is given them, will repudiate Him." And we just didn't know that there was "anyone specifically in hell except the devil and his cohorts."

But Stevens kept coming back "to the goodness of God." If God was good, how could he "allow all this evil in the world? So we went into free will and all that business." Of course Stevens was really "more of a poet than a Scholastic philosopher," Hanley pointed out. Stevens seemed to know "quite a bit about the Church," and "there were just a few little things that kept him from being a Catholic," like "this hell business." Hanley went on to explain that hell "was mentioned fifty-seven times in the Bible and that our Lord said there was a hell, so we believe what our Lord said." Stevens nodded. That seemed logical enough. The Socratic catechesis continued until Stevens returned home on May 11 to continue his recovery. For nine days Elsie, despite her own disabilities, insisted on taking care of him, by which time he and Holly both realized that it would be better for Elsie and him both if he continued his recovery elsewhere. Thus, on May 20, he was moved to the Avery Convalescent Home on New Britain Avenue, five miles from home, where he would stay for the next month, walking about the park-like grounds of the hospital each day.

The day he left for the Avery he received a letter from Professor Reuben A. Holden informing him that he was to receive an honorary Doctor of Letters from Yale on June 13. In spite of his weakened condition, he was going to "allow nothing to interfere" with his being there, he told Holden, "because the degree at Yale is precious to me." He did not, however, think it advisable to attend the dinner in his honor the night before. Instead Holly would drive down with him on the morning of the ceremony.

When the day came, Holly and "one of the colored men from the office" came for him "in a good, big, comfortable car" and drove him to New Haven, where they parked in front of the building where the candidates were donning their robes. "I was in very good shape," he told Barbara Church two weeks later, "and I don't think that anyone seeing me march in the procession would have noticed anything unusual except the loss of weight." He'd been given a seat at the end of the front row on the platform. The ceremonies had been "pleasant and brief," and afterward he and the other recipients had lunched with the president. It was the strawberries that did him in that day. "I must have been in particularly good shape because I had perhaps ten big ones," he confessed, after which he'd had such a battle keeping them down that even they were off his list for now.

Four days before going down to Yale, he'd received an honorary Doctor of Humanities from the Hartford School of Music. It was the first time he'd ever been officially recognized in his own city.

Each week the Sigmans visited him at the Avery. Stevens was "pretty much a changed man," Sigmans remembered. In fact until then, he'd never seen Stevens sick at all. They took him for rides, one time to the Passionist Monastery in Hartford. When Sigmans's wife asked Stevens if he wanted to get out and walk around the monastery's extensive grounds, Sigmans, knowing Stevens was not a religious man, interrupted. No, he said, Wallace did not want to get out. But as he started to drive off, he heard Stevens say, "I certainly do. I want to get out. I want to go down and see the church." Sigmans, a practicing Catholic himself, was surprised. Stevens had never talked about religion, "except on a rare occasion," when he mentioned how he liked to sit in St. Patrick's and meditate. Years before, when someone had asked him about his religious beliefs,

Stevens had dismissed the question by saying that he was just a "dried-up Presbyterian." But once, Sigmans recalled, Stevens had told him that, if he ever did join a church, it would be the Catholic Church.

Mengel too would remember visiting Stevens at the Avery with Holly. He was "feeling pretty well that day," and Mengel asked Holly if her father knew he had cancer. By that point, Holly thought he probably did, though he had said nothing about it. During that visit Stevens began talking about his time at Harvard with Santayana. "He obviously was enjoying this, speaking of the past," Mengel recalled. He also noticed a copy of the New Testament on Stevens's bedside table. It was the last thing he ever thought Stevens would be reading.

Avery, Stevens wrote his niece Eleanor that June, was "a place on high ground at one edge of the city . . . pretty much of a park with a great deal of woodland and a wonderful place in which to do nothing except get well." He was sure his strength was returning along with his appetite, and he was "always more than ready for breakfast and about half ready for lunch," though the rest of the day was "not so hot." Not being home meant that Elsie could spend all the time she wanted in her garden, which did her "a world of good." When he telephoned, he said, Elsie always sounded cheerful, and before long she was going to be completely over her disability.

Finally, on June 20, he was back home, returning that same day to the office to show Jainsen he was ready to carry on as before. Yes, he was "back in the office after an absence of about two months," he wrote McGreevy, during which time he had spent his days "in hospitals growing blanker and blanker." Even now he hardly had voice enough "to dictate this letter." Actually, he spent "only two or three hours a day at the office, principally to accustom myself to the idea of being back and also to get over this initial period commonly so full of interruptions." If just now he was "completely lacking in all vigor," he hoped that was "merely temporary."

The following day he dictated a letter to Barbara Church, who was back in France. It was going to take a while before he was working full days again, he told her. At the Avery he'd been able to roam the grounds in cooler weather, whereas here at home he was getting "almost no exercise . . . because of the heat." When he'd received his honorary degree from the Hartford School of Music, they'd given him a black hood with brilliant red highlights. Peter had been there with his mother, and when the hood was placed on Stevens's shoulders, the boy had turned to his mother and said, "Grandfather got the best one of all!" Stevens liked that. Actually he was surprised his grandson hadn't fallen asleep.

Sleep. What was it he'd said about his grandson the previous summer in a poem he'd called "A Child Asleep in Its Own Life"? "Among the old men that you know," he addressed the boy, there is one, not unlike his grandfather, who seems to brood "on all the rest, in heavy thought." But who are those old men, really, "except in the universe / Of that single mind." But whose single mind? The mind of the boy asleep, or the mind of an old man asleep in his own life, the beginning and end of it, each

The sole emperor of what they are,
Distant, yet close enough to wake
The chords above your bed to-night.

Even Peter's mother could not say what Grandfather's poem was about, since the words were meant only for those who could read them. Even Mengel was not sure what Stevens's dream song meant. "Dear Elias," Stevens would inscribe a copy of his *Collected* soon after, "When I speak of the poem . . . I mean not merely a literary form, but the brightest and most harmonious concept, or order, of life; and the references should be read with that in mind."

He'd said something similar to his "Korean Gypsy Scholar," Peter Lee, who had finally told Stevens that many of his poems baffled him. "When you say . . . that you feel as if you did not know English when you read those parts and sit and look into space and despair," Stevens had told him, that difficulty is what thousands of others no doubt feel.

> Content yourself with the thought that every poet's language is his own distinct tongue. He cannot speak the common language and continue to write poetry any more than he can think the common thought and

> continue to be a poet. . . . No one tries to be more lucid than I do. If I do not always succeed, it is not a question of my English, nor of yours, but I should say of something not communicated because not shared.

Sleep. "Most of the time when I am at home I drowse," he confessed to Sam Morse early that July. "I am without energy even to read the numerous things that are sent to me." A few days before, he'd received a manuscript in French. But, as he explained, he just couldn't bother himself about such things when he was so limp. People still wrote him for poems. But there would be no more poems.

He'd been at the office for two weeks now, "coming at 10:00 and leaving at 1:30 and doing very little in the meantime except seeing people who want to know how I feel." He could see that he would have been better off staying at the Avery because "living there was putting no one to any trouble and because it was cool and comfortable and, finally, because during the thirty-one days that I spent there I was able to retain everything that I ate." But then the hospital couldn't be expected to keep anyone indefinitely. Many nights it had been so cool there that he'd slept under a winter blanket. Now he was just trying to get through "this appalling July heat," which made the house feel like an oven. Unable to concentrate any longer, he wrote Barbara Church on July 15 to say he was sending her the French manuscript he'd received two weeks earlier because he could no longer enjoy even poetry.

Hale Anderson Jr., one of Stevens's associates at the Hartford, would remember what a stoic Stevens had been during those last days at the office. Stevens would sit in the reception room at lunch time and "put his thumb and forefinger under his chin and just rest, with his eyes closed, and never indicate by word or manner that he didn't feel well." Then, as the staff "began to hustle back to work, he would get up and go back to his office and tackle that pile of files again." "He'd almost crawl to do a job he was supposed to do," Manning Heard added. He could see that Stevens was suffering a great deal, though Stevens, stoic that he was, said nothing to anyone.

• • •

WITH THE CANCER SPREADING to his liver, it was time to return to St. Francis Hospital. He was taken there on July 21, by which time he could no longer keep food down, so that he had to be fed intravenously. When he saw Father Hanley this time, Stevens told him it was time now to get "into the fold." What Stevens assented to is probably what Santayana had wanted, the beauty of the idea of an idealized Catholic Church, and—being a surety lawyer—he opted to sign on the dotted line at the end, perhaps to assure himself (insofar as he could assure himself of anything) that Love, Beauty, and Mercy were parts of a Supreme Fiction he could sign off on. Perhaps there was something more, since he'd been leaning toward a resolution of the aesthetic and the religious for decades now. In any event it was at this point that Hanley baptized him in the presence of Sister Philomela, one of the nurse sisters on the floor. The following day Hanley brought Stevens communion.

"The first time he'd been at St. Francis," Hanley explained, Stevens still believed he was on his way to recovering. But time was running out, and a decision had to be made one way or the other. But "because his wife was not a Catholic and because it might seem that we got people into the hospital to drag them into the Church at the last minute, Archbishop O'Brien told me not to let it be known." Stevens had not needed "an awful lot of urging on my part except to be nice to him," Hanley added. There'd been a correspondence years before, he said, with a Sister Madeleva, a poet and president of St. Mary's College, who had known Stevens when he lived on Farmington Avenue and had tried to bring him into the faith. Now she wrote Hanley asking if Stevens had finally joined the Church. He had. As for Stevens being buried in a Catholic cemetery, Hanley believed the thought had never occurred to him. "He had gotten into the fold and that was it."

When Hanley told Holly that her father had been received into the Church, it seemed to make little impact on her. She seemed to brush off the priest as a minor nuisance. As for Elsie, Stevens had confided to Hanley that he and his wife had not gotten along for years, what with her living in one section of the house and him in another. When Hanley told him that it was important to forgive everyone, Stevens replied that one didn't "have to continue relationships when there is too much sharpness, or criticism or even—he used some word like—'acerbity.' " Stevens was always "using big words," Hanley added. "I suppose he was a man who lived on a higher or a different plane than she did." Through all of this, Stevens kept his sense of humor, joking with the nurses and reciting passages from Longfellow, which would surely be easier for them to grasp than his own poems.

When another colleague, Herbert Schoen, visited him at St. Francis, he was surprised to see how happy Stevens seemed. He was a veritable "jolly Santa Claus to the nurses." Schoen did not know "the reason for the transformation," simply that there had been one. Perhaps Stevens knew that "the end was coming," but in any case "he was a changed person—this time for the better." The nurses, Schoen could see, enjoyed being around him. Whatever the reason, his last days were "light and tripping and gay, which certainly impressed me." But when Schoen told Jainsen back at the office what he'd witnessed, Jainsen had retorted, "Unless they told me he had a heart attack, I never would have known he had a heart."

In those last days, when Holly came to see him, the sick man would tell her over and over of a time, fifty-two years before, when he'd bathed in the bright sublimities of the British Columbia Rockies. There, at the earliest end of August 1903, when afternoons began their long retreat, there in the Kootenays, in the remote outback where the windswept barrenness of blank rock glistened above the shagged timber line, something in the landscape had seemed to greet him.

On Monday, August 1, he slipped quietly into a coma. That evening his family visited him for the last time. Holly had had to bring Peter to the emergency room, and afterward she and Peter had stopped by her father's room. He'd regained just enough consciousness so that they were able to say their goodnights to each other. Later that night, alone, he fell back into a coma, and his fever intensified. At 8:30 the following morning he stopped breathing. The struggle was over.

• • •

JOHN CLEARY, OBITUARY EDITOR for the *Hartford Times*, got a call from the James T. Pratt Funeral Home in Hartford, the one "most patronized by rich Protestants." The man said he had an obit for the papers, so Cleary put on his headset "and started to type down the information he gave me, which was the man's name, his address, the place where he died and the date he died. And the fact that the funeral would be private." "Wait a minute," Cleary interrupted. "Wallace Stevens? Is that the poet, the Pulitzer Prize winner? We can't go on that one with this little information." "Well, that's the way the family wants it," the voice replied.

There was a brief service at the funeral home on August 4, where Elsie remained in the shadows, apart from the few who came to pay their respects. "It was a stark funeral parlor," Margaret Powers would remember. "No beautiful music, no beautiful service. There was some kind of eulogy. I was so horrified." She wondered what Stevens would have had to say about it. "No feeling of an afterlife or anything like that." A small room, with Holly and Elsie in purdah, "behind a screen." Later Holly would write Margaret to tell her that the St. Christopher medal that had belonged to her daughter, Julie, and which Margaret had given to Stevens, had been buried with him.

Jim Powers would remember a crucifix on Stevens's pillow "that his nurse or somebody had given him." Stevens had wanted that and the St. Christopher medal "pinned on his pillow right where he could see it." "How many times Jim and Stevens had talked about religion," Margaret remembered. Once Jim had told her that he thought Stevens would have liked to be in the Church but just couldn't do it. And yet he would seek out "these little churches all over Manhattan, mostly Roman." He seemed to love "the feeling of the Church, the atmosphere of churches," Jim had told her. And once, when the three of them were in New York together, Stevens had insisted on showing Margaret the inside of St. Patrick's, which she'd never seen. Together they had entered through the high portal and walked through the various chapels and up to the high altar.

The casket remained open for those few who wished to view the body before it was transported to Cedar Hill Cemetery, whose grounds Stevens had viewed from the knoll at the Avery on his daily walks behind the hospital. "Here a world celebrity dies and is buried," Sigmans would report years later, "and a handful of people are there. Just a handful." The pallbearers were from the Hartford, Sigman among them. "Just those around the office, no president of this-or-that, the mayor or the governor." He remembered too that "lots of people from the company, people that Stevens would see in the hall thousands of times, didn't bother to come over 'cause a lot of them didn't understand him. They didn't like him. They thought he was abrupt. They thought he was in a class by himself. He wasn't understood. You had to live with Mr. Stevens in a sense, as we did, to know him."

• • •

IT WAS GIVEN TO William Carlos Williams to write Stevens's commemoration piece for *Poetry*, where both had started out forty years before. "To me there was something in the dogged toughness of his thought that gave it a Germanic quality," Williams wrote that October. "He always reminded me of Goethe, in his youth," when zitronenbäumchen—lemon trees—filled his dreams, before the devastations of the moral sense had overcome him." First there was Stevens the New York dandy, the Stevens he had known most intimately, before he assumed the New England conscience of a Dickinson or a Hawthorne.

There was always a cryptic quality to the man's verses, Williams pointed out, a ritualistic quality, as if he were following a secret litany he revealed to no man. "Over and over again, as he reached his later years and . . . began to be recognized for what he was, a thoroughly equipped poet, even in such a late book as *The Auroras of Autumn*, he could be detected, to the surprise of the world, in this secret devotion." The truth was that, "in the midst of a life crowded with business affairs," Stevens had shown himself to be "a veritable monk."

By then he had "seen and possessed what he wanted in this world," Williams believed. "Henceforth contemplation, vividly casting its lights across his imagination, sufficed for him." Stevens had always seemed a "frightened man drawing back" from a world which for too long had ignored him. Which of course, Williams knew, was the way Stevens had wanted it. By the 1940s he'd "earned an undeserved reputation for coldness if not sterility," a condition which only time would rescue him from." Though Williams had "no confidence" that anyone would be reading Stevens tomorrow (or himself, for that matter) what Stevens could give you, if you read him carefully enough, was "something to cure our neuroses and make us whole again in the face of much that is sordid and cheap in the world."

But one read Stevens, finally, for the sheer pleasure of his lines, which offered something "difficult to isolate and capture in a phrase." Still, this much was certain: Stevens had written English as no Englishman had ever written it. After Dante's *Vita Nuova*, "which marked a peak in musical verse," Williams believed, poetry had forgotten how to dance. In fact, English poetry, and so the poetry of the New World, "had not danced since the Reformation had bred Milton with his *Paradise Lost*. There was no joy in it."

Then along had come Stevens. Stevens had been so gay when he was young, but then conscience had overcome him, leaving only isolated flecks of that gaiety, "like a caper half-heartedly performed with . . . a backward look over his shoulder to show the man he had been." Now that Stevens had entered that "other world," Williams thought his friends would want him to remember that young gay poet just starting out. Norman Holmes Pearson, who'd attended Stevens's funeral, had sent Williams a letter afterward, from which he quoted now: "There were only four there . . . remotely connected with him as a literary figure: Jack Sweeney, [the Yale scholar] Donald Gallup, Samuel French Morse, and myself. And no neighbors, or just a few; the rest were from the insurance company. It was very special, but perhaps becoming. I dunno; anyhow I miss him."

• • •

IN THE SIXTY YEARS since Stevens's death, his poetic reputation has continued to grow, until today it would be no stretch of the imagination to say that he is among the most important poets of the twentieth and the still-young twenty-first century, sharing a place—at least among poets, first-rate critics, and scholars—with Rilke, Yeats, and Neruda.

But such a reputation has come only by degrees, as if a sleeping giant had, to our astonishment, begun to awaken. In his own lifetime he garnered both the dismissal of critics like Yvor Winters and the praise of American poets such as William Carlos Williams and Hart Crane, as well as prominent critics like R. P. Blackmur and Randall Jarrell. In time his reputation spread to England and Ireland, then to France, Germany, Italy, and the rest of Europe. Thanks to Knopf and Random House, his collected, selected, and uncollected poems continue to appear to this day, not only in English, but French and Italian, among other languages.

His daughter, Holly, continued to edit and publish his work: first the massive *Letters* in 1966, followed by *The Palm at the End of the Mind: Selected Poems and a Play by Wallace Stevens* in 1971 and, six years later, her edition of the early letters of her parents. The letters of Stevens and Feo were published in 1986 and Stevens's commonplace book, *Sur Plusieurs Beaux Sujets*, in 1989. Forty-two years after his death, the Library of America published Stevens's *Collected Poetry and Prose*. That was followed by *The Letters of Wallace Stevens to Elsie* in 2006 and John Serio's very useful *Selected Poems* in 2011. Back in the mid-1970s, Peter Brazeau did us an invaluable service by interviewing many of those who had known Stevens during his Hartford years and publishing an oral biography. A decade later Joan Richardson's two-volume critical biography of Stevens gave us a fuller view of Stevens by integrating much of the life and poetry. And there is the invaluable *Wallace Stevens Journal*, which has been published semiannually for the past four decades.

It says something, too, that so many of our finest scholars and critics have paid such careful attention to Stevens's poetry and thought, increasingly since the 1990s. Among them of course are Harold Bloom and Helen Vendler, as well as J. Hillis Miller, George Lensing, James Longenbach, Joseph Riddell, Glen MacLeod, Alan Filreis, John Serio, Thomas Lombardi, Tony Sharpe, Bart Eeckhout, Jacqueline Vaught Brogan, Edward Ragg, Eleanor Cook, Charles Doyle, Lisa Goldfarb, Charles Altieri, and Alison Johnson.

As Helen Vendler noted some thirty years ago, it took fifteen years to learn Stevens's language and instruct others "in its odd grammar and lexicon. It was a delightful period, in which his poems were still fresh and (especially the later ones) relatively unknown." It was also a period in which readers asked if Stevens's poetry was good or even great and original, or reactionary and conservative. For decades the emphasis has been on Stevens the poet—heady, cerebral, aloof, an edifice as imposing as the Hartford insurance building that he inhabited for more than thirty years. Many to this day will, if they know anything about Stevens's poetry, cite something from *Harmonium*—poems still crisp though they were composed a century ago. But if many of the poems remain out of the comfort zone of most readers, especially those poems Stevens composed in the last, bountiful twenty years of his life, they will yield their richness to those willing to enter into his brilliant, funny, haunting, musical, dark, and often consoling world. In the end, he is capable not only of revealing your very self to you, but of delighting and consoling you, and even of breaking your heart.

ACKNOWLEDGMENTS

My deep thanks to Brendan Rappel and the research staff at Boston College, who answered hundreds of research queries over the past fifteen years and who so generously supplied me with endless articles and papers pertaining to Stevens and his circle. Thanks too to Natalie Russell and the staff at the Huntington Library in San Marino, California, who graciously furnished me with copies of letters and photographs from their extensive Wallace Stevens Collection. Thanks as well to the staff at Emory University for help in securing images from their Arthur Gary Powell Collection, as well as to the manuscripts collections at the Beinecke Library at Yale and at SUNY Buffalo for once again making available so many letters and manuscripts from their various collections, especially their extensive William Carlos Williams collections.

Thanks especially to the indefatigable Alison Johnson, both for her biography of Stevens and for inviting me to take part in reading and commenting on Stevens's poems, early and late, in the film documentary *The World of Wallace Stevens.* I began reading Stevens's poetry some fifty-five years ago, while an undergraduate at Manhattan College, and have never ceased. In that time so many critics and scholars have informed and deepened my understanding and appreciation of one of the most extraordinary poets of the twentieth century, whose influence continues to flourish in our time. Among the voices to whom I have returned: Holly Stevens, Peter Brazeau, Harold Bloom, J. Hillis Miller, Helen Vendler, Charles Altieri, Albert Gelpi, Joan Richardson, George Lensing, James Longenbach, Alan Filreis, John Serio, Glen MacLeod, J. Donald Blount, William Van O'Connor, Frank Kermode, R. P. Blackmur, Robert Buttel, Walt Litz, Hugh Kenner, Milton Bates, Eleanor Cook, Charles Berger, Steven

Gould Axelrod, Joseph Riddel, David Jarraway, Janet McCann, Robin Schulze, Tony Sharpe, Jacqueline Vaught Brogan, Mark Halliday, and John Irwin. Thanks to Daphne Fox Williams for permission to quote from the poems of her grandfather, William Carlos Williams, and to Peter Hanchak for allowing me to reproduce the photograph of him and his grandfather. And, of course, there are others.

I also want to acknowledge the poets with whom I have spoken over the years as we mused about the wonders Stevens had wrought: Allen Mandelbaum, Robert Pack, John Montague, Philip Levine, Donald Justice, Bill Heyen, Marvin Bell, Mark Strand, Robert Hass, Carolyn Forché, Mark Jarman, Edward Hirsch, and Dana Gioia.

Then too there are the necessary ghosts—William Carlos Williams, Ezra Pound, Hart Crane, Allen Tate, Marianne Moore, John Berryman, Robert Lowell, Randall Jarrell, Elizabeth Bishop, Sylvia Plath, and others—to whom I have offered my life's blood, willingly pouring it out into the Odyssean trench that they might drink from it and whisper (or mutter) into my one good ear.

My gratitude to so many of my former students in the various Stevens seminars I have been privileged to teach at the University of Massachusetts/Amherst and at Boston College over the past forty-five years, a number of whom have themselves taught Stevens over the years, and to the many who, from the blaze in their eyes, clearly saw something transformative in the man and his poems.

A very special thanks to my agent, Jill Kneerim, and her very capable associate, Lucy Cleland, who offered so much support, practical guidance, and—yes—wisdom.

And to the indefatigable, unflappable and seasoned editor Bob Bender, who went over every jot and tittle and quotation mark again and again, to ensure that the book met the standards he as senior editor at Simon & Schuster expected, as well as to his attentive and very helpful associate, Johanna Li. As it turns out, standing in the wet snow at attention for months, years, watching for those half-invisible enemies we call Errors, does bestow a certain vigilance and humility.

A word of acknowledgment as well to the permissions staff at Knopf for help in securing all necessary permissions for my biography.

And of course my lasting thanks to my sons and their wives, my grandchildren, and especially my wife, Eileen, to whom I dedicate this book. For more than half a century she has been my editor, guide, and muse, during which time I have poured thousands on thousands of hours into the lives of so many poets, while she waited patiently for my return from that strange, heady world of shadows.

ABBREVIATIONS USED IN NOTES

Brazeau — Peter Brazeau, *Parts of a World: Wallace Stevens Remembered* (Random House, 1983).

CPP — *Collected Poetry and Prose* (Library of America, 1997).

CS — J. Donald Blount, ed., *The Contemplated Spouse: The Letters of Wallace Stevens to Elsie* (University of South Carolina Press, 2006).

Filreis — Alan Filreis, *Modernism from Right to Left: Wallace Stevens, the Thirties and Literary Radicalism* (Cambridge University Press, 1994).

HL — Huntington Library.

HR — "Letters to Ferdinand Reyher," ed. with afterword by Holly Stevens, *Hudson Review* 44, no. 3 (1991).

Letters — *Letters of Wallace Stevens*, edited by Holly Stevens (Knopf, 1966).

S&P — Holly Stevens, *Souvenirs and Prophecies: The Young Wallace Stevens* (Knopf, 1977).

WCW — William Carlos Williams.

NOTES

CHAPTER 1. THE HEAVEN OF AN OLD HOME: 1879–1897

1 "What strange places!": WS to Elsie, 4 September 1913, *Letters*, 181.

2 "Happy the man": "Sonnet from the Book of Regrets," *CPP*, 516.

5 "damned ass": WS to his mother, 23 July 1895, *Letters*, 4–5.

5 "flotsam": WS to his mother, 4 August 1895, *Letters*, 7.

5 "self-sacrificing": WS to his mother, 31 July 1896, *Letters*, 9.

7 thrown kisses: 22 June 1900, Journal entry, *Letters*, 39.

7 "Piano Practice at the Academy of the Holy Angels": 1919, *CPP*, 549.

8 "all the things": WS to Elsie, 21 January 1909, *Letters*, 125.

8 "The Thessalians,": *Reading Eagle*, 24 June 1897, *CPP*, 755.

9 "dumped into a hole": WS to John Zimmerman Harner, 23 July 1945, *Letters*, 509.

9 "a hardware store": WS to Elsie, 16 May 1920, *Letters*, 219.

9 "When you are young": WS to Eleanor Stevens Sauer, 4 April 1950, *Letters*, 674.

9 "I am out of touch": WS to Emma Stevens Jobbins, 22 December 1953, *Letters*, 806.

CHAPTER 2. HARVARD: 1897–1900

11 a seat "of Unitarian optimism": Filreis, 27.

12 "an unfamiliar practice": Norton to Santayana, 23 April 1905, *The Letters of George Santayana, Book 1*, 304n.

13 "Autumn": *CPP*, 481.

13 a man's sense: CF. "Effects of Analogy" (1948), *CPP*, 710.

13 "Who knows": Garrett Stevens to WS, 27 September 1897, *Letters*, 14.

14 "for the campaign": Garrett Sr. to WS, 6 March 1898, *Letters*, 9.

14 "the remembrance of youth": WS Harvard journal, fall 1898, *S&P*, 20.

15 "Who Lies Dead": *CCP*, 481.

15 "where Faith and Hope": "Vita Mea," *CPP*, 482.

15 "from an allegorical": 27 December 1898, journal entry, *Letters*, 20.

15 "the natural tower": "Credences of Summer," *CPP*, 323 ff.

16 "modest, simple, and delightful": *S&P*, 37.

16 the creeps: WS to Donald Hall, 16 February 1950, *Letters*, 667.

16 "a paper doll": 7 July 1899, journal entry, *Letters*, 27.

17 "just such unexpected": 18 July 1899, journal entry, *Letters*, 28.

17 "into thin whiteness": 19 July 1899, journal entry, *Letters*, 29.

17 "dark ground at evening": 1 August 1899, journal entry, *Letters*, 32.

17 "Deer walk upon our mountains": "Sunday Morning," *CPP*, 56.

17 "the apple pungency": 7 July 1899, journal entry, *S&P*, 43.

18 "fine reserve and quietness": 21 July 1899, journal entry, *S&P*, 47.

18 "There must surely exist brains": 21 July 1899, journal entry, *S&P*, 47.

18 "To Stella": *CPP*, 489–90.

19 "the lyrics of song-sparrows": 26 July 1899, journal entry, *Letters*, 30.

19 "toward the splendid clouds": 1 August 1899, journal entry, *S&P*, 52–53.

19 "the real note of despair": 5 August 1899, journal entry, WS's afterthought 14 June 1904, *S&P*, 59.

19 "silly, affected": Notation by WS, dated 14 June 1904, *SP*, 59.

20 "an ode": *CPP*, 494–95.

20 "the most humorous poem": Floyd DuBois to WS, 28 January 1942, *S&P*, 63.

21 Stevens had dined with George Santayana: *S&P*, 68–69. Stevens journaled this encounter with Santayana on two blank pages at the end of his copy of Santayana's *Lucifer*. He also placed Santayana's holograph copy of the poem next to his own poem in the book, dating both 1 May 1900.

22 "Cathedrals are not built along the sea": *CPP*, 486.

22 "Reply to a Sonnet": George Santayana, *A Hermit of Carmel and Other Poems* (New York: Scribner's, 1901).

23 "Sparklets were": WS to José Rodriguez Feo, 4 January 1945, *Letters*, 482.

23 Copey stared at him: Witter Bynner to WS, 11 December 1954, *S&P*, 68.

CHAPTER 3. STARTING OUT: 1900–1903

26 "a bosom a foot and a half thick": 15 June 1900, journal entry, *Letters*, 37–38.

26 "A Window in the Slums": *Letters*, 40.

26 "brave fellow": 16 June 1900, journal entry, *S&P*, 73–74.

27 "a dirty hole": 18 June 1900, journal entry, *S&P*, 75.

27 "four different kinds of oil": 19 June 1900, journal entry, *S&P*, 75.

28 "a wretched, rag, tag, and bobtail": 28 June 1900, journal entry, *S&P*, 78.

28 "several birds": 19 July 1900, journal entry, *S&P*, 82.

28 "And hear the bells": 4 July 1900, journal entry, *Letters*, 42.

29 "thin, sweet-smelling wisps": 8 August 1900, journal entry, *S&P*, 85.

29 "clattering trucks and drays": 21 October 1900, journal entry, *S&P*, 88.

30 "in a level, unemotional": 29 December 1900, journal entry, *S&P*, 92–93.

30 "Long ago": "The Figure of the Youth as a Virile Poet," August 1943, *CPP*, 678.

31 "the mysterious spirit of nature": 7 February 1901, journal entry, *S&P*, 98.

32 "sitting on a park bench": WCW 1955, *Poetry*, January 1956.

32 an editorial: WCW to William van O'Connor, 22 August 1948, *S&P*, 76.

32 "If I only had": 12 March 1901, Journal Entry, *Letters*, 89.

34 "Froebel be hanged!": "To Miss Gage," July 1902, *CPP*, 498.

35 "Oh, Mon Dieu": 9 August 1902, journal entry, *S&P*, 103.

35 "incessant murmurs": 10 August 1902, journal entry, *S&P*, 104.

35 "one of the most beautiful scenes": 17 August 1902, journal entry, *S&P*, 106.

35 "dirty and dangerous": 24 August 1902, journal entry, *S&P*, 107.

36 "two thrushes": 15 September 1902, journal entry, *Letters*, 65.

36 "by discreet flattery": 8 October 1902, journal entry, *Letters*, 61.

36 "before twelve candles": late December 1902, journal entry, *Letters*, 62.

37 "great morality": 11 March 1903, journal entry, *S&P*, 113.

37 "Why there's Eddie": 12 July 1903, journal entry, *S&P*, 115.

38 "domesticated": 26 July 1903, journal entry, *S&P*, 115.

38 "a cigarless, punchless": WS's journal for 26 July 1903, *Letters*, 72.

38 "a delicious calf's": 26 July 1903, journal entry, *Letters*, 72.

38 "not the faces": Ibid.

38 "a coarse animal": 26 July 1903, journal entry, *S&P*, 116.

CHAPTER 4. TWO VERSIONS OF THE AMERICAN SUBLIME: 1903–1906

39 "What fat farms": 2 August 1903, journal entry, 64.

40 "through burnt timber": 1 September 1903, journal entry, *Letters*, 67.

40 "through icy mountains": 18 September 1903, journal entry, *S&P*, 127.

41 "the distant company": 20 October 1903, journal entry, *S&P*, 127.

41 "sound shoes": 20 October 1903, journal entry, *Letters*, 67–68.

41 "see somebody": 14 February 1904, journal entry, *Letters*, 69.

41 "one of the finest comedies": 8 March 1904, journal entry, *S&P*, 129.

41 "delightful up to": 17 March 1904, journal entry, *S&P*, 130.

42 "suspiciously long hair": 31 March 1904, journal entry, *S&P*, 131.

42 "and many a good honest woman": 4 April 1904, journal entry, *S&P*, 131.

42 "sat & smoked": 9 April 1904, journal entry, *S&P*, 132.

42 "sentimental, sketchy": 9 April 1904, journal entry, *Letters*, 71.

42 "God! . . . What a thing blue is": 18 April 1904, journal entry, *S&P*, 132–34.

43 "to shut out the face": 18 April 1904, journal entry, *Letters*, 71–72.

44 "ravishing hand": 6 August 1904, journal entry, *S&P*, 138.

44 "an extremely attractive fellow": WS to Philip S. May, 4 April 1937, *Letters*, 317.

44 "were about to say": 26 September 1904, journal entry, *S&P*, 142.
45 "office and theatre": 5 February 1905, journal entry, *S&P*, 144.
45 "Work, concerts, letters": 5 March 1905, journal entry, *S&P*, 144.
45 "mere blots on the calendar": 10 April 1905, journal entry, *S&P*, 144.
45 *une vrai princess* [sic] *lointaine*: 27 April 1905, journal entry, *S&P*, 146.
46 "Are you really fond": fragment of letter from WS to Elsie, 1905, *CS*, 33.
46 "I thought today": fragment of letter from WS to Elsie, 1906, *CS*, 34.
46 "I want to be": fragment of letter from WS to Elsie, 1904–1905, *Letters*, 74–81.
46 "the worn, the sentimental": WS to Elsie, April 30, 1905, *S&P*, 146.
46 "Mary Stuart": 30 April 1905, journal entry, *Letters*, 98.
47 "a thousand times as long": 8 May 1905, journal entry, *S&P*, 146–7.
47 "cheerful": 23 May 1905, journal entry, *S&P*, 147.
47 "drinking gin & courting the moon": 18 June 1905, journal entry, *S&P*, 147.
47 "as happy as a lark": late July 1905, journal entry, *S&P*, 149.
47 "same whiskers": Undated, but July 1905, *SP*, 149.
48 "vicious, dark mind": 7 August 1905, journal entry, *S&P*, 150.
48 "women chopping wood": 11 August 1905, journal entry, *S&P*, 151.
48 "minute knowledge": 31 December 1905, journal entry, *S&P*, 156.
49 "soon would have become blacker": 5 February 1906, journal entry, *S&P*, 158.
49 "a doddering girl": 5 February 1906, journal entry, *Letters*, 86.
49 "It is such splendid": *Letters*, 90.
50 "the Christian fears life": 24[?] April 1906, journal entry, *S&P*, 165.
50 "starved, nonchalant": 29 July 1906, journal entry, *S&P*, 169.
51 "Read such things": 5 September 1906, journal entry, *S&P*, 171.
51 "New office": 10 October 1906, journal entry, *S&P*, 171.
51 "I am afraid to review": 5 December 1906, journal entry, *S&P*, 171.

CHAPTER 5. WINGÈD VICTORY: 1907–1913

53 "just coming out of sparrow church": March 10, 1907, WS to Elsie, *Letters*, 95–96.

54 “all very Roman and wonderful”: 4 January 1907, journal entry, *Letters*, 94.

54 “nothing but mud”: 21 March 1907, to Elsie, *Letters*, 97.

54 “more or less unmanageable”: 1 April 1907, journal entry, *S&P*, 174.

54 “noble conception”: *Letters*, 127.

55 “I am in the mood”: 6 June 1907, journal entry, *S&P*, 179.

55 “intent on getting”: WS’s journal, undated, but probably late October 1907, *Letters*, 133.

56 “transcripts of common-place Nature”: 5 January 1908, journal entry, *S&P*, 189.

56 “Suppose some glimmering”: *S&P*, 188; also see revised version in *CPP*, 508, where the poem is titled “Chiaroscuro.”

57 “Fog now, and a bell”: “On the Ferry,” *S&P*, 191.

57 “Wall was in town”: Catharine to Elizabeth, 22 November 1908, *S&P*, 196.

58 “Tell me what you wear”: WS to Elsie, 3 December 1908, *S&P*, 196.

58 “down-town—the very last place”: WS to Elsie, 17 January 1909, *CS*, 128–29.

59 “more absorbing”: WS to Elsie, 31 January 1909, *Letters*, 129.

59 “Oh, what soft wings”: *CS*, 145; also *CPP*, 508–9.

60 “to see what symbols”: WS to Elsie, 2 May 1909, *CS*, 185–86.

61 *The Little June Book: W.S. to E.V.M. June 5, 1909, CPP*, 509–16.

61 “two very large rooms”: WS to Elsie, 9 August 1909, *Letters*, 155.

61 “to walk violently”: WS to Elsie, 31 August 1909, *Letters*, 159.

61 “terribly insidious”: Ibid.

62 “Our house is under the mark”: postcard from WS to Elsie’s parents, with p.s. added by Elsie, 28 September 1909, *S&P*, 246.

63 “her that I love”: “A Valentine,” 1910, *CPP*, 517.

63 “looking at an old scene”: WS to Elsie, 7 June 1910, *CS*, 290.

64 “experience and a willingness”: WS to Elsie, 6 August 1911, *Letters*, 169.

65 “like wells of sweet water”: WS to Elsie, 6 August 1911, *Letters*, 169.

65 "About a year ago": 25 June 1912, journal entry, *Letters*, 172–73.

66 "a little collection of verses": WS to Elsie, 7 August 1913, *Letters*, 180.

CHAPTER 6. AN EXPLOSION IN A SHINGLE FACTORY: 1913–1916

69 "Just as my fingers": "Peter Quince at the Clavier," *CPP*, 72.

69 Wallace wrote her: WS to Elizabeth, 30 November 1912, *Letters*, 177.

70 "an uninteresting cemetery": WS to Elsie, 11 August 1914, *Letters*, 182.

71 "An odor from a star": *CPP*, 522.

71 Williams would later point out: WCW to William Van O'Connor, 22 August 1949, *HL*. Quoted in George S. Lensing, *Wallace Stevens: A Poet's Growth*, 105.

72 "As they sat": Donald Evans, from *Two Deaths in the Bronx*, Nicholas L. Brown, Philadelphia, p. 17. Among those to whom Evans dedicated the book were Stevens's friends Pitts Sanborn and Carl Van Vechten.

72 "What . . . has impelled me": *HR*, 393.

73 "blushing and holding": All Carl Van Vechten anecdotes in this chapter are from "Rogue Elephant in Porcelain," *Yale University Library Gazette* 38 (October 1963), 41–50.

77 "the thought of Eve": "Dolls," *CPP*, 517.

77 "Cy Est Pourtraicte": *CPP*, 17.

82 "I do not go to New York": Marcel Duchamp to Walter Pach, 27 April 1915, written from the Hotel-Americain, Paris, in *American Artists, Authors and Collectors: The Walter Pach Letters, 1906–1958*, Bennard B. Perlman, ed. (New York: State University of New York Press, 2003), 155.

83 "like sparrows": WS to Elsie, 3 August 1915, *Letters*, 185.

84 "Arensberg could afford": WCW, *Autobiography*, 136.

84 "I finally came": WCW, *Autobiography*, 173.

85 "a cheerful, healthy": WS to Barbara Church, 27 August 1953, *Letters*, 797.

85 "I had not myself noticed this": WS to Weldon Kees, 10 November 1954, *Letters*, 850.

85 "When we went there": Ibid.

85 "He seemed like a cat": WS to Harriet Monroe, 24 August 1922, *Letters*, 228.

86 "the best poetry written today": from *Poetry*'s editorial policy, printed in the first issue, 1912.

86 "a pack of brown cards": Harriet Monroe in *Chicago Daily Tribune*, 23 February 1913.

87 "cab-horse at the corner": This and the following poems were published in the November 1914 issue of *Poetry* under the collective title *Phases*.

87 "recondite, erudite": Harriet Monroe to WS, 27 January 1915, quoted in Lensing, *A Poet's Growth*, 247.

91 "thirty-five years old": contributor's note, *Poetry Magazine*, November 1915.

91 "the disuse into which things fall": WS to Harriet Monroe, 23 June 1915, *Letters*, 183.

92 "an erratic and inconsequential thinker": to Elsie, 29 August 1915, *Letters*, 186.

92 "the view of the Jersey meadows": Alfred Kreymborg, *Hidden New Jersey*, http://www.hiddennj.com/2013/08/creativity-in-palisades-art-colony-of.html.

93 "I was a little different": Marianne Moore, interview with Donald Hall, *The Paris Review*, no. 26 (Summer–Fall 1961).

93 "daring to omit capitals": WCW, *Autobiography*, 136.

94 There they assembled: see two photographs taken that day, the first of the men, the second of the women, in Paul Mariani, *William Carlos Williams: A New World Naked* (New York: Norton, 1990), 460.

94 "of anything of importance": WCW to WS, 8 June 1916, Stevens papers, HL.

94 "be handled in the usual broad": *Hartford Agent*, April 1916.

95 "You sign a lot of drafts": WS, "Surety and Fidelity Claims," *Eastern Underwriter*, 25 March 1938, reprinted in *CCP*, 796–97.

CHAPTER 7. THE EYE OF THE BLACKBIRD, 1916–1918

99 "The lilacs wither in the Carolinas": "In the Carolinas," *CCP*, 4.

99 "more inane": WS to Elsie, 23 April 1916, *Letters*, 193.

99 *Three Travelers*: *CPP*, 601–14.

99 "create a poetic atmosphere": WS to Harriet Monroe, 22 May 1916, *Letters*, 194.

100 "formative moment": Harriet Monroe, "Prize Announcement," *Poetry*, June 1916, p. 160.

100 "quite out of the question": WS to Alice Corbin, 1 June 1916, cf. Alan Filreis, "Voicing the Desert of Silence: Stevens' Letters to Alice Corbin Henderson," *Wallace Stevens Journal* 12, no. 1 (1988), 15.

100 "properly and sensitively": WS to Alice Corbin.

100 "So much water": WS to Harriet Monroe, 4 March 1920, *Letters*, 216.

100 "truth, not pose": Ibid.

101 "an Hotel for Homelovers": Highland Court Hotel, *'Round Hartford in an Hour* (Hartford, CT, 1920).

101 "abominably": *HR*, 381.

101 "become fervent": WCW to WS, 2 June 1916, *HL*.

101 "on winning 'ARRIET'S prize!": WCW to WS, 8 June 1916, HL.

102 "Eminent Vers Libriste": WS to Elsie, 19 June 1916, *Letters*, 196.

103 "It was very nice": WS to Elsie, 27 June 1916, *CS*, 357.

103 "a regular blowout": WS to Elsie, 26 January 1917, *CS*, 361.

104 "His intention was not to produce": WS to Bancel LaFarge, 17 June 1917, *Letters*, 200.

105 "in proving anything": WS to Harriet Monroe, 31 October 1917, *Letters*, 203.

105 "the purpose of this kind": Ralph Block, *New York Tribune*, 11 October 1917.

105 "would have been in saying": WS to Harriet Monroe, 31 October 1917, *Letters*, 203.

105 "been more interested in the theatre": WS to Ronald Lane Latimer, 5 November 1935, *Letters*, 290.

105 "returned to Milwaukee": WS to Ferdinand Reyher, 15 November 1917.

106 "I think, after all": WS to WCW, 9 April 1918, quoted in WCW "Prologue" to *Kora in Hell* (Boston: The Four Seas Company, 1920), 17.

110 "I've had the blooming horrors": WS to Harriet Monroe, 8 April 1918, *Letters*, 206.

111 "sleep in a big chair": WS to Elsie, Chicago, 15 March 1918, *S&P*, 369.

111 a trainload of "Negro" draftees: WS to Elsie, 1 May 1918, *Letters*, 209.

112 "To fight with his brothers": Cf. WS's *Lettres d'un Soldat (1914–1915)*, *CPP*, 538–45, which WS prefaces with this passage in French: *"avec des yeux dessillés."* Author's translation.

112 "If I should fall": *CPP*, 529.

114 "Dear Stevens": WCW to WS, 24–25 December 1918, Mariani, *A New World Naked*, 156.

114 "Shine alone": WCW, "El Hombre," *The Collected Poems of William Carlos Williams*, Vol. 1, p. 76.

CHAPTER 8. HARTFORD ON THE HARMONIUM: 1919–1921

115 "a substantial sum": WS to Elsie, 17 January 1919, *Letters*, 210.

116 "a heavenly change": Ibid., 211.

116 "dingy, grimy, and sooty": WS to Elsie, 5 May 1919, *CS*, 377.

117 "Barque of phosphor": *CPP*, 18.

118 "fifty with white hair": WS to Elsie, 12 May 1919, *CS*, 380.

118 A friend of hers: letter from Constance M. Hallock to Stevens family, *CS*, 382n.

119 "a job for a man": WS to Elsie, 1 June 1919, *CS*, 384.

119 "unselfishly and devotedly": WS to Elsie, 29 May 1919, *CS*, 383.

119 "as dismal as": WS to Harriet Monroe, 16[?] August 1919, *Letters*, 215.

120 "Here is one of thirteen ways": Carl Sandburg to WS, October 1919, *Letters*, 215n.

120 "The cows are down": WS to Harriet Monroe, 25 April 1920, *Letters*, 218.

121 "I have not had a poem in my head": WS to Elsie, 16 May 1920, *Letters*, 219.

122 "no more heft": WS to Carl Zigrosser, 13 March 1920, *Letters*, 219.

123 "just started something called *Contact*": 31 January 1921, *HR*, 387.

124 "nigger hucksters": WS to Alice Corbin, Henderson, April 11, 1921, Filreis, "Voicing," 15.

124 "Mow the grass": "Two at Norfolk," *CPP*, 92.

124 "to do about the damned Indians": WS to Alice Corbin Henderson, 11 April 1921, Filreis, *Voicing*, 15.

125 "Kreymborg described your build": Robert McAlmon to WS, July 21, 1921, *HL*.

126 "bicycling with Wyndham Lewis": 30 June 1921, *HR*, 395.

126 "aesthetic theory back of it": 13 May 1921, *HR*, 390.

126 "hideous ghosts": WS to Harriet Monroe, 29 October 1921, *Letters*, 222.

127 "Not less because": *CPP*, 51.

128 "put it in our pipes": 13 May 1921, *HR*, 392.

CHAPTER 9. THE COMEDIAN AS THE LETTER C: 1921–1923

129 "such a must": WS to Harriet Monroe, 29 October 1921, *Letters*, 223.

129 "the rudiments of tropics": *CPP*, 65.

130 "made life a bore": WS to Harriet Monroe, 21 December 1921, *Letters*, 224.

130 "determined to have": WS to Monroe Wheeler, 10 December, *Letters*, 224.

130 "I have just come back": WS to Hervey Allen, 5 May 1922, *Letters*, 226.

131 "a very unlady-like thing to do": WS, *From the Journal of Crispin*, Louis L. Martz, *Wallace Stevens: A Celebration*, eds. Frank Doggett and Robert Buttel (Princeton University Press, 1980), 4.

131 "eye most apt": *CCP*, 22–37.

133 "a cypher for Crispin": WS to Hi Simons, 12 January 1940, *Letters*, 351.

133 "a pretty hard thing": WS to Hi Simons, 12 January 1940, *Letters*, 350.

134 "drinking beer and singing": Ibid., 352.

141 a postcard of a coconut tree: WS to Elsie, 8 January 1922, *CS*, 395.

141 "We must come together": WS to Elsie, 10 January 1922, on stationery of the Florida East Coast Hotel Company Flagler System, Long Key Fishing Camp, *CS*, 397.

142 "Now that trip to Florida": 2 February 1922, *HR*, 398.

142 "My poems seem so simple": WS to Alice Corbin Henderson, 27 March 1922, Cf. Alan Filreis, "Voicing the Desert of Silence: Stevens' Letters to Alice Corbin Henderson," *Wallace Stevens Journal* 12.1 (Spring 1988), p. 16.

144 "greatest of living American poets": Yvor Winters, in his review of E. A. Robinson, *Poetry*, February 1922, 287.

144 "I pride myself": April 1922, *HR*, 401.

144 "to be persnickety": WS to Gilbert Seldes, 5 May 1922, *Letters*, 227.

145 "the roller of big cigars": *CPP*, 50.

146 "frightfully uncertain": WS to Carl Van Vechten, 17 July 1922, *Letters*, 228.

146 "Alfred did desire to examine": Van Vechten, *Porcelain*, 47.

147 "A few weeks ago": WS to Harriet Monroe, 24 August 1922, *Letters*, 228.

147 "although we were both": Ibid.

147 "About the Crispin poem": WS to Harriet Monroe, 23 September 1922, *Letters*, 229.

148 "Gathering together the things": WS to Harriet Monroe, 28 October 1922, *Letters*, 231.

149 "an awful job to typewrite": WS to Carl Van Vechten, 18 November 1922, *Letters*, 232.

149 "Knopf has my book": WS to Harriet Monroe, 21 December 1922, *Letters*, 232.

149 "I do not remember": Van Vechten, *Porcelain*, 49–50.

149 "pure nonsense": WS to Elsie, 24 January 1923, *CS*, 398.

150 "a matter of $700": WS to Elsie, 26 January 1923, *CS*, 399.

150 "out at sea fishing": WS to Elsie, 29 January 1923, *CS*, 400.

150 "Nothing but the most gorgeous weather": WS to Elsie, 2 February 1923, *CS*, 403.

151 "a nigger policeman": WS to Elsie, 4 February 1923, *Letters*, 234.

151 "Bellisimo, pomposo": "The Revolutionists Stop for Orangeade," *CPP*, 80.

152 Fancy having your name: WS to Elsie, 11 February 1923, *Letters*, 236.

153 "THE GRAND POEM": WS to Alfred Knopf, *Letters*, 237.

153 "USE HARMONIUM": WS to Alfred Knopf, 18 May 1923, *Letters*, 238.

CHAPTER 10. A BABY AMONG US: 1923–1934

155 at $2 a copy: Ninety years after its publication, a signed first edition of *Harmonium* sells for $18,500.

155 "accoucheur": WS to Carl Van Vechten, 11 September 1923, *Letters*, 241.

155 "first (and, no doubt, only) book": WS to Alice Henderson, September 9, 1923. It was his last letter to her.

156 "The sea as flat and still": Elsie's journal entry, 28 October 1923.

156 "Cool this morning": Elsie's journal entry, 1 November 1923.

156 Cf. George S. Lensing, "Mrs. Wallace Stevens's *Sea Voyage* and "Sea Surface Fall of Clouds," *American Poetry* 3, no. 3 (Spring 1986), 76–84.

157 "Red Loves Kit": *CPP*, 556–57.

159 "You do not understand": *CPP*, 554–60.

161 "At the moment I have nothing": WS to Monroe Wheeler, 11 December 1924, *Letters*, 242.

161 "one or two things": WS to Harriet Monroe, undated (July 1925), *Letters*, 243.

161 "fictitious reality": John Gould Fletcher, "The Revival of Aestheticism," *Freeman*, 10 December 1923.

162 "somewhat misanthropic": WCW to Marianne Moore, 27 December 1923, WCW, *Selected Letters*, 57.

162 "out of the blue": WCW, *Autobiography*, 174.

162 "There is the love of magnificence": Marianne Moore, "Well-Moused, Lion," *Dial*, January 1924.

163 "The impeccability of the dandy": Gorham Munson, "The Dandyism of Wallace Stevens," *Dial*, November 1925.

164 "continually heavy and noisy": Holly Stevens, *Letters*, 242.

164 "Holly grows prettier": WS to Harriet Monroe, 12 January 1925, *Letters*, 244.

164 "Though Valentine brings love": February 1925, *CPP*, 557.

165 "seen very few litérateurs": WS to WCW, 14 October 1925, *Letters*, 245.

165 "evolve a mainland": WS to Marianne Moore, 19 November 1925, *Letters*, 246.

165 "Carlos the Fortunate": WS to Marianne Moore, 3 December 1926, *Letters*, 248.

165 "its foster-children": WS to WCW, 15 January 1927, *Letters*, 249.

165 "most curious about it": WS to Harriet Monroe, 3 February 1926, *Letters*, 246.

166 Princess Wamsutta Percale: Holly Stevens, "Bits of Remembered Time," *Southern Review*, Summer 1971, 651.

166 "a glorious trip": WS to Harriet Monroe, 3 February 1926, *Letters*, 247.

167 "Believe me, signor": WS to WCW, 7 September 1927, Huntington Library, *Brazeau*, 245.

167 "Undecipherable letter": WCW to Ezra Pound, 4 October 1927, *Brazeau*, 244.

167 "converting a piece of mysticism": WS to L. W. Payne, 31 March 1928, *Letters*, 250.

168 "A purple woman": *CPP*, 558.

168 "No doubt you know": cited in *Poetry*, August 1928, along with Monroe's response.

168 "Thanks for the pleasant letter": WS to Louis Untermeyer, 11 June 1929, *Letters*, 252.

169 "along the edges": *CPP*, 558.

169 "lashed the palms": WS to James A. Powers, 19 February 1930, *Letters*, 258.

169 "The exceeding brightness": Lincoln, *CPP*, 108.

171 "nothing short of a coup d'état": WS to Lincoln Kirstein, 10 April 1931, *Letters*, 261.

171 "Whatever else I do": WS to Harriet Monroe, 5 August 1931, *Letters*, 262.

171 "Dear Louis Untermeyer": Hart Crane to Louis Untermeyer, 24 July 1931, *O My Land, My Friends: The Selected Letters of Hart Crane*, ed. Langdon Hammer and Brom Weber (New York: Four Walls, Eight Windows, 1997), 478.

172 "wise parents": Kingswood Oxford School History, Kingswood oxford.org.

172 "was growing up": Anthony Sigmans, *Brazeau*, 80.

172 "Is there not fundamentally": Gorham B. Munson, "The Dandyism of Wallace Stevens," *Dial*, 79, (November 1925), reprinted in Brown and Haller, *The Achievement of Wallace Stevens*, 41–45.

174 "The only thing of any interest": WS to Jim Powers, 27 December 1932, *Letters*, 263.

174 "You say that spite": "Good Man, Bad Woman," *CPP*, 558.

175 "a deliberately commonplace costume": WS to William Rose Benét, 6 January 1933, *Letters*, 263.

175 "dances, feasts, parades en masque": WS to Holly Stevens, February 1933, *Letters*, 264.

176 "unpublished manuscript": WS to Morton Zabel, 13 March 1933, *Letters*, 265.

176 "Since Stevens has passed now safely": Morton Zabel, "The Harmonium of Wallace Stevens," *Poetry* 39 (December 1931), 148, reprinted in Brown and Haller, *The Achievement of Wallace Stevens.*

176 "uncommon in English poetry": R. P. Blackmur, "Examples of Wallace Stevens," *Hound & Horn* 5 (Winter 1932), reprinted in R. P. Blackmur *Language as Gesture: Essays in Poetry* (Harcourt Brace, 1952), and later in Blackmur, *The Double Agent: Essays in Craft* (Harcourt Brace, 1935). Also in Brown and Haller, *The Achievement of Wallace Stevens*, 52–80.

177 "twenty-five pages to say": WS to José Rodríguez Feo, 26 January 1945, *Letters*, 484.

177 "It seems to be": WS to Jim Powers, 12 May 1933, *Letters*, 266.

179 "Melodious skeletons": "A Fish-Scale Sunrise," *CPP*, 130.

180 "spent his life in rejecting": preface, reprinted in *CPP*, 768–71.

180 "sick of the constant aping": WCW to Horace Gregory, undated, 1948, WCW, *Selected Letters*, 265.

181 “elaborate bit of perversity”: WS to Harriet Monroe, 12 February 1934, *Letters*, 267.

181 “holiday-makers”: WS to Elsie, 23 February 1934, *Letters*, 268.

182 “if the Communists”: WS to Jim Powers, 23 March 1934, *Letters*, 269.

182 “wildly needed”: WS to Martin Jay, June 1933 *Letters*, 256.

182 “with his best work”: Morton Zabel, “Recent Magazines,” *Poetry* 45 (December 1934), 176.

183 “impersonal to the point”: WS to Alcestis Press, 8 October 1934, *Letters*, 257.

183 “every day or night or both”: WS to Ronald Latimer, 28 November 1934, *Letters*, 271.

183 “Dear James Albert Mark”: Willard Maas to Ronald Latimer, December 1934, *Letters*, 270.

183 “He was a bisexual avant-gardist”: Alan Filreis, http://afilreis.blogspot.com/2009/06/soul-collected.html.

184 “Dear Bynner”: WS to Witter Bynner, 6 April 1934, *Letters*, 270.

184 “Dear Sherlock Holmes”: WS to WCW, 13 May 1936, *Letters*, 311.

CHAPTER 11. THE IDEA OF ORDER AT KEY WEST: 1934–1936

188 “Poet, be seated”: *CPP*, 107.

190 “behold the sublime”: *CPP*, 106–7.

190 “If you do not like these”: WS to Morton Zabel, 6 December 1934, *Letters*, 272.

191 For a young: “Turmoil in the Middle Ground,” *New Masses*, 1 October 1935, 41–42.

191 “I explained”: Arthur Powell, memoir, quoted in *Brazeau*, 100–101.

191 “In the far South”: *CPP*, 121.

193 “Yesterday I put on ear muffs”: WS to Ronald Latimer, 10 December 1934, *Letters*, 272.

194 “cheerless to anyone”: Ibid.

194 “I sit down every evening”: WS to Ronald Latimer, 8 January 1935, *Letters*, 273.

194 “The cold wife”: WS to Ronald Latimer, January 1935(?), *Letters*, 274.

195 "Many thanks for everything": WS to Philip S. May, 21 February 1935, *Letters*, 274.

195 "walked up the boulevard": WS to Elsie, 25 February 1935, *Letters*, 275.

195 "The cocktail party": WS to Harriet Monroe, 13 March 1935, *Letters*, 278.

196 "look up such things": WS to Robert Frost, 4 March 1935, *Letters*, 275.

196 "the prettiest kind of stand-off": Robert Frost to WS, 28 July 1935, Dartmouth College Library, quoted in Jay Parini, *Robert Frost: A Life*, 292.

196 "an abridgment": WS to Ronald Latimer, 12 March 1935, *Letters*, 277.

197 "It is the word": *CPP*, 99.

198 "not only a complete disintegrator": WS to T. C. Wilson, 25 March 1935, *Letters*, 278.

198 "published in Atlanta": WS to T. C. Wilson, 1 July 1935, *Letters*, 281.

198 "unaffected, witty": "A Poet That Matters," *Life and Letters Today* 13 (December 1935), 61–65, *CPP*, 775–80.

199 "merely finding myself in that *milieu*": WS to Ronald Latimer, 21 November 1935, *Letters*, 296.

199 "To many readers": Stanley Burnshaw, "Turmoil in the Middle Ground," *New Masses* 17 (October 1, 1935), 41–42.

200 "I hope I am headed left": WS to Ronald Latimer, 9 October 1935, *Letters*, 286.

202 "I took a look at *Ideas of Order*": WS to Ronald Latimer, 15 November 1935, *Letters*, 293.

202 "We give our good qualities": WS to Ronald Latimer, 21 November 1935, *Letters*, 295.

203 "life without poetry": WS to Ronald Latimer, 10 December 1935, *Letters*, 299.

204 was never Teutonic: WS to Ronald Latimer, 19 December 1935, *Letters*, 302–3.

205 put out of the question: WS to Phil May, 10 January 1936, *Letters*, 307.

205 "hell raising": WS to Phil May, 27 January 1936, *Letters*, 307.

206 *The Ordeals of Ida*: WS to Ronald Latimer, 9 March 1936, *Letters*, 309.

206 Probably on the evening: Hemingway reported the incident in a draft letter to Sara Murphy in late February 1936. Cf. *Selected Letters* (1917–1961), ed. Carlos Baker, 438–40.

207 as Hemingway would remember it: Ernest Hemingway to Sara Murphy, Key West, ca. 27 February 1936, Carlos Baker, ed., *Hemingway Selected Letters, 1917–1961* (New York: Scribner's, 1981), 438–40.

208 "squiring a damsel": WS to Phil May, *Letters*, 308.

208 "gone up to Pirates Cove": Hemingway to Sara Murphy, *Hemingway Selected Letters, 1917–1961*, 439.

209 "A tramp thawing out": WCW, "The Sun Bathers" (1934), *The Collected Poems of William Carlos Williams*, eds., A. Walton Litz and Christopher MacGowan, New Directions, vol. 1, 371.

210 "Most people don't think of Hemingway": WS to Henry Church, 2 July 1942, *Letters*, 410.

211 "violently affective": WS to Samuel French Morse, 27 May 1943, *Letters*.

212 "go on, high ship": *CPP*, 97–98.

CHAPTER 12. THE MAN WITH THE BLUE GUITAR: 1936–1937

213 "My expedition is over": WS to May, 9 March 1936, *Letters*, 308.

214 "There are people who think": WS to Ronald Latimer, 17 March 1936, *Letters*, 309.

214 "a stuffed goldfinch": Ibid.

214 "in spite of the owlishness": WS to Ronald Latimer, 16 May 1936, *Letters*, 311.

214 "It is hard to realize": WS to Morton Zabel, 6 October 1936, *Letters*, 312.

214 "into contact with": "In Memory of Harriet Monroe," *Poetry*, December 1936, *CPP*, 780–81.

215 "at a time when politics": Ruth Lechlitner, *New York Herald-Tribune*, 6 December 1936, 40.

215 "burned down": WS to Ronald Latimer, 7 December 1936, *Letters*, 313.

215 The real problem with Stevens: "The Violent Mind," Ben Belitt, *Nation* 143 (12 December 1936), 708.

215 Stevens wrote Belitt: WS to Ben Belitt, 12 December 1936, *Letters*, 314.

215 "the way one must look forward": WS to Ronald Latimer, 7 December 1936, *Letters*, 313.

215 "the transaction between reality": "The Irrational Element in Poetry," *CPP*, 781–92.

217 "in the midst of a circle of trees": "Owl's Clover," *CPP*, 567–91.

218 "white forelegs taut": Ibid.

220 "armed, gloriously": From "The Greenest Continent," *Owl's Clover, CPP*, 575–81.

221 "The trees": *CPP*, 581–86.

222 "During the winter": WS to Ronald Latimer, 17 March 1937, *Letters*, 316.

223 "rising in the heat": "The Men That Are Falling," *CPP*, 177.

228 "Copernicus, Columbus": WS to Renato Poggioli, 12 July 1953, *Letters*, 790.

228 "I imagine that I chose": WS to Renato Poggioli, 25 June 1953, *Letters*, 783.

229 "A good many years ago": WS to Ronald Latimer, 6 May 1937, *Letters*, 320.

230 "to have someone to knock round with": WS to Jim Powers, 15 June 1937, *Letters*, 321.

231 "difficult for anyone": WS to Leonard C. van Geyzel, 31 December 1937, *Letters*, 327.

231 "a horror of poetry pretending": WS to Ronald Latimer, 16 September 1937, *Letters*, 326.

231 "The story is that Stevens": WCW, "On Wallace Stevens," *New Republic*, November 17, 1937, 50.

CHAPTER 13. THE NOBLE RIDER AND THE SOUND OF WORDS: 1938–1941

234 "shilly-shallying": WS to Ronald Latimer, 21 January 1938, *Letters*, 329.

234 "an affair of weekends": WS to Ronald Latimer, 28 June 1938, *Letters*, 333.

235 "Day creeps down": *CPP*, 184–86.

237 "the silence was": *CPP*, 186.

237 "I suppose": *CPP*, 187.

237 "We are at a time of the year": WS to Leonard van Geyzel, 12 April 1939, *Letters*, 337.

238 "in restoring to the imagination": WS to Henry Church, 1 June 1939, *Letters*, 340.

238 As much as: WS to Allen Tate, 10 May 1939, *Letters*, 339.

238 "It depresses me to think": WS to Pitts Sanborn, 26 June 1939, *Letters*, 341.

239 "the primordial importance": WS to Hi Simons, 29 December 1939, *Letters*, 346.

239 "tried to change": Hi Simons, " 'The Comedian as the Letter C': Its Sense and Significance," *Southern Review* 5 (Winter 1940), reprinted in Brown and Haller, *The Achievement of Wallace Stevens*, 97–113.

240 "one happened to be playing checkers": WS to Hi Simons, 29 December 1939, *Letters*, 346.

240 "A music more": *CPP*, 212.

242 he shared the nation's feeling: WS to Leonard van Geyzel, 20 September 1939, *Letters*, 342.

242 "a habit of mind": WS to Hi Simons, 9 January 1939, *Letters*, 348.

242 "sovereign sight": *CPP*, 103.

243 from "romanticism to realism, to fatalism": WS to Hi Simons, 12 January 1940, *Letters*, 350.

244 "furiously literary": WS to Hi Simons, 30 April 1940, *Letters*, 355.

244 "too academic": This exchange was first reported by Lawrence Thompson in *Robert Frost: The Later Years*, Lawrence Thompson and R. H. Winnick (New York: Holt, Rinehart and Winston, 1976), 61.

245 That May: WS to Leonard van Geyzel, 24 May 1940, *Letters*, 355–56.

245 "My God, Elizabeth": Jane MacFarland Wilson, *Brazeau*, 267.

245 "a little woman": Anna May Stevens, *Brazeau*, 278.

246 "This has not been a good summer": WS to Henry Church, 23 August 1940, *Letters*, 364.

246 “difficulty of imposing”: WS to Hi Simons, 28 August 1940, *Letters*, 369.

246 “produce a poem equivalent to”: WS to Hi Simons, 29 August 1940, *Letters*, 371–72.

247 “The prologues”: *CPP*, 226–27.

249 “that in their presence”: WS to Hi Simons, 30 August 1940, *Letters*, 373.

249 “brimming white in a perspective of trees”: Ibid.

249 “the essential poets”: WS to Henry Church, 15 October 1940, *Letters*, 376.

249 “attempt to disclose the truth”: WS to Henry Church, 27 December 1940, *Letters*, 383.

250 “trace the idea of nobility”: WS to Henry Church, 30 January 1941, *Letters*, 386.

250 If Stevens’s talk: *CPP*, 643.

254 “what a lot of serious reading”: WS to Hi Simons, 8 July 1941, *Letters*, 392.

254 “very nice piece”: a story Elias Mengel recalled years later, *Brazeau*, 286. Richard Mervin Bissell, president of the Hartford, died of coronary obtrusion 18 July 1941 at the age of seventy-nine. The VP who popped his head in the door of Stevens’s office was Wilson Jainsen, and the antagonism between Jainsen and Stevens continued until Stevens’s death. A fellow officer at the Hartford, the circumspect E. A. Cowrie, admitted that Jainsen, who bracketed more and more of Stevens’s responsibilities after Stevens turned seventy, was “a bit disgusted with [Stevens] at times” because he found Stevens too independent. But though Stevens could be difficult to work with, Cowrie added, “he was affable a great deal of the time” (*Brazeau*, 292).

254 “I love to hear from you”: WS to Henry Church, 28 January 1942, *Letters*, 401.

CHAPTER 14. THE SON RESTORES THE FATHER: 1941–1945

256 “figures in an idyll”: undated typescript in Huntington Library, quoted in *Brazeau*, 270.

257 "I felt like a perfect ninny": Holly Stevens, "Bits of Remembered Time," *Southern Review*, July 1971, 656.

257 "For a long time": Holly Stevens to WS, 30 September 1942, *HL*, quoted in *Brazeau*, 283–84.

257 "For my own part": WS to Holly Stevens, 7 October 1942, *Letters*, 422.

258 "You may remember": WS to Ruth Wheeler, 23 October 1942, *Letters*, 423.

259 "a source of unfailing happiness": WS to Holly Stevens, 26 October 1942, *Letters*, 426.

259 "the faintest idea": WS to his sister Elizabeth, 2 October 1942, *Letters*, 421.

260 "She was positively radiant": Jane MacFarland Wilson, *Brazeau*, 282.

260 "You lost your brother": WS to Henry Church, 2 March 1943, *Letters*, 440.

261 "We walked along the Parkway": Jane MacFarland Wilson, *Brazeau*, 269.

261 she felt his strong disapproval: Jane MacFarland Wilson, *Brazeau*, 282.

262 "Everyone in the family": WS to John Sauer, 25 October 1944, *Brazeau*, 285.

262 "Who could ever": WS to Emma Jobbins, 19 February 1945, *Brazeau*, 270.

262 "after muddling round": WS to W. N. P. Dailey, 16 May 1945, *Letters*, 499.

262 "horse thieves": John Sauer, *Brazeau*, 275.

262 "Recitation after Dinner": renamed "Tradition," *CPP*, 595.

263 "Outside of Wedlock": *CPP*, 592.

264 "substitute for the reading": WS to John Sauer, 3 October 1944, *Brazeau*, 273.

265 "structure of ideas": "The Bed of Old John Zeller," *CPP*, 287.

265 "to have been both poor": WS to Howard Althouse, 9 August 1944, *Letters*, 470.

265 "Unlike the Puritans": WS to Lila James Roney, 4 October 1943, *Brazeau*, 274.

266 "We were with him": Anna May Stevens, *Brazeau*, 279.

266 "When one has": WS to Arthur Powell, 12 December 1946, *Brazeau*, 285.

266 "When a poet": WS to Hi Simons, 18 February 1942, *Letters*, 402.

267 "On an Old Horn," *CPP*, 210.

267 "He may not": WS to Hi Simons, 18 February 1942, *Letters*, 403.

267 "the bird kept": *CPP*, 216.

268 "the order of the spirit": WS to Hi Simons, 18 February 1942, *Letters*, 403.

268 "They are building a new house": WS to Barbara Church, 27 February 1942, *Letters*, 404.

268 "Your package": WS to Katharine Frazier, 30 December 1941, *Letters*, 397.

269 "Weather by Franz Hals": *Notes toward a Supreme Fiction*, "It Must Be Abstract," VI, *CCP*, 333.

270 "Dear Miss Frazier": WS to Katharina Frazier, 19 May 1942, *Letters*, 407.

270 "a way of saying in a scrawl": WS to Henry Church, 11 June 1942, *Letters*, 409.

270 "the merit of delineating": WS to Henry Church, 8 September 1942, *Letters*, 418.

271 "perky and pensive": Frank Jones, "The Sorcerer as Elegist," *Nation*, 7 November 1942, 488.

272 "His intricately subtle mind": Elizabeth Drew, "First Person Singular," *Atlantic Monthly*, November 1942.

272 "with his damned hoobla": WS to Hi Simons, 12 January 1943, *Letters*, 433.

275 "reached a point": WS to Henry Church, 8 December 1942, *Letters*, 430.

276 In July 1942: WS to Harvey Breit, 27 July 1942, *Letters*, 412.

276 "Has the mystery man": Charles Henri Ford, "Verlaine in Hartford," *View Magazine*, September 1940, I, 1.

278 "I like to hear you say 'Pooh!' ": WS to José Rodríguez Feo, 20 June 1945, *Letters*, 505.

278 If only Americans: WS to Harvey Breit, 29 July 1942, *Letters*, 413–15.

279 "The belief in poetry": WS to Henry Church, 30 March 1943, *Letters*, 446.

279 would give a paper: WS to Jean Wahl, 9 April 1943, *Letters*, 447.

280 "It appears": "The Figure of the Youth as Virile Poet," *CPP* 666–85.

283 "Wallace Stevens is beyond fathoming": Marianne Moore to WCW, 12 November 1944, 453.

283 "A man with your [last] name": WS to Theodore Weiss, 14 November 1944, *Letters*, 476.

284 "My father wasn't": WS to Jane MacFarland, 13 September 1943, *Letters*, 454.

CHAPTER 15. FAREWELL TO AN IDEA: 1944–1947

285 "moral difficulties": John Crowe Ransom, "Artists, Soldiers, Positivists," *Kenyon Review*, Spring 1944.

286 "What particularly interested me": WS to John Crowe Ransom, 17 June 1944, *Letters*, 468.

286 "I hope you will like it": WS to John Crowe Ransom, 28 July 1944, *Letters*, 469.

286 "I think of something": WS to Henry Church, 31 August 1944, *Letters*, 472.

287 "writing letters home": *Esthétique du Mal, CPP*, 277–87.

290 has heard the commotion: Manning Heard, *Brazeau*, 251.

290 "very glad for Holly's happiness": *Brazeau*, 284n.

291 "no longer anything": WS to Oscar Williams, 4 December 1944, *Letters*, 479.

291 "What a curious world": WS to Henri Amiot, 11 December 1944, *Letters*, 480.

292 "I had hoped that": WS to Paule Vidal, 20 March 1945, *Letters*, 491.

292 "You ask about Truman": WS to Paule Vidal, 25 April 1946, *Letters*, 528.

292 "a taste for Braque": WS to Paule Vidal, 23 January 1947, *Letters*, 545.

292 "happy little drawings": WS to José Rodríguez Feo, 4 January 1945, *Letters*, 481.

293 "as bright and cheerful": WS to José Rodríguez Feo, 26 January 1945, *Letters*, 483.

293 "secretaries of the moon": "A Word with José Rodríguez-Feo," *CPP*, 292.

293 "from the Catholic point of view": WS to José Rodríguez Feo, 19 March 1945, *Letters*, 491.

294 "time passed": WS to Helen Head Simons, 13 April 1945, *Letters*, 497.

294 "What bothers me": WS to James Guthrie, 25 June 1945, *Letters*, 506.

295 "benumbing effect of the war": WS to Henry Church, 19 July 1945, *Letters*, 507.

295 "territorial or material gain": Sumner Welles, "Vision of a World at Peace," *Virginia Quarterly Review*, Autumn 1945.

295 "Description without Place": *CPP*, 296–302. The poem first appeared in *Sewanee Review*, Autumn 1945.

296 "If God made a progress": WS to Henry Church, 18 May 1943, *Letters*, 448.

297 "an expectation": "Description Without Place," *CPP*, 296–302.

297 "A Place (Any Place) to Transcend All Places": *Collected Poems of William Carlos Williams*, vol. 2, 163–66, originally published in *Kenyon Review*, Winter 1946.

298 "lamb-like urban talent": WCW to Marianne Moore, 7 November 1944, *Selected Letters*, 233.

298 Williams had written: WCW to James Laughlin, 24 January 1943, *Selected Letters*, 83.

298 "You know": WCW to WS, 21 July 1944, *Selected Letters*, 229.

299 "generate an assembly": WCW to WS, 24 July 1944, *Selected Letters*, 230.

299 "What is going on": WS to James Guthrie, 18 October 1945, *Letters*, 515.

299 "to be quoted": WS to Charles Norman, 9 November 1945, *Letters*, 516.

300 "A friend": WS to Theodore Weiss, 5 September 1947, *Letters*, 565.

300 "The misery of Europe": WS to José Rodríguez Feo, 5 March 1946, *Letters*, 525.

300 "we never understand": WS to Rolf Fielde, 16 April 1946, *Letters*, 526.

300 "the inaccessible jewel": WS to Henry Church, 21 January 1946, *Letters*, 521.

301 "Now" the poem: "Credences of Summer," *CPP*, 323–26.

304 "New York seems to go": WS to Henry Church, 6 August 1946, *Letters*, 531.

305 "for some fifteen or twenty years": "About One of Marianne Moore's Poems," *Quarterly Review of Literature*, Summer 1948, *CPP*, 703.

305 "of both the visible": WS, "About One of Marianne Moore's Poems," *CPP*, 704.

306 "in the exact form": WS to Victor Hammer, 11 December 1946, *Letters*, 541.

306 "I write poetry": WS to Hi Simons, 6 September 1944, *Letters*, 473.

306 That December he wrote Feo again: WS to José Rodríguez Feo, 10 December 1946, *Letters*, 540.

306 "At San Miguel de los Baños": "Attempt to Discover Life," *CPP*, 320.

307 "infallible Dr.": WS to Henry Church, 14 December 1946, *Letters*, 542.

307 "Taking a new": WS to José Rodríguez Feo, 19 December 1946, *Letters*, 543.

307 one of the significant components: "Three Academic Pieces," *CPP*, 686–98.

309 "I saw a photograph": WS to Henry Church, 19 March 1947, *Letters*, 550.

310 "put in a dictaphone system": WS to Karl Shapiro, 6 March 1947, *Letters*, 551.

310 "so completely crushed": WS to Barbara Church, 9 April 1947, *Letters*, 552.

310 "Two forms": *CPP*, 371–75.

311 "an exquisite happiness": WS to Barbara Church, June 1947, *Letters*, 558.

311 "who lived in a certain luxury": WS to Barbara Church, 26 November 1947, *Letters*, 570.

312 "to exhibit the fecundity": F. O. Matthiessen, "Wallace Stevens at 67," *New York Times*, 20 April 1947.

312 "This is where": *CPP*, 355–63.

CHAPTER 16. THE EYE'S PLAIN VERSION: 1948–1949

319 There were those: *CPP*, 365.

319 "to follow very attentively": WS to Barbara Church, 7 January 1948, *Letters*, 573.

321 "Effects of Analogy": *CPP*, 706–23.

321 "After I have walked home": WS to José Rodríguez Feo, 17 February 1948, *Letters*, 579.

322 "The other day I read": WS to Allen Tate, 6 April 1948, *Letters*, 583.

323 "Either the cocktails were too good": WS to Allen Tate, 31 March 1949, *Letters*, 634.

323 "relaxed, easy": *Brazeau*, 173–74.

323 "another bugaboo": WS to Norman Holmes Pearson, 6 February 1951, *Letters*, 706.

324 "I also said": WS to Barbara Church, 29 April 1948, *Letters*, 592.

324 "memorabilia of someone": WS to Thomas McGreevy, 6 May 1948, *Letters*, 596.

324 "at its worst in England": WS to Thomas McGreevy, 12 May 1948, *Letters*, 597.

324 "I have a new correspondent": WS to José Rodríguez Feo, 14 June 1948, *Letters*, 598.

324 "not one of those frightful": WS to Barbara Church, 19 August 1948, *Letters*, 609.

325 "would come to one": WS to José Rodríguez Feo, 14 June 1948, *Letters*, 599.

325 "very serious thing to say": WS to Thomas McGreevy, 15 June 1948, *Letters*, 600.

325 "without the interventions": WS to Barbara Church, 22 June 1948, *Letters*, 601.

325 "rather be in that church": Ibid.

325 "each morning to paint": WS to Barbara Church, 19 August 1948, *Letters*, 610.

326 "Nuns Painting Water-Lilies": *CPP*, 456.

326 "Sweet peas I love": WS to Wilson Taylor, 23 June 1948, *Letters*, 603.

326 "It would not surprise me": WS to Thomas McGreevy, 25 August 1948, *Letters*, 611.

328 "at least making notes": WS to Norman Holmes Pearson, 12 July 1948, *Letters*, 605.

328 "various professors": WS to Barbara Church, 7 September 1948, *Letters*, 613.

328 "the mistress of error": "Imagination as Value," *CPP*, 724–39.

329 make "any convent": Ibid.

330 "One goes to the Canoe Club": WS to José Rodríguez Feo, 25 October 1948, *Letters*, 621.

331 "of two minds": WS to Paule Vidal, 9 November 1948, *Letters*, 623.

331 "when one has more elbows": WS to Barbara Church, 25 November 1949, *Letters*, 627.

332 "Somehow modern art": WS to Thomas McGreevy, 27 March 1949, *Letters*, 630.

332 "When I was in New York": WS to Barbara Church, 21 June 1949, *Letters*, 639.

333 "in quite normal time": WS to Barbara Church, 21 June 1949, *Letters*, 638–40.

333 "We seem to be coming closer": WS to Barbara Church, 23 August 1949, *Letters*, 646.

333 "I am glad that you share": WS to Paule Vidal, 9 March 1949, *Letters*, 637.

333 "so much cooler": WS to Paule Vidal, 30 September 1949, *Letters*, 649.

333 "the Venetian glass bowl": WS to Paule Vidal, 5 October 1949, *Letters*, 650.

334 "I am the angel": *CPP*, 423.

334 "Every fresh beginning": WS to Barbara Church, 21 June 1949, *Letters*, 639.

CHAPTER 17. THE OBSCURITY OF AN ORDER: 1950–1951

343 "the longest and dreariest month": WS to Barbara Church, 1 February 1950, *Letters*, 663.

343 "a winter of mist": WS to Thomas McGreevy, 17 February 1950, *Letters*, 668.

344 "a Catholic spirit": WS to Barbara Church, 23 March 1950, *Letters*, 671.

345 "so many tall black-haired girls": WS to Thomas McGreevy, 1 June 1950, *Letters*, 680.

345 "sustained by a habit": WS to Barbara Church, 13 June 1950, *Letters*, 682.

345 "I suppose that in reality": WS to Eleanor Stevens Sauer, 4 April 1950, *Letters*, 674.

346 "intelligent and hard-working": WS to José Rodríguez Feo, 24 April 1950, *Letters*, 676.

346 "set the Hudson River on fire": WS to Barbara Church, 13 June 1950, *Letters*, 683.

346 "so many that we have known": WS to Barbara Church, 27 April 1950, *Letters*, 677.

347 "one of the colored boys": WS to Barbara Church, 13 June 1950, *Letters*, 682.

347 "he was the king": Naaman Corn, *Brazeau*, 248.

347 "that everything": WS to Barbara Church, 17 July 1950, *Letters*, 684.

348 "provided one isolates oneself": Ibid.

348 "Another sunlight": "As at a Theatre," *CPP*, 455.

348 "a particularly pleasant summer": WS to José Rodríguez Feo, 15 August 1950, *Letters*, 687.

348 "A year ago": WS to Emma Stevens Jobbins, 11 October 1950, *Letters*, 693.

349 "The Relations between Poetry and Painting": *CPP*, 740–51.

350 "feather-headed": Marianne Moore to Elizabeth Bishop, 26 January 1951, Bonnie Costello, ed., *The Selected Letters of Marianne Moore* (New York: Knopf, 1997), 484.

351 "There is no life": *CPP*, 255–57.

351 "I had a perfect time": Marianne Moore to Elizabeth Bishop, 26 January 1951, *Selected Letters of Marianne Moore*, 484–85.

351 "I had not the slightest expectation": WS to Alfred Knopf, 23 February 1951, *Letters*, 708.

351 "I thought it best": WS to Barbara Church, 9 March 1951, *Letters*, 709.

352 "well-disposed toward": Ibid.

352 "There has been entirely": WS to Sr. M. Bernetta Quinn, 26 March 1951, *Letters*, 710.

353 "Well," he said, "we didn't need": Theodore Weiss, "Lunching with Hoon: Wallace Stevens," *American Poetry Review* 7, no. 5 (1978), 43; Paul Mariani, *William Carlos Williams: A New World Naked* (New York: Norton, 1990), 630.

353 "saddened and disturbed everyone": WS to WCW, 23 April 1951, *Letters*, 716.

353 "for though I know": WCW to WS, 25 April 1951, John Thirlwall, ed., *The Selected Letters of William Carlos Williams* (New York: New Directions, 1957), 295.

353 "One grows accustomed": WS to Theodore Weiss, 5 April 1951, *Letters*, 712.

354 "to do any writing now": WS to Thomas McGreevy, 13 April 1951, *Letters*, 714.

354 "Two or Three Ideas," Mount Holyoke College, 28 April 1951, *CCP*, 839–50.

355 "tremendous blow-out": WS to Barbara Church, 25 June 1951, *Letters*, 720.

355 "for the hell of it": WS to Eleanor Stevens Sauer, 7 September 1951, *Letters*, 726.

356 "double-chocolate ice cream": WS to Barbara Church, 2 October 1951, *Letters*, 729.

356 "vacations as they are practiced": WS to Thomas McGreevy, 10 September 1951, *Letters*, 727.

356 "got no farther": WS to Joseph Bennett, 8 December 1950, *Letters*, 701.

357 "Light the first light": *CPP*, 444.

358 "that poetry is supreme": WS to Barbara Church, 2 October 1951, *Letters*, 729.

358 "To say that philosophers": WS to Barbara Church, 30 November 1951, *Letters*, 734.

358 "not believe to-day": WS to Sr. M. Bernetta Quinn, 21 December 1951, *Letters*, 735.

358 "shutting out something crude": WS to José Rodríguez Feo, 27 December 1951, *Letters*, 735.

CHAPTER 18. A NEW KNOWLEDGE OF REALITY: 1952–1954

359 "to an older": WS to Norman Holmes Pearson, 24 January 1952, *Letters*, 737.

359 "confront fact": "About One of Marianne Moore's Poems," *Quarterly Review of Literature*, Summer 1948, *CPP*, 699–706.

360 "It is easy to say that Marianne": WS to Norman Holmes Pearson, 24 January 1952, *Letters*, 737.

360 "a woman of natural goodness": WS to Barbara Church, 30 November 1951, *Letters*, 734.

360 "I knock this morning": WS to Marianne Moore, 29 January 1952, *Letters*, 738.

361 "a particularly good time": WS to José Rodríguez Feo, 19 February 1952, *Letters*, 740.

361 "two trunks": WS to Barbara Church, 24 March 1952, *Letters*, 820.

361 "the figures": *CPP*, 432.

362 "I grieve to hear": WS to Barbara Church, 29 September 1952, *Letters*, 761.

363 "always bowed": quoted by WS in a letter to Bernard Heringman, 3 May 1949, *Letters*, 637.

363 "Notwithstanding all the talk": WS to Paule Vidal, 18 June 1952, *Letters*, 755.

363 "in order to procure": WS to José Rodríguez Feo, 30 June 1952, *Letters*, 757.

364 "I suppose that if": WS to Barbara Church, 4 August 1952, *Letters*, 758.

364 "Over here": WS to Barbara Church, 10 September 1952, *Letters*, 760.

364 "in this world, in this house": "The Irish Cliffs of Moher," *CPP*, 427.

365 "To-day there is a light": WS to Barbara Church, 29 September 1952, *Letters*, 761.

365 "extremely kind": Elias Mengel, *Brazeau*, 286.

368 "One turns with something like ferocity": "John Crowe Ransom: Tennessean," *CPP*, 820.

369 "At my age": WS to Thomas McGreevy, 24 October 1952, *Letters*, 763.

370 "When I consider": WS to Bernard Heringman, 7 January 1953, *Letters*, 765.

370 "A young man in a new scene": WS to José Rodríguez Feo, 13 January 1953, *Letters*, 767.

372 "I was in rather a chaotic state": WS to Marianne Moore, 27 March 1953, *Letters*, 771.

372 "Reality Is an Activity of the Most August Imagination": *CPP*, 471.

373 "after a cautious drive": WS to Barbara Church, 16 October 1953, *Letters*, 800.

373 "For that alone would be new": WS to Barbara Church, 21 October 1953, *Letters*, 801.

374 "a structure of little blocks": WS to Richard Eberhart, 7 December 1953, *Letters*, 803.

374 "Someone telephoned me": WS to Barbara Church, 16 November 1953, *Letters*, 802.

374 "the loss of all religious significance": WS to Jim Powers, 21 December 1953, *Letters*, 805.

374 "too lively": WS to Emma Stevens Jobbins, 22 December 1953, *Letters*, 806.

375 "a tremendous kick": WS to Barbara Church, 10 February 1954, *Letters*, 817.

375 "melted candy": WS to Norman Holmes Pearson, 27 April 1954, *Letters*, 830.

375 "and his large ones flops": WS to Barbara Church, 4 June 1953, *Letters*, 836.

375 "greatly admired": WS to Barbara Church, 15 March 1954, *Letters*, 825.

375 “Your Easter message”: WS to M. Bernetta Quinn, 21 April 1954, *Letters*, 828.

376 “a machine-made title”: WS to Alfred Knopf, 25 May 1954, *Letters*, 834.

376 “go on writing”: WS to Barbara Church, 6 May 1954, *Letters*, 832.

376 *The Sail of Ulysses: CPP*, 462–7.

376 “Perhaps I shan’t throw it away”: WS to Babette Deutsch, 2 June 1954, *Letters*, 834.

377 “What there is left”: WS to Horace Taylor, 27 September 1954, *Letters*, 834.

377 “Presence of an External Master of Knowledge,” *CPP*, 467.

378 “many pages of extraordinary analysis”: WS to Robert Pack, 7 June 1954, *Letters*, 837.

379 “growling not only”: WS to Leonard van Geyzel, 25 June 1954, *Letters*, 838.

379 “that heavenly time”: WS to Barbara Church, 23 July 1954, *Letters*, 841.

380 “super-duper”: WS to Barbara Church, 31 August 1954, *Letters*, 842.

CHAPTER 19. A FINAL SERIOUSNESS: 1954–1955

383 “an imposing structure”: Lewis Nichols, “Talk with Mr. Stevens,” *New York Times*, October 3, 1954.

384 “a stuffed one”: *New York Times*, 3 October 1954.

384 “a year younger”: WS to Louise Seaman Bechtel, 4 October 1954, *Letters*, 847.

385 “everybody and everything”: WS to Alfred Knopf, 6 October 1954, *Letters*, 848.

385 “The Whole Man: Perspectives, Horizons”: 21 October 1954, *CPP*, 872–77.

386 “living in the suburbs”: WS to Richard Eberhart, 22 November 1954, *Letters*, 851.

387 “filled up to the roof”: WS to Knopf, 9 November 1954, *Letters*, 849.

387 “a monumental presence”: *Brazeau*, 287.

387 “taking up the routine”: WS to Archibald MacLeish, 29 November 1954, *Letters*, 853.

387 "Everything I've got": WS to Barbara Church, 4 January 1955, *Letters*, 864.

388 "to be able to grow old": WS to Peter H. Lee, 4 January 1955, *Letters*, 865.

388 "When a poet comes out of his cavern": *CPP*, 877.

389 "This resolution": WS to Alfred A. Toscano and John Wassung, clerks, respectively, of the Senate and House of Representatives of the General Assembly of the State of Connecticut.

389 "Mrs. Stevens had a thrombosis": WS to Barbara Church, 18 February 1955, *Letters*, 874.

390 "I can remember": E. A. Cowrie, *Brazeau*, 292.

390 "Taken by itself": WS to Barbara Church, 18 February 1955, *Letters*, 874.

391 "the possibility that the evening train": WS to Barbara Church, 21 March 1955, *Letters*, 876.

391 "in a world": Ibid.

391 "Oh, hell!": Anthony Sigmans, *Brazeau*, 289.

392 "In spite of its solemnity": WS to Peter Lee, 1 April 1955, *Letters*, 879.

392 "Easter and the rabbits": WS to Barbara Church, 7 April 1955, *Letters*, 880.

392 "Your use of the word nobility": WS to Robert Pack, 14 April 1955, *Letters*, 880.

392 "I hope you don't really feel": WS to Robert Pack, 22 December 1954, *Letters*, 861.

392 "more fatal": WS to Robert Pack, 28 December 1954, *Letters*, 863.

392 "Here / In Connecticut": "A mythology reflects its region," *CPP*, 476.

392 "This is Connecticut": "Connecticut Composed," *CPP*, 894–96.

393 "The thrift and frugality": "Connecticut Composed," *CPP*, 894.

394 "Of Mere Being": *CPP*, 476–77.

395 "I expect to be able to leave": WS to Barbara Church, 2 May 1955, *Letters*, 882.

395 "to see all the patients": Arthur Hanley, *Brazeau*, 294.

397 "allow nothing to interfere": WS to Reuben A. Holden, 20 May 1955, *Letters*, 883.

397 "one of the colored men": WS to Barbara Church, 14 June 1955, *Letters*, 886.

397 "pretty much a changed man": Anthony Sigmans, *Brazeau*, 290.

398 "feeling pretty well": Elias Mengel, *Brazeau*, 291.

398 "a place on high ground": WS to Eleanor Stevens Sauer, 13 June 1955, *Letters*, 885.

398 "back in the office": WS to Thomas McGreevy, 23 June 1955, *Letters*, 886.

398 "almost no exercise": WS to Barbara Church, 24 June 1955, *Letters*, 886.

399 "The sole emperor": *CPP*, 468.

399 "Dear Elias": Elias Mengel, *Brazeau*, 288.

399 "When you say": WS to Peter Lee, 17 February 1955, *Letters*, 873.

400 "Most of the time": WS to Sam Morse, 5 July 1955, *Letters*, 888.

400 He'd been at the office: Ibid.

400 Unable to concentrate: WS to Barbara Church, 15 July 1955, *Letters*, 890.

400 "put his thumb and forefinger": Hale Anderson, *Brazeau*, 292.

400 "He'd almost crawl": Manning Heard, *Brazeau*, 292.

401 "into the fold": Arthur Hanley, *Brazeau*, 294.

402 "jolly Santa Claus": Herbert Schoen, *Brazeau*, 293.

402 the bright sublimities: It was his daughter who remembered her father recalling his time in the Canadian Rockies as he lay dying, *S&P*, 117.

402 "most patronized": John Cleary, *Brazeau*, 296.

403 "It was a stark funeral parlor": Margaret Powers, *Brazeau*, 296.

403 "that his nurse or somebody": Jim Powers, *Brazeau*, 297.

403 "Here a world celebrity": Anthony Sigmans, *Brazeau*, 297.

404 "To me": William Carlos Williams, *Poetry*, January 1956, 234–39.

406 "in its odd grammar": Helen Vendler, "The Hunting of Wallace Stevens: Critical Approaches," in *The Music of What Happens: Poems, Poets, Critics* (Harvard University Press, 1989), 75–90.

BIBLIOGRAPHY

WORKS BY WALLACE STEVENS

The Auroras of Autumn. Knopf, 1950.

Bowl, Cat, and Broomstick, 1917. Printed in *The Palm at the End of the Mind*, 1971.

Carlos among the Candles: A Monologue, Poetry Magazine 11, 3 (December 1917).

The Collected Poems of Wallace Stevens. Knopf, 1954, reprinted, Random House, 1982.

Collected Poetry and Prose. Library of America, 1997.

Esthétique du Mal. Cummington Press, 1945.

Harmonium. Knopf, 1923, revised edition, 1931.

Ideas of Order. Alcestis Press, 1935, enlarged edition, Knopf, 1936.

Letters of Wallace Stevens. Edited Holly Stevens. Knopf, 1966.

The Man with the Blue Guitar, and Other Poems. Knopf, 1937.

The Necessary Angel: Essays on Reality and the Imagination. Contains "The Noble Rider and the Sound of Words," "The Figure of the Youth as Virile Poet," "Effects of Analogy," "The Realm of Resemblance," "Someone Puts a Pineapple Together," and "Of Ideal Time and Choice." Knopf, 1951.

Notes toward a Supreme Fiction. Cummington Press, 1942.

Opus Posthumous. Edited by Samuel French Morse. Knopf, 1957, reprinted Random House, 1982.

Owl's Clover. Alcestis Press, 1936.

The Palm at the End of the Mind: Selected Poems and a Play by Wallace Stevens. Edited by Holly Stevens. Knopf, 1971.

Parts of a World. Knopf, 1942.

Poems by Wallace Stevens. Edited by Samuel French Morse. Vintage Books, 1959.

Preface to William Carlos Williams, *Collected Poems, 1921–1931*. Objectivist Press, 1934.

A Primitive Like an Orb. Gotham Book Mart, 1948.

Raoul Dufy: A Note. Pierre Beres, 1953.

The Relations between Poetry and Painting. Museum of Modern Art, 1951.

Selected Poems. Fortune Press, 1952.

Selected Poems. Faber, 1953.

Selected Poems. Edited by John N. Serio. Knopf, 2011.

Sur Plusieurs Beaux Sujects: Wallace Stevens' Commonplace Book. Edited by Milton Bates. 1989.

Three Academic Pieces: The Realm of Resemblance, Someone Puts a Pineapple Together, Of Ideal Time and Choice. Cummington Press, 1947.

Transport to Summer. Knopf, 1947.

LETTERS

Blount, J. Donald, ed. *The Contemplated Spouse: The Letters of Wallace Stevens to Elsie*. University of South Carolina Press, 2006.

Coyle, Beverly, and Alan Filreis, eds. *Secretaries of the Moon: The Letters of Wallace Stevens and José Rodriguez Feo*. Duke University Press Books, 1986.

MAGAZINES CONTAINING WORKS BY STEVENS

Accent, American Letters, Botteghe Oscure, Broom, Contact, Dial, Halcyon, Horizon, Hound and Horn, Kenyon Review, Life and Letters Today, Little Review, Measure, Modern School, Nation, New Republic, Others, Poetry, Poetry London, Quarterly Review of Literature, Rogue, Secession, Soil, Southern Review, Voices, Wake.

WORKS ABOUT STEVENS

1950–1960

Alvarez, A. *Stewards of Excellence: Studies in Modern English and American Poets*. Scribner, 1958.

Borroff, Marie, ed. *Wallace Stevens: Twentieth Century Views: A Collection of Critical Essays.* 1959.

Kermode, Frank. *Wallace Stevens.* Oliver & Boyd, 1960.

O'Connor, William Van. *The Shaping Spirit: A Study of Wallace Stevens.* Regnery, 1950.

Pack, Robert. *Wallace Stevens: An Approach to His Poetry and Thought.* Rutgers University Press, 1958.

Quinn, M. Bernetta. *Metamorphic Tradition in Modern Poetry: Essays on the Work of Ezra Pound, Wallace Stevens, William Carlos Williams, T. S. Eliot, Hart Crane, Randall Jarrell and William Butler Yeats.* Rutgers University Press, 1955.

Tate, Allen. Philip Wheelwright, Cleanth Brooks and I. A. Richards. *The Language of Poetry.* 1960.

Thirlwall, John C., ed., *The Selected Letters of William Carlos Williams.* McDowell, Obolensky, 1957.

1961–1970

Baird, James. *The Dome and the Rock: Structure in the Poetry of Wallace Stevens.* Johns Hopkins University Press, 1968.

Blackmur, R. P. *The Double Agent: Essays in Craft and Elucidation.* Peter Smith, 1962.

Blessing, Richard Allen. *Wallace Stevens' "Whole Harmonium."* Syracuse University Press, 1970.

Borroff, Marie, ed. *Wallace Stevens: A Collection of Critical Essays.* Prentice-Hall, 1963.

Brown, Ashley, and Robert S. Haller, eds. *The Achievement of Wallace Stevens.* Lippincott, 1962.

Brown, Merle E. *Wallace Stevens: The Poem as Act.* Wayne State University Press, 1970.

Burney, William. *Wallace Stevens.* Twayne, 1968.

Buttel, Robert. *Wallace Stevens: The Making of "Harmonium."* Princeton University Press, 1967.

Doggett, Frank. *Stevens' Poetry of Thought.* Johns Hopkins University Press, 1966.

Donoghue, Denis. *Connoisseurs of Chaos: Ideas of Order in Modern American Poetry.* Faber, 1965.

———. *The Ordinary Universe: Soundings in Modern Literature.* Faber, 1968.

Enck, John J. *Wallace Stevens: Images and Judgments.* Southern Illinois University Press, 1964, reprinted 1968.

Lentricchia, Frank. *The Gaiety of Language: An Essay on the Radical Poetics of W. B. Yeats and Wallace Stevens.* University of California Press, 1968.

Morse, Samuel French. *Wallace Stevens: Poetry as Life.* Pegasus, 1970.

Nasser, Eugene Paul. *Wallace Stevens: An Anatomy of Figuration.* University of Pennsylvania Press, 1965.

Pearce, Roy Harvey, and J. Hillis Miller. *The Act of the Mind: Essays on the Poetry of Wallace Stevens.* Johns Hopkins University Press, 1965.

Riddel, Joseph N. *The Clairvoyant Eye: The Poetry and Poetics of Wallace Stevens.* Louisiana State University Press, 1965.

Scott, Nathan A., Jr. *Four Ways of Modern Poetry: Wallace Stevens, Robert Frost, Dylan Thomas, W. H. Auden.* John Knox Press, 1965.

Stern, Herbert J. *Wallace Stevens: Art of Uncertainty.* University of Michigan Press, 1966.

Sukenick, Ronald. *Wallace Stevens: Musing the Obscure.* New York University Press, 1967.

Tindall, William York. *Wallace Stevens.* University of Minnesota Press, 1961.

Van Vechten, Carl. *The Yale University Library Gazette* 30, no. 2 (October 1963), 41–50.

Vendler, Helen Hennessy. *On Extended Wings: Wallace Stevens' Longer Poems.* Harvard University Press, 1969.

Walsh, Thomas F. *Concordance to the Poetry of Wallace Stevens.* Pennsylvania State University Press, 1963.

Wells, Henry W. *Introduction to Wallace Stevens.* Indiana University Press, 1964.

1971–1980

Beckett, Lucy. *Wallace Stevens.* Cambridge University Press, 1974.

Benamou, Michel. *Wallace Stevens and the Symbolist Imagination.* Princeton University Press, 1972.

Bloom, Harold. *Figures of Capable Imagination.* Seabury, 1976.

Bloom, Harold. *Wallace Stevens: The Poems of Our Climate.* Cornell University Press, 1976.

Bornstein, George. *Transformations of Romanticism in Yeats, Eliot, and Stevens.* University of Chicago Press, 1976.

Borroff, Marie. *Language and the Poet: Verbal Artistry in Frost, Stevens, and Moore.* University of Chicago Press, 1979.

Brown, Ashley, and Robert S. Haller. *The Achievement of Wallace Stevens.* Lippincott, 1973.

Buttel, Robert, and Frank Doggett, eds. *Wallace Stevens: A Celebration.* Princeton University Press, 1980.

Doggett, Frank. *Wallace Stevens: The Making of the Poem.* Johns Hopkins University Press, 1980.

Ehrenpreis, Irvin, ed. *Wallace Stevens: A Critical Anthology.* Penguin, 1973.

Hines, Thomas J. *The Later Poetry of Wallace Stevens: Phenomenological Parallels with Husserl and Heidegger.* Bucknell University Press, 1976.

Kenner, Hugh. *A Homemade World: The American Modernist Writers.* Knopf, 1975.

Kessler, Edward. *Images of Wallace Stevens.* Rutgers University Press, 1972.

Litz, A. Walton. *Introspective Voyager: The Poetic Development of Wallace Stevens.* Oxford University Press, 1972.

McNamara, Peter L., ed. *Critics on Wallace Stevens.* University of Miami Press, 1972.

Middlebrook, Diane Wood. *Walt Whitman and Wallace Stevens.* Cornell University Press, 1974.

Morris, Adalaide Kirby. *Wallace Stevens: Imagination and Faith.* Princeton University Press, 1974.

Perlis, Alan. *Wallace Stevens: A World of Transforming Shapes.* Bucknell University Press, 1976.

Stevens, Holly. *Souvenirs and Prophecies: The Young Wallace Stevens.* Knopf, 1977.

Wallace Stevens Journal. Semiannual since 1977.

Weston, Susan B. *Wallace Stevens: An Introduction to the Poetry.* Columbia University Press, 1977.

Woodward, Kathleen. *At Last, the Real Distinguished Thing: The Later Poems of Eliot, Pound, Stevens, and Williams.* Ohio State University Press, 1980.

1981–1990

Axelrod, Steven Gould, and Helen Deese. *Critical Essays on Wallace Stevens.* G. K. Hall, 1988.

Bates, Milton J. *Wallace Stevens: A Mythology of Self.* University of California Press, 1985.

Berger, Charles. *Forms of Farewell: The Late Poetry of Wallace Stevens.* University of Wisconsin Press, 1985.

Bevis, William W. *Mind of Winter: Wallace Stevens, Meditation, and Literature.* University of Pittsburgh Press, 1989.

Brazeau, Peter. *Parts of a World: Wallace Stevens Remembered.* Random House, 1983.

Carroll, Joseph. *Wallace Stevens' Supreme Fiction: A New Romanticism.* Louisianna State University Press, 1988.

Fisher, Barbara M. *Wallace Stevens: The Intensest Rendezvous.* University of Virginia Press, 1990.

Gelpi, Albert. *Wallace Stevens: The Poetics of Modernism.* Cambridge Studies in American Literature and Culture. Cambridge University Press, 1985.

LaGuardia, David M. *Advance on Chaos: The Sanctifying Imagination of Wallace Stevens.* University Press of New England, 1983.

Leggett, B. J. *Wallace Stevens and Poetic Theory: Conceiving the Supreme Fiction.* Duke University Press, 1987.

Lentricchia, Frank. *Ariel and the Police: Michel Foucault, William James, Wallace Stevens.* University of Wisconsin Press, 1988.

Leonard, J. S., and Christine E. Wharton. *The Fluent Mundo: Wallace Stevens and the Structure of Reality.* University of Georgia Press, 1988.

Quirk, Tom. *Bergson and American Culture: The Worlds of Willa Cather and Wallace Stevens.* University of North Carolina Press, 1990.

Richardson, Joan. *Wallace Stevens: The Early Years, 1879–1923.* William Morrow, 1986.

———. *Wallace Stevens: The Later Years, 1923–1955.* William Morrow, 1988.

Sexson, Michael. *The Quest of Self in the Collected Poems of Wallace Stevens.* Edwin Mellen, 1981.

Vendler, Helen. *Wallace Stevens: Words Chosen out of Desire.* Harvard University Press, 1986.

Walker, David L. *The Transparent Lyric: Reading and Meaning in the Poetry of Stevens and Williams.* Princeton University Press, 1984.

Woodman, Leonora. *Stanza My Stone: Wallace Stevens and the Hermetic Tradition.* Purdue University Press, 1983.

1991–2000

Berry, S. L. *Wallace Stevens.* Creative Education (Mankato, MN), 1997.

Dickie, Margaret. *Lyric Contingencies: Emily Dickinson and Wallace Stevens.* University of Pennsylvania Press, 1991.

Filreis, Alan. *Modernism from Right to Left: Wallace Stevens, the Thirties and Literary Radicalism.* Cambridge University Press, 1994.

Grey, Thomas. *The Wallace Stevens Case: Law and the Practice of Poetry.* Harvard University Press, 1991.

Jarroway, David R. *Wallace Stevens and the Question of Belief: Metaphysician in the Dark.* Louisiana State University Press, 1993.

Jenkins, Lee M. *Wallace Stevens: Rage for Order.* Sussex Academic Press, 1999.

Leggett, Bobby J. *Early Stevens: The Nietzschean Intertext.* University of North Carolina Press, 1992.

Lensing, George S. *Wallace Stevens: A Poet's Growth.* Louisiana State University Press, 1991.

Lentricchia, Frank. *Modernist Quartet.* Cambridge University Press, 1994.

Lombardi, Thomas F. *Wallace Stevens and the Pennsylvania Keystone: The Influence of Origins on His Life and Poetry.* Susquehanna University Press, 1996.

Longenbach, James. *Wallace Stevens: The Plain Sense of Things.* Oxford University Press, 1991.

MacLeod, Glen. *Wallace Stevens and Modern Art: From the Armory Show to Abstract Expressionism.* Yale University Press, 1993.

Maeder, Beverly. *Wallace Stevens' Experimental Language: The Lion in the Lute.* Palgrave Macmillan, 1999.

McCann, Janet. *Wallace Stevens Revisited: "The Celestial Possible."* Twayne, 1995.

Murphy, Charles, M. *Wallace Stevens: A Spiritual Poet in a Secular Age.* Paulist Press, 1997.

Newcomb, John Timberman. *Wallace Stevens and Literary Canons.* University Press of Mississippi, 1992.

Penso, Kia. *Wallace Stevens, Harmonium, and the Whole of Harmonium.* Archon Press, 1991.

Rae, Patricia. *The Practical Muse: Pragmatist Poetics in Hulme, Pound, and Stevens.* Bucknell University Press, 1997.

Riddel, Joseph N. *The Clairvoyant Eye: The Poetry and Poetics of Wallace Stevens.* Louisiana State University Press, 1991.

Rosu, Anca. *The Metaphysics of Sound in Wallace Stevens.* University of Alabama Press, 1995.

Rotella, Guy. *Reading and Writing Nature: The Poetry of Robert Frost, Wallace Stevens, Marianne Moore, and Elizabeth Bishop.* Northeastern University Press, 1991.

Sampson, Theodore. *A Cure of the Mind: The Poetics of Wallace Stevens.* Black Rose Books, 1999.

Schaum, Melita C. *Wallace Stevens and the Feminine.* University of Alabama Press, 1993.

Schulze, Robin G. *The Web of Friendship: Marianne Moore and Wallace Stevens.* University of Michigan Press, 1995.

Schwarz, Daniel R. *Narrative and Representation in the Poetry of Wallace Stevens: "A Tune beyond Us, yet Ourselves."* Palgrave Macmillan, 1993.

Serio, John N. *Teaching Wallace Stevens: Practical Essays.* University of Tennessee Press, 1994.

Serio, John N. *Wallace Stevens: An Annotated Secondary Bibliography.* University of Pittsburgh Press, 1994.

Sharpe, Tony. *Wallace Stevens: A Literary Life.* Palgrave Macmillan, 2000.

Voros, Gyorgyi. *Notations of the Wild: Ecology in the Poetry of Wallace Stevens*, Iowa Press, 1997.

Whiting, Anthony. *The Never-Resting Mind: Wallace Stevens' Romantic Irony.* University of Michigan Press, 1996.

2001–2010

Andersson, Daniel. *The Nothing That Is: The Structure of Consciousness in the Poetry of Wallace Stevens.* Acta Universitatis Upsaliensis, 2006.

Barone, Dennis, and James Finnegan. *Visiting Wallace: Poems Inspired by the Life and Work of Wallace Stevens*. University of Iowa Press, 2009.

Brogan, Jacqueline Vaught. *The Violence Within / The Violence Without: Wallace Stevens and the Emergence of a Revolutionary Poetics*. University of Georgia Press, 2003.

Cleghorn, Angus J. *Wallace Stevens' Poetics: The Neglected Rhetoric*. Palgrave Macmillan, 2001.

Cook, Eleanor. *A Reader's Guide to Wallace Stevens*. Princeton University Press, 2009.

Critchley, Simon. *Things Merely Are: Philosophy in the Poetry of Wallace Stevens*. Routledge, 2005.

Eeckhout, Bart. *Wallace Stevens and the Limits of Reading and Writing*. University of Missouri Press, 2002.

Eeckhout, Bart, and Edward Ragg. *Wallace Stevens across the Atlantic*. Palgrave Macmillan, 2008.

Mariani, Paul, Martica Sawin, and Oriole Farb Feshbach. *LUMINATIONS: Images by Oriole Farb Feshbach for the Poem "Auroras of Autumn" by Wallace Stevens*. Midmarch Arts Press, 2008.

Quinn, Justin. *Gathered beneath the Storm: Wallace Stevens, Nature and Community*. University of Dublin College Press, 2002.

Ragg, Edward. *Wallace Stevens and the Aesthetics of Abstraction*. Cambridge University Press, 2010.

Renza, Louis A. *Edgar Allan Poe, Wallace Stevens, and the Poetics of American Privacy*. Louisiana State University Press. 2002.

Riggs, Sarah. *Word Sightings: Poetry and Visual Media in Stevens, Bishop, and O'Hara*. Routledge, 2002.

Rosenthal, Edna. *Aristotle and Modernism: Aesthetic Affinities of T. S. Eliot, Wallace Stevens, and Virginia Woolf*. Sussex Academic Press, 2008.

Schaum, Melita C., and John N. Serio. *Wallace Stevens and the Critical Schools*. University of Alabama Press, 2003.

Serio, John, ed. *The Cambridge Companion to Wallace Stevens*. Cambridge University Press, 2007.

Surette, Leon. *The Modern Dilemma*. McGill-Queen's University Press, 2008.

Woodland, Malcolm. *Wallace Stevens and the Apocalyptic Mode*. University of Iowa Press, 2005.

2011–2015

Altieri, Charles. *Wallace Stevens and the Demands of Modernity: Toward a Phenomenology of Value*. Cornell University Press, 2013.

Clarke, Edward. *The Later Affluence of W. B. Yeats and Wallace Stevens*. Palgrave Macmillan, 2011.

Cohen, Milton A. *Beleaguered Poets and Leftist Critics: Stevens, Cummings, Frost, and Williams in the 1930s*. University of Alabama Press, 2011.

Cook, Eleanor. *Poetry, Word-Play, and Word-War in Wallace Stevens*. Princeton University Press, 2014.

Deshmane, Chetan. *Wallace Stevens: A Lacanian Reading*. McFarland, 2012.

Doyle, Charles. *Wallace Stevens*. Critical Heritage series. Routledge, 2013.

Ford, Sara J. *Gertrude Stein and Wallace Stevens: The Performance of Modern Consciousness*. Routledge, 2011.

Goldfarb, Lisa. *The Figure Concealed: Wallace Stevens, Music, and Valéryan Echoes*. Sussex Academic Press, 2011.

Goldfarb, Lisa, and Bart Eeckhout. *Wallace Stevens, New York, and Modernism*. McFarland, 2012.

Johnson, Alison. *Wallace Stevens: A Dual Life as Poet and Insurance Executive*. Cumberland Press, 2012.

———. *The World of Wallace Stevens*. A Johnson/Startzman Film, produced and directed by Alison Johnson. DVD. 2015.

Kleinberg-Levin, David. *Redeeming Words and the Promise of Happiness: A Critical Theory Approach to Wallace Stevens and Vladimir Nabokov*. Lexington Books, 2012.

Mazur, Krystyna. *Poetry and Repetition: Walt Whitman, Wallace Stevens, John Ashbery*. Routledge, 2014.

Santilli, Kristine S. *Poetic Gesture: Myth, Wallace Stevens, and the Desirous Motions of Poetic Language*. Routledge, 2014.

Serio, John, and Christopher Beyers, eds. *Wallace Stevens: The Collected Poems: The Corrected Edition*. Vintage International, 2015.

Tompsett, Daniel. *Wallace Stevens and Pre-Socratic Philosophy: Metaphysics and the Play of Violence*. Routledge, 2012.

Vendler, Helen. *The Ocean, the Bird, and the Scholar: Essays on Poets and Poetry*. Harvard University Press, 2015.

POETRY CREDITS

“Of Modern Poetry,” “Not Ideas about the Thing but the Thing Itself,” “The Idea of Order at Key West,” “The Planet on the Table,” “The Latest Freed Man,” “The Man with the Blue Guitar,” “Final Soliloquy of the Interior Paramour,” “Asides on the Oboe,” “A Postcard from the Volcano,” “Angel Surrounded by Paysans,” “Our Stars Come from Ireland,” “Like Decorations in a Nigger Cemetery,” “Mozart, 1935,” “Notes toward a Supreme Fiction,” “Sailing after Lunch,” “Esthétique du Mal,” “Credences of Summer,” “Farewell to Florida,” “Large Red Man Reading,” “To an Old Philosopher in Rome,” “The Auroras of Autumn,” “The Men That Are Falling,” “An Ordinary Evening in New Haven,” “Variations on a Summer Day,” “The Sun This March,” “Of Mere Being,” “Some Friends from Pascagoula,” “A Fish-Scale Sunrise,” “Owl’s Clover,” “On an Old Horn,” “Certain Phenomena of Sound,” “The Bed of Old John Zeller,” “Attempt to Discover Life,” “St. Armorer’s Church from the Outside,” “A Child Asleep in Its Own Life,” “Reality Is an Activity of the Most August Imagination,” “Red Loves Kit,” “The Woman Who Blamed Life on a Spaniard,” “The Widow,” “Outside of Wedlock,” and “Tradition” from THE COLLECTED POEMS OF WALLACE STEVENS by Wallace Stevens, “The Sun Bathers” by William Carlos Williams quoted with permission of Daphne Williams Fox and the Estate of William Carlos Williams.

ILLUSTRATION CREDITS

1, 3, 4, 8–11, 13, 14, 16–18: Courtesy of the Huntington Library
2: Photo by Paul Mariani
5: Courtesy of Boston College Library
6: Courtesy of the Philadelphia Museum of Art
7: Courtesy of the State University at Buffalo
12: Courtesy of Alison Johnson
15: Courtesy of Emory University Archives
19: Courtesy of Peter Hanchak

INDEX

ABOUT THE AUTHOR

PAUL MARIANI is the author of eighteen books, including biographies of William Carlos Williams (a finalist for the National Book Award), John Berryman, Robert Lowell, Hart Crane, Gerard Manley Hopkins, and Wallace Stevens. He has also published seven volumes of poetry, most recently *Epitaphs for the Journey* (2012). In addition, he has published critical studies of Hopkins and Williams, two volumes of critical essays, *A Usable Past* and *God and the Imagination*, as well as *Thirty Days*, a spiritual memoir. He has lectured and read his poetry widely, has served as an editor for various journals, is the author of more than two hundred published essays, and has been the recipient of multiple awards from the National Endowment for the Humanities and the National Endowment for the Arts. In 2009 he received the John Ciardi Award for his lifetime achievement in poetry. He holds a chair as University Professor of English at Boston College, where he has taught since 2000. From 1968 until 2000 he taught at the University of Massachusetts / Amherst, where he was Distinguished University Professor.